A TOUCHSTONE BOOK
PUBLISHED BY SIMON & SCHUSTER INC.
NEW YORK LONDON TORONTO SYDNEY TOKYO

THE PULITZER PRIZES

1988

EDITED BY

KENDALL J. WILLS

TOUCHSTONE
Simon & Schuster Building
Rockefeller Center
1230 Avenue of the Americas
New York, New York 10020

TOUCHSTONE and colophon are
registered trademarks of Simon & Schuster Inc.

Designed by Bonni Leon
Manufactured in the United States of America

10 9 8 7 6 5 4 3 2 1
10 9 8 7 6 5 4 3 2 1 Pbk.

Library of Congress Catalog Card Number: 88-641507
ISBN 0-671-67255-x
ISBN 0-671-67202-9 Pbk.

The editor is grateful to the following for permission to reprint:

Pulitzer Prize nominating letter by Charles E. Shepard. Used by permission of Charles E. Shepard.

"Jim Bakker Resigns from PTL: Jerry Falwell Assumes Leadership" by Charles E. Shepard, March 20, 1987, page 1. Reprinted with permission of *The Charlotte Observer*.

"Businessman Says He Negotiated Hahn Settlement with Dortch" by Charles E. Shepard, March 27, 1987, page 1. Reprinted with permission of *The Charlotte Observer*.

"Contradictions Cloud Bakker Case Reports" by Charles E. Shepard, April 11, 1987, page 1. Reprinted with permission of *The Charlotte Observer*.

"PTL '86 Payments to Bakkers: $1.6 Million" by Charles E. Shepard, April 18, 1987, page 1. Reprinted with permission of *The Charlotte Observer*.

"3 PTL Directors Didn't Know What Bakker Was Paid" by Charles E. Shepard, April 22, 1987, page 1. Reprinted with permission of *The Charlotte Observer*.

"Dortch Used PTL Money to Pay Hahn" by Charles E. Shepard, April 28, 1987, page 1. Reprinted with permission of *The Charlotte Observer*.

"Tax Status of PTL Attacked" by Charles E. Shepard, April 28, 1987, page 1. Reprinted with permission of *The Charlotte Observer*.

"Jessica Hahn: The Woman Behind the Headlines" by Jody Jaffe, May 21, 1987. Reprinted with permission of *The Charlotte Observer*.

"PTL Dealings Defied 'All Business Practices,' Official Says" by Charles E. Shepard, May 23, 1987, page 1. Reprinted with permission of *The Charlotte Observer*.

Pulitzer Prize nominating letter by Jim Tharpe, managing editor of *The Alabama Journal*. Reprinted with permission of *The Alabama Journal*.

"Death Comes at Early Age for Some of Alabama's Poor" by Susan Eggering, September 14, 1987, page 1. Project directed and edited by Jim Tharpe and Ann Green. Reprinted with permission of *The Alabama Journal*.

(*continued on page 554*)

ACKNOWLEDGMENTS

One luxury of an annual anthology is that it provides the editor the opportunity in the latest volume to correct any deficiencies in the previous issue. Fortunately, I have just one glaring omission to set right. I did not adequately thank Peggy Piaskoski for her unfailing assistance in producing this anthology. She has cheerfully offered editorial advice at each stage of production and has greatly improved the final product. An editor's editor, Peggy has skillfully balanced honest criticism with welcomed encouragement.

I would also like to thank several colleagues at The New York Times. *Special thanks to Robert B. Semple Jr. for offering me a job that is an editor's delight and for trusting me not to make a mess of it. Howard G. Goldberg shared much valuable editing advice as well as his rarified sense of humor. He was equally generous in parting with some of the finer samples from his well-stocked wine cellar. Jeanne Pinder, Terry Neilan, Kevin McKenna, Tom Feyer, David Pitt and Bill Wellman each gave me valuable instruction in writing and editing.*

I am grateful to Diane Asadorian, Robert D. Stang, Alfred M. Taffae, Joanne Kenen, Justine Kaplan, Brian Manning, Patricia Ochs, Kirk Johnson and Frances Siciliano for their warm friendship and steady encouragement. A special thanks to my wonderful family whose continual support is greatly appreciated.

Thanks to Bud Kliment, assistant administrator for the Pulitzer Prize Committee, for tolerating my numerous inquiries and requests.

Finally, I would like to thank Carole Hall and James Nichols, my editors at Simon & Schuster, for their strong commitment to this anthology and for consistently being a pleasure to work with.

To Beth F. Nachreiner
and Mària E. Moll

CONTENTS

Contents

INTRODUCTION

The winners in the fourteen Pulitzer Prize journalism categories presented here are striking in their powerful reflection of the human condition. While each of the works is dramatic in its own right, the news articles, photographs and editorial cartoons tell a collective tale that is more significant than a simple assemblage of unrelated stories.

To be sure, this volume contains some of the year's biggest stories —the stock-market crash, the PTL scandal, the "crack" cocaine menace and others that will be remembered years from now as among the most important issues of the day. But there are also lesser-known dramas presented by some of the country's best journalists. Although some of these stories have not yet received much attention outside the circulation areas of the newspapers in which they were printed, they are equally compelling chapters in our nation's history and deserving of our attention.

The special value of this volume of *The Pulitzer Prizes* is the presentation, for the first time, of all the 1988 prizewinning works under one cover. This anthology includes fresh stories from around the country, told by some of the most seasoned as well as by some of the best emerging storytellers.

Jacqui Banaszynski, winner of the feature writing category, offers a moving account in the *St. Paul Pioneer Press Dispatch* of how an AIDS victim sacrificed his privacy, and his family harmony, by talking publicly about his disease, thus forcing a Midwestern community to confront his humanity. "I want to take the mask off the statistics and say we are human beings and we have feelings," Dick Hanson, the AIDS victim, said in explaining his decision to talk to reporters.

The Charlotte Observer delivers a drumbeat of revelations about the PTL financial scandals and the public airing of Jim Bakker's sexual liaison with Jessica Hahn.

Dave Barry, humor columnist for *The Miami Herald,* reveals a secret of his craft. "The theory I go on," he explains, "is that nothing you could ever make up is as funny as what real people actually do." He may have something there. But just as soon as he's got you snickering, he'll bring a tear to your eye with his next column.

The image of Wall Street came crashing down in two tales, one of greed and another of fear. James B. Stewart and Daniel Hertzberg, reporters for *The Wall Street Journal,* present an article that details the downfall of Martin A. Siegel as he exchanged privileged information for profit. The pair also present an insightful analysis of the frenetic events during the stock-market crash last October in which fortunes evaporated.

There's more. *Wall Street Journal* reporter Walt Bogdanich discovered through personal experience that many laboratory tests are faulty because they are conducted like piecework in a factory where profit but not accuracy is the guiding concern. In human terms, the faulty results can be devastating.

Jane Healy, an editorial writer for *The Orlando Sentinel,* tells how she broke away from more typical editorial writing style to campaign aggressively against "Florida's Shame," the consequences of mismanaged economic growth in Orange County.

It has long been "common knowledge" that Chicago's City Council was rife with corruption. Nearly everyone in town had taken that proposition for granted, but few had bothered to investigate it. The *Chicago Tribune* unleashed a team of reporters to get behind the mist of rumor. Unchallenged for so long, some council members didn't even try very hard to hide their abuses.

At the Pentagon, Tim Weiner of *The Philadelphia Inquirer* sifted through piles of documents and interviewed scores of people to shine light on the so-called black budget that funds clandestine activities and that has skyrocketed during the Reagan years. Shielded from public debate, the programs funded by this budget drip with waste and, some critics say, run counter to United States foreign policy according to the stories.

Thomas L. Friedman of *The New York Times* traversed the Middle East, a region known more for the dogma of retaliation than the delicate peace of reconciliation. Having earned a Pulitzer Prize in 1983 for his reporting from Lebanon, he proved his objectivity again by moving to Israel and skillfully outlining the causes of much of the region's conflict.

Closer to home, two stories that could have been written in many American communities were expertly presented by *The Alabama Journal* and the *Lawrence* [Massachusetts] *Eagle-Tribune.* The first is a sobering account of the tragically high number of infant deaths in

Alabama. Most disturbing is that many of the deaths were preventable. The second is a horrifying tale of how a Massachusetts prison granted furloughs to a convicted murderer who used this freedom to attack again.

Reviewing another medium, Tom Shales, television critic of *The Washington Post,* inexhaustibly analyzes shows. Unblinking, he flags our attention to both the "pearls" and the "garbage" and intelligently sizes up the programs that fall somewhere in between.

As in the 1987 edition, the articles in this anthology are interspersed with two chapters of prizewinning photographs and a chapter of editorial cartoons. Doug Marlette, a cartoonist who split the year between *The Charlotte Observer* and *The Atlanta Constitution,* takes aim at self-appointed leaders as well as the ones elected to public office.

For several days last October, the nation's attention focused on a small town in Texas where rescue workers frantically worked to free 18-month-old Jessica McClure from a well shaft. Scott Shaw waited above ground, photographing the scene for *The Odessa American.* When Jessica surfaced, surrounded by exhausted townsfolk, Shaw's shutter clicked, framing a dramatic moment.

Finally, Michel duCille of *The Miami Herald* planted himself in the middle of a cocaine operation in Miami and secretly used his camera to illustrate a story about drug activities that are infecting communities across the country.

Again this year, each chapter is introduced by the winners' descriptions of the background to the news events and the "inside stories" of how they turned the works into prizewinners. These essays are as compelling and instructive as the articles, photos and cartoons that follow.

Despite the widespread interest in the Pulitzer Prizes and the significant publicity that surrounds almost everything related to them, I've discovered much confusion about how the works are nominated and who selects the winners. I think it's worthwhile, therefore, to describe briefly the selection process.

Anyone can submit an entry from a daily or weekly publication to the Pulitzer Prize Committee; all entries must reach the committee at the Columbia University campus by February 1 for works published the previous year.

The Pulitzer Prize Committee, composed of 17 members (listed on page 17), selects five jurors—journalists from newspapers across the country—in each of the 14 categories to review the entries. These 70 jurors serve one-year terms. After evaluating the entries, the jurors choose three finalists, which are nominated and presented to the Pulitzer Committee. The committee then reviews the nominations and may add to the lists presented to it. Committee members serve overlapping terms of three years. As vacancies occur, the committee chooses replacements.

In the spring, the Pulitzer Committee selects the winners and awards them $3,000 from the endowment established by Joseph Pulitzer, the late newspaper publisher who envisioned the awards. The first awards were conferred in 1917, six years after his death.

During the last 71 years, the selection process has successfully drawn attention to a treasury of outstanding achievement by American journalists. The winners have truly earned the respect that comes with being "the best in the business."

Kendall J. Wills
Honolulu, Hawaii
1988

THE PULITZER PRIZES

PULITZER PRIZE BOARD

ONE

THE PTL SCANDAL

1988 WINNER IN THE PUBLIC SERVICE CATEGORY

"For a distinguished example of meritorious public service by a news-paper through the use of its journalistic resources . . . a gold medal."

The Charlotte Observer
Staff

When news of Jim Bakker's sexual encounter with Jessica Hahn broke last October, the evangelist resigned from PTL in a scandal that shook the ministry's foundations. Equally troubling to the faithful, however, were revelations of financial deception that had become standard practice at PTL. *The Charlotte Observer* had been on the money trail for years.

For years *The Charlotte Observer* seemed the only obstacle in Jim Bakker's way. A marketing genius and a master with the TV medium, the evangelist turned a low-budget local Christian TV show into a corporation with annual revenues exceeding $100 million. While other TV evangelists opened universities, Bakker built an unrivaled resort, Heritage USA, which drew born-again Christians from across the country.

By 1986, his 13th year in Charlotte, it seemed that Bakker had neutralized *The Observer*. In January 1986, *The Observer* published a series of stories describing the secret findings of an earlier federal investigation of Bakker's money-raising practices. Bakker struck back with a campaign, "Enough is Enough."

He broadcast shrewd rebuttals on his nationally syndicated weekday TV program. He sought to intimidate the newspaper and its parent chain, Knight-Ridder, with appeals to his supporters to cancel subscriptions, pull ads and deluge his adversary with letters and phone calls. He hired private detectives to investigate the newspaper's publisher, editor and reporters and former coworkers he suspected were aiding the newspaper. He sought to discredit me by broadcasting a false charge that I had tried to buy the cooperation of a woman evicted by PTL. The charge was a fabrication, a fact Bakker kept from viewers even after his staff realized its mistake. By spring 1986, it seemed PTL's campaign was working: even those who once might have urged the newspaper on were beginning to agree that the newspaper was on a vendetta.

I continued to pursue the story. Top on my list was an effort to substantiate information I had obtained that PTL had paid money to hush up a 1980 sexual encounter between Bakker and a New York church secretary named Jessica Hahn.

I had learned of the allegations from Hahn herself. In December 1984, Hahn called *The Observer* and complained of continuing rumors about the sexual encounter. Three weeks later, she telephoned and retracted all she had said. She threatened to sue if anything was printed. It was at that time, I later learned, that Hahn's representative in California began threatening PTL with a lawsuit. In February 1987, that representative negotiated a private settlement with Bakker's number two man, Richard Dortch.

In late 1985, I learned that Hahn had been paid to stay silent. What had seemed merely an episode in the private life of a public figure had become a story about misuse of donors' dollars—the very kind of news *The Observer* had pursued at PTL since the late 1970s.

But my source demanded confidentiality. And he could supply no documents to back up his tip. *The Observer* had to proceed with stealth. Any overt attempt to report the story would give PTL the warning it needed to again silence those involved.

Over the next year I sought corroboration. I approached one man who knew all and had been described as ready to talk; the man refused to see me. But in January 1987, I won the confidence of the second source *The Observer* needed. I began reporting the story full time, first with public record background checks on the principals and a round of interviews with those who would not alert PTL.

In February, I approached the principals: Hahn, her California-based representative Paul Roper, Hahn's onetime go-between to Bakker, defrocked minister John Wesley Fletcher and, finally, the organization. At first PTL stonewalled, apparently convinced *The Observer* did not have the story or would not publish it. I continued my calls, to PTL board members and officials of the Assemblies of God denomination that had ordained Bakker and Dortch.

Inside the newsroom, Rich Oppel, editor of *The Observer*, insisted on for-the-record confirmation and documentary proof of a payoff. That seemed impossible. PTL had structured the Hahn settlement to avoid a paper trail and seal the lips of those involved. *The Observer* wanted enough evidence to convince its readers. After Bakker's

"Enough is Enough" campaign, Oppel was not content to ask readers to accept blindly the newspaper's word that the accusations were true.

I went back to the phone. By March 13, the newspaper had a copy of a February 27, 1985, check for $115,000 written by PTL's lawyer and the on-the-record statement by Roper that he had received the money on behalf of a woman who had accused Bakker of wrongdoing.

On March 13, managing editor Mark Ethridge received a call from Norman Roy Grutman, a New York lawyer. Grutman said he represented PTL, Bakker and Dortch. He threatened legal action if *The Observer* published its story that weekend. Grutman demanded that the newspaper interview Bakker and Dortch—precisely what *The Observer* had been refused for three weeks.

That same day, I learned that Bakker's denomination had begun a formal investigation, largely due to my inquiries with officials in its national and state headquarters.

On March 19, by telephone from his home in California, Bakker told *The Observer* he was stepping down. "I am not able to muster the resources to combat a new wave of attack that I have learned is about to be launched against us by *The Charlotte Observer* . . ."

Over the next six weeks, I broke a string of exclusives.

• PTL had paid $265,000 to Hahn and laundered the money through its building contractor.

• Dortch, who had taken over day-to-day control of PTL after Bakker's resignation, had negotiated the Hahn settlement personally.

• Jim and Tammy Bakker had been paid more than $1.6 million in 1986. The sum surprised even PTL board members who supposedly set their pay.

• PTL had raised more than $49 million from donors to build a $26-million hotel at Heritage USA. Yet the 500-room hotel remained unfinished, and PTL owed the builder millions.

On April 28, the new PTL board fired Richard Dortch and another top Bakker aide, David Taggart, who was the subject of an *Observer* profile that morning. Bakker had failed to regain control of PTL—his plan even as he resigned in March.

As he took control of PTL in the spring of 1987, Jerry Falwell, the new board chairman, applauded *The Observer*'s coverage. The newspaper, he said, had ushered in a new era of accountability for the TV evangelism industry. In February 1988, the National Religious Broadcasters adopted a new, tougher set of standards for ethics and financial accountability.

Within weeks of Bakker's thwarted return, federal investigators began a sweeping investigation of the previous PTL management, probing allegations of tax fraud, wire fraud and mail fraud. A grand jury was empaneled in the summer of 1987. It continued its confidential work a year later. In May 1988 Bakker predicted he would be indicted.

Meanwhile, PTL's new leaders—first Falwell, then David Clark, a former executive at Pat Robertson's Christian Broadcasting Network —sought to save PTL from what Falwell called the "fiscal sins" of its past leaders.

—Charles E. Shepard
The Charlotte Observer

JIM BAKKER RESIGNS FROM PTL; JERRY FALWELL ASSUMES LEADERSHIP

TV EVANGELIST CITES PERSONAL, CHURCH REASONS

FRIDAY, MARCH 20, 1987

BY CHARLES E. SHEPARD

PTL President Jim Bakker, who built a fledgling Christian TV show in Charlotte into one of the nation's most popular TV ministries, resigned Thursday from PTL "for the good of my family, the church and of all of our related ministries."

Bakker, 47, his voice trembling by the end of a telephone statement to The Observer, said fellow TV evangelist Jerry Falwell of Lynchburg, Va., would replace him as chairman of PTL's board.

Falwell named a new board of directors Thursday.

PTL Executive Director Richard Dortch told employees at the Heritage USA headquarters south of Charlotte that he will succeed Bakker as president and host of PTL's daily talk show, now called the "Jim and Tammy" show.

In the statement, Bakker said that seven years ago he was "wickedly manipulated by treacherous former friends" who "conspired to betray me into a sexual encounter." He did not identify those people.

Then, Bakker said, he "succumbed to blackmail . . . to protect and spare the ministry and my family."

"Unfortunately, money was paid in order to avoid further suffering or hurt to anyone to appease those persons who were determined to destroy this ministry.

"I now, in hindsight, realize payment should have been resisted and we ought to have exposed the blackmailers to the penalties of the law."

Bakker made the comments as The Observer was investigating allegations that a New York woman and her representatives received $115,000 in 1985 after she said she had sexual relations with Bakker in a Florida hotel room.

A lawyer representing PTL, Norman Roy Grutman of New York, refused Thursday to answer whether the money paid was from PTL, Bakker's personal funds or some other source. He also declined to say how much money was paid.

He said payment was made under a pledge of secrecy, and PTL would not violate that.

The Observer first sought comment from Bakker and other PTL officials Feb. 24. Dortch canceled an interview, declined to answer questions submitted in advance and issued a three-paragraph statement.

"We refuse to become bitter and respond to rumors, conjecture and false accusations," Dortch's statement said then. "We place ourselves and our ministry in the hands of those who have spiritual rule over us and submit to their disposition of any matters brought before them concerning us."

On March 13, lawyer Grutman agreed to make Bakker and Dortch available for an interview.

The interview began with Bakker's statement Thursday at 2:30 p.m.

PTL employees gasped and cried when told of Bakker's resignation during a closed staff meeting two hours later in the church at Heritage USA.

Falwell also spoke by phone to the employees, who numbered about 400.

The developments open a new chapter for PTL, which reported $129 million in revenues in 1986, employs about 2,000 people and owns the 2,300-acre Heritage USA retreat between Charlotte and Fort Mill, S.C.

Bakker, a Michigan-born preacher, moved to Charlotte in early 1974 and soon became the top figure at the fledgling PTL.

He became PTL's senior pastor, preaching before overflow crowds Sunday morning.

He used his personality and gift for TV to raise hundreds of millions of dollars from viewers. The weekday broadcast once known as the "PTL Club," for Praise The Lord or People That Love, is known today as the "Jim and Tammy" show.

He was Heritage USA's master planner, conceiving of two 500-room hotels, a water amusement park, homes for single mothers and street people and other buildings. There are plans for developments worth hundreds of millions of dollars more.

In other developments Thursday:

• Bakker announced he has resigned from his denomination, the Assemblies of God.

PTL and Dortch also are leaving the Springfield, Mo.–based denomination, lawyer Grutman said. Dortch will remain on the PTL board.

Denomination officials told The Observer March 13 that they had begun formally investigating allegations against PTL, including the charge of sexual misconduct by Bakker.

The investigation will continue, despite the resignations, church officials said Thursday.

• Bakker disclosed that "my and (my wife) Tammy's physical and emotional resources have been so overwhelmed that we are presently under full-time therapy at a treatment center in California.

"Tammy Faye and I and our ministries have been subjected to constant harassment and pressures by various groups and forces whose objective has been to undermine and to destroy us. I cannot deny that the personal toll that these pressures have exerted on me and my wife and family have been more than we can bear," he said.

On March 6, in a videotape shown to PTL viewers, Bakker and his wife of 26 years disclosed that Tammy Bakker was being treated for drug dependency. Since mid-January the Bakkers have been in the Palm Springs, Calif., area, where they own a home.

• The entire board of directors at PTL, which Bakker had chaired, resigned. At least two of eight members of the board had resigned in recent weeks.

One of those, the Rev. Charles Cookman of Dunn, is the N.C. district superintendent for the Assemblies of God. In that role, he is responsible for the investigation of Bakker and PTL.

Cookman confirmed Monday he had resigned. He did so, he said, to avoid a conflict of interest, not because he had reached any conclusion on the allegations' merits.

When an Assemblies of God minister is found guilty of a moral indiscretion, church procedure says, the minister will, at minimum, be suspended for two years. For at least some of that time, ministers are barred from preaching if they want to return to the ministry in the denomination, church officials say.

In more extreme cases, the minister is dismissed outright from the denomination.

• Falwell, speaking from Virginia on the same telephone hookup with Bakker and The Observer, said he agreed to take the PTL post in part because he feared "a backwash that would hurt every gospel ministry in America, if not the world."

Falwell, who will continue his ministry in Virginia, pledged the new PTL leadership will have an open-door stance toward the news media.

BUSINESSMAN SAYS HE NEGOTIATED HAHN SETTLEMENT WITH DORTCH

FRIDAY, MARCH 27, 1987

BY CHARLES E. SHEPARD

PTL President Richard Dortch personally negotiated the $265,000 settlement of a New York woman's claim against Jim Bakker, the businessman who represented the woman said Thursday.

Over lunch at a Los Angeles hotel, Dortch and Paul Roper agreed in February 1985 how much money would be paid and to create a long-term trust account, Roper said.

The woman, Jessica Hahn, had complained through Roper to PTL that a 1980 sexual encounter with Jim Bakker damaged her emotionally.

The Observer reported Thursday that Hahn—whom Bakker branded a "blackmailer"—has gotten monthly payments of about $800 to $1,200 since spring 1985 from a $150,000 trust account created by PTL's attorneys.

And on Feb. 27, 1985, after Hahn appeared in a hearing mediated by a retired judge from Los Angeles, PTL's attorneys gave Roper a $115,000 check on the woman's behalf, The Observer has reported.

One PTL attorney was Howard Weitzman, a Los Angeles criminal specialist. The check was drawn on his client's trust account, according to a copy of the check.

A source familiar with events inside PTL in February 1985 has said a $25,000 PTL check was wired from a Rock Hill bank into Weitzman's client's trust account on or about the same day the agreement was reached in Weitzman's office.

Dortch's involvement in payments to Hahn continued into 1986 as he expedited trust payments to Hahn and was sent correspondence from the California lawyer serving as trustee for the fund, according to Roper and copies of correspondence obtained by The Observer from another source.

Dortch, executive director of PTL since late 1983, was named president and TV show host for the Fort Mill, S.C.–based television ministry when Bakker resigned March 19.

Dortch has not publicly explained his role in handling the Hahn matter for Bakker since 1984. At a Thursday news conference, he shook his head when asked if he would answer questions.

He could not be reached for comment late Thursday.

Thursday morning on PTL's weekday TV talk show, new PTL board Chairman Jerry Falwell disclosed that his new board of directors unanimously ratified the decision to name Dortch president. The eight-member board, which includes Dortch, met Thursday for the first time.

"Last week, when the transition occurred, we had to be sure there would not be a gap here of any kind, not a hiccup, not a anything," Falwell told viewers about his decision to promote Dortch.

In a news conference later, reporters asked Falwell about Dortch's role in the Hahn matter.

"We had that discussion this morning. We have read the news reports. We have heard rumors. . . . An inquiry is being made by counsel and independent auditors," Falwell said.

Falwell—who was Bakker's handpicked successor—estimated the inquiry will take a month.

In recent weeks, PTL has been represented by New York lawyer Roy Grutman, who also represents Dortch and Bakker.

Asked if Grutman's role and Dortch's presence on the board during an investigation might create a public relations problem, Falwell said:

"It may be, and the board will certainly give that serious consideration. In our two hours 15 minutes today, we covered all that (time) allowed us to cover. That did not concern us enough to make it a priority in this meeting."

In stepping down, Bakker said money was paid to avoid disclosure of a sexual encounter seven years ago—a decision he termed "poor judgment."

But Bakker's resignation statement to The Observer and appearance Monday on a nationwide PTL broadcast made no mention of continuing payments.

Bakker and his attorney have refused to say how much was paid or if the money came from PTL, Bakker or another source. Falwell said Thursday he didn't know.

Roper, 43, said Dortch led him to believe the $265,000 was coming from a real estate deal Bakker was completing.

Roper said Dortch told him: "Jim Bakker's had to sell his house over this thing. All he is getting (from the sale) is $265,000. He's not getting enough in salary to support" a larger settlement.

Public records show Jim and Tammy Bakker sold a $100,000 home in the River Hills community on Lake Wylie south of Charlotte in November 1983. But they are not known to have sold a home in York or Mecklenburg counties when the $265,000 settlement was arranged in 1985. Records show the Bakkers cleared $40,808.41 from the River Hills home sale.

Home sales have been cited before to explain Bakker's financial dealings.

In October 1984, Dortch told The Observer the Bakkers sold a Charlotte-area home to raise the down payment on a $449,000 Palm Desert, Calif., vacation home. The Bakkers paid $150,000 down on the home, which they are close to selling.

The Bakkers moved last month into another Palm Springs home, valued at $600,000.

Roper said the source of the settlement money had been important for Hahn and him.

"Neither Jessica nor myself wanted any money that came out of any (PTL supporter's) Social Security check or any donations given to the Lord," Roper said.

Lawyer Grutman refused comment Thursday.

Last week, Grutman said his clients could not elaborate on the money used because they were bound by a "covenant of confidentiality" accompanying the payment.

Hahn, who has declined to say what she was paid, is bound by a gag clause as well, according to sources.

Until Thursday, Roper had been unwilling to confirm that Hahn was getting payments from a trust account.

A trust agreement is in operation, although it has never been signed, according to documents and sources.

The agreement says Hahn, a 21-year-old church secretary in 1980, would receive the full $150,000 after 20 years of receiving interest from the principal. She also pledged, as part of the settlement, to surrender her right to seek damages, sources say.

The trust account began earning interest in about March 1985. For 1985, Hahn received $10,045 in interest, according to a Bank of Los Angeles statement. Payments have continued, according to a source, although the total isn't known.

Among the issues not yet resolved, according to a source, is the name of the trustor of the Jessica Hahn Trust. The trustor of a trust is customarily the person or entity supplying the money in the trust.

Weitzman's former partner, lawyer Scott Furstman, discussed that question in a July 2, 1985, letter to Dortch quoted in The Observer Sunday. In the letter, Furstman refers to the Jessica Hahn Trust.

"I have done additional research," Furstman wrote, "and am of the opinion that the Trustor can be designated as a corporation as opposed to an individual."

Weitzman has refused to comment on the matter, and Furstman has not returned a reporter's calls.

Documents and interviews with Roper and other sources have provided new details of the Hahn affair, which is being investigated by the Assemblies of God—the Pentecostal denomination from which Bakker and Dortch sought to resign last week.

The new information includes a copy of the draft lawsuit sent to PTL by Roper Jan. 14, 1985. The eight-page document said Hahn suffered emotionally from the Dec. 6, 1980, afternoon encounter with Bakker in a Clearwater Beach, Fla., hotel room.

The suit was never filed in court. Roper has said he sent the draft after failing to get PTL to return his telephone calls regarding Hahn's accusations.

Roper—who is studying law at a California university—challenged Bakker's claim of blackmail, as has Hahn.

"After a thorough investigation, I had a good faith belief that this lady had been damaged by the conduct of Jim Bakker. And having that good faith belief I had every right to pursue a claim for compensatory damages" for her.

"She was emotionally impaired in her ability to make a living," Roper said. "It had been represented to me she had been unable to hold a job."

Hahn, now 27, was a church secretary at the Massapequa Tabernacle on Long Island, N.Y., in 1980.

Roper told The Observer he wanted to follow the Bible's mandate that he meet with the accused, but Bakker refused to meet. Instead Dortch came.

They met Feb. 7, 1985, in a Newport Beach, Calif., office after Dortch flew out on PTL's jet. Roper said he told Dortch he wanted a Christian conciliation procedure, with each side naming a representative and those two naming a third.

Then, the three-member panel would hear the facts and render a binding decision, Roper said.

He said Dortch told him Bakker objected to the procedure because it was not to be done through the Assemblies of God church. Later, Dortch instructed him to handle the matter, privately, through Weitzman, Roper said.

Several weeks later, Roper said, he and Dortch agreed on a settlement over lunch at the Century Plaza Hotel in Century City, Calif., a short walk from Weitzman's office.

Roper said he wanted some "official sanction" on the settlement, out of concern that he and Hahn might be accused of blackmail.

On Feb. 27, 1985, Hahn, Roper, Furstman and Weitzman met for about two hours at Weitzman's office with Charles Woodmansee, a retired Los Angeles judge.

Woodmansee's role was, in part, "to pass his blessing on the legality and propriety of the proceedings," Roper said. "His comment was, 'This would pass muster in my courtroom.' "

Woodmansee could not be reached Thursday.

Before leaving, Roper said, he was given the $115,000 check.

About $20,300 went to Hahn directly, Roper has said. The rest was used to pay her expenses—including payment to Roper for handling the matter and providing help with tax returns and other matters over the 20-year trust term, Roper said.

Roper said Hahn's monthly checks have been late at times, prompting him to contact Furstman.

"If I couldn't get money out of Furstman, I would call Dortch," Roper said. That occurred three or four times, he said, most likely in 1985.

An April 10, 1986, letter from Furstman to Roper containing tax information on interest paid to Hahn's account in 1985 shows that a copy was to be sent to Dortch.

Roper declined to say how many times he has talked with Dortch since February 1985.

Dortch's critics—most notably a former close friend, TV evangelist Jimmy Swaggart—have suggested Dortch should step down.

In an interview Monday, Swaggart confirmed he met three days earlier in Palm Springs, Calif., with several key players in the Hahn matter. Swaggart was visiting the desert resort—coincidentally the same place Bakker has been since mid-January.

Among those present were Roper, Chattanooga TV minister John Ankerberg and John Stewart, an Orange, Calif., minister, Christian radio show host and law school professor whom Roper asked to draft the lawsuit sent to PTL on Hahn's behalf in early 1985.

Swaggart said he met with Roper because Roper had told an intermediary he trusted Swaggart and he was reluctant to give evidence he had to the Assemblies of God.

Monday, Bakker accused Swaggart of a "diabolical plot" to use the sexual allegation to take over PTL. The attack, carried on national TV, helped ignite a cross fire between some of the nation's leading TV evangelists in newspaper accounts and network TV shows.

Wednesday, in a session that ran from midafternoon to about 11 p.m., Roper, Ankerberg and others presented evidence to the Assemblies of God's executive presbytery in Springfield, Mo.

Staff writers Elizabeth Leland and Pam Kelley contributed to this article.

CONTRADICTIONS CLOUD BAKKER CASE REPORTS

SATURDAY, APRIL 11, 1987

BY CHARLES E. SHEPARD

For six years there were only whispers.

Today the rendezvous between two strangers in a Florida hotel room is front-page news.

But Jessica Hahn and former PTL leader Jim Bakker are saying next to nothing as press reports unfold, in explicit detail, what supposedly took place Dec. 6, 1980, in Clearwater Beach.

Their silence complicates the task of reconstructing what happened between the then-21-year-old secretary from a New York church and the 40-year-old Charlotte minister with a national TV audience and a crumbling marriage.

Accounts from one camp contradict stories told by the other.

Even the claims from within each camp—from the participants themselves—have not been entirely consistent.

Did Bakker plan a rendezvous to make his wife jealous or was he set up by scheming friends? Was he the insensitive seducer or hapless victim?

Did Hahn sip wine or water before the encounter? Did she have sexual relations with one man or two? Was she a virgin or sexually adept?

Consider these questions and the sometimes perplexing evidence in documents obtained by The Observer, statements Bakker and Hahn have made in public and to reporters, and comments attributed to the two by their associates:

WHY DID HAHN GO TO FLORIDA?

And who decided that Bakker and Hahn would have sex?

Oklahoma City evangelist John Wesley Fletcher, a close associate of Bakker in 1980, told The Observer he invited Hahn to Florida after Bakker told him he wanted to make his wife, Tammy, jealous.

Fletcher and Hahn have told The Observer that Hahn did not expect a sexual encounter. She said she had never before had intercourse.

In two December 1984 interviews with The Observer, Hahn said Fletcher led her to expect to meet Bakker and to watch him film a telethon.

Bakker painted a much different picture in his March 19 resignation statement and in private talks with Jamie Buckingham, a writer for a charismatic magazine.

"Treacherous former friends and then colleagues," aided by a female confederate, "conspired to betray me into a sexual encounter," Bakker said.

Buckingham, after a visit with Bakker, said Hahn "just got hold of a Pentecostal preacher who didn't know how to handle it and it just devastated him," according to The Washington Post.

WHAT DOES BAKKER SAY HAPPENED?

Bakker's comments on TV and to associates suggest several interpretations.

Buckingham told The Post that Bakker "was very surprised that this gal was able to perform the way that she did. . . . He described her as very professional for 21 years of age, (that) she knew all the tricks of the trade."

The Rev. Robert Schuller, a California TV minister, talked to Bakker by phone three days after his resignation:

"The whole thing was such a crazy idea, that the 15 minutes I spent in the room with this girl, I was so scared I couldn't have done it anyway," Bakker told Schuller, according to the Los Angeles Times.

On a videotape made the day before Schuller called, Bakker suggested he used the sexual encounter to recapture his wife's affections.

In the videotape, broadcast March 23 by PTL, Bakker said: "Tammy and I were having difficulty in our marriage, and I got some idea, in my hurt, that I could make Tammy jealous and somehow win her back to my love. Oh, I made a mistake, and it was wrong."

Bakker, speaking from the Palm Springs, Calif., home where he has been in seclusion, made the comments with Tammy Bakker at his side.

Asked about Bakker's comments, Paul Roper, the California businessman who confronted PTL with Hahn's story and negotiated a $265,000 settlement, told The Observer he found "it curious that Jim Bakker can't make up his mind which story he's going to tell."

"First I hear that he's confessed," Roper said. "Next I hear that he blamed his wife. The next thing I hear is that it was a setup by an evangelist friend. Next story was he confided in Robert Schuller that he spent 15 minutes and he was so frightened he couldn't do anything . . . and now I hear that he is surprised and shocked that Jessica Hahn was so experienced and that she took advantage of a poor little Pentecostal preacher."

HAS HAHN'S STORY CHANGED?

In her December 1984 interviews with The Observer, Hahn offered to take a lie detector test.

"I know the story is hard to believe," she said. "I'd swear in front of any judge that what took place is the truth."

The 1984 interview is mostly identical to her comments in a taped interview with Roper Jan. 3, 1985.

They also closely match a third account obtained by The Observer —an unsigned five-page letter sent to Bakker's personal aide, apparently in early 1984, after Bakker and his aide failed to return Hahn's phone calls. The author described herself as "a Christian lady" who knew Hahn and believed the young woman had been hurt.

But the three accounts do contain inconsistencies:

—**Sex with a second man.** According to a 30-page transcript of Hahn's comments to Roper, Hahn said a second man, a PTL associate, had sex with her against her wishes after Bakker left.

The man, named in the transcript, has told The Observer he did not have sex with Hahn. He said he believes she accused him to assure his silence.

In Hahn's Observer interview and the unsigned letter, no mention was made of sex with a second man. Hahn has refused to discuss the differing accounts with The Observer.

—**Water or wine.** In her taped comments, Hahn said evangelist Fletcher gave her a glass of wine before Bakker arrived.

She felt nauseous. "I thought it was because I hadn't eaten. . . . I was in a daze. Personally I think there was something in the wine."

In the Observer interview, Hahn said she believed something had been put in her drink to make her sick.

But Hahn said then the drink was water, not wine.

On March 28, Fletcher told The Observer he remembered a glass of wine in Hahn's hotel room. Asked if he had suggested Hahn drink from it, he said, "No, not to my knowledge."

In fall 1981, Fletcher was dismissed from the Assemblies of God denomination for what he says was a drinking problem. Once a regular guest on PTL shows, he has ever since been an outcast at PTL.

—**Requests for money.** In December 1984, Hahn told The Observer she had not asked PTL for money, as claimed in a document she said PTL pressured her to sign.

However, the unsigned letter sent to PTL earlier sought for Hahn an apology from Bakker, an end to gossip—and $100,000.

"Miss Hahn requires and deserves an opportunity to pick up the pieces of her life and rebuild it," the letter says. "That amount would not seem excessive to you if it had been your daughter or my daughter who had been violated."

DID BAKKER "ASSAULT" HAHN?

In a draft lawsuit Roper sent to PTL two weeks after interviewing Hahn, Roper suggested Hahn might sue Bakker for millions of dollars, alleging assault and battery, intentional infliction of emotional distress and false imprisonment.

No suit was filed.

But the draft suit achieved its purpose—getting PTL's attention. In February 1985, then-PTL Executive Director Richard Dortch agreed to the $265,000 settlement, Roper has said.

In his resignation statement, Bakker told The Observer: "I categorically deny that I've ever sexually assaulted or harassed anyone."

Bakker said his enemies "falsified, distorted and exaggerated the facts so as to make the occurrence appear many times worse than it ever was. Anyone who knows Jim Bakker knows that I never physically assaulted anyone in my life."

In Hahn's 1985 taped statement—which was sent to PTL with the draft lawsuit—Hahn did not use the term assault or imprisonment.

Hahn is quoted as saying she felt ill, speechless, out of control and out of breath, and tried several times, unsuccessfully, to stop Bakker.

"He did everything he wanted to do, and just didn't care," she said.

In The Observer interview in December 1984, Hahn was asked about giving consent.

"It certainly wasn't what I wanted . . . I didn't ask for it . . . it wasn't like I was sitting there laughing. I was crying, I was sick," she said.

Hahn told The Observer she should have left the room when Bakker, clad in a white terry-cloth swimsuit, started confiding intimate marital problems.

"I should have done a lot of things. I wasn't sure what was going on," she said. "I honestly didn't believe what was happening."

After Bakker left, Hahn said, she "felt like I wanted to call somebody, but I didn't know who to call."

She did not call police. She also apparently kept the incident from her mother and stepfather, then a police officer.

WHAT ELSE TROUBLED HAHN?

In the 1984 interview, Hahn expressed concern about continuing gossip and prank calls, about possible reprisals and about any misuse of the document she said Dortch and another PTL board member pressured her to sign a month before.

According to Hahn's taped interview with Roper, the PTL document she signed accused her of extortion and defamation, blamed the incident on her and said she had never been touched or abused.

"It made me feel like I was accused of raping them and then stealing their money," she told Roper.

PTL's effort to cover up the incident began within days of the sexual encounter, Hahn told Roper.

Bakker telephoned her, she said, and asked for assurances she wouldn't talk. "He told me I would be accountable to God if I caused trouble."

She also talked by phone and in person with Dortch, who took over last month as PTL president. Dortch has declined comment.

"He said they could guarantee my protection if I would protect them. . . . He said he could even get me a job if it came to that."

Dortch also told her she would have no spiritual peace until she signed the PTL document. He warned, too, Hahn told Roper, that Bakker might commit suicide if a scandal broke.

HOW HAD HAHN BEEN DAMAGED? AND WHY DID SHE WAIT TO SEEK A SETTLEMENT FROM PTL?

In her 1985 interview with Roper, Hahn said she had lost 20 pounds, gone to a psychiatrist and been nervous, upset and emotional since the incident.

"You must be wondering why Miss Hahn waited three years before coming forward," the 1984 unsigned letter to PTL said.

"Well, quite frankly, the pain doesn't go away. She has tried and tried to forget, but then someone else opens a mouth to gossip, and yet another lends an ear, and so it goes . . . The worst, most degrading and permanent effects are just now truly manifesting themselves."

PTL '86 PAYMENTS TO BAKKERS: $1.6 MILLION

SATURDAY, APRIL 18, 1987

BY CHARLES E. SHEPARD

Jim and Tammy Bakker received nearly $1.6 million in pay from the PTL television ministry last year and an additional $640,000 the last three months, The Observer has learned.

And between January 1984 and last month, the cohosts of PTL's weekday talk show received a total of $4.8 million in salary, bonuses and other payments, according to a source with access to ministry records.

Bakker, 47, stepped down as PTL president and chairman a month ago after acknowledging a 1980 extramarital sexual encounter and a subsequent agreement to make payments—later reported to be $265,000—to quiet complaints from Jessica Hahn, the woman involved.

Figures made available to The Observer show other PTL executives —including PTL's new president, Richard Dortch, and both Bakker's personal aide and secretary—received bonuses in 1986 more than twice their regular salaries.

And in the early months of 1987, Dortch and Bakker aide David Taggart received bonuses approaching what they received in all of 1986, the source said.

Bakker's choice as PTL's new board chairman, the Rev. Jerry Falwell of Lynchburg, Va., has ordered a halt to bonuses and other payments besides regular salaries, The Observer has learned.

Under IRS rules for tax-exempt organizations such as PTL, a private individual may not receive its funds except as reasonable payment for goods or services.

Last month, Falwell said the new PTL board had agreed to continue paying the Bakkers indefinitely. Falwell said then he did not know what the Bakkers were paid, and he did not reveal what the continuing pay would be.

The Bakkers have spent all but a few days of 1987 out of town and off the air, first at their Gatlinburg, Tenn., home and then in Palm Springs, Calif., where they purchased a home this year.

Two weeks before Jim Bakker's resignation, he disclosed publicly that his wife had been under treatment for drug dependency in California, and that he, along with their two children, had been in counseling. On March 19, Bakker said his and his wife's "physical and emotional resources have been so overwhelmed that we are presently under full-time therapy."

PTL last divulged the Bakkers' salaries—though not apparently bonuses or other compensation—in January 1979.

PTL said then the Bakkers earned $72,800 a year, including $1,000 a week for Jim Bakker and $400 for his wife.

The PTL ministry reported contributions of $28 million in 1978 as it began developing its Heritage USA retreat south of Charlotte. Last year, revenues totaled $129 million. PTL employs about 2,000 people.

In recent years, as Bakker's lifestyle and purchases of vacation homes and luxury cars have attracted media scrutiny, Bakker and PTL officials have said PTL's board of directors asked him to refrain from disclosing his pay.

Bakker—son of a machinist from Michigan—has said PTL's board sets his pay, with him out of the room, and takes good care of him. He has rejected suggestions that he is wealthy.

Bakker, Dortch and Taggart have determined bonuses for other PTL executives, according to two individuals familiar with ministry procedure.

Bonuses of about $470,000 and salaries of about $120,000 make up most of the $640,000 in pay the Bakkers received between January and March, the source said. In addition, Bakker received a loan of $150,000.

According to the source, Dortch, Bakker's personal aide David Taggart, Bakker's secretary Shirley Fulbright and PTL finance director Peter Bailey were paid between about $115,000 and $350,000 in 1986.

Specifically:

• Dortch, then PTL's executive director, earned about $350,000 in 1986, including bonuses of about $220,000 and a retirement account contribution of more than $80,000. Dortch was—and still is—a PTL board member.

In the first three months of 1987, Dortch received about $270,000, most of it in a $200,000 bonus.

In 1985, Dortch was paid about $240,000.

Dortch, 55, was an Assemblies of God district superintendent in Illinois before joining PTL's staff in late 1983. He has taken over hosting Bakker's talk show but also has come under fire for his role in negotiating the $265,000 settlement in 1985, and for his assurances to PTL board members that rumors of Bakker's sexual misconduct and payments were untrue.

• Taggart, Bakker's aide and a PTL vice president, was paid about $360,000 in 1986, including bonuses of about $275,000 and a salary of approximately $90,000.

From January through March of this year, Taggart got bonuses of $220,000, plus about $30,000 in salary.

Taggart, 29, once a performing pianist, was in charge of running Bakker's office, arranging his travel and buying his clothes, cars and homes.

• Fulbright, who has the title of executive assistant to the president, received about $160,000 in 1986, including bonuses of about $110,000.

From January through March of this year, she got about $50,000 in salary and bonuses.

Fulbright was also identified as assistant secretary-treasurer of PTL earlier this year.

• Peter Bailey, PTL's finance director, was paid about $115,000 last year, including $60,000 in bonuses and a salary of about $55,000. The first three months this year, he received about $70,000.

Bailey, reached Friday night, declined comment.

The compensation figures apparently do not include pay received by family members such as the Bakkers' children and Dortch's wife, son and daughter.

They also apparently do not include all the executives' fringe benefits, such as the lakefront home Dortch lives in. The house is valued at $256,170 for tax purposes.

In addition to a PTL home in a ministry compound on Lake Wylie, the Bakkers have been supplied cars, most recently Mercedes-Benzes. The ministry also has paid for their utilities, maids, grounds keepers and around-the-clock security.

After the Bakkers bought the mountainside home in Gatlinburg last year, PTL paid to erect the stone, wrought iron and chain-link fence put up around the property at a cost of more than $35,000. PTL's board had approved the expenditure for Bakker's security, according to former board member J. Don George.

In past comments on the air, Bakker has complained that the press misrepresented his financial resources and held an unfair standard for a minister's lifestyle.

"You won't win in this public opinion with the press because—you know one time they accused me of being a wealthy man," Bakker told viewers Oct. 13, 1985. "They kept saying if Jim would reveal this, reveal that, and it said in the article we don't reveal things."

So, Bakker said on the broadcast, he ordered an outside audit.

"Do you remember my net worth when they did that audit several years ago?" he asked a PTL employee nearby. Turning to the camera, he said, "My net worth came out to be $15,000."

Bakker did not tell his audience the year of the audit—1977.

The audit, made public by PTL, listed Bakker's and his wife's net worth as $23,568.

In that year, PTL said Bakker was paid $24,000 and his wife about $8,000 annually. Bakker also received a housing allowance of $2,868 and a $6,864 annuity contribution.

In a February 1983 television interview, Bakker told a reporter he was making a "living salary" but was not a millionaire.

By the next year, however, the Bakkers' combined compensation was more than $1.2 million, according to the source.

In October 1984, after an Observer story prompted Bakker to disclose his purchase of a California home, new Mercedes-Benz and antique Rolls-Royce, Bakker, Dortch and other PTL officials sought to counter any impression that Bakker was rich.

"You know what the net worth of Jim Bakker is," Dortch told viewers Oct. 8, 1984. "It's the amount of money that he paid down on the house he just bought . . . and the pension that he has."

Dortch did not disclose either figure. According to public records, the Bakkers paid $149,000 down on their first California vacation home, sold recently. Before that sale, they paid $350,000 down on the Palm Springs house.

In fall 1984, Bakker told viewers he had no secrets and did not try to disguise his lifestyle:

"If you're a partner with PTL, you know we've never hidden anything from you, except the normal things that you don't discuss on television."

3 PTL DIRECTORS DIDN'T KNOW WHAT BAKKER WAS PAID

WEDNESDAY, APRIL 22, 1987

BY CHARLES E. SHEPARD

Three former PTL directors say they didn't know what Jim Bakker was paid and don't remember authorizing all of $1.1 million in bonuses Bakker received during his last 15 months as the TV ministry's president and chairman.

The directors—a retired Charlotte businessman, a Texas hotel executive and a Texas pastor—expressed surprise that Jim and Tammy Bakker drew nearly $1.6 million in 1986 and PTL's executive director got more than $350,000 in salary and bonuses.

"Whew!" A. T. Lawing of Charlotte, a PTL board member since 1973, said late Friday. "Well, I just, I can't hardly believe that."

Bakker has said publicly that PTL's board set his salary and benefits, a common corporate practice.

The three board members acknowledge they voted hundreds of thousands of dollars in bonuses for the Bakkers last year on the recommendation of the executive director, fellow board member Richard Dortch.

But the former directors' statements, in separate interviews, raise a question about whether some money may have been paid without board approval.

Not only were last year's totals surprising, they said, but the board approved no bonuses or salary increases in 1987.

Figures obtained by The Observer show that Jim and Tammy Bakker and Dortch were paid $670,000 in bonuses the first three months of this year and also may have been receiving higher salaries.

It's not known who decided to make the questioned payments, who had authority to approve them, or whether any money was disbursed without proper authorization.

A 1983 copy of PTL's bylaws does not state who sets executive compensation.

Under IRS rules, a charity jeopardizes its tax-exempt status if employees receive unreasonable compensation or benefit financially solely because of their position. In considering such allegations, the IRS may consider whether a charity's accepted procedure has been circumvented.

PTL officials did not respond to an inquiry Tuesday. Efforts to interview the other five members of the former PTL board were unsuccessful.

On TV Tuesday, Dortch, PTL's new president and its only continuing board member, announced that he would give up his salary and benefits for 12 months.

Dortch was paid more than $350,000 last year and, for the first three months of 1987, received about $270,000 in salary and bonuses, according to figures obtained by The Observer.

In interviews over the last five days, former directors Lawing, Ernie Franzone and the Rev. J. Don George said they cannot document specifically the amount of bonuses they agreed to pay Bakker because they were not allowed to keep minutes and other PTL papers shown at board meetings.

Lawing and Franzone were among the directors who stepped down at Bakker's request a month ago.

Bakker, acknowledging a 1980 sexual encounter and subsequent payment for Jessica Hahn, resigned March 19 and handed the Fort Mill, S.C., ministry over to the Rev. Jerry Falwell, a Lynchburg, Va., Baptist evangelist.

George, who joined the PTL board in 1985, resigned in January. He said he felt the board had little influence.

"Perhaps I would, with hindsight being 20–20, be more inquisitive if I had it all to do over again," said George, whose Irving, Tex., Assemblies of God church has 4,500 members. "But I don't regret trusting in people, believing in them."

Said Franzone, of Bedford, Tex., "We played 'follow the leader. . . .'

"I completely trusted Jim Bakker. I completely trusted Rev. Dortch. If you want to call it a blind trust, I guess you could say it was."

Franzone, 58, is executive vice president of the Brock Hotel Corp., which manages PTL's Heritage Grand Hotel.

The three board members said they didn't know Bakker's base salary.

"The salaries were completely secret from the board," said Lawing, 67, retired owner of a service station equipment firm. He said he did not know why.

Bakker and PTL officials have rebuffed queries about Bakker's salary in recent years by saying the board asked him not to disclose the figures.

"The information I had was (Bakker) lived a kind of hand-to-mouth existence, that he lives from one paycheck to the next," said George. "That was the impression that I got from conversations that the board had with Brother Dortch."

It was Dortch, the board members say, who suggested Bakker's bonuses, after Bakker left the board room.

George, 50, said he had assumed Bakker's salary was $50,000 to $75,000. That, he said, left him inclined to approve large Christmas bonuses for Bakker.

Bakker's salary in 1985 and 1986 was $265,000 a year, according to a source with access to ministry records.

Figures obtained by The Observer show Bakker drew about $88,000 in salary between January and March. Treated as a quarterly sum, that would indicate a $352,000 annual salary.

Figures obtained by The Observer indicate the salaries of Tammy Bakker and Dortch may have increased as well this year.

The three former directors say the board had been called on to approve bonuses, but not salaries, for Tammy Bakker and Dortch in recent years.

In Dortch's case, figures obtained by The Observer show he drew more than $30,000 in salary the first three months of this year. That $120,000-a-year pace compares with a full-year's salary of about $45,000 for Dortch in 1986.

According to Lawing, PTL's board did not set or know Dortch's salary when Dortch became Bakker's deputy in late 1983. Dortch has been a PTL board member since the late 1970s.

Lawing and the two other directors said they also didn't know who decided how much board members would receive—$16,000 last year.

About the bonuses, the board members said, proposals came tied to the Bakkers' specific needs.

One time, Franzone said, "it came up that they needed the money for taxes or . . . some kind of financial situation."

More recently, George said, the board was told that Bakker needed money to help remodel and improve security at their new home in Gatlinburg, Tenn.

George said he remembered two bonuses in 1986 for Bakker. Each was for $100,000, George said, but Dortch would ask that PTL also provide the money Bakker needed to pay taxes on the bonus, he said.

Assuming Bakker was in the top tax bracket, PTL would have had to spend roughly $200,000 for such bonuses—half for Bakker and half to pay taxes. Under tax rules, PTL would have to report the full $200,000 as income to Bakker.

Figures obtained by The Observer show Jim Bakker received $800,000 in bonuses last year. "Wow, that surprises me," said Franzone when told the number.

George said the board voted one bonus at a mid-December meeting last year. The other, he said, came up in midyear and was portrayed to board members as a belated Christmas bonus from 1985.

Franzone and Lawing said they believed the board approved two or three bonuses in 1986.

When the board voted bonuses for Bakker, the three said, they typically also voted $50,000 after-tax bonuses for Tammy Bakker and for Dortch.

Tammy Bakker was cohost of PTL's flagship TV program and her own program, George said. Dortch "was a key man in the organization," he said.

Usually after the board voted on bonuses for the Bakkers, board member Charles Cookman or Almee Cortese would suggest "we must also do something for Brother Dortch," George said.

George, along with Lawing and Franzone, said the board has voted on no bonuses this year.

"Nothing has gone to them this year at all," said Lawing.

But figures obtained by The Observer show Bakker received $300,000 in January, February and March, Tammy Bakker about $170,000 and Dortch about $200,000.

George offered a possible explanation for at least some of the 1987 money.

Last year, he disclosed, the board voted to finance the Bakkers' and

Dortch's purchases of the Lake Wylie homes the ministry provides each.

The transfer was to take five years, with PTL covering any taxes due.

George said he never knew the homes' value. Dortch's is valued at $256,170 for tax purposes. No value is available for the Bakkers', bought in 1981 for $340,000. Both homes have undergone extensive renovation, remodeling and expansion at PTL expense.

"We were never privy to the type of information that would have allowed us to know the financial impact" of our decisions, George said.

Dortch, in an on-air announcement Tuesday, said he "will continue to live in the parsonage of this ministry . . . but I will not accept any salary whatsoever, nor pension benefits or any other benefits" for the next 12 months.

"God has spoken to my heart, and he will provide for my needs," he said.

Dortch, 55, has come under fire for his role in negotiating the $265,000 settlement for Jessica Hahn, the woman involved with Bakker, and for his assurances to PTL board members that rumors of sexual misconduct and payments were untrue.

DORTCH USED PTL MONEY TO PAY HAHN

TUESDAY, APRIL 28, 1987

BY CHARLES E. SHEPARD

PTL President Richard Dortch used ministry money to pay Jessica Hahn, channeling the $265,000 payment through PTL's building contractor, The Observer has learned.

Dortch asked Kansas contractor Roe Messner to send the money to a California lawyer handling Hahn's complaint over a 1980 sexual encounter with Bakker.

According to sources, Dortch told Messner to include the expenditure on one of his company's invoices to PTL. PTL later paid the bill, the sources say.

Explaining his need for help, Dortch, then PTL's executive director, told Messner that PTL needed to settle a threatened lawsuit confidentially.

New PTL Chairman Jerry Falwell confirmed the account Monday and said he believed Messner was manipulated. "I am personally convinced that Roe Messner is an honorable businessman," Falwell said.

"In my opinion, his chief error in the Jessica Hahn affair was lack of information and bad judgment."

Dortch could not be reached. Messner has declined to detail his role before today's PTL board meeting.

Messner, one of the nation's biggest church builders, has built more than $60 million in facilities at PTL's Heritage USA headquarters since 1984.

Falwell criticized PTL for using ministry money for Hahn.

"The part that bothers me most is that the settlement was on behalf of Jim Bakker, not PTL," Falwell said. "The sexual encounter was a result of Jim Bakker's misbehavior—not PTL's—and all settlements should have been covered by Rev. Bakker personally."

Falwell did not explicitly criticize Dortch, who took the president's post when Bakker resigned March 19. Dortch is the only former PTL executive on the board Falwell appointed last month.

Bakker resigned acknowledging a 1980 sexual incident and subsequent payment to quiet allegations by Hahn. He has refused to answer questions about whether he, PTL or someone else paid the money.

According to The Observer's sources, Dortch approached Messner in February 1985, after Dortch and Hahn's representative, Paul Roper, had worked out the proposed settlement over lunch in Los Angeles.

The sources gave this account:

Dortch told Messner that Bakker had had a sexual encounter with Hahn, then a 21-year-old church secretary, and Hahn was threatening to sue Bakker, PTL and other PTL officials.

He said he wanted to keep other employees at PTL from learning of the settlement.

Dortch asked Messner to send the money to Howard Weitzman, the Los Angeles lawyer handling payments and a trust for Jessica Hahn.

Acting at Dortch's request, Messner told his staff to wire the money to Weitzman's client's trust account. The amount was then included with construction items in a routine invoice sent to PTL for payment.

On Feb. 27, Weitzman paid Hahn's representative $115,000, The Observer reported last month. And a $150,000 trust account was set up in the woman's name.

Of the arrangement generally, Falwell criticized the decision to use ministry money without approval of directors then sitting on PTL's board.

"If the Jessica Hahn payment were in fact an out-of-court settlement to limit damage to the PTL ministry, it should have been so indicated in the board minutes, and should have been a board decision to pay those funds directly from PTL," Falwell said.

"It is my understanding that the board knew nothing of the Jessica Hahn affair until the general public did."

Four former PTL board members have told The Observer they did not know about the financial settlement for Hahn until news of it emerged in the press.

Dortch and Bakker also sat on PTL's board.

In at least three interviews during the last month, Messner has declined to discuss his role in helping make payments to Hahn. He said he was bound by promises to PTL officials to say nothing until after today.

"I don't fear anything anyone is going to write because I sure haven't done anything wrong," he said April 9. "I told the board I would remain silent, and that's what I'm going to do."

At the time Dortch approached Messner, the builder was completing work on PTL's Partner Center, which included the 500-room Heritage Grand Hotel, a shopping mall, cafeteria and conference center. PTL officials have said the project cost about $43 million.

Messner is building the $26 million Towers Hotel at Heritage USA.

The 51-year-old contractor acknowledges PTL owes his company about $12 million. That apparently makes him the ministry's biggest creditor.

Messner also is expected to build the new Calvary Church off N.C. 51. He is a candidate to build a new 10,000-seat church in Lynchburg for Falwell.

It is not known what Bakker knew of the arrangements. Bakker could not be reached for comment Monday, but the sources' account conflicts with claims advanced by people close to the 47-year-old former PTL president.

Jamie Buckingham, a writer for a charismatic magazine, told The Washington Post last month after visiting with Bakker that the Assemblies of God minister told him an "anonymous donor" provided the money for Hahn.

"He doesn't know where it came from," Buckingham said. "He knows it was not laundered through PTL. But he said he had a group of people around him who said, 'We'll handle this.' "

TAX STATUS OF PTL ATTACKED

IRS SAYS EXEMPTION SHOULD BE REVOKED

TUESDAY, APRIL 28, 1987

BY CHARLES E. SHEPARD

The IRS has told PTL it wants to revoke the TV ministry's tax-exempt status for 1981–1983 because a "substantial portion of PTL's net earnings" those years went to benefit Jim Bakker, his relatives and other PTL officers, IRS documents show.

In a confidential 1985 report, the IRS contends Bakker was paid nearly $1 million more than was reasonable those three years.

It also asserts that Bakker and other officers spent money lavishly, holding $8,000 dinner parties and renting $350-a-night hotel rooms. And the IRS says PTL failed to report all of Bakker's income on his W-2 forms.

In a separate matter, the S.C. Tax Commission is demanding PTL pay $5.5 million in penalties, interest and back taxes for 1984–1985, documents obtained by The Observer show.

PTL expects the two tax agencies to extend their claims to cover more recent years, according to undisclosed portions of PTL's 1986 financial statements obtained by The Observer.

Such a move would jeopardize the ministry's tax-exempt status for 1984 and 1985 and result in another S.C. claim for at least $4.5 million in sales and accommodations taxes.

PTL, which has refused to answer past tax questions, is appealing the findings inside the two tax agencies.

"PTL officials . . . indicate that they do not agree with any issue raised in the report," the IRS's Nov. 13, 1985, letter to PTL says.

If the Fort Mill, S.C., TV ministry lost its tax-exempt status, its contributors would no longer be able to deduct donations on their tax returns. That would make such gifts more costly for donors, likely hurting the ministry's ability to raise money.

And PTL would have to file back tax returns and likely pay back taxes.

It is not known how much PTL would owe the federal government if it lost its tax-exempt status. PTL's auditors indicated, however, that the IRS claim would have a "material" or significant effect on PTL's financial statements.

PTL reported $129 million in revenues in 1986.

The agencies' claims are described in two documents obtained by The Observer—the November 1985 IRS "examination report" sent to PTL, and notes contained in the undisclosed portion of PTL's 1986 audited financial statements.

The IRS documents provide the first publicized evidence that government officials have objected to PTL's spending on the Bakkers.

Bakker has told viewers that ministers and their followers should not have to live with "junk." He also has complained that the IRS won't tell him what he can do.

The IRS document asserts that "numerous expenditures and transactions were made, or entered into, for the personal and private benefit of some of the officers of PTL, primarily James O. Bakker."

In return for the privilege of tax exemption, federal law prohibits charities from allowing individuals to pocket funds except as reasonable payment for goods or services.

The IRS document portrays the ministry as making little effort to explain specific expenses to IRS auditors.

"They have presented no documentation but contend that all expenditures questioned were expended for exempt (or charitable) purposes," the IRS says.

It is not known what documents PTL has supplied the IRS in their continuing dispute. It is also not known whether the IRS has changed its position since November 1985. PTL's audited financial statements make no reference to any such shift.

The documents detail auditors' findings for the 1981–83 years on these points:

• Unreasonable compensation—The IRS said Bakker drew $967,648 more than he should have over the three years, based on his duties and the pay of his counterparts in other ministries.

PTL responded that "the compensation was reasonable because

(Bakker) is the guiding light of the ministry and is the key to PTL's success in fundraising."

The IRS documents show Bakker was paid $638,112 in 1983, $400,766 in 1982 and $259,770 in 1981.

During PTL's fiscal year 1983, for example, the IRS found Bakker's salary was $301,506.

But he also received a $24,000 living allowance, $91,101 in pension contributions, a $18,548 discount on the purchase of two condominiums at Heritage USA, $130,494 in benefits for his use of a home furnished and owned by PTL, and $66,663 in other expenses for his personal benefit.

The IRS said Bakker should have received $121,000 that year, not the more than $600,000 he did get.

The Observer reported earlier this month that Bakker and his wife, Tammy, received compensation of nearly $1.6 million in 1986, not including fringe benefits.

In the first three months of this year, The Observer reported, the couple drew $640,000 in salary, bonuses and other compensation. In addition, they received a $150,000 loan.

The Rev. Jerry Falwell, Bakker's successor as PTL board chairman, called the pay given the Bakkers and other PTL executives "horrendous" and "indefensible."

• Expenditures for the private benefit of officers. In 1981–83, about $841,000 was spent without substantiation that it was for PTL's charitable purpose.

The totals were not included on the officers' W-2 forms, the IRS said.

Bakker bought the two condominiums at Heritage USA for about $90,000, getting the $18,548 discount.

PTL told the IRS all employees could get such discounts, making the fringe benefit nontaxable. But the IRS says the general discount was not offered until two months after Bakker's purchases.

In another incident, PTL claimed that two 1982 cash advances totaling $25,000 were for a medical trip by Bakker and his aide, David Taggart, to Palm Springs, Calif.

But the records did not say what illnesses had been treated or what medical procedures performed.

"Also, the records submitted . . . reflected numerous personal-type expenditures not related to medical treatment, e.g. floral gifts, newspapers, magazines, parsonage decor items, etc."

In addition, the IRS said, the medical claim was never submitted to PTL's group medical plan.

The IRS got no or insufficient documentation of the purposes of checks written to officers, of advances to officers that were forgiven, and of travel expenses reported by officers.

In some cases, the IRS wrote, documentation "indicated that the expenditure was for the personal or private benefit" of a PTL officer.

In other cases, it said, expenditures appeared "lavish or extravagant."

"There were numerous instances of payment of excessive tips for restaurant dining and limousine service," including one that exceeded 110%, the IRS letter says.

Travel items purchased included "briefcases costing $418 and $800, an address book for $70, a Gucci toilet kit for $74, and a Gucci pen for $120."

The IRS also questioned restaurant and hotel bills.

In a late 1980 trip to Hawaii, Bakker and his family rented a $350-a-night hotel suite.

A Christmas party for 90 PTL executives at Charlotte's Cafe Eugene restaurant cost nearly $8,700, or $96.46 a person. A 20th wedding anniversary party for the Bakkers at the same restaurant cost $8,500.

• Interest-free use of funds. PTL money was used to buy personal items or for private expenses of Bakker and his family.

After inquiries, the IRS said, PTL tallied the expenditures involved and in April 1983, Bakker reimbursed PTL $75,908.57.

• Assets for Bakker's personal use. The ministry in 1982 bought and decorated an oceanfront condominium for Bakker and his family. The condominium, whose existence was disclosed by The Observer in February 1983, was bought for $390,000.

The IRS letter also reveals that furniture and fixtures for the unit cost $202,566.34. PTL sold the unit after the news accounts.

• Benefits to Bakker family members. PTL leased cars to Bakker's father and father-in-law at cost. But payments during the four months audited show PTL was paid $716 less than it had paid.

In April 1982, PTL's directors voted a $2,000 bonus to Tammy Bakker, then a cohost of and singer on the "Jim Bakker" show.

But PTL records show that on that day, Tammy Bakker was paid $4,651, more than twice what the board had authorized.

According to PTL's 1986 audited financial statements, PTL has been granted a hearing before the IRS's regional appeals director. The ministry's next step would be to go to court or submit to the IRS decision.

The IRS letter suggests an alternative position if PTL succeeds in keeping its tax-exempt status.

First, the IRS said, PTL should be classified not as a church, but as a religious organization—subject to tougher reporting requirements.

The IRS argued that PTL was not a church because its TV operation, not its local services, are its primary activity and the TV operation does not meet IRS standards for churches.

Second, it said, PTL should be taxed on the unexplained expenditures cited in support of the tax-exempt status revocation.

IRS documents are confidential, and IRS officials have declined to say what demands they have made from PTL.

S.C. officials also won't elaborate on their dispute with PTL. Sources say PTL is appealing to the S.C. Tax Commission.

The commission staff says the $1,000 "lifetime partnership" payments PTL received in return for a lifetime promise of free lodging at its hotels are subject to the state's 7% tax on hotel rooms.

PTL's financial statements say the commission staff has said PTL owes $5.5 million for fiscal 1984 and 1985, including penalties and interest.

If that position prevails, the commission would likely seek the same tax on more than $67 million in "partnerships" not included in the pending S.C. claim. At a 7% tax rate, PTL would owe more than $4.5 million more.

JESSICA HAHN

THE WOMAN BEHIND THE HEADLINES

THURSDAY, MAY 21, 1987

BY JODY JAFFE

NEW YORK—Jessica Hahn's life has been a search for the embrace of family. First the family of her mother and father, then the family of God she found in Pentecostalism.

Pentecostalism led her to evangelist John Wesley Fletcher. Fletcher led her to Jim Bakker. And that 1980 encounter made her name a household word in 1987.

The story broke March 19. Jim Bakker resigned over his sexual encounter with a 21-year-old church secretary.

Five days later, a color picture of Jessica Hahn, the secretary, hit the newsstands. The world saw a flame-haired, chesty woman in tight black jeans, spike boots, a clingy black V-neck and heavy gold chains.

Hardly America's vision of a church secretary.

To understand, it is necessary to understand where and how she grew up.

Jessica Hahn is a child of Long Island.

For the rich, the island's rural outreaches make perfect playgrounds —close enough for a jaunt to the country home, still distant from suburbia.

Closer in, the landscape changes from overstated houses and understated women to understated houses and overstated women. The postwar working class looking to do better on a quarter-acre. Retired cops who dream of staying at the big hotel in Hershey, Pa. Wives—once office workers, now homemakers—redecorating their children's rooms into dens for their husbands.

Girls who dress Long Island-style, where more is better, jeans are tighter, jewelry and makeup heavier, all of it as expected on Long Island as khaki slacks, add-a-beads and a hint of blush are in Charlotte.

"When I saw her picture in the paper, I didn't think twice about it," says Jessica Hahn's childhood best friend, Mary Beth Erhard, 29. "That's how I would dress. I think that looks really good like that. That's typical for New York, anything goes."

Jessica Hahn's mother, also named Jessica, followed the script: Marry young; have babies. She met a handsome utility splicer and thought she was on her way to happiness.

"He was very domineering, very handsome but cold," says Jessica Moylan. "I used to think he was the strong silent type because he didn't talk much."

The marriage disintegrated; they eventually divorced.

Dropped by her friends and later excommunicated from her church, Moylan was alone with three children.

She found work at $60 a week. Rent was $55 a month and there were four mouths to feed.

Jessica Hahn was 2 years old.

After six months alone, Jessica Moylan was having lunch with a friend. In walked a big, friendly Irishman who started talking to them.

"I thought he was interested in my friend," Jessica Moylan recalls. "I didn't consider myself single. I had three children; who'd want to take a woman with three children?"

Eddie Moylan did. He courted his flame-haired beauty for three years before they married.

Jessica Hahn was 5.

Moylan became Hahn's father in everything but name.

As a New York cop, Eddie Moylan made a decent living. But he was already sending money to his mother and a daughter.

He scraped, and bought the American dream—a house in the suburbs where *his* kids could play outside, in safety.

Jessica Hahn was 8 years old when they moved in.

"I remember," Moylan says, "we gave each of the kids $2 for dinner that night. That was all we had left."

She grew up in that house on Massachusetts Avenue, in Massapequa. The lots are manicured, the houses cared for. Her blue ranch is two houses in from the dead end, with a front yard of white gravel, a driftwood centerpiece and a hand-carved sign announcing "The Moylans."

"WHEN I LEFT THE HOUSE, SOMETIMES I WANTED TO GO RIGHT BACK; THAT'S HOW INSECURE I WAS."

—Jessica Hahn

From the start it was a house with structure, order and rules.

"The big joke," Eddie Moylan chuckles as he sinks into his overstuffed chair, "was there were always lists on the refrigerator. 'Jeffery's chores, Cheryl's chores, Jessica's chores.' When I got married, my friends kept joking, 'Where's Eddie's list of chores?' "

"I always had rules," says Jessica Moylan, shoulders square, back straight.

In the Moylan home, Eddie Moylan wears the emotions. Quick to laugh and joke, he answers his door in an old T-shirt and baggy pants, his belt unbuckled. Jessica Moylan is the doer, the disciplinarian who's dressed by dawn, color-coordinated, perfectly coiffed and flawlessly made up.

Says Jessica Hahn: "She always made me wear ribbons in my hair. She used to say, 'When you don't go out with ribbons, it's like going out without panties.' "

Jessica Moylan remembers her daughter required little discipline. A few times she got sent to bed early. But mostly, her mother remembers, Jessica Hahn was eager to please.

"Even now if we have a fight on the telephone and it's my fault, she calls back in five minutes and says, 'I'm sorry, Mom.' She always tries to save me. Maybe she feels because I've had enough in my life. Jessica always treats me like I'm the daughter. I always say to her, 'You're not my mother. I'm your mother.' "

As a child, Hahn often picked flowers for her mother from neighbors' gardens. "Don't worry, Mom," she would say, "I asked first."

But she was also mischievous. She feigned sleep in nursery school and organized games when the teacher left the room. She would put off her chores, then beg her sister for help.

She was a sloppy tomboy, her mother remembers, clumsy, careless of her appearance and rarely cried when she got hurt.

"She was always embarrassing me, walking around with mud hanging off her socks," Jessica Moylan says.

On Massachusetts Avenue, a neighbor remembers her as "a lovely girl who never caused any trouble."

"Jessica was a bubbly type of person," says Joan Clifford, mother of Hahn's friend Mary Beth Erhard. "Jessica never overdid. She wasn't overtalkative, wasn't shy."

Says Erhard: "She was a normal kid. She was talkative, outgoing. We'd play Barbie dolls, go to the movies and have sleep-over parties."

Meanwhile, a trinity had formed on Massachusetts Avenue among 8-year-old Jessica, Mary Beth and another neighborhood girl, Carol. For the next six years, they were inseparable.

Until late April 1974, Mary Beth pounded on Jessica's door. Carol was dead. A brain tumor. Pain had shot through her arm while she was at a New Jersey amusement park. She had died that night.

"We were hysterical," Erhard says. "Jessica couldn't stop crying the whole night. We took a walk to the Catholic church and stopped in there awhile. Then we came back and talked some more. The next day we went to the funeral. It took us a long time to get over it. It was always the three of us. We didn't talk about Carol for a year because it hurt too much. After that we talked about it once in a while."

Jessica Hahn was 14 years old. Her religious rebirth was about to begin.

"I remember my mother held me and said, 'Just think, right now like I'm holding you, God is holding her.' I didn't know the Lord then, but I was grateful she had a God to go to. That's when I started thinking about death and heaven and God."

Reared Catholic, Hahn went to Mass each week. But she says she never felt as though she knew the Lord; there was always a middleman.

By junior high, Hahn says, she was chubby and insecure.

"When I left the house, sometimes I wanted to go right back; that's how insecure I was. I had a group of friends, but I didn't go out much. I felt very out of place. I always found a void, but rather than trying to figure it out, I walked away."

During free periods in school, Hahn remembers helping in the office or the nurse's station.

"I loved teachers; I always had this thing for older people, people that could teach me things. Authority or whatever it is."

Outside, Hahn lived for her baby brother, born when she was 12.

"I had to be at the bus stop every day at a quarter to 3 with the carriage for Jessica to take Danny," Jessica Moylan says. "If I wasn't there, she would throw a fit."

Friends would ask Hahn to join them. Friday night movies, Saturday at the mall or an afternoon at the local hangout, an old schoolyard they called Pickin Field.

"You could tell she didn't really want to do it," Erhard says, "When we went out places, she said she wanted to stay in."

One day she did go out.

"IT WAS VERY DIFFERENT, VERY EMOTIONAL. I THOUGHT, 'THIS IS CHURCH?'"

—Jessica Hahn

On June 21, 1974—two months after Carol died—Hahn strolled Danny to Pickin Field. Music was coming from the yellow-and-white striped tent pitched next to the Full Gospel Tabernacle Church.

"She wanted to check it out," Erhard says, "She wanted me to go over, and I said I wasn't really interested. I was really involved in the Catholic Church."

It was a hot, sunny morning. Hahn, in jeans and a white halter, followed the soft strains of "I Just Want to Praise the Lord."

"It sounded like a love song to the Lord, soft and peaceful," Hahn says. "It was very different, very emotional. I thought, 'This is church?'"

She saw people walk to the altar, declaring their acceptance of Jesus. She walked to the altar.

"It immediately drew me in. I watched and listened and went back that night. I felt for the first time I fit in somewhere, except for my family. I always felt content with my family."

Eddie Moylan never misses Sunday mass, and he didn't like his daughter's conversion to Pentecostalism. But any church is better than no church, his wife convinced him.

"It was exciting for her," Jessica Moylan says. "Ours is a quiet religion. It's a very quiet church. Let's face it, it's solemn."

That was the summer Hahn met John Wesley Fletcher, a fiery, self-proclaimed faith healer who preached at the revivals.

"I thought, 'This is God.' "

Hahn dedicated herself to the church with the zeal of a budding Olympic athlete. Meetings with friends ended, and school interfered with where she wanted most to be—the Full Gospel Tabernacle.

"By this time in my life—ninth grade—I'm totally in love with my life," Hahn says. "I feel complete, content and happy. I have a personal relationship with God that I never really had. It was like a family; they took me under their wing."

While her friends dated, Hahn spent her time at the church, talking about God.

"It's like when you fall in love," she says, "You want to learn what a person's about, everything they say and do."

What free time she had, she spent with her brother Danny.

"She never dated much," says Erhard. "When I would go out with my boyfriend, I would talk about him. . . . I didn't know why she didn't date. I never asked because I didn't want to hurt her feelings."

Hahn remembers one date, a boy named Craig. She also remembers a crush. A musician at the church. "I thought he was the best thing in the world. I stared at him every five minutes."

Hahn's mother noticed her daughter's solitary life, but was not bothered. She didn't want Jessica to make the same mistake she had.

"I can understand; I entrusted myself to my first husband," she says. "But the next time, I looked for something else. I looked for security—is he going to be a good father to my children; will he make me happy the rest of my life?"

"SHE'S A GOOD GIRL. WE KNOW WHAT SHE WAS; WE KNOW WHERE SHE CAME FROM AND WHAT SHE IS."

—Jessica Moylan

Jessica Hahn made little impact on her 1977 graduating class at Massapequa High—until Bakker's March 19 revelation. Its most famous alumni had been Brian Setzer, guitar player for the Stray Cats, and Timothy Van Patten, who played Salami in the TV show "White Shadow" and Romeo to Hahn's Juliet in senior English.

After graduation, Hahn got a job at her church as a secretary, where she worked for the next 10 years. She still didn't date. Weekends and evenings were at the church or at nearby dinners with church members.

"I never thought seriously about marriage," Hahn says. "When I pictured my life, I always thought about my life being alone. I don't know why."

In December 1980, John Wesley Fletcher asked her to go to Florida to watch the PTL show being taped and meet Jim Bakker.

Jessica Hahn was 21.

She was a fan of Bakker's and had been sending his ministry $15 a month. "I thought this man is doing it all, and PTL must be a little piece of heaven," Hahn says.

She returned from Florida early, saying nothing to her mother and father about the trip. Her parents noticed nothing different.

"I always thought a mother's supposed to sense things like this," says Jessica Moylan. "I try it over and over in my mind. When she came home, was she sick, did she act funny?"

Five years passed. Hahn moved out. It was time, she told her parents, that she be on her own.

"I loved living there," Hahn says. "But I knew the story was going to break, and I didn't want to get them involved."

Two more years passed. On March 19 a New York Post reporter drove down Massachusetts Avenue. Eddie Moylan was in his garage looking for a can of wood stain. The reporter asked about Hahn and Bakker.

Eddie Moylan immediately called Hahn.

"She said, 'Tonight everything's coming out. I thought you would be spared,' " Eddie Moylan says.

The next day, a reporter gave them a copy of The Observer. They read of their daughter and Bakker. Of the Florida hotel room and money paid to her. Weeks later, they read more. Hahn's taped transcript, which she confirms is her voice, was leaked to Star magazine. Hahn says she doesn't know by whom. It describes a naive young woman, lured to Florida, given alcohol and then forced to have sex with Bakker.

"Hook me up to a lie detector," she says, "roll in the machines."

Hahn has yet to tell her parents what happened.

Jessica Moylan never talked to her daughter about sex. Hahn learned from a library book.

"I was brought up by my grandmother," Jessica Moylan says. "You just didn't talk about it. It embarrassed me. Even today I don't talk about private matters. We're the kind of family that gets embarrassed when a nude scene comes on the VCR."

The Moylans think their daughter has been painted as something she is not.

"They make jokes because she's pretty," Eddie Moylan says. "I'll tell you what's the worst. It's like a stab; the biggest thing that hurt and tears us apart is when they say 'the Jim Bakker affair.' This was not an affair."

Says Jessica Moylan: "It's almost as if she died. The ache is so bad, and we're helpless. I know and Eddie knows. She's a good girl. We know what she was; we know where she came from and what she is."

These days, Hahn spends her time in her three-room upstairs apartment in West Babylon. A life-size poster of Elvis Presley greets her as she walks in. Over her living room sofa hangs another Elvis portrait.

She has stopped working at the church. She doesn't want to get them involved, she says. Her only companion is her dog, Missy, who gets two Lean Cuisine dinners each night. (Glazed Orange Chicken is the dog's favorite.) Hahn's telephone rings constantly.

Reporters. Book agents. Movie producers.

Another family for Jessica Hahn.

PTL DEALINGS DEFIED 'ALL BUSINESS PRACTICES,' OFFICIAL SAYS

SATURDAY, MAY 23, 1987

BY CHARLES E. SHEPARD

They were unusual days for PTL, that early winter of 1985–86.

Instead of plans for buildings, Jim Bakker talked to his TV audience day after day about paring spending, trimming staff, lowering his sights.

On Christmas Day 1985, viewers watched a PTL executive hand Bakker what the evangelist called "one of the presents I wanted more than anything else"—PTL's first balanced budget.

Within three months, the executive sat before Bakker in his Palm Desert, Calif., home, awash in frustration. Spending, said budget director Mark Burgund, is out of control. Bakker's determination to build at the Heritage USA resort was forcing the ministry into the red.

And, Burgund recalled in an interview this week: "The employees themselves were not taking the budget seriously. They knew they would be rewarded for pleasing Jim."

The swift demise of that budget was a lesson in the rules of finance within the television ministry's pyramid-shaped headquarters south of Charlotte.

According to Burgund and longtime chief financial officer Peter Bailey, the practices included:

• No internal accountability for spending on the executive payroll and checking accounts, and the top executives' MasterCard and Visa credit cards. Bakker and a small group of executives controlled these from the third floor.

• Little communication between the third floor and those in finance on the second floor, who knew how much the ministry had to spend.

• An antiquated records system that left the ministry ignorant for months about its finances. Among the uncertainties: how many

$1,000 "lifetime partnerships" it had sold in return for the promise of free lodging in PTL's hotels.

"It defies all business practices," PTL's new chief operating officer Harry Hargrave said Friday. "There has to be control and accountability of every department of any organization. Even the very top echelons of business are responsible to internal audit and corporate controllers."

Last year, PTL raised nearly $44 million in contributions and $57 million more in partnerships.

PTL's auditors have begun finding evidence of questionable spending in the once-secret third-floor accounts:

Item: On April 9, Bakker aide David Taggart signed a $100,000 check to his brother James Taggart's interior decorating company, according to a source. PTL's board fired David Taggart on April 28, though apparently unaware of the April 9 check.

James Taggart had done interior decorating for PTL and the Bakkers. A notation on the check indicates he was being paid for consulting services, according to the source. He was also receiving $120,000 a year from the executive payroll, for consulting.

Item: In their final 18 months, Bakker and David Taggart took $640,000 in cash advances on the third floor's two credit cards, Hargrave confirmed Friday.

Of that, Taggart took $45,000 shortly before taking a European vacation last year. PTL officials want to know if any was used for personal expenses.

Ministry officials have found no documents showing how the $640,000 was spent.

Bailey says David Taggart told him that he, not finance, would keep all credit card records, to assure confidentiality. In a phone call since his dismissal, Taggart told Bailey he has the receipts and will turn them over, Bailey said. Taggart could not be reached.

PTL's top executives began to be paid from a separate payroll in late 1983 or early 1984, after longtime board member Richard Dortch became executive director.

Dortch wanted to protect Bakker's image and was secretive by nature, says Burgund, who had worked for Dortch before.

"It doesn't matter if there's nothing wrong with it. He doesn't want anyone to know," says Burgund.

PTL's outside auditors managed the executive payroll, sending checks when the third floor called. When the account ran low, the auditors wrote for more money.

Former PTL board members have said they do not remember authorizing some bonuses paid Bakker, his wife, Tammy, and Dortch.

Burgund, though a close Dortch associate, knew nothing of the top salaries, including $1.6 million for the Bakkers in 1986. "I was so angry," he says.

Bailey says recent disclosure of the pay scale confirms what he suspected. He says he had told Dortch of his worries about the growing cost of the payroll.

Dortch, he says, made no comment. "You just couldn't discuss it."

Bailey, who was also on the executive payroll, received $55,000 in salary last year, plus a $60,000 bonus.

Money also flowed from the two credit cards and an executive checking account.

One expense of the checking account, Bailey says, was $40,000 to $50,000 spent each month to reduce the balance on the credit cards. Besides Bakker and Taggart, the cards were used by Dortch and Bakker's secretary, Shirley Fulbright, Bailey said.

The outstanding balance on the cards recently was a combined $120,000, Bailey said. Up to about $100,000 could be charged on each card.

Bakker's management style created a second set of financial problems.

"I'm sure he's well-meaning and had good intentions," said Bailey. "But he did not understand the cash crisis we were constantly in."

When he raised a chunk of money, Bakker would immediately spend it, perhaps to landscape the grounds or start a building, Bailey says.

"It was as though we didn't exist any more," Burgund says. "He would just go ahead and do what he wanted to do and all of a sudden we were a million short. . . ."

Dortch tried to restrain the spending, Burgund says. Time after time, he said, Dortch would tell PTL's managers: "When Jim Bakker says get it built, he doesn't mean bankrupt the ministry to get it there."

While they juggled cash to pay for what Bailey calls Bakker's "agenda," PTL's staff was more successful applying professional standards to areas where Bakker was uninvolved.

In many areas, says Burgund's successor as budget director, Dana Cadwell, "we had budgets and we were accountable and it was run very professionally."

The spending squeeze compounded problems in finance, says Burgund.

"We've got a 21st century Christian campground with an 18th century bookkeeping system," says Burgund. "We couldn't get $2 million to put a (computerized) bookkeeping system in."

Compounding the problem was Bakker's disdain for his financial staff.

"Time and time again," says Burgund, "he would call us pencil pushers. 'If pencil pushers had their way we'd still be in tents.' "

After hearing that comment at one meeting, Burgund says, Bailey leaned over and whispered to him, "And they'd be paid for."

TWO

A DEATH IN THE FAMILY AND WHEN FURLOUGHED MURDERERS STRIKE AGAIN

1988 WINNERS IN THE GENERAL NEWS REPORTING CATEGORY

"For a distinguished example of reporting within a newspaper's area of circulation that meets the daily challenges of journalism such as spot news reporting or consistent beat coverage . . ."

The Alabama Journal
Staff
and
Lawrence Eagle-Tribune
Staff

A DEATH IN THE FAMILY

Alabama has the highest infant death rate in the nation, a statistic that compares to rates in Third World countries where the resources to prevent such deaths are scarce. Sadly, most of the deaths in Alabama could have been prevented, *The Alabama Journal* reports.

They are the poor, the silent. And their children continue to die.

Alabama has the highest infant death rate of any state in the nation. In 1986, nearly 800 babies did not live to see their first birthday.

Faced with those grim statistics, *The Alabama Journal* in 1987 embarked on a three-month investigation of the state's infant mortality crisis. The result was a series of more than 20 articles that ran five consecutive days, September 14–18, beginning each day on *The Journal*'s front page.

A few weeks later, the series was reprinted in tabloid form and 5,000 copies were distributed to lawmakers, school officials, doctors, public health experts and other shakers and movers in the state. Many have used the tabloid to prod the governor and Legislature into action.

The result has been the first serious proposal in Alabama's history to combat infant mortality.

What emerged from *The Journal*'s investigation was a story that went beyond the numbers. It was a story of human beings and human suffering. Many of the families interviewed had been snared so long in the web of poverty that infant deaths were viewed as just one more cruel fact of life. They had no political spokesman, no hope for a better future.

The project was a major undertaking for a small (20,000 circulation) newspaper, requiring thousands of hours of staff time and a considerable financial commitment.

Major obstacles had to be overcome. Reluctant, often distrusting mothers who had lost babies had to be convinced their stories could help save future lives. Reams of documents and statistics had to be obtained and analyzed.

At one point, the governor refused to grant an interview on a subject that was obviously embarrassing to the state. Only after we pointed out his refusal to talk about the subject would be prominently displayed in the series did he change his mind.

Reporters traversed Alabama and several other southern states in order to get a firsthand view of victims' lives. Often the poverty-stricken families were suspicious of our efforts. In many instances, early morning drives of several hundred miles ended with weary photographers and reporters returning to the office with stories of families who refused to talk.

Editors, however, vowed the series would not be published until the human story behind the numbers was told.

That tenacity paid off. Some families did talk, and we believe it is their stories, in their own words, about life and death in the hamlets of our state that will make a difference in Alabama's fight against infant mortality.

Our findings were many. Infant deaths were directly tied to poverty and the state's severely limited Medicaid system as well as inadequate rural health care. We also found infant deaths are a tragedy not only for the families involved, but also for the state as a whole as the infant mortality rate affects everything from health care costs to industrial recruiting. Perhaps most important, we found the state can actually save money by reducing infant mortality rather than dealing with its consequences.

The newspaper's efforts already are bearing fruit. In October, the governor appointed an Infant Mortality Task Force to study the problem. In December, he announced plans to seek $6 million from the Legislature to confront the tragedy. The December announcement was the most ambitious proposal ever in Alabama to reduce infant deaths.

—Jim Tharpe, Manager Editor
The Alabama Journal

DEATH COMES AT EARLY AGE FOR SOME OF ALABAMA'S POOR

MONDAY, SEPTEMBER 14, 1987

BY SUSAN EGGERING

The photo album tells the story.

There, beneath sheets of protective plastic, lie Tarneisha and Star-neisha Lewis, frozen in 3-by-4-inch glossy Polaroids. In identical caskets of baby blue, they are stiff and cold, unable to feel the warmth of the blankets that swaddle their tiny bodies.

The terse newspaper blurbs beneath the photos announce to the world their deaths.

A handful of photos. A few scraps of newsprint. They're all that's left to remind Eutaw mother Josephine Lewis of her twin girls. That, and the question that will remain unanswered forever: Why?

Why did they die? Why did they become two more statistics in Alabama's infant mortality crisis?

Josephine, 24, can only think it was the will of God. It is this knowledge that makes the losses bearable. It is this knowledge that she would share with another mother agonizing to understand the reason behind an infant's death, a death in the family.

"Only thing I could tell her is like what everybody's been telling me," Josephine said. "It was God's will. Maybe he took them for a reason."

Josephine's story, in many ways, is the story of the hundreds of infant deaths that occur each year in Alabama. Each baby that dies lives on only as a statistic, a pathetic sort of immortality.

Alabama has the highest infant mortality rate of any state in the nation, outranked only by concentrated pockets of poverty in the District of Columbia. For every thousand Alabama babies born in 1986, 13.3 failed to make it to their first birthday, according to the Bureau of Vital Statistics.

Only a dozen years shy of the 21st century, those grim statistics put the state on a par with developing nations in terms of quality of life.

"We're talking about Third World conditions right here in Alabama," said Dr. Roseanne Cook, the sole physician staffing the Pine Apple Rural Health Clinic in Wilcox County. "You don't have to go to Africa or South America to see Third World conditions. They're right here in the rural South. All you have to do is drive through the county, open up your eyes and visit a few homes."

While government office buildings in Montgomery hum with state-of-the-art computers and researchers in Huntsville probe the mysteries of celestial travel, our babies continue to die.

For Alabama has been unable, or unwilling, to ensure a basic right to its youngest citizens—the right to a fair shot at life.

Last year, of the 59,441 births in the state, 788 infants died. And there will be many more funerals in the years to come unless the state acts decisively to save its children.

The problem is a critical one. During a three-month investigation of infant mortality, The Alabama Journal found that:

• Infant deaths can be dramatically reduced if the state only will make the commitment.

• Infant mortality is directly linked to poverty, poor education, lack of transportation and insufficient access to medical care both during pregnancy and after birth.

• It costs much less to provide medical care for pregnant women than to pay the hospital and medical bills of the underweight and handicapped infants often born to women who receive no prenatal care.

• The poor, who are the main victims of infant mortality, have no political spokesman to bring their cause to the attention of legislators and others who could rectify the problem.

• Without help from the Legislature, the vicious cycle of poverty, illiteracy, teen pregnancy and inadequate medical care will continue unabated generation after generation.

• The Legislature has paid little more than lip service to the problem even though infant deaths have plagued the state for years.

• Alabama has funded such ventures as the Alabama Shakespeare Festival and dozens of local festivals honoring everything from chitlins to blueberries while ignoring a life-and-death issue.

• The infants of Medicaid mothers have a much better chance of surviving than do the babies of women who have no money, insurance or financial assistance of any kind.

• Other states with social problems similar to those in Alabama have confronted the infant mortality problem head-on and have succeeded in reducing their infant mortality rates.

• The ramifications of infant mortality extend beyond the affected families to the state as a whole. Industry interested in locating in Alabama looks at quality-of-life indicators, and a high infant mortality rate is an automatic strike against a state.

• The typical mother whose child becomes an infant mortality statistic is young, single, poor and, very often, black.

Consider a profile of such a woman: She probably has not visited a doctor at all or only infrequently during her pregnancy.

The doctor who delivers her child doesn't know if she has a history of hypertension and diabetes in her family—most common among poor black families.

She seldom eats a well-balanced diet, and she is more likely to give birth to a low-birth-weight or nutritionally deprived infant, ill-equipped to survive the first year of life.

Providing medical care to all pregnant mothers would go a long way toward solving Alabama's infant mortality problem, doctors say.

But such a simple, common-sensical, preventive approach lacks the appeal of high-tech medicine.

"It's not glamorous to provide prenatal care," said State Health Officer Dr. Earl Fox. "It is exciting to see a one-pound infant kept alive on a respirator, but it's much more expensive."

It costs on average $1,000 a day to keep a baby in a hospital neonatal unit. And though many don't realize it, this is a cost that all taxpayers ultimately share, Fox said.

The prudent thing to do would be to invest in preventive care.

"This is an issue in my mind where there's a lot of return for the money," Fox said.

"For every dollar spent on prenatal care, $3.38 is saved in the short term and more in the long term. The issue is not are we going to pay for it. We're already paying for it. The issue is really only what we're going to pay for and how we're going to pay for it."

But little money has been allocated for such things in the past. Though infant mortality is far from a new problem, state lawmakers are just now beginning to take an interest in the issue.

There's been speculation that the complaints of those affected by infant mortality have gone unaddressed for so long because those people constitute no valuable voting bloc, have no political clout.

"It hasn't been an issue up until now," Fox said. "I don't know why."

The reason no one has made infant mortality an issue may be simple. It is a complex problem.

There are no parades and precious few cheers for those who try to save babies.

Yet much can be done. Studies have documented that babies of Medicaid mothers—the poorest of the poor in Alabama—are less likely to die after a year of life than their richer counterparts.

But in Alabama, to be eligible for Medicaid, a family of four can earn no more than $118 per month.

In bureaucratic terms, that's 16 percent of the federal poverty level. In the real world, that's 97 cents per day for each person.

No other state has a lower Medicaid eligibility standard.

Tommy McDougal, executive director of the Alabama Hospital Association, joins virtually every other health expert in the state in contending that Medicaid should be expanded.

He concedes, however, the problem cannot be solved solely by expanding the program.

"The number of people eligible in the state for the last five years has increased," he said, "yet the number of people getting benefits has dropped in the last five years. I think it's a failure to make it as easy as possible to get into the Medicaid program. We've sort of had the mentality in this state to hold the line and not spend any more dollars."

Other states have successfully implemented programs which have significantly reduced the rate of infant mortality.

Rather than protesting that funds for reducing infant mortality are too costly for their limited means, Mississippi, South Carolina and Kentucky have implemented an array of wide-ranging, inexpensive and innovative programs.

In fact, Mississippi, long at the bottom of almost all indicators of health care, has surpassed Alabama in the battle against infant mortality.

Through a number of programs, the state dropped its infant mortality rate from 14.4 infant deaths per 1,000 births in 1984 to 12.3 in 1986.

South Carolina also has established programs that lowered its infant mortality rate below Alabama's.

And seven years after Kentucky watched its infant mortality problem reach critical proportions, the state's infant mortality rate has been reduced by nearly 30 percent.

By not correcting the problem, the entire state of Alabama—not just the poor—will continue to suffer, for the problem is multifaceted.

It is an issue at once economic, legislative, health-related, social and moral.

"I think we have a moral responsibility," Fox said. "However, in the end, everything gets reduced to economic terms. I think this is one of those things that is right and humane and moral to do, but it's also efficient from a cost standpoint."

By not doing anything, more than just huge debts are incurred.

"When babies die, that's an early warning signal that something is greatly wrong in the society," said Christiane Hale, director of the maternal child health program at the University of Alabama at Birmingham. "Half the babies don't have to die. That's a personal tragedy."

Potential income is lost because industries have no interest in relocating to a state where even one or two quality-of-life indicators are poor.

"We take every opportunity to get mothers to seek out prenatal care," said Calvin Michaels, personnel director for Burlington Industries of Greensboro, N.C. "Of all the things that can be done, prenatal concern is number one. We would like to know employees have access to all medical care if we were locating a plant. That's always on our checklist."

The time to do something is now, according to Fox, who has a two-fold plan of action in mind.

What's needed, he said, is financial aid plus the development of a statewide system to provide prenatal and postpartum care to all women who currently are not receiving it. Each is essential.

"You need the financing and the system," Fox said. "I look to

Medicaid for the funding. You've got to have a system (too). That's where I see the (public) health departments coming in."

While Fox has mandated within the past nine months that all of Alabama's county health departments provide prenatal care, the problem remains that there is inadequate physician support for the public health nurses, he said.

But by taking advantage of matching federal funds, the cost of implementing a program to combat infant mortality would not be prohibitive.

"Because Alabama is so poor, all it has to do is pay 28 cents to buy a dollar," Hale said.

"It's the best bargain around. Alabama may be facing its last chance to move in a cost-efficient way."

Once people understand the true nature of infant mortality and the feasibility of reducing it, they will be eager to help, Fox said. And improvement will be visible in just a few years.

Maybe then the needless deaths that plague families like Josephine Lewis's will cease.

Until then, babies will continue to die needlessly, their only legacy one of parental heartache and cold statistics.

That, and perhaps a handful of photos, a few scraps of newsprint.

Journal staff writers Frank Bass, Emily Bentley and Peggy Roberts contributed to this story.

1986 STATE INFANT MORTALITY RATES

HIGHEST		LOWEST	
State	Rate	State	Rate
Alabama	13.3	Wyoming	6.87
S. Carolina	13.1	Montana	6.95
Georgia	12.3	N. Hampshire	7.21
Louisiana	12.1	Maine	7.68
Illinois	11.8	Iowa	7.94
N. Carolina	11.7	Mass.	7.95
S. Dakota	11.6	Vermont	8.23
Mississippi	11.5	Kansas	8.32
Missouri	11.4	Wisconsin	8.88
Tennessee	11.4	Oregon	8.92

Source: National Center for Health Statistics   Journal graphic by Phyllis Perry

DEATH OF TWIN GIRLS SAD REMINDER OF ALABAMA'S SOCIAL PROBLEMS

MONDAY, SEPTEMBER 14, 1987

BY SUSAN EGGERING

EUTAW—From the yard come the robust cries of neighborhood children at summertime play. But inside the brick house, all is quiet, still. The mother, a tired 24, sits in the dim front room, a photo album open before her.

Most of the memories preserved between the album's covers are of pleasant, happy times. But the pictures of Josephine Lewis's twin girls only bring sadness to their mother. These pictures are not a celebration of life, but a reminder of death.

Yet she will keep them, even treasure them, for they are all that she has left of Tarneisha and Starneisha Lewis. Both died before reaching their first birthday—two more of Alabama's infant mortality statistics.

Josephine's case is not that unusual.

Numerous extenuating circumstances made hers a high-risk pregnancy, according to Dr. Sandral Hullett, her delivering physician.

Like all pregnant patients who come to Eutaw's West Alabama Health Services, Josephine was rated on a numerical scale. She received points for those pre-existing conditions she had which, doctors know, increase a baby's chances of dying before its first birthday.

Ten is high.

"Her risk scale shows she had a risk factor of 25," said Hullett, health services director, as she glanced at Lewis's patient file.

Her high-risk factor was no surprise given Josephine's background.

She was a sophomore in high school the first time she became pregnant. She had five children by the time she was carrying the twins at age 22. She never finished high school, never married. Her income remains minimal, borderline poverty.

One of her children required a transfusion after birth due to jaundice. A risk of premature birth, hypertension and anemia associated with previous pregnancies pushed her risk factor still higher.

Despite her troubled medical history, Josephine did not seek out prenatal care until almost her third trimester with the twins, Hullett said. She came in only twice to see a doctor before she delivered.

This inattention was not unusual. Transportation was difficult. She owned no car and had to depend on family and friends to get into town to the clinic.

Josephine's nutrition was less than adequate, so she did not gain the expected weight. In fact, maternity clothes were completely unnecessary as they had been with her previous pregnancies, she said. Nutrition simply was not a high priority.

"I just wouldn't eat no liver or drink no tomato juice," she said.

She was only in the 24th week of what should have been a 40-week pregnancy when she delivered prematurely on Oct. 3, 1985.

By the time Josephine arrived at the hospital, she was so far along in labor that Hullett had to deliver the twins in the corridor.

Tarneisha, who weighed only 2 pounds, died 30 minutes after birth. Her lungs were simply too immature to sustain her, Hullett said. Starneisha, who weighed a half pound more, remained in the newborn nursery for two months until she tipped the scales at 5 pounds.

"Then I got to bring her home," Josephine said.

Things were fine the first couple of weeks, and Josephine was careful to follow Hullett's instructions about when and how to administer drops of medicine to regulate Starneisha's sometimes erratic heartbeat.

"She got so she was growing," Josephine said.

The baby's premature clothes no longer fit. Things were looking up.

Then, a few days after Christmas, on Dec. 28, Josephine couldn't wake Starneisha at feeding time.

"I thought she was just sleeping," she said.

She tried to rouse her, but the infant wouldn't budge.

"Usually when I picked her up, she'd wiggle and move, so I knew she was okay," Josephine said.

But this time she didn't. Couldn't. She was dead. The cause of death—unknown and undeterminable—was attributed to the catch-all Sudden Infant Death Syndrome, Hullett said.

For Josephine, it was the second tragedy in less than three months.

"It just really shocked me," she said. "I couldn't believe this could happen to me. It isn't fair."

Her fiance, the father of the twins, was devastated.

"He took it more harder than I did," Josephine said.

Seven-year-old Lashanda, Josephine's oldest child whom she has "adopted out" to her mother, was told that Starneisha had died. But Josephine's other five children thought for a long time the baby was just in the hospital. They periodically pestered their mother about when the baby would be coming home.

Josephine couldn't tell them the truth.

Life—somehow—goes on.

She has had another child.

Josephine now cares for Carlos, 5; her 4-year-old twins, Santeini and Anteini; Dominique, 3; and Ashley, 11 months.

She does what she can with what little she has. Colorful photos of the family are hung all around in an attempt to brighten the drab walls of the small, government-subsidized house. In another room, Josephine has created a makeshift shrine of sorts, surrounding a large picture of Jesus with a border of red yarn.

The house is livable, nothing more. The battered screen door requires a Herculean push to open and close. Some of the living-room furniture is stained and worn, the rest of it shrouded beneath mismatched covers. The air smells faintly of stale urine.

Although Josephine's life as a full-time mother is busy, her thoughts still turn occasionally to the baby girls she lost. If they had lived, they would have rounded out her boisterous brood and given her a matched set of twins—one each of boys and girls.

Josephine and the dead twins' father continue to cope with the loss of the babies.

"We talk about it a lot," Josephine said, "and go visit the graves and take flowers and clean them off."

BLACK BABIES ARE MORE LIKELY TO DIE THAN WHITE COUNTERPARTS, FIGURES SHOW

MONDAY, SEPTEMBER 14, 1987

BY SUSAN EGGERING

It is a given, when dealing with the topic of infant mortality, that blacks in Alabama are at greater risk of losing their babies than whites.

The numbers say so.

Infant deaths are nearly twice as high among blacks as among whites throughout the country, according to Christiane Hale, director of the maternal child health program at the University of Alabama at Birmingham. Hale has studied national infant mortality rates from 1900 to the present.

"It's one of the most astonishing, constant relationships we see," she said. "At any time and any place, the infant mortality rate will be twice as high among blacks as among whites."

Statistics from the state Bureau of Vital Statistics clearly indicate this.

In 1986, of the 788 Alabama babies who died before they reached their first birthday, 374 were white and 414 were non-white, a category that is 98 percent black, said Dale Quinney, director of the bureau's Division of Statistical Analysis Services.

While only 40 more black babies than white babies died, the figures must be viewed in the context of the number of babies born to each race. Whites had more babies than blacks, but blacks lost more babies proportionately than whites.

The number of deaths translates to a rate of 9.7 deaths per 1,000 live births for whites, while the corresponding rate for non-whites is 19.9.

Alabama's population is 76 percent white, 23 percent black and 1 percent Hispanic.

But infant mortality is not a "black" or racial problem. Rather, experts say, it is an economic problem—one that arises out of poverty and poor access to medical care.

"They're poorer," said Dr. Roseanne Cook, a physician in Wilcox County. "It has to do with economics."

Jim Coleman, director of West Alabama Health Services in Eutaw, agreed.

"To me, it's not so much race but the economic index," he said.

Blacks were not guaranteed the right to vote until the 1960s and have often been relegated to the lowest-paying jobs. Generation after generation, they have been trapped in a cycle of poverty, teen pregnancy and welfare. Today, they continue to struggle against the economic hardships in the wake of decades of racism.

Though not scientifically proven, Hale suspects that the effects of poverty linger on even long after a family breaks out of its vicious grasp.

A study done in 1980 seems to support this. It compared a group of black and white women, all of similar background. They were each between 25 and 29 years of age, had four years education past the high school level, were married and had had successful first pregnancies, Hale said. Yet the black women had a much higher percentage of low-birth-weight babies—5.5 percent—when compared with the whites —2.8 percent.

One of the major problems remaining today is that the system of prenatal and postpartum health services available to poor blacks is simply not adequate, Coleman said. "We have too many people falling through the cracks," he added.

"Let's face it," he said. "Why do we have the so-called best health care system in the world and such a high infant mortality rate?

"If you have money, you can get the best care there is. If you don't, you can't."

Even where services for the poor exist, the system is fraught with layers of bureaucracy that can scare, confuse and tire potential clients.

"What the average person needs to do is pretend he is poor and see if he can interface with the human service organizations," Coleman said. "You spend all your time going from one to another. The programs are not designed to make it convenient for the individual. That's the real problem with the health-care delivery system."

But even when health services are available, black women sometimes don't seek out prenatal care.

"A lot of it is cultural and just not knowing the importance of it," said Dr. Sandral Hullett, health services director at the Eutaw clinic.

Many don't fully understand the significance of pregnancy.

"People take it for granted that when they're pregnant, they're going to have this wonderful baby," she said. "It doesn't always happen that way."

Whatever the reason, as a direct result of receiving little or no prenatal care, poor black mothers tend to have low-birth-weight babies—the babies who are at highest risk of dying.

"Low birth weights among the black population tend to be a problem, and low birth weights are a major contributing factor to infant mortality," said State Health Officer Dr. Earl Fox.

Little has been done to combat infant mortality in Alabama in the past, Fox said. There simply hasn't been much interest.

Only at the end of this year's legislative session did lawmakers begin to express any interest in the issue.

When asked whether, as a black legislator, he felt he had a greater responsibility than whites in fighting infant mortality, Sen. Hank Sanders, D-Selma, replied, "No."

"I've never had any citizen raise the issue with me," Sanders said.

"I feel I am particularly sensitive to the issue, but I don't feel the responsibility should be allocated to black legislators," he said.

"I think it's a poor people's issue."

What needs to be done is to develop a health care system that is a partnership between public and private sectors, Coleman said.

"The public sector and the private sector are going to have to work together to solve these issues," he said. "Government alone cannot solve it, and the private sector can't do it alone either."

But more than accessible health services is needed to lower Alabama's infant mortality rate, Coleman said.

"Money alone is not going to solve these problems," he said.

Needed as well are self-help, health classes in schools to encourage the next generation of parents to take care of themselves. In addition, increased job opportunities and better training are necessary.

And for those who question the fiscal soundness of such measures, Coleman is quick to point out that prevention is the most cost-effective measure when it comes to infant mortality and other health issues.

"If we could spend more time, energy and money on prevention, we could really reduce the cost of health care," he said.

Journal staff writer Emily Bentley contributed to this story.

HIGH TEEN PREGNANCY, INFANT MORTALITY RATES GO HAND-IN-HAND

TUESDAY, SEPTEMBER 15, 1987

BY EMILY BENTLEY

Of the 788 babies under age 1 who died in Alabama last year, one-fourth were born to teen-age mothers.

According to experts like State Health Officer Earl Fox, Alabama's high teen-age pregnancy rate goes hand-in-hand with the state's high rate of infant mortality.

A teen-age pregnancy is a set-up for low-weight birth and other complications—and, therefore, for infant death.

While babies born to teen moms made up only 17.4 percent of the state's deliveries in 1986, they accounted for 25 percent of the infant deaths, according to figures from the state Bureau of Vital Statistics.

In 1985, Alabama's overall infant mortality rate for babies of mothers of all ages was 12.6 per 1,000, while babies of teen-age mothers —looked at alone—had a mortality rate of 18.7 per 1,000.

Doris Barnette, head of the state Department of Public Health's Division of Family Health Services, said addressing the number of teen-age pregnancies would help solve the infant mortality problem.

In Alabama in 1986, 788 babies died before their first birthday; 199 of those were the children of teen-age mothers, according to Department of Public Health records.

The 1984 figures—the latest national comparisons available—show Alabama ranked fourth among states in the number of teen-agers giving birth.

According to 1986 figures, Alabama is first among states in infant death.

But Fox said while a teen-age mother is at an increased risk of delivering a low-birth-weight baby and of having other complications, the consequences of teen-age birth can be almost neutralized through proper prenatal care and education.

Fox said the incidence of teen-age pregnancy has decreased in the past few years. State Bureau of Vital Statistics records show Alabama's teen pregnancy rate declined from 18.2 in 1984 to 17.4 in 1986.

"I think that's evidence that you can make a difference," Fox said.

Those who do get pregnant are faced with a family of their own when they should be concerned with school, friends and their parents and siblings.

Barnette said because a teen-ager's body is not fully mature, pregnancy for teens is more risky than for slightly older women.

"Teen-age mothers are more likely to deliver low-birth-weight babies," Fox said.

Also, teen-agers tend to deny—even to themselves—that they could be pregnant. They put off finding out for sure, and they delay seeking medical care or alternatives, such as adoption or abortion, to keeping the baby.

The lack of accessibility to medical care that plagues many women —26 counties in Alabama have no obstetric services—puts hurdles in front of even well-intentioned young women who know they should see a doctor.

If the baby's father is not around and the family is not willing or able to provide transportation, a one- or two-hour trip to a city for a doctor's visit can be inconvenient to impossible.

And that is if the teen-ager has the money or insurance to convince a doctor to see her. She may not know of locally offered prenatal education classes or pregnancy screenings or she may shy away from them to avoid exposing her pregnancy to local people.

A pregnancy is not the ideal news to bring home to parents. Often because of social or familial pressure, young mothers-to-be find themselves on their own, probably for the first time in their lives, without experience in taking care of their own needs.

Even for teen-agers who are in a better home situation, poor nutrition plays a big part in the poor start a baby born to a teen-ager often gets, Barnette said.

Teen-agers frequently do not recognize the need for a balanced diet and the need to stay away from substances like alcohol, tobacco and caffeine during pregnancy.

A female teen-ager often does not take good care of herself, much less an infant growing inside her, said Fox.

Ted Williams, chairman of the Alabama chapter of the American Academy of Pediatricians, said even teen-agers' babies who are delivered without serious complications often develop nutrition-related problems after they are taken home.

"A woman leaves the hospital with the baby, and it may be a poor feeder," Williams said. "The mother is most likely under 21."

In addition, because of the new pressures of motherhood and the immaturity of teen-agers, child abuse is a greater danger for the baby of a teen mother.

To a woman who is herself still a child, the round-the-clock responsibility of caring for an infant can be overwhelming, experts say.

Fox said through educating young mothers on how to care for themselves and their babies, the tendency toward child neglect and abuse—and more unwanted pregnancies—can be diminished.

"We can almost neutralize the effects of teen pregnancy with prenatal care and reduce the risks—if we get them into the (health care) system," Fox said.

PORTRAIT OF A HIGH-RISK INFANT

PRENATAL CONDITIONS

- Race. *The infant death rate for blacks is almost twice the rate for whites.*
- Age. *Women younger than 17 or older than 35 are more likely to lose babies.*
- Poverty. *Babies born to poor women are at a higher risk.*
- Number of births. *A woman who has never had a baby, or one who has had more than four children, is considered high-risk.*
- Weight. *An underweight mother is more likely to have an underweight baby. A mother who was a premature infant or weighed less than 5 pounds, 5 ounces at birth falls in the high-risk category.*
- Disease. *Diabetes or chronic hypertension contributes to the risk factor.*
- Obstetrical history. *A mother who already has had a low-birthweight baby or more than one spontaneous abortion is considered high risk.*
- Complications during pregnancy. *Bleeding, cervical problems, etc., contribute to the risk factor.*
- Health. *Smoking, poor nutrition and alcohol and drug abuse by the mother are all dangerous to the health of the unborn child.*

DELIVERY CONDITIONS

- Birth trauma. *Experts say treating a patient in labor who has no prenatal record is the highest of risk factors. The delivering physician has no way of knowing what prenatal conditions are involved.*

POSTNATAL CONDITIONS

- Abnormalities. *Heart and respiratory problems are most common in premature newborns.*
- Poor living conditions. *The environment to which the newborn goes home is important.*
- Health care. *Poor child care, lack of immunizations, nutrition, etc., contribute to the risk factor.*

Journal graphic by Phyllis Perry

POLITICS, COSTS DOOM STATE'S BABIES

WEDNESDAY, SEPTEMBER 16, 1987

B Y   F R A N K   B A S S

Alabama babies have been dying for a long time.

For decades, the death of children during their first year of life has been nothing more than something to attribute to fate.

But earlier this year when it was revealed that Alabama had the highest infant mortality rate of any state in the nation, it wasn't so easy to dismiss the problem as a simple matter of fate.

It's a well-established fact that infant mortality can be curtailed by providing access to prenatal care for the mother.

Access to prenatal care, according to experts, prevents low birth weight, which in turn lowers infant mortality.

And providing access to prenatal care should be simple.

But it's not.

Why?

"I don't think it's resistance," said Doris Barnette, head of the Alabama Department of Public Health's Division of Family Health Services. "I think it's inertia."

The failure of Alabama to take action on a problem is not without precedent.

Efforts to solve similar social problems, like teen pregnancy, poverty or racism, have met the same resistance. Time after time, the attempts have been thwarted.

Part of that inertia must be attributed to the costs inherent in solving any social problem.

Ironically, it's been shown that the costs of ignoring infant mortality are higher than the costs of reducing it.

Yet, according to Tommy McDougal, director of the Alabama Hospital Association, "We've sort of had the mentality in this state to hold the line and not spend any more dollars."

Dale Quinney of the Alabama Department of Public Health's Bureau of Vital Statistics agreed. "Traditionally, we've kind of lived off the milk of the federal government in this area," he said. "Now, that revenue is being withdrawn, and Alabama is really feeling it."

Many politicians in Alabama are elected on a platform of reducing taxes and continuing services. The short-term benefits of that political strategy are clear. But the long-term ramifications often are not examined by an electorate placing style over substance.

The apathy preventing Alabama from reducing infant mortality also may be attributed to the nature of the tragedy. Dead children do not vote, and the parents of dead children seldom are willing to bare their pain for the rest of the world to see.

More likely than not, parents of dead children are black, poor and ill-educated women. So the issue of infant mortality has not always been a burning one in a predominantly white, conservative state. The issue is further removed from the mainstream when a dead baby is perceived to be someone else's problem.

"There are no lobbyists for children," said Rae Grad, executive director of the National Commission to Prevent Infant Mortality. "So this one has to come from the heart or the pocketbook."

However, none of these factors alone—the costs, politics or isolation—has placed Alabama in the shameful position of losing 788 infants last year and having the highest infant death rate among the 50 states.

What has given Alabama a high infant mortality rate, most experts agree, is a lack of education—or, put less politely, ignorance.

"Education and infant mortality go hand-in-hand," said Barnette.

This lack of education has manifested itself in many ways. Since most teen-agers do not know enough about their bodies, they become pregnant. And since teens do not know enough about their bodies or their babies, children die.

The state has given some pregnant mothers—those whose incomes are 16 percent of the federal poverty level—the opportunity to have people take care of them and their babies.

But access to prenatal care in Alabama is hardly universal. In 26 of Alabama's 67 counties, no obstetric care is available. Most attribute the lack of obstetric care to greedy insurance companies, litigation-happy lawyers or incompetent physicians.

In the counties where such care can be found, the people who need it the most often don't know how to manipulate the health care system to their advantage.

The recriminations continue. Some have charged the Alabama Medicaid program is inadequate, the state Department of Public Health's budget is a shambles, the legislators are timid, the lawyers are conspiring to run the physicians out of business, and the insurance companies, charging high rates for liability coverage and health insurance, are going to slay everyone.

But in the meantime, small children, who have no comprehension of the arguments being advanced, are dying. Their parents, who often have no understanding of the machinations used to deny their children health care, are grieving.

And almost everyone continues to ask, "Why?"

1 ANGRY PHYSICIAN QUITS POST

WEDNESDAY, SEPTEMBER 16, 1987

BY PEGGY ROBERTS

Dr. Felix Tankersley was in the shower just before 7 a.m. when the emergency room doctor at Jackson Hospital called to say a walk-in patient was ready to have her baby.

Being the obstetrician on call, Tankersley left the house without shaving and hurried to the maternity ward, where he delivered 27-year-old Valisha Jones's third baby.

Since it was to be his next-to-last rotation as an obstetrician in Montgomery, the doctor was hoping for a slow day that sweltering morning in late July.

But before he had finished his 24-hour shift, six pregnant women he had never seen before needed his attention.

"That's the reason I'm quitting," he said. "You just never know what you're going to be facing, and there's no way to avoid being on that rotation."

Before the end of this year, there may be as few as 10 obstetricians still delivering babies in Montgomery.

In the last few months, at least two have left, and several others are considering quitting.

Tankersley and other local obstetricians are angry about the deteriorating conditions in the Montgomery emergency room rotation.

They argue the system encourages indigent patients to neglect prenatal care by allowing them to drop into the emergency room when they go into labor.

In an emergency room, a certified obstetrician is obliged by law to deliver their babies.

And what the doctor on call faces is a threat to both the mother's and the infant's health and to his own legal security.

"I want someone to know what kind of horror I'm facing," said Tankersley after his 24-hour shift was over.

Three of the patients Tankersley cared for on that shift delivered healthy babies.

Two of them, including a 28-year-old who on that day had her sixth child, he offered to sterilize.

"I told them I'd tie their tubes for nothing.

"People might criticize that, but you can't tell me it's not easier to feed three or six than 12," he said.

The mother of six accepted Tankersley's offer and had the procedure done after she delivered. The other woman opted not to have her tubes tied.

"My husband said he might want more," she explained. "No time soon, though."

A 22-year-old unmarried Prattville woman, arriving at the emergency room in mid-afternoon, miscarried in her fourth month of pregnancy.

And a 16-year-old girl who checked in bleeding at about 4:30 p.m. delivered a 2-pound infant who died shortly afterward.

"I had no way of knowing how long she was bleeding," Tankersley said. "She was infected, too, and I don't know how long she had been that way."

His most serious case that day was a 20-year-old woman, bleeding and in labor, who hadn't seen a doctor since she delivered her third child last October.

"I saw her about 12 times over a three-day period, and during that time her bleeding got worse, so I sent her over to Baptist (Medical Center) to the neonatal unit, where I did a C-section on her," Tankersley said.

The 3-pound baby boy lived through the birth, and the doctor said his chances of survival would double each day. "But there will be a $150,000 medical bill," he said, referring to the hospital charges for intensive care the baby will need.

The woman had no health insurance of her own and wasn't covered under Medicaid.

Only one of the six patients had private insurance, but the 17-year-old mother who had insurance coverage didn't seek the care of a private doctor before delivery.

Tankersley said the girl's mother is a maid at a medical office building, and he's known her for years. "She has insurance, and yet she let her daughter get her care from the county clinic," he said.

When asked why she didn't take her daughter to see Dr. Tankersley, the woman just shrugged.

Tankersley did his last emergency room rotation July 12 and delivered his last private patient at the end of July. He will allow his obstetrical malpractice insurance to lapse. He'll still see patients for gynecological services.

One patient Tankersley has cared for through two pregnancies sat in his office with her husband and cried when the doctor told her he wouldn't be delivering her third child.

"I understand what you're up against, but what's going to happen when there's nobody left?" she asked.

"I really feel for them, and I'd like to keep delivering babies, but I can't afford to do it the way they've got it now," he said.

Tankersley has long been a vocal critic of the Medicaid system.

He charges that public funds are being misspent. "If you ask them (the state health department) for a breakdown of how every penny of that money is spent, you'll find out that it's costing more to provide poor obstetrical care through the clinics and the emergency room than through private doctors," he said.

Tankersley would rather see the funds that are currently spent on Medicaid diverted into the private sector. He suggested a pilot project in which private obstetricians would provide total care for women throughout their pregnancies.

"I've been criticized for my views because they've said I have a vested interest in this," he said. "But now I won't because I won't be delivering babies, and I still feel the same way."

In an effort to avoid being included in the emergency room rotation, Tankersley and two other local obstetricians offered to take on six patients per month, which is the average number of walk-in patients whose babies he delivers. They would become his own, private-care patients.

But most of the other obstetricians in town opposed the idea because it would mean fewer doctors on the rotation, and each one's turn would come around every 12 days instead of every 15 days.

That was the only way Tankersley would stay in obstetrics—if he could deliver only the babies of mothers he had provided total prenatal care from the outset.

To best describe his feelings of frustration over being forced to deliver babies of women he had never seen before, he told the story of a woman who walked into the Jackson Hospital emergency room on Thanksgiving Day two years ago.

The indigent patient's doctor had sent her from Troy to a Montgomery hospital, where an obstetrician was sure to be on call. "She wasn't too far along in her labor, and I didn't want to be responsible for delivering another one I had never seen before, so I told her to go back to Troy," said Tankersley.

"She said, 'I'm going to have my baby right here, and you're going to deliver it, or I'm going to sue you.' She knew she had me. And I delivered that baby," he said.

Tankersley sat back in his chair and shook his head. "It's not a question of money, really. It's just too much of a risk going in there and not knowing what kind of situation I might have to face that day."

HEALTH EXPERTS SAY MEDICAID WOES CONTRIBUTE TO INFANT MORTALITY RATE

WEDNESDAY, SEPTEMBER 16, 1987

BY PEGGY ROBERTS

Sixteen-year-old Terri's voice shook as she described her ordeal since she discovered she was pregnant three months ago.

"I'm overjoyed about it," she said, obviously more sadly determined than happy. "Maybe it'll change me. I was bad."

A diminutive girl dressed in a Montgomery high school drill team sweatshirt with the nickname spelled out in iron-on letters on her back, Terri, not her real name, is facing more exasperating problems than the average pregnant teen-ager.

When she applied for Medicaid to cover her prenatal care and delivery, she first was told she didn't qualify. Although her mother, a single parent, has no work income, she wasn't eligible because her younger sister collects Social Security benefits.

Even when she finally got Medicaid, she couldn't find a doctor in Montgomery who would take her as a patient.

Medicaid in this state pays $450 to deliver a baby. That includes six prenatal care visits and the doctor's expenses in delivering the child.

Doctors receive an average of $2,000 for a delivery paid for by the patient or by private insurance.

And with the number of delivering obstetricians in Alabama dwindling, it is getting tougher to find a doctor who'll accept the minimal Medicaid payments.

Health experts are worried the Alabama Medicaid system is part of the reason infant mortality in the state is so high.

Each year in Alabama, teen-agers like Terri fail to receive proper prenatal care and lose their babies before the infants reach age 1.

The Medicaid system is fast becoming one of the most hotly debated issues in the state. Experts can't agree whether Medicaid reform is the answer to reducing the state's high infant mortality rate, but they do agree the system needs changing.

Terri was disgusted and confused over her predicament. "I called every one of those doctors on the list they gave me, but nobody would take me," she said, choking on her words.

She doesn't know if the obstetricians she called turned her down because she was too far along in her pregnancy (most doctors won't take new patients after they reach their fifth month) or because there are now too few local obstetricians to care for the private patients who are willing to pay the entire fee.

She will continue to attend the Montgomery County Family Health Clinic, where she waits with 45 other women to see a volunteer doctor for a few moments. When she goes into labor, she'll go to the emergency room and be delivered by an obstetrician who knows neither her nor her medical history.

"The Medicaid system isn't helping many of those most in need," said Dr. Earl Fox, the state's health officer. "The public doesn't appreciate the importance of Medicaid in health care."

One option to expand Medicaid currently being considered in the Legislature is participation in a federal program that would match three-to-one funds raised on the state level for the care of mothers and children.

Known as the Sixth Omnibus Budget Reconciliation Act, or SOBRA, it has gained strong support among Alabama's physicians. It would allow pregnant women who earn more than the $1,440 annual limit allowed under the current Medicaid system to get medical benefits during their pregnancies and for the first year of the baby's life.

To be eligible for Medicaid benefits in Alabama, a candidate must earn less than $118 a month, or 16 percent of the poverty level as set by the federal government.

And even those pregnant, indigent women who are eligible under the current system often fall through the cracks.

Nineteen-year-old Debbie Edwards earned $75 a week as a waitress at a local restaurant until she got too far along in her pregnancy to work. She had no health insurance, and although she took a leave of absence from her job, she isn't sure the job will still be open when she is ready to go back to work.

But she was ruled ineligible for Medicaid.

"I was four months along before I even knew I was pregnant," she said. She is healthy and is receiving some prenatal care at the Montgomery County Family Health Clinic, and when she is ready to have her baby, she'll have to go to the emergency room to deliver.

When the baby arrives, she plans to take on two jobs to pay her hospital bills.

Debbie Edwards probably would have gotten Medicaid coverage, if she'd simply said she wasn't working.

"You have to know how the system works to make it work for you," remarked another woman at the county clinic.

The unemployed aren't the only ones passed over when the Medicaid money is doled out.

Faye and Randy Ford, a Chisholm couple, had their third baby in mid-December, just 10 months after their second child was born.

Brittany should have been a full year younger, but she came early. "Some people say she might have been premature because she was so soon after Taylor Michelle, but the doctor didn't say for sure," Faye explained.

The new baby didn't have extensive complications, but she was just small and weak enough to require hospitalization for the first three weeks of her life.

When the Fords took their baby daughter home, they also took home a bill for $15,000.

Neither Randy's job as a welder nor Faye's job in a Montgomery factory offered health insurance benefits, and Faye said they don't earn enough to purchase a private insurance policy.

"We had enough money saved to cover the cost of a regular delivery," she said.

Now they're hoping to work out a monthly payment schedule that will allow them to pay their medical bills little by little, without devouring their total income. But it will take years.

Former Medicaid Commissioner Faye Baggiano, who is writing her doctoral dissertation on the relationship between Medicaid and infant mortality in Alabama, agreed.

"The system is working for those who are eligible and receive the benefits," she said. "Medicaid has had some impact, and it has been positive."

Critics find little merit in the current Medicaid system.

"It pays less than in any other state in the country," said Dr. Robert Beshear, a Montgomery pediatrician who has been active in drawing lawmakers' attention to the state's infant mortality problem.

"It actually penalizes a poor family in which the parents are making an effort but maybe only earning a minimum wage and receiving no health benefits," he continued. "It seems to me that in a system where a family who earns more than $118 per month can't get assistance is tragic."

Beshear is especially critical of state officials who haven't made better mother and child health care in Alabama a top priority. "They have no long-term vision when they say we don't need money for these programs," he said. "It's a great silent tragedy."

INFANT MORTALITY PRICE TAG EXCEEDS PREVENTION COSTS

FRIDAY, SEPTEMBER 18, 1987

BY FRANK BASS AND EMILY BENTLEY

The death of a baby in Alabama is not without a price.

In terms of emotional suffering, the death is likely to be the most expensive loss of the parents' lives.

But there are real financial costs of the tragedy as well. And these costs greatly exceed the cost of preventing the tragedy.

The financial costs can be measured in dollars: Alabama spends $42 million per year on health care for low-birth-weight babies, said Dr. Earl Fox, state health officer. Inadequate prenatal care and teen-age pregnancies often result in low-birth-weight babies.

Care for disabled children, often born to women who receive inadequate medical care before birth, is even more costly.

Hospitals and doctors bear some of the costs when patients cannot pay. Most of the costs eventually are shifted to paying patients through higher fees.

But the financial toll of infant deaths can be illustrated in ways more difficult to quantify. It is the cost of lost productivity, the loss of badly needed jobs when business and industry see Alabama's high infant death rate as a sign of a continued lack of progress.

Last year, 788 babies died before their first birthday, giving Alabama the highest infant mortality rate of any state in the nation.

For every baby who dies, statistics show eight to 10 babies are born with complications or disabilities that require additional care. And more care means more cost.

"We are an instant gratification society," Fox said. "We want to see our results now. The infant death rate is only the tip of the iceberg. I think people tend to forget that."

Fox said having an underweight baby kept alive for weeks in a hospital neonatal unit—with high-tech equipment and highly trained nurses and doctors—is more exciting, more glamorous than providing prenatal care in every county.

But it is more expensive, he said.

Fox and other experts suggest a solid investment in prenatal care, which could dramatically reduce infant deaths.

For now, most of the state's burden of providing health care for expectant mothers falls on the Alabama Medicaid Agency and the Alabama Department of Public Health.

Most taxpayers and politicians tend to view appropriations to these agencies as a necessary evil. Funding for the agencies is often given grudgingly.

Yet for every $1 spent on prenatal care, $3.38 is saved in the treatment of a low-birth-weight infant, according to the Institute of Medicine, a Washington-based health care research group.

For every $1 spent on prenatal care, $10 is saved on the long-term costs for the treatment of a mentally disabled person.

The costs of infant mortality, then, are high—but how high?

Former Medicaid Commissioner Faye Baggiano estimates close to $20 million annually is spent on prenatal and delivery services for Medicaid mothers. That figure, she said, does not include the average of between $5,200 and $13,000 charged for a neonatal intensive care unit for a low-birth-weight baby.

Nor, she said, does that figure include the $43 per day charged for placing an extremely disabled baby into a nursing home for life. However, most extremely disabled children don't live to adulthood.

For children who spend weeks in a neonatal care unit, costs can run from $14,000 to $150,000, said Sarah Shuptrine, a human services consultant from South Carolina.

A healthy birth costs about $2,000.

"We're paying for our neglect in a big way," Shuptrine said.

Rae Grad, executive director of the National Commission to Prevent Infant Mortality, said the cost of placing five children in a neonatal intensive care unit is equal to providing 150 women with prenatal care.

"When you look at those kinds of comparisons, how can it be we're not putting our emphasis on prevention?" she asked.

Costs are not limited to the state, however. Hospitals incur huge losses from providing obstetric care to expectant mothers.

Tommy McDougal, executive director of the Alabama Hospital Association, estimates somewhere between 20 percent and 40 percent of all hospital bad debts are related to obstetrics. He said the debt could be reduced by expanded Medicaid coverage.

"In Alabama, that's a total of about $250 million," McDougal said.

Expanding the Medicaid program, agreed Baggiano, would cost money. But she said the cost would be minimal.

A recent study by Baggiano shows the 1985 infant mortality rate among Medicaid mothers was only 10 deaths per 1,000 live births. The figure was a substantial decrease from the figure of 13.2 for all mothers.

"We know the infant mortality rate for Medicaid mothers is not as high as the (rate for the) general population," agreed Medicaid Commissioner Mike Horsley. "That appears to be the answer."

Medicaid mothers have a lower infant death rate than the rest of the population, experts say, because Medicaid enables women without private insurance to get prenatal care. He said once a woman is brought into the health care system, she is educated about prenatal care, parenting and birth control.

But the Medicaid Agency must discover a constant revenue source to raise money for a 3-to-1 ratio of federal matching funds, said Horsley.

Once the state commits to raise money for the matching funds, it must continue to use that amount of money or a greater amount to continue receiving matching funds.

Medicaid is not the only state agency with a tight budget.

Like his colleagues, Fox must fight for every dollar he gets in the state budget. But Fox also realizes that the cost of ignoring infant mortality exceeds the cost of curbing it.

"I think the prenatal system is shaky enough without having to go six or 12 months with no dollars," Fox said. "And we don't need to rob Peter to pay Paul. What we need is to maximize Medicaid and have some money available for non-Medicaid eligibles."

State agencies, hospitals and parents can give estimates on how much inadequate prenatal care costs them. But there are costs to the state and its people that are not as evident as a hospital bill.

The administration of Gov. Guy Hunt has announced its intentions to boost the state's business climate. Yet for every child who dies for a lack of adequate prenatal care, the business community suffers.

And in an era of competitive infighting among states for new industry, that's bad news for Alabama. Potential new businesses, using infant mortality as an indicator of the quality of life, are less likely to locate in the state.

"Industry knows. Infant mortality is a surrogate variable; it captures the quality of life," said Christiane Hale, director of the maternal child health program at the University of Alabama at Birmingham.

Hale equated the state's infant mortality rate with a "canary in a coal mine." Miners used to take the small birds with them to make sure there was enough air and no noxious gases escaping. They would watch the canaries. If the birds acted strangely or became ill, the miners retreated from the mine shaft.

"When the canaries died, the miners got out. When babies die, that's an indication something is wrong."

She said that unless Alabama lowers its infant mortality rate, people will continue to perceive the state as being backward. Industry, she said, will continue passing Alabama by for other, more progressive states.

"I don't know how to put a cost in dollars of infant mortality to society," said McDougal. "There's just no way to get a handle on that. But we're smart enough to know that reducing infant mortality has a ripple effect."

VICIOUS CYCLE OF HIGH DEATH RATES CAN BE BROKEN, HEALTH EXPERTS SAY

FRIDAY, SEPTEMBER 18, 1987

BY EMILY BENTLEY AND FRANK BASS

Alabama's high infant mortality rate is part of a vicious cycle that robs children of life.

But health experts say the cycle can be broken by getting proper prenatal, or before delivery, care for women who haven't been getting it.

In Alabama in 1985, there were 59,663 births—999 to women who received no prenatal care. About 6,000 of the women received inadequate prenatal care.

Statistics show that the rate of infant deaths is five times greater among babies born to mothers who have not had at least four medical checkups during pregnancy.

According to health officials and doctors, the way to begin tackling Alabama's number-one-among-the-states infant mortality rate is to make prenatal care and delivery services more readily available.

Ted Williams, a Dothan pediatrician and president of the Alabama chapter of the American Academy of Pediatricians, said Alabama's prenatal care and infant mortality problems will only worsen unless care is made more accessible.

"A significant number of those bad outcomes could be prevented with good prenatal care," Williams said.

"We don't have to have an obstetrician in every hamlet, but we do need to have prenatal care available," he said.

Rural and poor areas offer the least opportunities for prenatal care.

Williams said if mothers-to-be get adequate prenatal care, the rest of the solution to the infant mortality problem will fall into place.

Top priority—by consensus—should be to expand Medicaid eligibility.

State Health Officer Earl Fox said the state's Medicaid eligibility standard—16 percent of the federal poverty level—encourages a cycle of infant mortality.

The cycle involves mothers-to-be who have had little or no prenatal care going to a hospital or doctor for delivery. Because of the increased risk associated with lack of prenatal care, doctors face increased liability risk and the possibility they'll have to foot indigents' bills.

Because of the risk and cost, doctors stop delivering babies, and that only decreases the availability of care and increases the chances of bad pregnancy outcomes for women and the burden on doctors who continue to deliver.

"What we need is to maximize Medicaid and have some money available for non-Medicaid eligibles," Fox said.

Medicaid eligibility traditionally has been contingent on eligibility for Aid to Dependent Children, welfare money available to single mothers and their children.

The problem with that, however, is it eliminates many married women from Medicaid coverage.

Through a federal Medicaid expansion program called SOBRA, which stands for the federal Sixth Omnibus Budget Reconciliation Act, Medicaid eligibility no longer is tied to welfare eligibility.

Fox said Medicaid expansion is the answer, with 73 cents in federal money for every 27 cents the state spends.

Doris Barnette, head of the state Department of Public Health's family health services division, agreed.

A pregnant woman in Alabama whose family income is more than 16 percent of the federal poverty level currently is not eligible for Medicaid.

In Alabama, that means a three-person family can earn no more than $1,416 annually.

The state's Medicaid eligibility standard is the lowest in the nation.

For those mothers eligible for Medicaid, there is little doubt the program works. The infant mortality rate in 1986 for babies of mothers on Medicaid was only 10 deaths per 1,000 live births.

If the state can pull together $8 million, matching funds from the

SOBRA can be used to triple the investment to about $24 million for expanding Medicaid coverage.

The matching funds would enable about 10,000 mothers who earn as much as 100 percent of the federal poverty level to be brought into the Medicaid program if the state matched the federal funds.

The money would ensure health care for women and their children younger than a year old. The money also would be used to increase nurse-midwife and obstetrician fees.

By gaining access to those medical visits, women also would be exposed to education and family planning information, Fox said.

Medicaid Commissioner Mike Horsley has proposed legislation to help get a continuous funding source for the state money needed to get the federal match.

"I can't expand a program without assuring continuous funding, and we just don't think the money is available through the General Fund," he said.

Horsley said he and Gov. Guy Hunt developed the plan to pool indigent care funds from local governments through creation of the Mothers and Babies Indigent Care Trust Fund. The plan was approved by the Legislature.

The local money will be channeled through the fund to obtain the federal matching funds, Horsley said.

Legislators also appropriated $1 million to go toward implementation of SOBRA.

Fox said in his department, money is needed to hire doctors and to provide education. Women who do not get perinatal education sometimes do not know how to care for themselves or their babies.

In 26 of the state's 67 counties, no obstetrical services are available, so public health is being forced to shoulder much of the burden of providing prenatal care.

"We need medical manpower sufficient to serve the state of Alabama," said Barnette. "We are facing some dire situations up in the northern part of the state. We're hoping they'll hang on."

Fox said he eventually hopes to have one health department physician for every three counties and a nurse practitioner in every county.

Currently, nurses are the only public health professionals providing obstetrical care in many parts of the state, Fox said.

"I'm forcing my nurses to do things we can't get the physicians to do," he said. "They're kind of left high and dry. The physicians are out there. But it's the question of money."

"One of the major contributors to infant mortality," said Barnette, "is the lack of planned deliveries. The ideal situation is to have plenty of coverage in your clinic, but to also have public nurses out there riding the circuit."

But Fox said not everything to solve the access-to-care problem requires millions of dollars.

He said two non-money moves the state could take under SOBRA would make Medicaid expansion easier.

One change would allow a pregnant woman to go into a local health department and immediately be approved for a 45-day period of eligibility as long as she applies with the Medicaid office within two weeks.

Even if she later is found ineligible, Medicaid would pay for medical expenses she incurred during that 45-day period, Fox said.

That change would make it easier to get people on Medicaid, he said.

Another possible change would eliminate the requirement for tests to see if items her family owns would disqualify a mother-to-be from Medicaid eligibility.

Horsley said those two policy changes will be made later.

Sarah Shuptrine, a human services consultant from South Carolina, said expanding Medicaid through SOBRA "is the best bet."

"Every baby should have the opportunity to be healthy," Shuptrine said. "That benefits everyone, and the less you will have to spend of taxpayers' money."

Shuptrine said reducing the infant mortality rate can be done.

In 1979 in South Carolina, where she worked as former Gov. Richard Riley's special assistant for human services, infant mortality was at 17 per 1,000 births.

By 1986, the rate had dropped to 13.1 per 1,000.

"Overall, 50 fewer babies died; 250 fewer were born with life-threatening conditions," Shuptrine said.

Shuptrine said expanding Medicaid coverage in Alabama to cover more mothers and children would go a long way toward eliminating barriers to prenatal care, delivery services and postnatal care.

And that availability of care would increase babies' chances to survive.

The state also must begin to implement inexpensive, innovative programs already being tested or used in other states. Grants are available for increasing prenatal care through such groups as the Southern Governors Association.

Programs such as those in Kentucky, Mississippi or South Carolina should be considered by state officials, experts said.

Rae Grad, the executive director of the National Commission to Prevent Infant Mortality, said those programs also should be geared less toward advancing technology and more toward preventive measures.

"We are improving," said Grad, "but the way we are improving is through technology, not prevention. And that's not the way it should be. The focus should be on prevention. In other words, instead of saving a low-birth-weight baby through high technology, we should concentrate on making sure that the baby is not a low-birth-weight baby to begin with."

LEGISLATION ON INFANT MORTALITY HAS BEEN LONG TIME COMING, SOME FEEL

FRIDAY, SEPTEMBER 18, 1987

BY EMILY BENTLEY

Although Alabama legislators made a last-ditch attempt in the 1987 session to provide money for more prenatal care for the state's mothers-to-be, many say lawmakers could have—and should have—done more, sooner.

The little money that was appropriated to fight Alabama's worst-state-in-the nation infant mortality problem was given primarily because of the efforts of a few senators and prenatal care advocates.

Sen. Jim Bennett, D-Birmingham, said the $1 million appropriated for more Medicaid coverage for mothers and babies was approved without any help from the governor's office.

Another effort—a joint resolution sponsored by Bennett, along with Sens. Hank Sanders, D-Selma, and Michael Figures, D-Mobile —called for the implementation of Medicaid expansion and an increase in how much doctors are paid to deliver Medicaid babies.

Gov. Guy Hunt pocket-vetoed it.

Sanders said legislation addressing infant mortality has been a long time in coming because his colleagues were more concerned with helping the rich avoid lawsuits than helping the poor keep their children alive.

Sanders said legislators failed to see the importance of infant mortality sooner because they were focusing their energies on "tort reform," a set of laws changing the way civil lawsuits are handled in the state.

The Legislature passed tort reform as its first priority in 1987, portraying the law changes as the way to bring down insurance rates for everyone, including doctors. By decreasing malpractice insurance rates, tort reform also would increase the availability of health care, proponents said.

"I don't think the tort reform issue was about providing more services to the poor; it was about providing more money to the rich," Sanders said.

And because issues are made by lobbyists, Sanders said, funding to combat the state's high infant mortality rate got bumped aside.

"This concerns, essentially, poor people. And there's no lobby for poor people," Sanders said.

Lt. Gov. Jim Folsom Jr. named some of the issues before the Legislature during this past session, including tort reform, parental consent for minors' abortions and the budgets. Amid all of the issues, infant mortality "did not emerge as a premier issue," he said.

A lack of awareness among lawmakers that there was an infant mortality problem also kept the issue in the background, Folsom said.

A week before the Legislature's regular session began, State Health Officer Earl Fox announced that Alabama had moved into the number one spot among states in infant deaths.

"Before Dr. Fox came along, nobody had all the information and compiled it the way he had and distributed it," Sanders said.

Now that legislators have been informed, "it should have the highest possible priority in the next Alabama Legislature," Sanders said.

Folsom said only recently has enough attention been focused on the problem to get the Legislature to look at ways to combat infant mortality.

The small group of senators initiated an additional $1 million appropriation for the Alabama Medicaid Agency to begin to expand Medicaid coverage, or government-subsidized health insurance, to more pregnant women.

The program would allow pregnant women who earn more than the $1,416 annual income limit allowed under the current Alabama Medicaid system to get medical benefits during their pregnancies and for the first year of the baby's life.

The senators began their effort after a Democratic Issues Forum brought the issue to the forefront—only six working days before the legislative session was to end.

They attempted to give the Medicaid Agency $5.2 million, but that was reduced to $1 million when Medicaid Commissioner Mike Horsley said he could not use all the money in the first year of such a program.

Full implementation of the expansion will cost between $7 million and $8 million in state funds and draw three times that amount in federal dollars, according to Horsley.

But reorganizing eligibility procedures and paperwork would take awhile, Horsley said.

He said Medicaid expansion under SOBRA, the federal Sixth Omnibus Budget Reconciliation Act, would need a continuous funding source, and he does not think enough would be available in the 1988 General Fund budget.

But Sen. Mac Parsons, D-Hueytown, said Horsley "sandbagged" the Legislature on what the options were for fighting infant mortality.

Although Horsley said his agency would need time to set up the expanded Medicaid program, Parsons said, "I found out later it's a program you either put into effect or you don't.

"It's like being pregnant. You're not a little bit pregnant," he said.

Folsom said he worked with Horsley on how to fund and how much to fund the Medicaid expansion program.

While the Medicaid expansion program was not fully funded, the Department of Public Health was able to keep $2 million for its perinatal education programs throughout the state despite money juggling that threatened the appropriation more than once.

The programs are important in teaching local nurses how to handle problem deliveries and in educating women on how to avoid problems, Fox said.

Fox said legislators weren't willing to step out on a limb and support a 5½-cent cigarette tax increase to save the babies of Alabama.

Fox said his proposal to increase cigarette taxes never got off the ground because of a general anti-tax attitude in the Legislature and Hunt's administration.

Fox worried whether tobacco lobbyists would be too persuasive to let such a measure pass, and, in fact, he never was able to get a sponsor for the bill.

Fox said the increase would have raised $23 million annually for the Medicaid expansion and for cancer prevention efforts.

"We may bring it back again next year," Fox said.

Fox said when it costs $1.25 for a pack of cigarettes, he does not think an extra 5½ cents will hurt smokers.

Fox said the money situation can be traced at least partially to the lack of a state trust fund for health.

"The Health Department and Medicaid have to depend on the General Fund, probably the most strapped of the state government," Fox said.

Fox said state government is much like the members of a poor family who can only see themselves through one day at a time. There is little planning for the future.

He said the cigarette tax would have helped alleviate that problem.

Fox said whether it is new money raised through certain tax measures or redirected funds the state already collects, money spent for prevention of problems—through accessible prenatal care—would be a wise investment.

But Sanders said it was "extraordinary that we were able to do what we did. I think we made a major contribution in what was done."

Folsom said legislators addressed it as well as possible this year.

"We'll come back next year, and the problem is still going to be there. My guess is that it will require more money," Folsom said. "We're going to have to come up with the bucks. . . ."

Fox said legislators are just realizing the implications of infant mortality.

"In a state like Alabama, you're talking about where are you going to get the money—we're talking about somewhere between $5 million and $7 million dollars to implement that program (SOBRA). I guess I'm a little prejudiced, but I feel if it's a priority, funding could be found."

WHEN FURLOUGHED MURDERERS STRIKE AGAIN

When a convicted killer is sent to prison, most people breathe easier, knowing the murderer cannot attack again. But a Maryland couple had their lives shattered because Massachusetts prison officials gave a furlough to William Horton, who went on a rampage. The *Lawrence Eagle-Tribune* explains how it happened.

On April 8, 1987, the *Lawrence Eagle-Tribune* was in the midst of covering a major flood when word came of what sounded like a tragic but routine crime story:

In Maryland, a young couple had just been taken hostage, assaulted and terrorized for 12 hours by a convicted killer, William R. Horton Jr.

Horton had fled 10 months earlier after being given a secret weekend furlough from a Massachusetts prison. He was serving a life sentence, with no chance of parole, for killing a 17-year-old gas station attendant in Lawrence, a small industrial city tucked off in Massachusetts' northeast corner.

The Maryland story was published that day. For days *Eagle-Tribune* reporters pounded on the doors of the Massachusetts Department of Corrections in an attempt to find out why Horton was furloughed, and whether steps were being taken to ensure that incidents like the one in Maryland would not recur.

They were given a clear message: Go away.

A department spokesman would give no information about Horton or how furloughs were granted. Corrections Commissioner Michael Fair said through an aide that he would never be available for questioning about the case. Governor Michael Dukakis would not return phone calls.

But the *Eagle-Tribune,* a small newspaper in the shadow of huge and powerful metropolitan papers used to having heavy influence on state governmental affairs, did not go away.

Dogged, basic reporting over the next nine months produced revelation after revelation about Massachusetts' out-of-sight furlough program, one operating basically without guidelines or proper record keeping.

The *Eagle-Tribune* obtained access to Horton's prison records, which revealed he had been far from a model prisoner. The paper accomplished something no other newspaper had managed to do—it obtained an exemption to Massachusetts' infamous Criminal Offenders Records Information Act, which shields the records of criminals from the public in the name of protecting their privacy.

The paper rebutted prison officials' contention that Horton would have been considered for furlough in most other states by conducting a 50-state survey that proved this contention simply was not true.

The newspaper published more than 175 stories in all—and got officials, politicians and people of Massachusetts to pay attention to the issues of opening public information to the public, coddling of murderers and laxity in state bureaucracy. Here are the results:

—A bill to ban furloughs in Massachusetts is progressing through the legislature and is expected to pass.
—A successful statewide petition drive yielded 57,000 signatures, enough to put an anti-furlough measure on the Massachusetts ballot in 1988.
—Embarrassment for Governor Dukakis, who is running for president and who faced anti-furlough demonstrations in New Hampshire, a key primary state. At year's end he halted furloughs and hinted that he would sign a bill banning them after a study by his anti-crime commission.
—A state commission was established by the governor to modify the Offenders Records Information Act. The Massachusetts Newspaper Publishers Association has begun a campaign to repeal the act.

The *Eagle-Tribune*'s proudest accomplishment was to tell the story of the two Maryland victims in a way that was both non-intrusive and healing. After months of working up to it, Angela and Clifford Barnes spoke publicly about their ordeal, discovering in the process that they desperately needed someone to care about what happened.

"I will never be able to understand it," Angela Barnes told *Eagle-Tribune* reporter Susan Forrest. "But at least I feel a big weight has been taken off my shoulders." They have since become public advocates for change in the Massachusetts criminal system.

KILLER'S RETURN COULD TAKE YEARS

MARYLAND WANTS TO JAIL HIM FIRST

FRIDAY, APRIL 17, 1987

BY SUSAN FORREST

A top prison official in Maryland says Massachusetts may have to wait years to get convicted murderer William Horton back because that state wants to punish him first.

Maryland does not "pussy-foot around" with first-degree murderers, Samuel Saxton, director of the department of corrections in Prince George's County, Md., said yesterday.

"He is facing some pretty serious charges down here and I imagine he's going to get a bundle of time, if not something more deadly than that," said Saxton. "If he's found guilty of the crimes committed in Maryland, and my guess is that he will be found guilty, then it could be many years before you see him back in Massachusetts," Saxton said.

Horton, 35, formerly of Acton Street, Lawrence, is a convicted first-degree murderer sentenced to life in prison because he stabbed a Lawrence youth 19 times in 1974. He was approved for furloughs last year and skipped out on a weekend pass June 12.

Police in Prince George's County, Md., say that two weeks ago today—while still a fugitive from justice—Horton held a Maryland couple hostage in their home for 12 hours. Police say he raped the woman several times and tied the man up in the basement and slashed him with a knife.

Horton was caught after a high-speed chase that ended with police bullets in his arm and abdomen.

Saxton said Horton is still in Southern Maryland Hospital under 24-hour armed guard.

"As soon as he is reasonably stable he will be taken from the hospital to the jail and I will lock him up in the medical ward, the high security medical ward," Saxton said. "He will be escorted by two officers everywhere he goes. He will not ever get away from us.

"We don't pussy-foot around down here with first-degree murderers and it's wrong to be letting folks out of jail who ought not to be out in the first place," he said. "I hear you folks up there in Massachusetts got quite a liberal prison system. I'm rather hard-nosed about murderers."

Saxton's willingness to discuss Horton's current status is in sharp contrast to the reticence of officials at the Massachusetts Department of Corrections, who refuse to talk about Horton at all.

Area legislators say Horton's actions in Maryland and the publicity now surrounding the case have created turmoil in the Massachusetts corrections department.

"They obviously made a grave mistake in allowing William Horton access to a furlough program and I think they're not quite sure how to handle the pressure now," said state Rep. Joseph Hermann, D-North Andover.

Massachusetts State Police Lt. Thomas Spartichino, head of the Essex County Crime Prevention and Control Unit, said he is aware of at least two other convicted murderers in the state who are still at large after being furloughed from prison. Roy White, 49, of Beverly, is one of them. White was convicted of second-degree murder in 1968 and he skipped out on a weekend pass from state prison in Concord on March 18, 1986.

When contacted specifically about White, Massachusetts corrections spokesman Mary McGowen did verify he is still a fugitive.

The reporter then called the department of corrections in Prince George's County to get up-to-date information on Horton. The call was immediately put through to Saxton, the top official.

"What can I help you with, young lady?" Saxton asked. "Yeah, we got Willie Horton, but he's actually under another alias because he got hold of fake I.D.'s somewhere along the way. The alias is Tony Franklin, but we know he's Willie Horton because the FBI positively identified him through fingerprints."

Saxton said Horton has been charged with first-degree rape but several other serious charges are expected to come in a grand jury indictment.

"It could be years before Mr. Horton goes back to your state or it could be just a matter of months," Saxton said. "The specifics will be determined at a later date. My guess is we will try him here and he will serve the time for what he did to that couple. Whether Massachusetts will want Horton extradited right away I don't know. Why don't you ask corrections officials in your state about that?"

"I have no comment," Massachusetts spokesman McGowen said when asked.

Carol Landrum, a police officer in Prince George's County, Md., familiar with the Horton case, said, "Everyone down here is asking how a convicted murderer got out on furlough in Massachusetts. "It is unfortunate that a criminal such as this fell through the cracks of a correctional system," she said. "Maryland is stricter. I suppose every state prison system is different but I am not aware of any other furlough program for first-degree murderers."

Hermann and Rep. Larry Giordano, D-Methuen, said they cannot get answers from Massachusetts officials. They said at least 100 Greater Lawrence residents have asked them how Horton got out of jail in the first place.

Giordano filed a bill earlier this week that would abolish a 1972 furlough law for first-degree murderers sentenced to life in prison. It was under this law that a three-member board made up of corrections officials approved Horton's weekend passes.

Yesterday both lawmakers said they were busy talking to state officials about gaining access to the minutes of Horton's furlough hearing last year. They say the CORI Act—Criminal Offenders Records Information Act—which was established in 1972, is the stumbling block because it protects the privacy of convicts' records.

"I have given a copy of the CORI Act to statehouse attorneys because I want to find a loophole that would allow access to Horton's files," Hermann said. "Frankly I think Mr. Horton has at this point given up all rights to privacy. The department cannot simply say, 'Hey we're sorry but everyone makes mistakes.'

"If there was gross misconduct on the part of the furlough board then I want to see the evidence," Hermann said. "I want to know what questions Horton was asked at that hearing and I want to hear his answers. I think a lot of people would love to hear his answers."

MASSACHUSETTS PRISON CHIEF 'WILL NEVER BE AVAILABLE'

Since Wednesday, the Eagle-Tribune has repeatedly phoned Massachusetts Corrections Commissioner Michael Fair. His secretary and public affairs officers always say he is at meetings or unavailable.

Last night the fifth and final call of the day was placed:

"He is not available," corrections spokesman Mary McGowen said.

"Do you know when he will be available?" the reporter asked.

"No I don't."

"Will he be available tomorrow?"

"Nope."

"The day after tomorrow?"

"No."

"Next week?"

"No."

"Will he ever be available for me?"

"No, he will never be available."

"Can you answer how many other murderers furloughed by your department have escaped and how many have gone on to commit violent crimes while out on passes like Horton?"

"I don't know."

"Could you get me that information?"

"No."

"Could I get that information from someone else in the department?"

"No, we have a strict media-access policy. I don't have that information and the media can only deal with this office."

PROSECUTOR ASSURED WITNESSES KILLER JAILED FOR GOOD

THURSDAY, MAY 7, 1987

BY SUSAN FORREST

LAWRENCE—The man who prosecuted William Horton Jr. said he believed the cold-blooded killer was behind bars for good when the guilty verdict was read.

"I had given these assurances to reluctant witnesses when they walked out of the courtroom in 1975," said Lawrence attorney Michael Stella Jr., a former Essex County assistant district attorney.

"It turned my stomach when I read what happened in Maryland, and I'm upset because I was not told as a prosecutor about this furlough program for first-degree murderers," Stella said. "I had no idea Horton was approved for furloughs."

The First-Degree Lifer Law went into effect in 1972, two years before Joseph Fournier, 17, was stabbed 19 times during an armed robbery at the Marston Street Mobil Station in Lawrence.

"Horton was not the typical murder defendant I came across," said Stella, who prosecuted 18 murder cases as an assistant district attorney. "I knew if he was ever let out, someone else would be a victim. Maybe if the furlough board had contacted me I could have told them these same things."

When asked how he felt on May 22, 1975, when a Superior Court jury declared Horton, Alvin Wideman and Roosevelt Pickett guilty of Fournier's murder, Stella replied, "If there was ever a case to argue for the death penalty in Massachusetts, the Horton-Wideman-Pickett situation would have been it."

All three men were sentenced to life without parole.

Mary McGowen, a spokesman for the Massachusetts Department of Corrections, cited a privacy law when asked whether Wideman and Pickett have been authorized for furloughs. She would only confirm that neither man is at the state prison in Concord where Horton was held before he skipped out on a weekend pass last June.

Stella said it was never officially determined at the trial which of the three men actually stabbed the Fournier youth. There were no eyewitnesses, he said, and Horton and Wideman blamed one another during initial questioning by former Lawrence Police Chief Patrick Schiavone, then a sergeant, and the late Capt. Stephen Sciuto.

"Who of the three actually did the stabbing was not an issue the jurors were concerned with because the case was based on the joint venture theory," Stella said. "But from the beginning of the investigation, Capt. Sciuto, myself, Pat Schiavone and Assistant D.A. Robert O'Sullivan were of the opinion that Pickett was the driver of the car, Horton and Wideman went in to rob the gas station, Horton had the knife and it was Horton who stabbed Fournier 19 times.

Schiavone, who owns Executive Detective Agency in Lawrence, echoed Stella's theory about Horton's role in the murder.

"Horton would have you believe that the other two stabbed the Fournier boy and he stayed in the car, but we all know he did it," Schiavone said. "Horton was the one who was the coldest throughout the trial. Pickett and Wideman showed remorse almost immediately. Horton showed no remorse at all, no sorrow.

"I don't know who in holy hell allowed this guy out of prison," he added. "That was a crime in itself."

Stella said he believes in the prison furlough program, but not for first-degree murderers. He said officials in the corrections department who make the final decisions should be held accountable.

"A statement saying 'We made a mistake,' 'We blew it' or 'We're sorry' is simply not good enough," Stella said. "I don't mean to sound like a radical, but if a murderer doesn't come back from a weekend pass, the people on the furlough board should finish out his sentence because they are responsible for the crimes he committed on the outside.

"I think the woman Horton allegedly raped in Maryland has a good lawsuit against someone in the Massachusetts Corrections Department," he said.

On April 3 and 4, Maryland police said Horton broke into the home of a young couple, terrorized them for 12 hours, raped the woman at gunpoint, slashed her boyfriend after tying him up, rammed a police cruiser and threatened to shoot at the four officers chasing him.

He was finally brought down by two police bullets in his arm and abdomen.

Horton is now in the medical ward of Prince George's County, Md., state prison, charged in a 44-count grand jury indictment, including assault with intent to murder, first-degree rape and assault and battery. He is scheduled to be arraigned May 15.

NO ONE RECALLS FREEING KILLER

WEDNESDAY, MAY 27, 1987

BY SUSAN FORREST

State prison officials who recommended that William Horton Jr. be furloughed in 1986 cannot recall specific details about the case.

A preliminary investigation just completed by the Executive Office of Human Services, which oversees the Massachusetts Department of Corrections, found that:

THE DEPUTY commissioner of the Department of Corrections, whose signature is on Horton's furlough release, does not remember approving it.

THERE ARE NO minutes to show what took place during Horton's many furlough hearings.

A PRISON CASEWORKER, unidentified in the probe report, was "very supportive" of his furlough application.

Still, the report finds that Horton's furloughs were conducted properly under the law. It says "established procedures" were followed.

The report did criticize the corrections department for a lack of detail in documents filed by prison caseworkers on Horton's evaluation for furloughs and it found fault with the absence of other documentation, such as minutes of his furlough hearing.

Among the lack of details:

A THREE-MEMBER PANEL, consisting of Horton's assigned caseworker, a correctional officer and a correctional counselor at Concord, voted to approve Horton for furloughs. When interviewed for the state report, "None could recall any specific details" about the hearing.

FOUR OF THE FIVE OFFICIALS at the central office of the corrections department, designated by the commissioner to serve as panel members for all furlough candidates, could not "specifically recall sitting on the panel that considered the request for the furlough from which this inmate escaped.

"Only one individual could recall sitting on a panel which considered a furlough request by the inmate," the report continued. "Others indicated a strong likelihood that they served on a panel which considered the inmate's application, but none could specifically recall when."

THE DEPUTY COMMISSIONER, who frequently serves as acting commissioner and who approved the furlough from which Horton escaped, "did not specifically recall approving the furlough under investigation," according to the report that was compiled by a special Investigative Unit at the Department of Human Services. Although several officials were involved in Horton's furlough process, according to the report, no names were released.

A CASEWORKER made an oral presentation to the three-member prison panel about Horton but "there were no minutes or record of the panel's discussions, other than the vote," the report said. "At the central officer level, there was documentation to verify that the panel met and voted on the inmate's request . . . but "there was no document reflecting the central office caseworker's assessment or the basis of the panel's recommendation.

"Such an absence of central office documentation has the potential to reduce the scrutiny which each individual (furlough) request receives," the report further stated.

The investigation into Horton's furloughs was ordered last month by Secretary of Human Services Phillip Johnston after the convicted killer failed to return from a weekend pass in June and then, according to Maryland police, went on a violent spree there which included the rape of a young woman.

The report says that the official police version of the brutal murder that Horton committed in 1974 was submitted as part of his furlough process.

The Lawrence police said yesterday they were never asked by prison officials to give an official version of the murder.

The report also said that a background check of whether Horton had a drug and/or alcohol problem was used as part of the furlough process. Two weeks ago first-degree murderers from state prison in Norfolk told the Eagle-Tribune that Horton was a heroin and cocaine addict in prison.

"The panel did not find anything unusual not to give Horton a furlough," Human Services spokesman Madeline Hardart said. "That implies there was not a problem with substance abuse."

The prison superintendent at Concord, where Horton was before he fled to Maryland, told state investigators that Horton was "a good furlough risk," according to the report. The superintendent also said that Horton's unidentified caseworker "did not recall any unusual problems about the inmate or the application that would have caused him to look more closely at the inmate's institutional file or to deny the request."

The state investigation was headed by Carmen Russo, chief investigator for the human services department. He wrote that Horton's furloughs were granted properly and that "elaborate" and established procedures were followed.

At the same time, he noted, the investigation uncovered several weaknesses which need to be addressed—absence of sufficient detail in Horton's prison evaluation sheets, absence of separate documentation at the corrections department's central office of review and assessment, and insufficient accountability of employees who reviewed Horton's furlough application.

HOW ONE FAMILY STOPPED FURLOUGHS FOR KILLERS

SUNDAY JUNE 7, 1987

BY SUSAN FORREST

UPPER MARLBORO, MD.—Stephanie Roper was a soon-to-be college graduate when she was kidnapped by two men, raped, mutilated and then burned alive.

It was April, 1982.

Stephanie's brutal murder in Prince George's County—the same county where police say furloughed killer William Horton Jr. of Lawrence terrorized a young couple two months ago—sent shock waves through the state of Maryland.

The men responsible said in court that they tortured and killed Stephanie because they were drunk and stoned.

Both killers were sentenced to death, but the death penalty in Maryland has not been used since 1961, even though 18 inmates sit on death row.

An appeals court—citing the drug and alcohol defense—reduced the sentences of Jack Ronald Jones, 26, and Gary Beatty, 17, to two consecutive life terms without the possibility of parole.

But in Maryland in 1982, life without parole really meant 11 years before parole eligibility.

From that moment on it was war for Vincent and Roberta Roper, who said they became outraged and disgusted with the lies and leniency of the criminal justice system in their state.

"Basically we had a death penalty which didn't mean death and a life sentence which didn't mean life," Mrs. Roper said Friday. "People from all over the state called us after the trial was all over to say that when the system failed Stephanie, it failed them as well."

Refusing to allow Stephanie's death to be in vain, the Ropers formed a grass-roots organization in 1983 to fight for the rights of victims of violent crimes.

And they named the organization after their 22-year-old daughter, who was the eldest of five Roper children.

"We started it certainly because of what happened to our daughter," Mrs. Roper said, "but now it has come to symbolize every victim of a violent crime in Maryland."

Today the Stephanie Roper Committee—with 11,000 members—is one of the most successful of the 5,000 or so grass-roots organizations in the United States that deal with victims' rights.

"What we have done can never bring Stephanie back to us, but it does in some way make us feel that our loss was not in vain," Mrs. Roper said. "Our goal is to spare future victims and their families from the criminal justice system.

"You see, what happens is that the criminal victimizes you, and then all too often the criminal justice system inflicts the second injury," she said. "Our organization strives to balance the system so it is truly just for victims."

Since 1983, the Stephanie Roper Committee has been instrumental in changing 12 Maryland laws that deal with criminals and victims.

Here are just a few:

LIFE WITHOUT PAROLE: Parole eligibility for murderers increased from 11 to 25 years, which means Stephanie's killers will be eligible for parole in the year 2032.

DRUGS AND ALCOHOL DEFENSES: The defenses used by Stephanie's murderers are no longer admissible in murder trials.

TRUTH IN SENTENCING: In the past, judges instructed juries that a life sentence meant a person will spend the rest of his natural life in prison "which was fiction," Mrs. Roper said. Now judges are required to instruct juries that a life sentence does not necessarily mean life and could mean parole in 25 years.

VICTIM IMPACT STATEMENT: Written and oral statements from victims of violent crimes and families of murder victims are now part of the court sentencing and parole processes.

VICTIM'S ADDRESS: Victims are no longer required to state their addresses and phone numbers before testifying in court.

TOUGHER ELIGIBILITY REQUIREMENTS: Requirements for admission to an innovative prison in Jessup, Md., called the Patuxent Institution, have been made tougher. The program focuses on rehabilitation, weekend furloughs and the early parole of all inmates who successfully go through the program, including murderers. But on July 1, a law goes into effect which says murderers are no longer eligible for the program.

Unlike Massachusetts, which currently has a state-wide furlough program for first-degree murderers, Maryland's cold-blooded killers had only the Patuxent Institution—and now that is gone, due to the perseverance of the Stephanie Roper Committee.

A bill now pending in the Massachusetts legislature, co-sponsored by Reps. Larry Giordano, D-Methuen, and Joseph Hermann, D-North Andover, would abolish the state's furlough program for first-degree murderers, which is designed to help inmates prepare for parole.

It was filed after William Horton, a first-degree murderer sentenced to life without parole because he stabbed a Lawrence youth 19 times, was furloughed in 1986, failed to return from a weekend pass and then ended up in Maryland where police say he raped a pregnant woman at gunpoint and stabbed her boyfriend.

HOW 12 HOURS SHATTERED TWO LIVES

COUPLE SAYS THEY WERE TERRORIZED BY FURLOUGHED KILLER

SUNDAY AUGUST 16, 1987

BY SUSAN FORREST

Some descriptions in this story are explicit and wrenching. We apologize. We felt, though, that the story could not be told without them.

LA PLATA, MD.—"I thought you were dead," she said.

"I knew you were alive because I heard you screaming for me and pleading with this animal," her fiance replied.

"I thought you would feel differently about me afterward," she said.

"Why?" he said. "You didn't do anything wrong. You're not the animal."

"I felt dirty," she said. "I was scared you wouldn't want me anymore."

Clifford C. Barnes, 28, paused for a moment, then turned to me.

"I'm glad you came down from Massachusetts to meet us. (She's) saying some things she never said before. I know she needs counseling. We both need counseling."

□ □ □

This conversation took place last week in a booth of the Szechuan Gardens, a Chinese restaurant in Waldorf, Md.

The speakers are a couple who police say were tortured, both physically and mentally April 3 and 4, by furloughed killer William Horton Jr. of Lawrence.

I wanted to meet them for so long, ever since I started writing

Horton stories back in early April. They invited me to Maryland. I got to know this couple as people, not as just "those victims."

The Eagle-Tribune is withholding the name of Barnes's 27-year-old fiancee as it does the names of other women who say they have been raped.

To clear up one thing, however, the victim says she is not, nor was she ever, pregnant, as was announced at a legislative hearing in Boston two months ago.

Anyway, what I learned from this courageous young couple is that any one of us could have been the victims.

They never returned to the house in Oxon Hill, Md., where police say their 12-hour ordeal took place. They did drive by there last Monday, to show where it happened. She would not get out of the car and wanted to leave almost immediately.

They are selling that home and buying another one. In the meantime they are renting a three-bedroom house located in the woods about 20 miles from Oxon Hill. The only way to get there is by dirt roads. They have five attack dogs that sleep outside.

"I couldn't ask her to go back to the house where she was raped by this animal," Barnes explained. "Would any man make his wife or girlfriend do that?

"This house is OK for now until we move into our new house because no one can get near here with the attack dogs," he said. "We can barely get near the attack dogs."

Why the convicted first-degree murderer from Lawrence ended up in Maryland after he failed to return from a weekend furlough from the Massachusetts Department of Correction last year remains a mystery.

Police said Horton did not know the Maryland couple. Police said he was apparently living in the same neighborhood of Oxon Hill and had staked out their house for three to four days before going on his rampage.

"We didn't learn that he was a furloughed killer from Massachusetts until four days after he did what he did to us," Barnes said.

"It's weird because the next morning after it happened we both said at about the same time that he looked and acted like he had killed before.

"We didn't know that he really had until we were told by police that his name was Horton and that he had stabbed a boy to death 19 times in 1974."

□ □ □

I pictured the couple to look and act the way they did—attractive and kind to others. She is a blond and blue-eyed woman and stands 5 foot 10. Barnes is rugged and handsome. He is 6 foot 1 and weighs 225 pounds.

"I had no fair shot with this animal because he put the barrel of the gun in my mouth, forced me to the basement, tied up every part of my body and then stuck a sweatshirt in my mouth so I couldn't yell or scream," Barnes told me, his voice cracking.

"I'd love to get this animal alone in a room with me now, one-on-one with no weapons."

The couple has been together three years. They were to be married last May 30 but postponed it until Sept. 26 because of the attack.

They work in Washington, D.C. Barnes is the manager of a car dealership and automotive repair center. She is an accountant with a prestigious company. She is still in school, working to become a certified public accountant.

Barnes's father died in 1974 and his mother, brother and two sisters live in neighboring Virginia.

Her father abandoned the family when she was an infant and her mother died when she was 17. She feels close to her brother and two sisters, but they are scattered across the country.

"I'm the only family she really has here," Barnes said.

He calls himself a Baptist, but says he no longer believes in God because of what happened.

She is Catholic and says she believes in God more than ever because she is still alive.

One thing Barnes is thankful for is that the AIDS tests they took right after the ordeal came back negative.

"That would have been cause for suicide," he said.

"I was suicidal anyway, you know," she said. "Lots of times suicide still isn't far from my mind."

"You never told me that," he replied.

"You never asked," she said.

□ □ □

I listened more than I usually do during interviews. I rarely had to ask questions during my three-day stay. I just let them talk.

"I got home from work first that night," Barnes recalled. "She was at a party."

An intruder burst through the door and he became the first victim.

"As I was tied up and being beaten by this man," he said, "I prayed so hard that she wouldn't come home that night. I prayed she would notice something strange and run back out.

"Every man out there who loves a woman or who has ever loved a woman probably can't imagine what it was like to be helpless while a maniac is violating, raping and beating that woman.

"I had resigned myself to dying, but I wanted to live for her sake."

□ □ □

For months I had tried to contact the couple for an interview, but they have an unlisted phone number and Maryland police said they could not give me any information.

As it turned out, Barnes wanted to find me as much as I wanted to find them.

He phoned me two weeks ago at the Eagle-Tribune.

"Is this Susan Forrest?" he asked. "I've been looking for you. Someone in your area has been sending us all your articles on William Horton. We like your stories. We feel like we know you. We feel a connectiveness with you."

□ □ □

I met them at my hotel in Maryland on Sunday and it was awkward. They were both wary of my intentions. They were afraid of her name being printed in the newspaper. She did not want her face in the newspaper.

She probably said about 10 words in five hours during our first meeting.

"I'm sure you're a good reporter, but I don't see how you're going to be able to explain the impact this had on us," Barnes said.

I told her I admired her courage—trying to grab Horton's gun at one point, trying to humanize the situation by asking him for a beer and then talking about a television show so that he would not rape her again, and untying her ropes knowing he could burst back in the bedroom any minute.

She finally admitted she was embarrassed about the rapes.

"You know, he liked having the metal knife on my body," she said. "When I realized he was going to rape me, I lied and told him I had herpes, hoping that would scare him off.

"Instead, he said, 'OK, let's see.' He put the knife down there and checked. He laughed and said, 'Nope, can't find anything.' Then he just did it."

"God," she added, "I never even told the police that part."

□ □ □

In my countless interviews with them—on their boat, in restaurants, in their home, in my hotel room and even in Prince George's County courthouse as we waited to see if Horton's case would go forward—I learned so much more about the attack, how it changed them both and how their relationship changed.

She went back to work shortly after the ordeal. She went to a few rape counseling sessions, but stopped because it was too difficult to face up to what had happened.

Barnes wants her to go back into therapy. He says they need help to replenish their relationship.

"I thought the scars would go away eventually if we pretended it never happened," she said.

"It won't get better by itself," Barnes said.

He looked at me and said, "She handles it real well in front of other people. I don't even know what she's thinking sometimes, anymore."

Then he got angry.

"We had everything going for us before. We are two of the nicest people I know. (She) is smart and giving and loving. We always did things for other people, especially our families. We keep going over and over in our heads why it happened to us, but we don't understand."

□ □ □

During the interviews they periodocally cried, got angry or became quiet. I saw her fear of everything that moved when we were out in public. I watched the way she walked around her house, expecting some maniac to jump out from behind every corner.

"I am angry, hurt and mostly afraid of my own shadow," she said. "I feel like a weak rag doll.

"The absolute terror I feel inside is that I don't have complete authority or control over who has my body or spirit," she said.

"It can be broken or stolen like a discarded piece of furniture. I am no longer in charge of my emotions or independent. I feel like I am at the mercy of any crazy person who decides to rape or kill me."

"She carries a knife all the time when she's in the house now, and she won't go to the bathroom until she checks behind the shower stall first," Barnes said. "Can you blame her? I mean, your home is supposed to be the place where you feel safest, but I was on the toilet when this maniac burst into the bathroom holding a gun."

"I'm afraid of my own shadow," she added. "I will go back to counseling and I am going to get better."

□ □ □

They said they used to fight about silly things, like who would do the dishes or make up the bed.

Now, they said, they fight about this.

They said they never had problems sleeping through the night before.

Now, they said, they are up and down all night.

"I keep hearing her screams over and over in my head," Barnes said. "I hated not being able to help her."

"I keep remembering him standing over me with his ugly face and sick laugh," she said.

They said they used to be very independent people. They said they used to go out separately with friends, like on the night they say Horton broke into their home.

Now, they said, they are always together, except during working hours.

"She never used to call me at work and now she calls me 12 times a day to make sure I'm all right," Barnes said. "And I'm no better. I'm always calling her during the day, for no reason, just to make sure she is where she is supposed to be."

They said they used to have a passionate, wonderful and constant sex life.

Now, they said, they make love maybe once every two weeks and she does not enjoy it much.

"It has definitely changed our love life," Barnes said.

□ □ □

There are some good things that have not changed, though, like the hobbies that brought them together in the first place—boating, dancing and watching old movies.

She is an avid animal lover like me. I will stop my car to help an injured squirrel off the road. She says she pulls over to assist slow-moving turtles.

"Horton's an animal," Barnes said.

"No," she replied. "My dogs are animals. I love my dogs. I love all animals. He's not good enough to be called an animal. He's a monster."

"You're right," Barnes said. "He's a monster. I'd like to kill him."

"I don't wish him dead," she said. "I want him to rot in jail."

Barnes said he believes Horton would have killed them both if Barnes had not escaped to a neighbor's house.

"It was like a cat and mouse game with this guy," he said. "He was like a cat who caught the mouse but wanted to watch it suffer first before it made the final kill.

"He never dug the knife straight into me. It was always a slow dragging motion."

Barnes has dozens of scars on his stomach as proof.

"Horton had no intention of just robbing this house. If he did, he could have left a long time before. We had three VCRs in that house and four color TV sets. He didn't take any of that stuff. He liked torturing me. He used the knife on me in such a way that I moaned and squirmed. He enjoyed it. He laughed.

"The reason he got caught was because he stole my red Z28. How many red Z28s are speeding on a highway at 6:30 in the morning?" Barnes asked. "He was an easy mark."

They said they do not know what would have happened to their lives if Horton had not been caught.

But he was caught. And, if convicted of all the charges Maryland has against him, and if he is sent back to Massachusetts to continue serving his life sentence before he serves his life sentence in Maryland, Horton will be a very old man before he sees the outside world.

The couple say they will sue the Massachusetts Department of Corrections for the hell they endured.

Through Eagle-Tribune articles, they sought out the man who prosecuted Horton in 1975, Michael Stella Jr.

Stella is now a private attorney in Lawrence. He is representing them.

□ □ □

As I waved goodbye to the couple last week, I felt like I was saying goodbye to old friends.

"We knew there was someone in Massachusetts we could talk to," Barnes said, "someone who could try and help us to understand how this ever happened in the first place."

"I will never be able to understand it," she said, "but at least I feel like a big weight has now been taken off my shoulders."

MOST STATES WOULD NOT HAVE FURLOUGHED HORTON

SUNDAY, DECEMBER 6, 1987

BY BARBARA WALSH

Forty-five states and the federal prison system say William Horton Jr. would not have been released on a weekend pass from one of their jails, a just-completed nationwide survey by the Eagle-Tribune shows.

The survey found that furloughs are not allowed in those states for prisoners serving a life sentence without possibility of parole.

It found that Horton might have been granted a furlough in four other states: Connecticut, Ohio, Wisconsin and Texas. They do not have a life-without-parole sentence.

The Eagle-Tribune surveyed the other 49 states on furloughs for prisoners to see how Massachusetts' furlough program compared nationwide. The Eagle-Tribune wanted to find out how many other states would have furloughed a first-degree murderer like Horton, who was serving a life-without-parole sentence.

Most said releasing Horton, "would be out of the question," as he posed too high a risk to the public.

Horton's only hope of release in most states was an eventual commutation of his sentence by the governor. However, the Massachusetts Department of Correction granted 10 home furloughs or unsupervised temporary releases for Horton despite a prison disciplinary and drug record.

Corrections officials said approval of Horton's furlough requests were "routine" and "done by the proper guidelines."

Horton, convicted of the brutal stabbing death of a 17-year-old Lawrence teen-ager, escaped on his 10th weekend pass. He fled to Maryland and held a couple hostage there for 11 hours, raping the woman twice at gunpoint and repeatedly stabbing her fiance.

The Horton case sparked public outrage and most likely furloughs for first-degree killers will be abolished in this state within the next year.

Currently there is a bill to ban furloughs for the state's 325 first-degree killers. In case the bill fails or is vetoed by Gov. Dukakis, a grass-roots group collected 57,000 signatures on a furlough petition, which will force the issue before voters on the 1988 ballot.

After Horton committed violent crimes during his escape, Massachusetts prison officials, in defense of their system, said 44 other states had furlough programs similar to theirs.

Information on furlough policies nationwide is not readily available. The most recent 50-state survey was done in 1984 by a private agency. However, it does not include information about furloughs for first-degree killers.

So the Eagle-Tribune phoned correction officials in 49 states and the Federal Bureau of Prisons, asking whether they furloughed any prisoners, if so whether lifers were eligible and under what circumstances.

Survey results showed several states do furlough first-degree killers, but their eligibility processes vary greatly.

First-degree killers in Massachusetts before Horton's escape were released after serving 10 years. Now, along with other changes, they are released after serving 12½ years. Correction officials here say murderers are furloughed to find out if they are able to act responsibly in society and should be paroled.

In almost every other state and the federal prison system it is the reverse.

Killers are not released unsupervised from jail until they have been cleared for parole and are within six months to two years of their release.

Furloughs, most states and the federal correction departments say, are for the purpose of re-establishing family ties before the convict is released back into society. There is no need to allow dozens of furloughs beforehand, they say.

William Toney, a spokesman for the federal prison system, said, "There's no way this Horton guy would have gotten out. It would be highly unlikely someone serving a sentence for that type of offense would receive a furlough in the federal system until they have proved over the years some sense of responsibility."

The average time span of a home furlough is anywhere from eight hours to three days. Some states, such as Florida, only allow them in the daylight.

Massachusetts has one of the most liberal furlough systems in the country, the survey shows. Other states such as Louisiana and Maryland have the toughest.

In Maryland following Horton's six-day trial in October, he was sentenced to two consecutive life terms plus 85 years for terrorizing the Maryland couple. There, the only way for a first-degree murderer to get a weekend pass is after the parole board recommends his commutation to the governor.

Samuel Saxton is Director of Prince George's County Department of Corrections. Horton was kept in the Prince George's County jail for seven months, from the time of his April capture until his conviction.

Said Saxton about releasing a first-degree murderer like Horton: "I don't know of a case where people on death row or having serious charges pending would be allowed that kind of latitude. I would have never let a guy like Horton out.

"We're in charge of protecting society," Saxton said. "If you want to know where a person is going you look at where they've been."

Saxton said Horton's past would show he is too high a risk for release. When Horton stabbed 17-year-old Joseph Fournier of Lawrence 19 times and stuffed him in a garbage pail in 1974, he was on parole after serving three years for assault with intent to murder in South Carolina.

"If a person commits a crime of passion it's one thing," Saxton said. "But when you've got a wild dog, that's different. You don't open up the gate and release him to pillage on the public."

In Louisiana "chances are nil," a correction official said, that someone like Horton would have gotten out on a weekend pass.

"When you're sentenced to life without parole that's it. You don't get good time, you don't get parole," Lynn McCloud, a spokesman for the Louisiana Department of Corrections, said. "Nothing. Maybe if you apply for clemency in 25 to 30 years you might be considered but it's doubtful."

If a lifer is applying for clemency in Louisiana, the law says he must publish a notice in his community's newspaper for three consecutive days alerting them of his intent.

"That gives the public, the victim's family and the district attorney the chance to know about it and object if they want to," McCloud said. "It's our way of notifying the people years down the road after the crime is committed . . .

"It's only fair," McCloud said of the newspaper ads. "The public has more rights than the murderer."

District attorneys pick up the local newspapers each day to check on potential clemency requests, McCloud said. If they object to the killer's release, he said, the murderer would most likely be kept in jail.

In Massachusetts there is a privacy law, the Criminal Offenders Records Act (CORI) which keeps prisoners' records secret. When a criminal is released on furlough or paroled the public is not told.

When McCloud was given Horton's background and told he was released, McCloud said: "You're kidding. That's crazy. That man is a prime escape risk. You never let a lifer out like that. What has he got to lose?

"We'd never consider that guy," McCloud said. "I can't believe they let that guy out. Is that common practice out there?" he asked.

"If we did something like that, we'd all be hanging," McCloud said. "When we let a man out we hope the worst thing that will happen on furlough is that he'll get drunk. We're trying to keep guys like him inside. That's our biggest nightmare to have something like that happen."

Alaska has a furlough program but like most states they release first-degree killers only after they are approved for parole and within months of release.

If a killer is sentenced to life without parole they could not be released, Richard Toenies, spokesman for the Alaska Department of Corrections, said.

"If a judge saw fit to give an individual a life-without-parole sentence that's pretty severe," Toenies said. "If he felt the person should be kept out of society for the rest of his natural life, we don't have any power to release him."

Indiana has a furlough program but prohibits first-degree murderers from temporary leaves. No one serving a term of 16 years or longer is released on furloughs.

"Considering Horton's background he would be considered a high risk and a danger to society," Judy Donahue, Indiana Department of Corrections spokeswoman, said.

Indiana's furlough program came under fire in the early 1980's when a first-degree murderer was allowed out to attend a funeral.

"He had served 30 years and they allowed him to go to a funeral," Ms. Donahue said. "The sister of the person he murdered found out and was outraged. She wrote a letter to the governor's office. The result was the furlough program was tightened up considerably."

Now if a first-degree murderer wants to attend a funeral his case and background are reviewed. If his request is granted, he may be allowed to go to the funeral in handcuffs with a prison guard at his side.

"They are never allowed out unescorted anymore," Ms. Donahue said.

Massachusetts' neighbor New Hampshire has a furlough program. However, they are "very, very different," from Massachusetts, a spokesman there said.

"Our furlough program is very, very limited," Mary Keniston, N.H. Department of Corrections spokesman, said. "We are very public safety orientated. No one like Horton would get out. If you're serving a life without parole sentence, that means you don't go outside the walls at all."

New Hampshire allows inmates out for two to 12 hours, if they are in a halfway house and within 90 days of release.

Eagle-Tribune reporter Cheryl Rock contributed to this report.

HOW ONE DAY CHANGED A SYSTEM

SOON KILLERS WILL STAY JAILED

SUNDAY, DECEMBER 27, 1987

BY BARBARA WALSH

Soon killers will not be let out of prison for unsupervised weekend trips to shopping malls, movie theaters or their old homes.

The records of convicts serving time in jail most likely will no longer be kept completely secret.

And a young couple who were terrorized by an escaped killer will have recovered, knowing they made a difference in the world and may have saved someone's life.

Since the morning of April 4, when Maryland police captured escaped killer William Horton Jr. after he terrorized the young couple, some things are very different in Massachusetts.

The Horton case might have died with his capture, but the crimes he committed while on furlough tapped a vein of outrage.

Many people realized it could have been their home Horton broke into. It could have been one of their family members he terrorized.

Lawmakers, citizens and victims' families vowed to do whatever was needed to stop murderers from walking the streets unsupervised.

Eight months later they are close to accomplishing what they set out to do.

Here is a look at what Horton and the furor over his case have produced:

THE REVELATION THAT the state was running what amounted to a secret program to qualify killers for commutation by giving them weekend passes from jail. The idea was to let them show they could be trusted in society, then to commute their sentences.

A PROPOSED LAW TO ban first-degree killers from getting furloughs, temporary passes out of jail. The law has been overwhelmingly passed by the House and is headed for Senate approval.

A CITIZENS' PETITION, signed by 57,000 people, also aimed at abolishing furloughs for first-degree murderers. The petition puts a proposal to ban furloughs of first-degree murderers on the ballot in

1988—a ballot question that may be made moot by the Legislature's own furlough law.

A CHALLENGE to a 15-year-old law that says prisoners' records must be kept secret. A state committee has been appointed to reevaluate the law and to recommend changes to provide a balance between the public's need to know and the convict's right to privacy.

The Horton case also produced more intangible results.

It united victims throughout the state and gave them a way to fight back at a system they said refused to listen to them.

Their efforts brought the young Maryland couple who had been terrorized by Horton out of seclusion and into the limelight to fight a system they felt was very dangerous.

Clifford and Angela Barnes forced lawmakers and citizens to think of the furlough program in terms of human lives rather than statistics.

On the morning of April 4, as police in Maryland captured Horton, the big news in the Merrimack Valley and in most of Massachusetts and New England was the flooding that followed heavy March and April rains.

Local state Reps. Larry Giordano, D-Methuen, and Joseph Hermann, D-North Andover, were busy trying to help their communities find help to repair washed out roads and flooded buildings.

Giordano, a freshman representative sworn in four months earlier, was also trying to adjust to life at the Statehouse.

Donna Fournier Cuomo was occupied with her real estate job and with caring for her family.

Maureen Donovan was also busy with her family and her part-time job coordinating meals for Methuen senior citizens.

And then the William Horton Jr. story broke.

Each one of their lives took a 180-degree turn. Day by day, as the story developed and public awareness increased, so did the outrage.

The first startling revelation was that first-degree killers who were supposed to be serving life in prison without parole were being given weekend passes after serving 10 years.

Even the judge, who sentenced Horton to life without parole, and the district attorney, who prosecuted him for murdering a Lawrence teenager, had no idea first-degree murderers were allowed out on unsupervised passes.

The Horton case also brought to light the fact that first-degree killers did not actually serve life in prison.

In a state that has no death penalty, most of the public believed killers like Horton never got back on the street.

"I would routinely tell witnesses they did not have to worry about retaliation and commonly tell the parents of a murdered son or daughter, the killer would never see the light of day again," said attorney Michael Stella Jr., who prosecuted Horton in 1975 for murdering 17-year-old Joseph Fournier of Lawrence.

"I was shocked to find out that wasn't true."

Donna Fournier Cuomo, the sister of Joseph Fournier, tried to find out how the man who murdered her brother was set free.

Her questions went unanswered.

"No one knew about furloughs for killers," Mrs. Cuomo said. "It was a secret program."

Several readers called the Eagle-Tribune Sound Off line expressing outrage Horton was released.

Said one: "I am horrified a killer like Horton was released on furlough. I do hope the authorities are satisfied."

Another said: "Whoever approved Horton's release should be fired from his position immediately."

The Department of Correction admitted there was "clearly a regrettable and tragic mistake made" but refused to say why Horton was released.

Correction officials said the Criminal Offenders Records Information Act (CORI), a privacy law that keeps prisoners' records secret, prevented them from talking about the Horton case.

The privacy law and the Department of Correction's arrogance infuriated newspaper editors, lawmakers and the general public, who believed correction officials were using CORI to shield their mistakes.

"People were furious over Horton, and they wanted to know what happened, how it could happen and who was responsible," Eagle-Tribune Editor Daniel J. Warner Jr. said. "Simple, basic questions. And to discover there was this law that bureacrats could use to cover up those answers is just mind blowing. We've got to get rid of that law."

The Eagle-Tribune began a battle to get Horton's records and find out why he was released on a weekend pass.

In May, the Eagle-Tribune officially applied for Horton's records through the two boards that rule over releasing convicts' records, the Security and Privacy Council and the Criminal History Board.

Five months later, the Security and Privacy Council made a landmark ruling and granted the Eagle-Tribune access to Horton's records. Never before had a newspaper received access to a criminal's records.

The council's attorney said releasing Horton's records could cripple the furlough system, but in the end the public's need to know outweighed the killer's rights.

In fact, the furlough system was already in trouble.

Giordano, a Methuen police officer for 17 years, filed a bill to abolish furloughs for killers.

"I clearly remember when that Lawrence boy was found stuffed in a trash barrel," Giordano said a week after Horton was recaptured in Maryland. "My heart nearly dropped when I read about what happened in Maryland. I vowed to do everything in my power to repeal this outrageous law that allows dangerous killers out of jail for weekend visits."

He was joined by Hermann and other local lawmakers.

Giordano and Hermann refused to back off the issue despite pressure from Dukakis' aides, who said they were embarrassing the governor.

Dukakis said the furlough program was a success, despite some problems, and refused to budge from that position.

While Giordano and Hermann fought their battle at the Statehouse, local residents began waging their own assault on the furlough program.

Talking about the Horton case over coffee one morning, four women got mad enough to form their own committee. They called it Citizens Against an Unsafe Society (CAUS) and began collecting signatures on a petition asking the governor to stop killers from walking the streets unsupervised.

The petition, signed by 15,000 citizens, was delivered to the Statehouse. State officials ignored it, CAUS co-founder Maureen Donovan said.

"I was appalled," Mrs. Donovan of Methuen said. "I thought maybe the voice of the people would mean something. But they couldn't have cared less."

CAUS members later approached Dukakis while he was campaigning in Andover. They asked him how he would feel if someone was murdered in his family and the killer later released.

He answered: "Probably just like you people, but I can't ban the furloughs."

Dukakis told CAUS furloughs were needed to control killers in jail and help him to decide if he should commute a murderer's sentence.

Mary Gravel, a North Andover CAUS member, whose daughter was murdered 18 months ago, told Dukakis: "Your commutations make me sick."

Shortly after they met with Dukakis, CAUS switched tactics.

If Dukakis would not listen to them, they would force the issue to a ballot vote through an initiative petition.

Mrs. Donovan, Mrs. Cuomo and a handful of other CAUS members, canvassed the state, gathering signatures and educating the public about furloughs for killers.

They collected 57,000 signatures, enough to bring the issue before voters in 1988.

"People did not believe us about this program," said Mrs. Donovan. "It was the shock of the century."

While CAUS canvassed the state, the young Maryland couple that Horton had terrorized struggled to put their shattered lives back together.

Clifford and Angela Barnes had immediately moved out of the house where Horton held them prisoner for 12 hours. In their new home, they still felt unsafe. They also felt angry, bitter and alone in their struggle.

They received no apologies or explanations from Massachusetts. They felt no one cared.

In Cancun, Mexico, they found out they were wrong.

There, on a trip to help them forget Horton, they happened to meet a couple from Lawrence.

The Barneses learned thousands here shared their anger and were appalled a first-degree murderer like Horton had been released to harm more people.

They linked up with CAUS and came to Massachusetts twice to convince lawmakers they had to stop furloughing killers.

They testified at the Statehouse, describing the brutal hours Horton tormented them, raping Mrs. Barnes and slashing her husband.

Their testimony brought home the human cost of the furlough program's failures, forcing lawmakers to view it through their eyes, instead of through the statistics provided by the Correction Department.

"You people suffer from disassociation," Clifford Barnes told the House Post Audit Committee at the Statehouse. "I don't think any of you could understand how it is to listen to your wife cry out as she is violated and beaten . . . I wish you could enter our dreams at night. I wish you could be there when the heater goes off at night or something creaks and we jump up in bed."

The young couple touched people's hearts throughout the state with their story. Fighting back also helped heal their own psychic wounds, they said.

Now, nine months later, the outrage wrought by the Horton case is still simmering.

Giordano's bill to abolish furloughs was approved overwhelmingly by the House of Representatives and is now before the Senate.

If it fails there or is approved and later vetoed by Dukakis, voters will have a chance to make their own decision next November.

"We know it will be passed overwhelmingly by the public," Mrs. Donovan said. "It's such a dangerous, wrong situation. Anyone with any sense of public safety would not let this situation go on."

The assault also continues on CORI, the law that makes prisoners' records secret and that allowed correction officials to withhold the simplest facts about Horton for months.

A committee appointed by Dukakis meets monthly to discuss the law and will recommend changes some time next year.

Andrew Klein, chief probation officer in the Quincy courts and a member of the Security and Privacy Council who favored release of Horton's records, said CORI was never intended to protect prisoners still in custody of the state.

CORI, Klein believes, was intended to keep records secret only after prisoners are released from prison. The Horton case has forced board members to look at the 15-year-old law in a different light, Klein said.

"A new feeling is beginning to emerge that criminals in the system have less rights to privacy than those on the outside," Klein said.

"A Horton still in the system serving time is now beginning to be looked at as someone with less privacy rights that someone who successfully has served time and been released."

Looking back on the past nine months, Giordano said he is sorry Horton tragically changed the lives of Clifford and Angela Barnes but believes their decision to speak out fed the public's outrage and forced lawmakers to listen.

"If Horton had been killed by one of those Maryland cops, I don't think a lot of things would have come to light," Giordano said. "The case would have died with him.

"No one likes to be victims, but because the Barneses stood up and were counted they may have saved other people from going through what they did."

THREE

THE SPOILS OF POWER

1988 WINNER IN THE INVESTIGATIVE REPORTING CATEGORY

"For a distinguished example of investigative reporting within a newspaper's area of circulation by an individual or team, presented as a single article or series . . ."

Chicago Tribune
Dean Baquet
Ann Marie Lipinski
William Gaines

Investigative reporters for the *Chicago Tribune* had listened to plenty of rumors about money purportedly being squandered by City Council members. Most people seemed satisfied with rumors, but the *Tribune* team took the next step and uncovered flagrant abuses.

When we decided to investigate the Chicago City Council, there were a lot of people—some of our colleagues among them—who were baffled. What new stories could be told about an institution that was legendary for corruption? What impact would such an investigation have in a city where politicians, with a certain perverse pride, and voters, with a certain bemused cynicism, embraced Chicago's unofficial slogan, *Ubi est mia?* (Where's mine?)

Moreover, hadn't this been done before?

As it turned out, no. Though the newspaper's files were replete with stories about federal indictments of Chicago officials, the occasional enterprising investigation of a specific aldermanic infraction, or reports of the city council's colorful, albeit debilitating, antics, the *Tribune* had never undertaken a systematic investigation of the institution as a whole.

If rumor and assumption were true, Chicago's City Council was among the most corrupt government bodies in history. We were interested in proving whether the reputation was deserved. If it was, the challenge was to document the extent of the corruption and the tariff it extracted—both in dollars and in the cost to the city's reputation and management.

As the first step in what became a six-month investigation of the largest municipal lawmaking body in the country, we began interviewing. We talked to local government lobbyists, city officials who were familiar with the council's members and its workings, and to the aldermen themselves. Intentionally, we started with people noted for their integrity, hoping that they would be inclined to tell us of irregularities that other people in Chicago might dismiss as business as usual.

Because many of these people were at first unwilling to talk on the record, we regarded the early interviews as a way of trolling for "tips." We encouraged the sources to think broadly. If they were reporters with unlimited time to investigate the council, what would they look at? We recited the list of the council's 50 members and asked our interview subjects what they knew of each alderman.

We accepted nothing we heard as fact but as suggestions to pursue. Whatever ultimately was included in the series, we agreed, would have to be documented by records or firsthand attribution.

At the same time we were interviewing people, we also began accumulating documents, including the statements by each alderman on public ethics as well as their campaign contribution reports. While little of what we found in these records was incriminating on its face, the names of many contributors and the businesses aldermen owned later emerged in ways that demonstrated conflicts of interest or influence-peddling.

At the end of each day, we would convene with our notes and records and go over our findings. As the weeks passed, we began to see some patterns and themes emerging. But prior to making a formal outline for the project, we agreed on a series of subjects to pursue further.

Not all of these pursuits bore fruit. We spent hundreds of dollars to obtain a municipal court computer list of cases handled by aldermen who were attorneys. Then we spent weeks studying it, but it proved little. A seemingly endless comparison of the attorneys' legal clients to the city's huge list of approved vendors was also disappointing.

Fortunately, other avenues did not fail us. One fact at a time, a series emerged.

Some stories were naturals. From the start, we suspected that a systematic review of council committee spending would easily support a story about waste. After several planning sessions with aides in the city comptroller's office, we devised a plan to obtain, through the Freedom of Information Act, every voucher for every purchase in the last 18 months by each of the council's 28 committees. The vouchers showed purchases of car telephones, gifts, plane tickets and office furniture authorized by the aldermen.

In addition, we obtained the payroll records for each committee to track the political connections of employees. But because these documents did not alone prove waste, we also reviewed the work records of each committee for the same period.

Surprisingly, some of the committees had not met even once in 18 months. Others convened occasionally but did no legislative work. The marriage of the spending and work records provided a classic profile of municipal waste. Quotes from the aldermen, some of whom were shockingly brazen about their spending, enlivened the series.

Other stories took us by surprise. During one of our first interviews for the series, an alderman made a passing reference to one of his colleagues' financial success. How was it, he wondered, that Joseph Kotlarz, only several years out of law school, had built such a thriving legal practice? Kotlarz—a young, low-profile freshman alderman—had not occurred to us as one of the council members most worthy of investigation. But during the first of what would be a series of interviews with Kotlarz, he convinced us otherwise. He explained that clients were attracted to him through the power of his office, not his legal acumen. His law partner, he said, claimed that Kotlarz "couldn't do a real estate closing if I tried."

Based on this sketchy beginning, we proceeded with a broad investigation that included research on each of his real estate holdings, his council spending, his aldermanic payroll, his divorce records and interviews with more than two dozen business partners, friends and campaign workers. What resulted was a kind of case study of a Chicago politician. In telling the story of Kotlarz' quick rise from a gas station attendant to a wealthy and well-connected alderman, we were able to tell the larger story of the opportunities made available to members of the City Council simply by virtue of their election.

But in order for the series to transcend an anecdotal approach, we wanted a story that would detail how the abuses by individual aldermen merged to cripple the city in a larger, more systematic way.

Then we looked at how zoning worked in Chicago. By tradition aldermen exercised complete control over zoning in their wards. No building could be constructed, no shopping center developed without the approval of the local alderman. The system was clearly susceptible to corruption; developers had no choice but to solicit aldermanic support, and aldermen, not known for their asthetics or interest in sensible urban development, could demand changes in the design and scope of major projects. To document the impact of this, we decided to examine every zoning application for a three-year period, enough time to spot patterns and draw conclusions.

To organize the information, we designed a form that included the name of each applicant and his lawyer, the date of the application and comments by the alderman. We discovered that aldermen routinely sponsored zoning changes in their own names. In these instances, the property owner was rarely identified. Later, by researching county property records, we were able to show that many of the beneficiaries were friends and political supporters, and in one case the father of an alderman. After we had gone through all of the more than 600 changes, we compared the names of zoning applicants to each alderman's lists of campaign contributors. In the end, we were able to conclude that timely campaign contributions and a friendship with an alderman were the best ways to assure approval of a project.

As these and other stories took shape, the series' opening piece began to emerge almost on its own. Numerous instances of corruption or profiteering that did not warrant a separate story, research that documented the Chicago's City Council as the largest and most expensive in the country, interviews in which aldermen bragged of their abuse of power or bemoaned their membership on a body that at times has served as a national laughingstock—all this combined to form what to us was a depressing but compelling curtain raiser.

For the kicker to this story, we selected a quote that we thought established a tenor for the series. After a section documenting council members' use of city funds to repave the streets on which they lived, we quoted one alderman's explanation for this practice: "If it needs it," he said of his street, "why should I suffer?"

What new stories could be told about an institution legendary for its corruption? A few. What impact would such an investigation have in a city like Chicago? Some. While the series prompted several changes—legislation that would make it difficult for aldermen to do favors secretly for friends, the loss of an elected Democratic party seat by an alderman we profiled—results are measured on a different scale in Chicago.

For starters, the series has radically changed the way the *Tribune* and other news organizations in Chicago report on the City Council. Many actions by the council that were routinely left uncovered are now reported on aggressively. Developments that were once relegated to a paragraph in a news roundup are now front-page stories.

The council provides us with many such Page One stories.

The day after the Pulitzer Prizes were announced, a *Tribune* columnist facetiously asked, in print, whether the city's aldermen would sponsor a congratulatory resolution in honor of the prize. They did, sort of.

At the next council meeting, the members of the most expensive municipal government body in the country voted themselves an increase for committee spending.

—Dean Baquet, Ann Marie Lipinski, William Gaines
Chicago Tribune

POLITICS, PETTINESS, PROFITEERING

REWARDS OF THE WARDS ARE CHICAGO ALDERMANIC TRADITION

SUNDAY, OCTOBER 4, 1987

BY DEAN BAQUET AND
ANN MARIE LIPINSKI

The Chicago City Council, the largest and most expensive in the country, is a corrupted and inefficient body that habitually puts aldermen's personal concerns before the public good.

It has squandered its chartered power to set the city's course and surrendered itself to political housekeeping and profligate spending.

The tradition of chicanery in Chicago government is long and notorious. Twelve Chicago aldermen in the last 15 years have been convicted of crimes involving misuse of their offices. Three recent aldermen are under federal indictment on bribery charges.

But those convictions represent only the most flagrant, criminal abuses. Day in and day out, council operations are dominated by petty profiteering and a myopic fixation on trivia. Aldermen have again and again enacted laws and structured city government to enhance their power to exploit public needs for personal gain.

As a result, the very purpose of government has been corrupted. And the cost is huge—not only in terms of misspent dollars and cents, but also through the incalculable loss of the council's potential for leadership.

In a six-month investigation, The Tribune has examined in detail the business of the Chicago City Council and the businesses of its 50 members.

Reporters conducted hundreds of interviews with aldermen, their employees, City Hall officials, lobbyists and constituents.

Reporters also reviewed thousands of documents that pinpoint the spending, the operations, the political organizations and the private interests of city council members.

What emerges is a portrait of a legislative body whose membership is riddled with conflicts of interest and obsessed with minutiae.

How does the Chicago City Council work? It works first and foremost for the aldermen. These are just a few examples uncovered in The Tribune's investigation:

• A North Side alderman hands out business cards for a friend's jukebox and pinball machine company to tavern owners awaiting approval of liquor license applications, urging them to employ the company's services.

• A West Side alderman, who persuaded a drugstore chain to stock a soft drink he markets, boasts that the chain also has secured his vote on the city council.

• In a Loop office shared with his ward's Democratic organization, a veteran alderman works as an officer of a company paid by the city to insure firms that lease city parking lots. Across the street in City Hall, the alderman votes on the city leases to those firms.

• After approving $296 million in city bonds for infrastructure repairs, 15 aldermen designate portions of the funds to repave streets in front of their homes.

"People talk about the privatization of government," mayoral chief-of-staff Ernest Barefield said. "But they don't realize that it's already privatized."

This pattern of behavior did not begin this year, or this decade. The Chicago City Council has a long, unsavory tradition of greed and indifference.

The "Gray Wolves" who ran Chicago during an era of weak mayors at the turn of the century were renowned for corruption. Under the modern-day Democratic machine and its most noted leader, Richard J. Daley, council corruption was carried out on a grand scale by such powerful members as Thomas E. Keane.

By the mid-1970s, federal prosecutions had raised the risks for those tempted by outright bribery and extortion. The collapse of the monolithic machine, along with federal court rulings that curtailed patronage hiring, closed other traditional avenues of political reward. In 1983, the election of Mayor Harold Washington created a deep political split that paralyzed the council but encouraged many of its members into the petty schemes of self-enrichment that mar the institution today.

At the same time, the Chicago City Council has extracted a growing tariff from taxpayers to govern the nation's third largest city. The 50-member council, with its $14.1 million budget, surpasses in cost and size the councils of all other large U.S. cities.

When the city council meets this month to begin hearings on next year's municipal budget—one that may require another tax increase —it will be faced with a bill for city government that has ballooned in part because of the council's patronage hiring and wasteful spending.

Though most of the council's 28 committees rarely meet, their operations will cost taxpayers $5.3 million this year. Records show that many committee chairmen have used those funds to buy car telephones and expensive video, camera and computer equipment.

Former Ald. Niles Sherman (21st) billed the council's Committee on Finance $5,279 in travel advances for a May trip to Denver and another to Washington in June. The advances were not repaid even though Sherman lost his election and his office in April.

The council is about to spend $125,000 to renovate its chambers, with Ald. Eugene Sawyer (6th) arguing that, "Visitors should see something that represents us better."

Such cosmetic tinkering with the council's image, however, overlooks a deeper problem. Mired in the role of custodian of basic city services, the city council largely ignores major policy issues, leaving significant initiatives to the mayor's office and a handful of committed aldermen.

Many council members say they spend as much as 90 percent of their time arranging for tree-trimming, pothole repairs and the removal of abandoned cars in their wards, despite a crushing agenda of urban problems that includes the crisis in the public schools, the deterioration of public housing and the erosion of Chicago's economic base.

During a conversation in his city council office, Ald. Bernard Stone (50th) mentally reviewed the matters up for his consideration and said he sometimes feels like a $40,000-a-year elected janitor. "If I go down in history, I don't want to go down as the guy who changed more light bulbs in the 50th Ward or picked up the most trash," he said. "But plenty of aldermen do."

At a recent council meeting, freshman Ald. Edwin Eisendrath (43d) got approval for 50 businesses in his ward to renew their permits for hanging canopies, an action required of aldermen under council-written rules.

Yet a resolution asking the Board of Education to permit the council's Committee on Education to take a fact-finding tour of Chicago's troubled schools—submitted by Eisendrath in May—has not been raised for even routine debate.

The education committee—with 14 members, a $95,400 budget and a staff of 6—has not met since July. Meanwhile, Chicago's teachers went on strike Sept. 8, putting 430,000 children out of school.

"It's frustrating, it makes me angry, it's inane," said Eisendrath, a 29-year-old former teacher and one of the council's most idealistic members. "Everybody told me when I decided to run that the Chicago City Council was not the most progressive body known to man, but I never expected this."

In the Tribune's investigation of the Chicago City Council, reporters examined every expenditure of the council's 28 committees for 18 months of 1986–87, records of ownership of all 50 ward offices, the council members' campaign finance reports and ethics statements, and the digests and summaries of council meetings for the last four years.

In addition, reporters reviewed each of the more than 600 zoning changes that have gone before the council during a three-year period —changes that reflect one of the council's greatest, most abused and least understood powers.

The investigation disclosed in sharp detail a legislative body so ineffective at managing the affairs of the city that some aldermen say they are embarrassed to be members.

In conversations with council members about their colleagues, not one listed more than 10 aldermen whose skills, enterprise or intellect they admire. One of the mayor's top Cabinet members said there are only 8 out of the 50 whom he would consider hiring.

Ald. Edward Burke (14th), whom colleagues routinely list as among the smartest and most effective members, said that when he meets strangers during out-of-town trips he never introduces himself as a Chicago alderman.

"If they ask, I tell them I'm a lawyer," said Burke, who rejects the faint praise of one administration official that "if nothing else, at least some of the aldermen have street smarts."

"The council wasn't meant to be street smart," Burke said. "It's supposed to be the board of directors for a $2 billion corporation. To excuse lack of intelligence or talent for street smarts is kind of pathetic."

Following a three-month hiatus, the first council meeting in September was devoted almost entirely to aldermen reading eulogies, offering tributes to athletic teams and approving routine ordinances for signs and taxi stands. Ald. David Orr (49th), the council's vice mayor and one of its most active legislators, shook his head and retreated to his office.

"I feel pretty ill about a lot of this," he said later. "I don't like what this city council does. I don't feel proud of it. . . . I often wish I hadn't run again, but I did and this is my lot."

Records of council expenditures show aldermen spending thousands of dollars each year on travel, gifts, office remodeling and the employment of business partners, campaign workers, family members and friends.

Ald. Joseph Kotlarz (35th) has put his law partner and precinct workers on the staff of the Committee on Claims and Liabilities and let a $2,000 consulting contract to a friend, State Rep. Alfred Ronan (D., Chicago), who produced no report.

As Sherman faced an April aldermanic runoff election—which he ultimately lost—he submitted a voucher for a $5,279 travel advance.

In a March 18 letter to the finance committee outlining his expenses for a planned five-day trip to Denver to attend a three-day May meeting of a National League of Cities committee, Sherman billed the city $632 in airfare, $1,800 for hotel lodging, $300 for "travel per diem" and a registration fee of $425. (A spokesman for the Washington, D.C.–based league said the registration fee for that conference was $175.)

That same day, Sherman submitted a second letter to the committee, outlining costs for a four-day trip to Washington to attend a two-day meeting of the same committee, this one in June. For that trip, Sherman's pre-billed expenses included $792 in airfare, $1,800 for hotels and $300 for "travel per diem."

Asked if he attended the conferences after he left office, Sherman, who is still Democratic committeeman of the 21st Ward, said: "Did I, did I, did I, did I? I'm trying to remember now myself." He then said he "might" have attended the Washington meeting but, "off the top of my head," couldn't remember what the conference was about. He said he did not know if he returned any funds to the city.

"Don't hold me to this now," Sherman added. "I don't know what the heck happened."

City records also demonstrate a brazen acknowledgement on the part of some aldermen that Chicagoans' ingrained, bemused cynicism toward their public officials is well deserved. Conflicts of interest are so routine among council members that many openly list them on the skimpy ethics reports they are required to file each year.

A new Chicago ethics law, passed by the council on the eve of this year's city elections, stiffens some disclosure requirements, but there is an active campaign by many aldermen to kill or dilute the law.

Former Ald. Wilson Frost (34th), who resigned last year to become a Cook County Board of [tax] Appeals member, admitted on his last aldermanic ethics report to receiving free downtown parking space. The company that gave him the space holds contracts to operate city-owned parking lots; Frost voted on those contracts while in the council.

Former Ald. Perry Hutchinson (9th) admitted that a company in which he held a partnership interest had bid for a city contract to remove snow at O'Hare International Airport—a violation of the council's ethics standards that bar aldermen from doing business with the city. Hutchinson is awaiting trial on a bribe-taking charge in another case.

Five other aldermen reported accepting free European vacations from American Airlines. The airline leases space at city-owned O'Hare, has benefited from council-approved city bonds and has battled the city on tax levies.

After the council's Committee on Finance voted to approve a $500,000 city loan to the then-fledgling Midway Airlines, committee chairman Burke signed on as an attorney for the airline. While serving as its lawyer, Burke later voted to renew Midway's city lease. Burke also has represented American Airlines and accepted travel from the company.

Burke acknowledged that his law firm represented Midway, but he said that business had no connection to the city loan or his lease vote.

"Technically, there was no conflict because I didn't have an ownership in Midway," Burke said. "However, to be doubly sure, I would have recused myself if I had known. It was probably a routine matter that just slipped through."

By the willingness of some to trade on their office for personal gain, council members have sent a message to constituents that the office of alderman is for sale, said Ald. Jesus Garcia (22d). In an interview, Garcia described the parade of favor-seekers who have approached him since his election last year—people who assume that nothing an alderman does is for free.

"Most of the people approaching me this way will be business people, though sometimes it's a resident," Garcia said. "They ask for a job, for me to take care of some violations, to give them a zoning change. Then they say, 'I'll give you money, I'll give you a contribution, I'll back you up.' I say, 'I don't do business that way.' "

Since becoming an alderman, Garcia said, he has been approached dozens of times by persons seeking to trade city contracts for a piece of the profits, insurance firms inviting him to join their offices and lawyers wanting Garcia—a non-practicing paralegal—"to funnel them cases" of constituents.

"They say, 'You're a member. You're part of the club of 50. Do you realize the money you could make?' " Garcia said. "A lot of people want to hustle the alderman. A lot of people want the alderman to hustle."

Ald. Danny Davis (29th) recounted a visit to his ward office by one of his West Side constituents: "A guy just came in, pulled out a roll of money and put it on my desk and said, 'I want a liquor license. Take care of this.' " Davis said he declined the offer.

Aldermen have not been shy about inviting temptation. Over the years they have made laws that give them a remarkable amount of power over constituents in need of the most basic government services. By requiring an alderman's blessing for even routine matters, Chicago's City Council has multiplied the opportunities for corruption.

By council ordinance, aldermen receive copies of all applications for liquor licenses, even though they play no legal role in the process by which the licenses are awarded. City officials say that some white aldermen use this information to lobby against black applicants, while some black aldermen try to keep out Arab-Americans.

Aldermen also require the Department of Inspectional Services to alert them each time a constituent requests a building permit, whether it is for the construction of a high-rise or the addition of a backyard deck.

Though aldermen have no legal authority to approve or deny those permits, the council requires the department to put a 10-day hold on every one of the 12,000 applications it receives annually while the applicant's alderman reviews the request, said John Power, an assistant to the commissioner of inspectional services.

"It's a tremendous headache," Power complained. "Here we are trying to provide expeditious service to the constituent and, by council rule, we can't."

Aldermen require council approval for businesses that want to hang a new sign or build a canopy. Except as "a way for aldermen to make money," said Ald. Eisendrath, "I don't know what it [the regulation] is there for."

Council members have given themselves such power over zoning that no skyscraper, shopping mall, factory, two-flat or parking lot can be built in a ward without the alderman's approval. Some critics say that aldermen have used this to gain control over business development and to influence the ethnic and racial makeup of their wards.

The investigation also found that, thanks to a council privilege that allows aldermen to sponsor zoning changes in their wards, 30 percent of all zoning applicants in Chicago are never identified in city records.

Aldermen, in turn, have used their tremendous control over zoning to raise thousands of dollars in campaign contributions, a comparison of zoning changes and council members' fundraising records shows.

Paul and Velma Maxwell found out how much influence their alderman had when they set out to build a house in the South Side 21st Ward then controlled by Niles Sherman. The Maxwells' lawyer told them that although it was a routine matter, the only way to get the necessary city permission was to visit Sherman and win his approval.

Velma Maxwell said she met with Sherman, and the alderman asked her to buy $160 worth of tickets for a political fundraiser.

"He didn't say I wouldn't get the change if I didn't buy tickets," she recalled. "He just said, 'You scratch my back and I'll scratch your back.' " Maxwell said she agreed and handed Sherman the money, although he did not give her any tickets.

A month later, still awaiting approval, Maxwell visited Sherman a second time to ask about the delay. She said Sherman asked her to buy two more tickets, for another $160.

Maxwell says she did. The zoning change cleared the city council.

Efforts to reach Sherman for a response to Maxwell's statements were unsuccessful.

In 1983, David Shelton was having trouble getting the city licensing he needed to open a juice bar. He turned to newly elected Ald. Bernard Hansen (44th), whose ward includes the Uptown neighborhood where Shelton wanted to locate Medusa's, a club that would serve nonalcoholic beverages and cater to teens.

Shelton says he got some business advice he hadn't asked for.

"The first thing he asked me was whether I have a vending service," Shelton recalled. "I said, 'No.' He said, 'Here's a name, these guys are really good guys.' "

The name that Hansen gave Shelton was that of Arrow Vending, a jukebox, pinball and cigarette machine company that until recently was owned by John Lahey. Hansen describes Lahey as a childhood friend and a contributor to the alderman's campaign fund.

Shelton declined to lease equipment from Arrow, and his club eventually opened without the alderman's aid. But Shelton says that he paid another price, maintaining that his refusal to use Arrow resulted in Hansen's attempts to shut down his bar.

In November, 1985, Hansen personally led a late-night raid on Medusa's that ended with the club being cited for overcrowding. Hansen also was the leader of a city council battle to restrict the hours of juice bars like Medusa's, a fight that Hansen won.

Hansen said he does not remember whether he recommended Arrow

Vending to Shelton, but he said Shelton's refusal to use the company had nothing to do with his juice bar legislation or with the raid.

Tim Sullivan, owner of Club Berlin, also visited Hansen while waiting for the city to approve a liquor license application for his Halsted Street bar. When Sullivan met with Hansen, the alderman handed him a card printed with the name "Arrow Vending."

"He said a friend of his owned it," Sullivan recalled. Sullivan said Hansen did not pressure him, but he took the alderman's suggestion and leased a cigarette machine from the company.

Hansen said in an interview that he routinely asked bars in his ward to lease from Arrow, though he did not know how many. "I don't think it was hundreds," he said. "I have no idea—40, 30, 50. I don't know." He said that bar owners were free to ignore his pitch.

Hansen said he stopped touting Arrow about a year ago, on the advice of his lawyer, when he learned that the FBI was investigating corruption in city licensing. He said that federal investigators have assured him he is not a target of their investigation but that his lawyer warned him that it might appear improper for an elected official to promote a private business.

Hansen insists that his conversations with bar owners were intended only as friendly advice.

"Here's a friend of mine who has a business," he said, describing his pitch. "Like you might say, 'My hair stylist is a great guy. Go see him.' "

On Oct. 31, 1983, Hedy Radner, a prominent community organizer and head of the Chicago Film and Video Studio Foundation, stood before a packed city council chamber and told a joint committee hearing about her plan to build a sprawling movie studio and sound stage complex on a blighted site on the Near West Side.

For three years, Radner had worked to line up support from artists' and actors' groups, unions and the city's Department of Economic Development, which helped her piece together an application for an $860,000 federal grant to buy the land.

Editorial writers applauded the nonprofit project as a boon to city and state efforts to serve Hollywood's growing interest in Chicago, which lacked a full-service production lot.

Administration officials liked the plan because it would create jobs, increase tourism and spending in Chicago and allow the city to tap into dormant federal land-purchase money.

Testifying before the council's committees on Cable Television, Economic Development, and Cultural Affairs and Historic Preservation, Radner explained that the deal had to be closed quickly because the land owner had another offer.

The committee members unanimously approved the grant and authorized the necessary zoning. That same day, the matter moved to the full council, and Radner was assured by a number of aldermen that the proposal would sail through.

But when the issue rose on the agenda, so did Ald. Edward Vrdolyak (10th), then the city's most powerful alderman. "I move to defer and publish," Vrdolyak said, invoking a time-worn method of burying unwanted legislation.

Six days later, the land owner sold the site of Radner's grand plan to another buyer.

Within a few months, a new group brought in its own, similar proposal. This group included former U.S. Rep. Morgan Murphy, a regular Democrat of long standing from Chicago's Southwest Side, and union leader John Serpico, both Vrdolyak allies.

Telephone calls made to Vrdolyak's office to ask him why he took the action to defer and publish received no response.

The Washington administration refused to help the new group get a city-backed loan. The group turned to the state, which recently awarded Murphy and his partners a $600,000 Build Illinois loan at 5 percent interest.

Following the city council's approval last year of a $130 million bond package to finance public works projects, Ald. Richard Mell (33d) fretted that the money going to each of the wards was scarcely enough to scratch the surface of infrastructure needs.

The council vote was the second of its kind in two years, resulting in an unprecedented total of $296 million in borrowed funds to shore up city streets, sidewalks, sewers and alleys. Combined with a state-funded street resurfacing program controlled by the council, aldermen had gained their biggest opportunity in city history to direct fix-up funds to the most broken-down corners of their wards.

But Mell expressed fear that the widely publicized program was heightening voter expectations that could not be met.

"It's not a lot of money," he said after the vote. "It's a very minimal amount in today's dollars. . . . I think the mayor holds out false hope to people."

What Mell did not say was that in appropriating the first year's bond money, charity had begun at home.

Among the 33d Ward streets Mell had selected for resurfacing was a four-block stretch of Mozart Street that includes the alderman's home. He also chose a strip of Roscoe Street fronting the R. F. Mell Spring and Mfg. Co., which he owns.

Mell was one of 15 aldermen who used the special city or state funds to redo the streets where they live. Some aldermen also selected the streets in front of the homes of family members or business partners, according to Department of Public Works officials and a Tribune analysis of two years of records.

Asked how he allocated the repaving resources in his ward, Ald. Kotlarz said: "Almost personally. In other words, I almost without exception have visited every street. . . . We did them on an as-needed basis. Clearly there was no personal attention given anyone."

Told that records show him to have repaved the streets fronting his house, the home of his law partner, the home of a top precinct captain and the home of one of his council committee employees, Kotlarz said: "A very casual observation [of the streets], I think, will vindicate me."

When former Ald. Vrdolyak decided last year to give up his 10th Ward seat to run for mayor, he selected his brother, Victor, to replace him. The year before, Vrdolyak had awarded his brother another perk, having directed some of the 10th Ward's resurfacing funds to a four-block stretch of Carondolet Avenue that passes Victor's house.

Ald. Michael Sheahan (19th) not only used city bond funds to repave a stretch of Winchester Avenue that includes his home but, using the state funds, has repaved a nearly complete grid of streets surrounding his Southwest Side home.

Former Aldermen Marian Humes (8th), Miguel Santiago (31st) and Gerald McLaughlin (45th) were ousted from the council by voters last spring, though not without a memento of their years in office.

Those three, as well as a representative mix of sitting members—Fred Roti (1st), Bobby Rush (2d), Alan Streeter (17th), Jesus Garcia (22d), Danny Davis (29th), Percy Giles (37th), Patrick O'Connor (40th), Eugene Schulter (47th) and Bernard Stone (50th)—also selected their own blocks for repaving.

"It's a very political game," said Ronald Johnson, assistant commissioner of the city Department of Public Works. The site-selection process turns into "an IOU program for aldermen," Johnson said. "It's one of the tools they use in getting re-elected."

It is an expensive tool. According to Johnson, it costs $25,000 to resurface an average Chicago block. Though the state and city programs have combined to give each ward about 9 miles, or 72 blocks, of repaving in the last two years, the demand for resurfacing has outpaced the resources in a city where residential streets have a life of 25 to 35 years.

Even Mayor Washington winks at the council's penchant for turning the most basic of city services into political spoils. When Ald. Lawrence Bloom (5th) asked the council at its Sept. 9 meeting to acknowledge the presence in the gallery of Miss Black Illinois, the mayor, standing at the rostrum, smiled at the young woman and asked, "Did we pave your street?"

The program has been further politicized by some aldermen who appear to have used their prerogative over site selection to exclude certain ethnic areas in their wards. Johnson said that a biased pattern by some aldermen prompted public works officials to step in and "negotiate" changes in about one-fourth of the wards.

"When you put [the sites] on a map and notice that all the work is being done in 25 percent of the ward, you say to yourself, 'This might be a little biased,' " Johnson said.

Officials found, for instance, that except for a small grid in the northeast corner of his ward, Ald. Robert Kellam (18th) had virtually ignored his ward's predominantly black neighborhoods east of Western Avenue.

Public works officials attempted to redress the imbalance in that ward and about eight others by lobbying aldermen and adding a written criterion for site selection that asks for "equity and geographic balance," Johnson said.

Kellam said his choices were "based on need," not ethnicity. "We try to spread it out around the ward," he said, "but nobody is ever satisfied."

Though Ald. Stone estimates that 30 to 40 percent of the streets in his Far North Side ward are in dire need of repaving, he said he "makes no excuses" for having singled out his block as a top priority.

"If it needs it," he said, "why should I suffer?"

William Gaines and Joel Kaplan contributed to this report.

COMMITTEES WORK A LITTLE AND SPEND A LOT

MONDAY, OCTOBER 5, 1987

BY ANN MARIE LIPINSKI AND DEAN BAQUET

On Sept. 17, 1985, as the Chicago City Council prepared for its annual budget hearings, Ald. Edward Burke (14th), chairman of the council's Committee on Finance, warned that the city was facing a $50 million revenue gap.

Thirteen days later, Ald. Patrick Huels (11th) sent his secretary to a Wabash Avenue store to pick up office supplies for his Committee on Licenses. The secretary returned with five picture frames and two pen-and-pencil sets, including a 10-karat gold-filled, green onyx Cross desk set. Taxpayers picked up the bill for $326.29.

Between that date and the end of the year, Huels's committee, with a budget of $107,044 in public funds, met only twice and approved no legislation, although 11 ordinances were pending before it.

In the following year, Huels used committee funds to pay for monthly car-phone bills ranging from $38.80 to $327.74; a $22-a-month beeper service; a $350 "hands free duplex" to allow him to use the phone outside his car; a $155 telephone delivered to his ward office; $100 in cab fare coupons; a $103 Polaroid camera; an oak computer cabinet, chair and hutch priced at $312; and a $621 unitemized Diners Club International charge for "office equipment."

Huels's purchases were typical of how the $5.3 million in taxpayers' funds budgeted for city council committees are spent by the aldermen who run them.

And although they are spending, most of the committees aren't working. Last year, fewer than half of the council committees met more than six times.

In a six-month investigation of the Chicago City Council, The Tribune reviewed the records of thousands of expenditures by city council committees for an 18-month period through last June. Reporters also examined the reports that document the committees' work.

Those records show that many of the council's 28 committees spend portions of their budgets under the control of committee chairmen, on items such as beepers, car phones, gifts, travel, computers, video equipment and office furniture.

Huels said that having a car phone was, if not a necessity, "convenient" for running his committee and that a pager was needed to keep in touch with his staff. Other purchases, he said, were made to decorate his office. Asked why a committee chairman required a gold-filled pen-and-pencil set, Huels responded, "As opposed to what?"

Burke seemed to ignore his own predictions of dire financial difficulty—which, as it turned out, proved exaggerated.

For example, he used a committee contingency fund to pay $6,000 in legal fees to defend himself in a libel case. He also authorized his committee to pay $471.34 for his bodyguard's stay at the deluxe Mayfair Regent Hotel in New York City. When a committee employee quit, Burke's staff used city funds to buy a $160 leather briefcase as a farewell present.

The council committees and their $5.3 million budget also are run as personal patronage fiefs. Numerous committee payrolls are stacked with political supporters and friends of chairmen and other aldermen.

When Ald. Bernard Hansen (44th) hired Marie Merlo for a $650-a-month job writing speeches and doing research for the Committee on Economic Development, he explained, "She's a very talented person." She is also the daughter of John Merlo, Hansen's ward committeeman, but the alderman said that played no part in her employment.

Former Ald. Niles Sherman (21st) lost his re-election bid in April, but not a place on the city payroll. After his ouster by constituents, Sherman was hired at $268 a month as a part-time investigator for Ald. William Beavers (7th), chairman of the Committee on Police, Fire and Municipal Institutions.

"He can do a lot of research for me," Beavers said. "He can do quite a bit."

The salaries of the council committees' staffs total $3.9 million. Because the chairmen have total discretion on how to use their salary budgets, the number of employees and the number of hours they work fluctuate constantly.

In addition to wages, according to city Budget Director Sharon Gist Gilliam, the city pays the cost of medical coverage—an additional sum equal to about 35 percent of each employee's salary—for staff members paid to work more than 80 hours a month.

"One of the reasons for getting on a committee payroll is not so much for the pay as the medical benefits, which are among the best in the Western world," Gilliam said. "It's worth it to work here for the medical benefits alone."

Later this month, aldermen will begin hearings on a 1988 city budget that may require a new tax increase, even after proposed cuts in city services and staff. And though Ald. Lawrence Bloom (5th), Budget Committee chairman, acknowledges that the committees present "a legitimate area of concern," the council's own spending is likely to escape review.

"It's kind of hard to bring on each alderman and ask them questions about what their committee does, the way we would with a department head," Bloom said. "Maybe we should, but let's just say that it hasn't been done before. No alderman likes to sit in judgment of another alderman."

"The question here is, Who's auditing the auditor?" said city Comptroller Ronald Picur, whose $6.3 million departmental budget will be scrutinized by the council during budget hearings while the council's comparable spending on its committees will go virtually unchecked. "It comes down to a process of self-review," Picur said, "and that's a fundamental problem in government."

In interviews, aldermen and administration officials describe the council's committee system as a political peace-keeping device more than a necessary legislative tool. Over the years, a system made up of many committees that show little evidence of work has been used by mayors and by their council opponents to woo obstinate aldermen by cutting them in on city patronage.

Jacky Grimshaw, who as director of intergovernmental affairs is Mayor Harold Washington's chief liaison to the aldermen, believes that the 50-member council is itself "too big by half," and that the proliferation of committees is "a bad precedent set four years ago" when, under the control of former Ald. Edward Vrdolyak (10th), the city council established an all-time high of 37 committees.

But Washington, who once characterized committee patronage as a "cesspool," also has used this coveted perquisite to reward allies. Last spring, after complaints from Ald. George Hagopian (30th), the administration created a Committee on Veteran Affairs to reward the Northwest Side alderman for voting to help the mayor reorganize the city council power structure.

"It's a two-edged sword," said Ald. Burton Natarus (42d), a Washington ally who in 1986 withheld his vote on a council reorganization plan until he was awarded the Committee on Local Transportation and its $553,000 budget. "People wanted peace, and it's the way the mayor found to have political peace."

Burke, a key engineer of the committees' expansion during the bitter "Council Wars" period that followed Washington's election in 1983, bluntly acknowledges that the proliferation of many do-little committees "was a political decision made to garner votes."

He added: "There are about nine committees that could handle all of the necessary work, and we could be done with the rest."

The City Council's Committee on Finance, with its $1.8 million budget, is the richest and most powerful of the committees. In tandem with the Budget Committee, the finance chairman and his staff have one of the largest committee workloads and are responsible for reviewing the city's $2.4 billion budget. In addition, the finance committee has jurisdiction over capital improvements, administrative efficiency and the maintenance of municipal services.

But that committee also serves as a clearinghouse for less visible matters. While acting as finance chairman, a post he lost in April, Burke used a contingency fund to pay attorneys representing the committee in lawsuits involving political "Council Wars" disputes and to hand out no-bid consulting contracts, records show.

The contracts included one to a Chicago public relations and consulting firm for "research on state legislation and related matters" for the finance committee. The company, Stanley D. Banash and Associates, billed the committee $100 an hour for a total of $5,400 in the first three months of this year.

More than $20,000 was paid to attorney Lawrence O'Gara to handle the committee's unsuccessful attempt to subpoena the records of a city consultant. O'Gara, though not a member of Burke's law firm, works out of the alderman's office and has practiced law with Burke's attorney wife, Anne.

The contingency fund also was used to pay legal fees for officials under federal investigation, including about $10,000 to hire attorneys for present and former city officials who testified before grand juries. The committee was billed $8,200 by a lawyer who represented former Corporation Counsel James Montgomery, a top Washington aide, before a federal grand jury investigating city contracts.

And nearly $6,000 was spent to represent Burke in a libel case resulting from a 1986 radio show in which the alderman made a personal attack on former mayoral aide Clarence McClain. The suit still is pending.

Burke defended the use of city money to pay the legal costs, citing a section in the city code that gives the Finance Committee control over funds to represent city officials in lawsuits. Burke selected O'Gara to handle the one suit because he is "experienced in trial law," the alderman said.

Through the contingency fund, the committee also paid $808 to service its 27 beepers and at least $7,000 for travel, including trips to Washington, D.C., and Denver for former Ald. Sherman. These trips were scheduled to be taken after his April election defeat, and Sherman says he cannot remember whether he took them.

When Ald. Eugene Schulter (47th) won re-election in April and announced his new-found support of Washington, Schulter was named chairman of the council's Committee on Beautification and Recreation, with its $101,835 budget.

"I'm putting my agenda together now," Schulter said in a June interview. "We're going to have a hearing at the park district on their reorganization plan to see how it impacts the neighborhoods. We're also going to take a look at the complaint system at the parks."

Schulter added that the committee would review the park district's efforts to market its facilities—"One of the best kept secrets in Chicago," he said—and convene to study park safety and lakefront erosion.

"To my knowledge, the council has never looked at the park district before, at least not in the past 12 years," he said. "But I feel it is our responsibility to see what is going on."

Freshman Ald. Kathy Osterman (48th), vice chairman of Beautification and Recreation, would hardly recognize the committee Schulter described.

"I call it the Boring Committee," said Osterman, who proceeded to describe the typical meeting of the 13-member panel.

"Usually it's just Gene Schulter and myself," she said. "We have a list of all the block-club parties and sidewalk sales for Wards 1 through 50, and you just go through the agenda and approve it. It takes about five minutes. There's never any discussion, except once we talked about a tree stump in the 11th Ward. There was a little discussion on that.

" 'Can't we get into lake erosion?' I asked Gene. 'This is the perfect committee for lake erosion.' He's thinking about it, he tells me. . . . I go to meetings to approve block parties and sidewalk sales when I want to talk about lake erosion, something that is killing our city."

Osterman's portrayal of the committee's agenda since April also fits its operations under its two previous chairmen, according to a review of the committee's records since January, 1984—a period in which the committee's budget rose by more than $45,000 and members did little work while awarding themselves perks of office.

In 1984 and 1985, the committee met eight times, according to quarterly reports on file with the city clerk. The committee, then under Ald. William Krystyniak (23d), voted perfunctory approval of several hundred carnivals, street festivals and sidewalk sales. Meanwhile, the committee debated but never acted on an ordinance by former Ald. Marion Volini (48th) requiring new safety regulations at playgrounds to protect children against injuries and government bodies against lawsuits.

Neither Krystyniak nor Ald. Allan Streeter (17th), who assumed control of the committee in June, 1986, filed any reports with the clerk's office detailing the committee's work during 1986.

During that same period, Streeter used the committee budget to buy a $795 typewriter, spent $346.61 on beepers and had $119.77

worth of computer equipment delivered to his ward office. Streeter did not return repeated telephone calls for comment on the billings.

Krystyniak charged taxpayers for his car phone bills as well as $490 for film bought in July.

"I'm a true believer that a picture tells a hundred stories," Krystyniak said of the film, explaining that it was used to document "complaints" and committee members' tours of park sites. "Maybe some people don't even know what a basketball looks like," he said.

Krystyniak said the car phone permitted him "to stay in full communication back and forth" with his staff. "I'm a true believer in it, and that kind of guy," he said. "I make myself accessible to the public wherever I am."

Krystyniak is one of at least five committee chairmen who used committee money to install telephones in their own cars in the last 18 months, records show.

In March, 1986, while chairman of the Committee on Cultural Development and Historical Landmark Preservation, former Ald. Gerald McLaughlin (45th), charged a $1,701.50 car phone to his committee. McLaughlin also used committee money to pay four car phone bills that year totaling $413.53.

McLaughlin, who lost his re-election bid in April, would not say whether he returned the phone to the city following his defeat. "I have no comment on that," he said.

During a nine-month period that ended last March, Ald. John Madrzyk (13th) charged taxpayers $683.15 for car phone bills, as well as $290.16 in car phone installation costs. Madrzyk also used 1986 funds of his Committee on Administration, Reorganization and Personnel to buy $3,200 in office furniture and to pay an $87 bill for decaffeinated coffee and paper goods. City clerk records show the committee met four times in 1986.

In April, Madrzyk lost his committee chairmanship, but he didn't lose his car phone. He said the Committee on Finance, now chaired by Ald. Timothy Evans (4th), is picking up his monthly tab—an arrangement confirmed by Evans.

"I don't think it's a big what-do-you-do," Madrzyk said. "I see waste that the press never writes about, and here we're going to talk about how much?"

Ald. Bernard Stone (50th) said he recently bought a car phone but believes it would be improper to charge it to the Committee on Historical Landmark Preservation he heads. He pays for the phone himself.

But last October, while chairman of the Committee on Ports, Wharves and Bridges, Stone spent $3,577.93, most of the committee's budget for supplies, on television and video-recording equipment.

Stone said he needed the equipment to record his committee meetings. The committee met twice in 1986.

Stone has taken the video equipment with him to the Committee on Historical Landmark Preservation. If Ald. Robert Shaw (9th), the new Ports, Wharves and Bridges chairman, asks him to return the equipment to the committee, Stone said, he will oblige.

"If he wants it, he can have it," Stone said. "I'll just go out and buy another one on the new committee."

The day before last spring's council reorganization, freshman Ald. Edward Eisendrath (43d) ran into Ald. Evans in City Hall.

"Tim asked me if I was going to open my ward office where my campaign office had been," Eisendrath recalled. "I said no, I wanted to move to a place where I can build a ramp for the handicapped. Boom! The next day I was made vice chairman of [the committee on] Aging and Disabled."

Eisendrath candidly acknowledges that he has no expertise in this area, nor was it a committee appointment he had sought during post-election negotiations. But interest or expertise seem to play little role in council expansion and staffing of committees.

Sixty years ago, the council made do with 16 committees, panels whose names—the Committees on Track Elevation and Railway Terminals—summon up an image of the Chicago of 1927. Special needs were met with the naming of temporary committees, giving rise to the short-lived and long-forgotten Knights of Pythias Convention Reception Committee, City Hall-County Building Street-Floor Rental Committee and the Herbert Hartley Reception Committee.

It wasn't until 1975 that the council added two more standing committees; four years later there were 20. And while that level seems modest by current standards, even then, reform aldermen complained about the proliferation.

"All that's scandalous," former Ald. Leon Despres (5th), now the mayor's parliamentarian, said in a recent interview. "It was swollen patronage."

By 1983, the council was presiding over 37 committees, a record number brought about by "Council Wars" and the stubborn insistence by aldermen both aligned and opposed to the newly elected Mayor Washington to stake their claim to what Ald. Bloom calls the "last real perk aldermen have left."

"We gave them all budgets," one of Washington's council allies said. "We were throwing money all over the place."

The council, which fell under Washington's control following the 1986 special aldermanic elections, has trimmed its committees by 9, though at 28 it is matched in size only by New York City's council, whose 35 members preside over 20 standing committees and 8 sub-committees.

In the last decade, the council has more than tripled its 1977 committee budget of $1.7 million. Today, the number of committees is so high that when Ald. Krystyniak was asked on which he served, he had to retrieve a sheet of his council stationery to name the six.

"It [the committee system] could probably be refined," Evans said. "We could probably do with fewer. But in practical, pragmatic politics, you need enough council votes to reduce it."

On May 8, 1986, Roosevelt University urbanologist Pierre de Vise received the first of three payments from the Committee on Municipal Code Revision to suggest ways to rewrite Chicago's dated municipal code. Former Ald. Jerome Orbach (46th), then chairman of that committee, authorized payment for what was to be the panel's central effort under his stewardship.

When de Vise showed up at the committee's City Hall office, he found his work was cut out for him.

"There was nothing," de Vise said. "It was even hard for them to find a copy of the municipal code. We finally found the alderman's only copy, and I had to give it back."

De Vise said Orbach urged him to finish the first half of the report before this year's aldermanic elections. De Vise said he rushed to complete the draft and gave it to Orbach several weeks before the April runoff elections.

In April, Orbach lost his election, and the committee was turned over to Ald. Richard Mell (33d).

De Vise was paid $3,500 in city funds for his initial work. He said no one has asked him to complete the study.

"I had no illusions about the practicality of doing a consultant's report for the council," he said later. "I knew this was not the reason you have committees."

William Gaines contributed to this report.

COMPARING MAJOR CITY COUNCILS

	SIZE OF COUNCIL	NUMBER OF COMMITTEES	SALARY PER YEAR	COUNCIL BUDGET IN MILLIONS	RESIDENTS PER COUNCIL MEMBER
CHICAGO	50	28	$40,000	$14.1	60,000
LOS ANGELES	15	15	53,000	11.7	200,000
BOSTON	13	13	45,000	2.8	69,000
NEW YORK	35	20	47,500	13.8	212,000
DETROIT	9	None	53,000	6.5	121,000
PHILADELPHIA	17	14	40,000	6.0	168,000

Note: Figures are for 1987

Chicago Tribune Graphic; Source: Chicago Tribune news reports

PUBLIC OFFICE A BOON TO PRIVATE INTERESTS

THURSDAY, OCTOBER 8, 1987

BY DEAN BAQUET AND WILLIAM GAINES

When Ald. Fred Roti (1st) is not conducting official city business, he serves as an officer of a Loop insurance agency. But sometimes when he is conducting official city business, Roti also serves his company and its clients.

As a member of the Chicago City Council's powerful Committee on Zoning, Roti supported zoning changes that permitted the owners of Standard Parking Inc. and General Parking Inc. to expand lots in his downtown ward. Both companies have purchased insurance through Roti's agency.

Roti's agency also sold insurance to American Truck Leasing Inc., which until recently rented five platform trucks to the city for $31,365 a month.

And, in a striking merger of public and private concerns, Roti's agency, Anco Inc., has handled insurance for 10 city-owned parking lots for more than 15 years.

Anco, hired by the firm that manages those 10 lots, receives city payments for providing worker's compensation and other insurance for the parking facilities. The alderman, meanwhile, has voted to extend the management firm's city contracts.

The relationship between Anco and the city demonstrates vividly how an alderman can use his public office to help his private business interests.

A six-month investigation by The Tribune found the Chicago City Council riddled with actual and potential conflicts of interest. But perhaps the most obvious, and the simplest, apparent conflict involves Roti and Anco, an insurance agency intertwined with the history of the downtown 1st Ward.

There are no middlemen, intricate partnerships or secret land trusts concealing Roti's relationship to Anco or the company's dealings with the city.

Anco shows up on the list of city vendors. Roti lists himself as Anco's secretary-treasurer on his financial disclosure statement.

The city administration knows that Roti—a former opposition alderman who now supports Mayor Harold Washington—is an officer of Anco, according to correspondence obtained by The Tribune.

But city officials have done nothing about this, despite their stated fear that the relationship might cause embarrassment to the administration and the possibility that the relationship violates city law.

After reviewing Anco's dealings with the city, attorney Robert Howard, a lead author of Chicago's new ethics ordinance, said: "It's exactly the kind of conflict of interest the ordinance was intended to prohibit, especially because of the influence an alderman has over zoning matters and parking contracts. The idea of an alderman selling insurance to people who need his support or approval in his role as a public official is a direct conflict of interest."

Howard said Roti may be in violation of city laws that prohibit aldermen from doing business with the city. Roti is a leader of an effort to soften one of these laws, the city's new ethics ordinance that took effect in August.

Former U.S. Atty. Thomas Sullivan, whose landmark 1986 corruption study ripped the Washington administration for letting politics influence city contracts, said Roti should recuse himself from voting on matters concerning Anco clients, or let people know when his vote affects a client.

"The failure to do so raises serious questions about the integrity of the political process," Sullivan said.

Roti declined to be interviewed for this article.

Anco began out of cluttered Loop offices, the same suite that once housed an insurance agency run by the legendary Michael "Hinky Dink" Kenna, a 1st Ward alderman in the early decades of this century when the downtown district was notorious for open vice and corruption.

Anco was founded in 1951 by then-Ald. John D'Arco Sr. and Frank Annunzio, who was state labor director at the time and is now a congressman.

Annunzio said they started the agency, which receives a fee for matching insurance companies to clients, to sell to 1st Ward businesses.

Just after Anco was formed, the Chicago Crime Commission reported that Annunzio was in business with D'Arco, whom the commission labeled as an associate of organized crime figures, and Annunzio was forced to resign from the company.

The FBI has investigated Anco and D'Arco several times, law enforcement sources said, but none of these investigations has resulted in any charges.

The U.S. Department of Justice declined to release records of its Anco inquiries. But it acknowledged, in response to a Freedom of Information Act request from The Tribune, that it has such files and that the company is currently the subject of a federal investigation. The Justice Department would not describe the reason for the latest investigation.

Anco began selling insurance to Sam D. Kaplan Auto Parks and an affiliate, Downtown Parking Stations Inc., in the 1950s, Kaplan said in a recent interview. At the time, he said, Anco provided insurance for some of the lots Kaplan owns.

There are dozens of insurance agencies in the 1st Ward, which includes the bustling Loop and Chinatown. But by tradition, Kaplan said, "in any neighborhood where you have a parking lot, they gave the insurance to the alderman."

In 1970, two years after Roti was elected to the Chicago City Council, the city gave Kaplan a no-bid contract to manage 10 city-owned lots, most of them small, neighborhood facilities. Kaplan's contracts were approved by the city council. They have been regularly approved since then, without change in parking rates or contract terms.

Roti, 66, formerly a state senator and city sewer inspector, was not an Anco executive when Kaplan first became a city contractor. He became a salesman in 1972, however, and secretary-treasurer in 1982. Since 1972, Roti has voted at least five times to extend Kaplan's city contracts, records show.

Under its contract with the city, Kaplan's firm, which receives a percentage of gross revenue, is reimbursed for many of its costs, including insurance for employees. Every month, Kaplan forwards the bills to the city, which in turn pays Anco, now located at 100 N. LaSalle St.

It is difficult to determine how much the city pays Anco for insuring Kaplan's workers.

From 1983 to 1986, the city wrote checks to Anco totaling $26,634. The money covered worker's compensation insurance at nine relatively small city-owned parking lots.

Anco also provides worker's compensation insurance at a much larger city parking facility that Kaplan manages at 553 S. State St., in the 1st Ward. But Kaplan pays Anco directly for insurance at this lot, and details of those payments were not included in city records. One city document shows that Anco billed Kaplan at least $19,270 for 1986, which city officials described as a typical year's bill.

The city records also show that Kaplan uses Anco for casualty insurance at the lots, and that the city reimburses the parking lot operator for this cost as well. The amounts of those payments were not included in city records, however.

Kaplan, one of the biggest downtown parking lot operators, said he also uses Anco for worker's compensation insurance at lots that he himself owns. He would not discuss these private contracts, except to say that Anco offered the best price.

Kaplan said he did not know Roti is an officer of Anco until a reporter told him. He said D'Arco, who is still Anco's president, is his friend, and the agency gives him a good rate.

"We don't just throw money around," Kaplan said. "They carry my home insurance, too."

Despite complaints within the Washington administration and the city council about declining revenues from city-owned parking lots and meters, the management contracts were not rebid until last month. The new bids are still pending.

In April, 1986, a city Department of Revenue official sent letters to all the parking operators, saying he wanted a 25 percent reduction in the costs reimbursed by the city. The official, Deputy Revenue Director Douglas Ellis, also asked for profit-and-loss statements so the city could determine how much money the operators are making.

That's when Ellis got a call from Kaplan.

"Sam Kaplan called me from a phone on his boat in Florida and said, 'Son, I've been doing business with this city for 30 years, and nobody has ever asked me for a profit-loss statement,' " Ellis recalled. "I retorted, 'Well, then no one has ever asked you to do business right.' "

All of the city parking lot operators complied with the requests except Kaplan, Ellis said. So the city had to make its own cuts, he said.

"When he told me there was no place to cut," Ellis said, "I looked, and that's when I found out about Lawrence and Broadway."

At that location, the city was paying for 24-hour staffing at a Kaplan-run lot. Ellis paid a visit and found only two cars parked on the overnight shift.

"When you have two people working the overnight and only taking in two cars, it doesn't take a Rhodes scholar to figure out there's something wrong," Ellis said.

Kaplan said that if the lot was overstaffed, it was not his fault. He said the hours were set by the city, and the rates by labor unions.

Records obtained by The Tribune show that at least some city officials were concerned that the city's business dealings with Anco would become public.

"Anco Insurance is owned by, or Ald. Roti is a major partner in, the firm," Thomas R. Devereux, an administrative assistant in the Department of Revenue's Bureau of Parking, wrote to Ellis on Oct. 27, 1986. "This business is dispensed by Sam Kaplan to whomever he wishes.

"If you or someone within the administration suggests a new underwriter, Kaplan would have to go along," Devereux wrote. "I don't know what the commission for this insurance would be. There might even be a press article if they were to find out about a change of underwriter. This information is offered without comment or suggestion."

City spokeswoman Rae Jones said the city did not learn of Roti's involvement with Anco until just before Devereux's letter. She said the city continued to pay Anco because officials feared a lapse in insurance coverage.

Standard Parking, a major parking lot operator with several facilities in the Loop, also has been an Anco client several times over the years, according to Myron Warshauer, the company's president. He said Standard has used Anco in "a variety of ways." He declined further comment, except to say that "they were professional," and that Roti himself never solicited business.

In the city council, Roti has supported legislation that has benefitted Standard Parking.

The company has a contract to manage one city-owned lot, at Delaware and Rush Streets. Roti has voted extensions on that contract several times, city records show.

Additionally, in January, 1986, Roti supported a proposal before the City Council Committee on Zoning that permitted Standard to expand a parking lot it owns in the 1st Ward.

By almost inviolate tradition, the council's zoning committee does whatever the local alderman recommends.

General Parking Inc., another major downtown operator, uses Anco for "a small amount of insurance" at lots it owns, said company spokesman Gary Dunlap. He said that General's president, Gordon Prussian, does not recall how the company came to use Anco, or the type of insurance it buys.

In November, 1986, Roti supported General Parking's application for a zoning change at one of its 1st Ward lots.

American Truck Leasing, another firm that has bought insurance from Anco, rented large platform trucks to the city from 1983 until this summer, city records show. The trucks were used to lift workers to fix street lights and traffic signals.

The council does not approve contracts like American Truck Leasing's. But every year its Committee on Finance, of which Roti is a member, approves the list of vendors who can do business with the city.

American Truck is one of the vendors the finance committee, including Roti, has approved to lease equipment to the Department of Streets and Sanitation, according to Kirsten Svare, a department spokeswoman.

In recent months, the city has stopped hiring vehicles from American Truck Leasing, Svare said. Streets and Sanitation Commissioner

John Halpin decided it was cheaper for the city to buy its own trucks, she said.

For example, the city was paying $75,276-a-year for each of the five trucks—a total of $376,380 annually. The city recently bought its own trucks, at a cost of $128,200 each. At the price it paid American Truck Leasing, the city could have bought them in less than two years.

"That's why we don't use them anymore," Svare said of American Truck Leasing. "When Halpin thinks of those trucks, he gets real hot." She said that the original lease was arranged under the Jane Byrne administration and that the city bought its own trucks as soon as it could afford to do so.

Edward Levitt, president of American Truck Leasing, said he has used Anco over the years but does not now. Levitt said he bought insurance from Anco because State Sen. John D'Arco Jr., son of the Anco president, is a friend of his son.

D'Arco Sr. did not return repeated telephone calls for comment on this article. Other Anco officials also declined comment.

ZONING MAKES THE ALDERMAN A KING

SUNDAY,   OCTOBER   11,   1987

BY   DEAN   BAQUET   AND
WILLIAM   GAINES

Chicago aldermen use their power over city zoning laws to reward friends and backers with multimillion-dollar opportunities, to amass thousands of dollars in campaign contributions and to determine who can live, do business and prosper in their wards.

By letting politics and narrow self-interest control how the City of Chicago is carved into business and residential strips, the city council has created a jumbled, arbitrary system of zoning often described by planners as one of the worst in the nation.

And since the council has the ability to transform land values virtually at will, property owners are forced to seek the indulgence of their alderman, creating opportunities for favoritism and corruption.

Chicago aldermen have almost complete authority to reject or approve any project in their wards, no matter the size, merit or impact of the proposed development. In the last three years, the Committee on Zoning overruled an alderman just once—when a team of politically connected developers persuaded the council to ignore then-Ald. Martin Oberman's objection to a high-rise development in Lincoln Park.

A six-month Tribune investigation of the Chicago City Council has revealed a body permeated by patronage, conflicts of interest and wasteful spending.

But no city council function is more subject to such abuses than zoning.

To examine the city council's role in zoning, reporters reviewed records of the more than 600 zoning changes that went before the council's Committee on Zoning from January, 1984, through December, 1986—changes that affected everything from tiny single-family houses on the Northwest Side to major downtown real estate developments.

Among the findings of the investigation:

• Near-total sway over zoning enables an alderman to shape development and population patterns in the ward. With no questions asked by the council, two Southwest Side aldermen have rezoned large sections of their wards in what business and civic leaders contend is an attempt to control business and residential development. A North Side alderman rewrote an entire section of the zoning law so a friend could add on to his house.

• Aldermen routinely generate campaign contributions from persons and firms seeking zoning changes, sometimes receiving contributions within weeks of their favorable votes. Developers say it is difficult to turn down such requests because of the local alderman's power to decide whether a project will be approved.

• A total of 191 zoning changes—more than 30 percent of all the changes approved by the council from 1984 through 1986—were requested in the local alderman's name, without disclosure of the property owners' identities. Many of these properties also were held in secret land trusts that usually make it impossible to identify the owners through other public records.

• In each of the 191 cases, the city, rather than the property owner, paid to notify neighbors and handle other paperwork required for rezoning. It is difficult to put a price tag on this service because the cost of a zoning change can vary with the number of neighbors who must be notified.

At the center of the council's role in zoning is the Chicago Zoning Ordinance, a 30-year-old book that governs the way property is used. The ordinance actually is a series of maps that defines the zoning designation of every plat of land in the city.

A change in zoning classification can mean a dramatic increase or decrease in land value. A change from R1 to R7, for example, is the difference between the right to build a single-family house or a huge condominium project.

Chicago zoning officials have acknowledged that the city's zoning system is outdated and largely unenforceable, a key reason why expressways are littered with billboards and neighborhoods are marred by incongruous building patterns.

The Committee on Zoning, which makes recommendations to the full city council, is supposed to make decisions based on presentations from the applicants and advice from city planners, but records show that these recommendations are often ignored by the committee, even in cases when the planners argue that rezonings are disruptive.

City law requires that a property owner applying for rezoning name himself and any co-owners. But when a Chicago alderman sponsors a rezoning request, the property owner's identity does not have to be disclosed.

Almost every other major U.S. city requires the disclosure of ownership in zoning cases.

"Most do it because they want to question the owner at the hearings," said Thomas P. Smith, editor of Zoning News, a publication of the American Planning Association. "They want to direct their questions to him about what he is doing with the property. They would ask different questions of a person who is in the hazardous waste business versus someone's grandmother."

Another reason for disclosure, said Dorothy Nepa, zoning administrator in Denver, is to make sure that a council member has no business or personal ties to someone who wants a zoning change.

A situation where property owners' identities routinely are kept secret, Nepa said, "would be ideal for graft."

In many cities, zoning hearings are run like court hearings. Council members are not permitted to meet privately with applicants beforehand.

"At the hearing, the council member from the district generally takes the lead in discussion," said Nepa. "But he must come to the council with clean hands—without having made a decision."

That is how zoning works in other cities.

This is how zoning works in Chicago:

On the chilly morning of Dec. 16, 1986, Josephine Fulton, 45, a housewife, took a bus from her West Side neighborhood to City Hall. For two hours, she sat in city council chambers, awaiting her turn to speak.

Fulton was upset because the Committee on Zoning was about to consider a change that would permit a grocery near her house to qualify for a liquor license.

The committee chairman, Ald. Terry Gabinski (32d), finally called on Fulton to testify. She said she believed liquor sales would attract loiterers and vandals to her residential neighborhood.

City planners backed Fulton's claim, telling the committee the change would be an "unwarranted intrusion" in the neighborhood.

Gabinski deferred the matter—not because of the objections of Fulton and planners but because the local alderman, Wallace Davis (27th), had been in a traffic accident the night before and could not make the meeting.

Later that day, according to both Davis and Fulton, a member of Davis's staff told Fulton that the alderman would oppose the change, although he had introduced it under the provision that does not require ownership disclosure. Davis said he changed his mind because of mounting community opposition.

Fulton went home thinking she had won the battle.

Today, the two-story grocery at Huron Street and Homan Avenue has its new zoning, and its owners have applied for a liquor license.

In the intervening months, Davis, facing federal indictment, was defeated by Sheneather Butler, whose father and political mentor, Rev. Jesse L. Butler, has a personal interest in the store.

Ald. Butler placed the zoning change back on the committee's agenda without notifying neighbors. With her support, the change cleared the committee and was approved by the council.

"Nobody told me," Fulton said recently when informed of the change. "Nobody around here knew about it."

In an interview, former Ald. Davis, now on trial in federal court on charges of taking bribes from a city contractor, said Jesse Butler owns the building, which is held in a secret land trust, and that Jesse Butler originally asked for the zoning change.

In an initial interview, Jesse Butler would not confirm or deny whether he owns the property. In a subsequent interview, he said he does not own it.

He admitted, however, that he has applied at various city agencies for building permits and permission to install a grease trap on the property. He also said he was leading the effort to obtain a liquor license for the building, though he would not explain why. Butler's name does not appear on any public records pertaining to the liquor license application.

Several times, Butler made statements to reporters that indicated he has an interest in the property.

For instance, asked whether liquor would be sold in the building, Butler said: "It wouldn't look good for a minister to have a liquor license. I just got rezoned for rehabilitation and enlargement."

Butler, who works as an aide to Cook County Sheriff James O'Grady, also claimed that Davis withdrew his support for the rezoning because his daughter decided to run against Davis. Davis denied that was his reason.

Ald. Butler, who wrote a letter asking the city's Department of Inspectional Services to move quickly in granting a building permit for the store, said she had no idea her father might have an interest in the building. She said another man, Ata Yasin, had told her that he owns it.

Yasin did not return telephone calls or respond to messages left at his store.

Jesse Butler would not describe his interest in the property or his relationship to Yasin in any detail except to say that he once sold Yasin another grocery. Jesse Butler said there was no need for reporters to talk to Yasin because, "Anything he can tell you, I can tell you."

The way in which the grocery was rezoned is not unusual. At least 35 of the 50 current aldermen have sponsored zoning changes for unidentified business and property owners.

In some cases, the aldermen were helping constituents who could not afford the $250 zoning fee, city records show. But the records also show that most of the nearly 200 private interests rezoned by the local alderman have been restaurants, liquor stores, bars, real estate developments, car washes and large private homes. By waiving the zoning application fee for 191 anonymous petitioners, the city lost $47,750 in revenue over three years.

Ald. Fred Roti (1st), for example, sponsored zoning changes that benefited a restaurant and an unidentified real estate developer. Ald. Edward Burke (14th) rezoned property for a convenience store. And

Ald. William Henry (24th) obtained zoning variances for a repair shop and a liquor store.

The general manager of La Mexicana, a tortilla manufacturer in the 12th Ward, said his property was rezoned without application fee or disclosure because he is a regular contributor to his ward's Democratic organization.

"It's like, you scratch my back and I'll scratch yours," said Rudy Guerrero, general manager. "They are always selling tickets for a dinner or a dance or getting contributions for something. There's nothing wrong with that, is there?"

Guerrero said former Ald. Aloysius A. Majerczyk sponsored this zoning change even though neighbors opposed his plan to expand onto adjacent property.

Majerczyk said Guerrero was not required to make campaign contributions in exchange for help with zoning.

"An alderman wouldn't be in his right mind to refuse something that is going to improve the neighborhood and bring in jobs," Majerczyk said.

Earlier this month, when the new zoning committee chairman, Ald. Danny Davis (29th), was told that so many changes go to unidentified property owners, he promised to sponsor legislation to require disclosure in all zoning applications.

Aldermen Patrick Huels (11th) and John Madrzyk (13th) have used zoning to reshape entire sections of their wards, an effort that city officials and business groups portray as a potentially dangerous result of an alderman's unchecked power over zoning.

Huels sponsored 29 zoning changes over three years, including the rezoning of several blocks along commercial South Halsted Street, city records show. In doing so, the alderman gained control of development in many sections of his ward.

Madrzyk altered zoning in mostly residential areas to make it harder to develop multifamily housing. He also has moved quickly to downzone business strips as stores become vacant. Some of these changes involve properties near the boundary between his mostly white 13th Ward and the predominantly black 15th.

City Planning Commissioner Elizabeth Hollander and other officials said that the aldermen are treading on dangerous ground. City planners insist that council members do not have the expertise or citywide vision to make such far-reaching decisions.

"The aldermen do it to control the property," Hollander said. "They will tell you they're doing it to stop obnoxious use, but it's not a good practice.

"There are other means to handle problems in the ward," Hollander said.

Downzoning is the practice of lowering a zoning classification to limit development. For instance, going from R4 to R1 changes an area from multifamily housing to single-family. It can have far-reaching impact on the makeup of a ward: Multifamily housing increases population and is considered more affordable for the poor.

If a commercial area is downzoned, an existing business does not have to shut down. But if the building is sold, the property converts to the new zoning.

Ald. Marlene Carter (15th), who is trying to reverse downzoning by her predecessor, pointed out that the practice creates opportunities for corruption because it forces property owners to go to the alderman to have zoning restrictions lifted.

"They have to come to you to negotiate," Carter said.

But Huels said downzoning is the only way to keep out bars and pornographic book stores.

"There are areas in my ward that are overrun with taverns, where neighbors just don't like them anymore," said Huels. "I don't need package liquor stores and 15 resale shops on Halsted Street."

But he acknowledged that downzoning is a powerful device and, if not used carefully, "you could impede the growth of some businesses."

Madrzyk did not return repeated telephone calls to discuss zoning in his ward. But Carter said the rezonings abutting her ward appear racially motivated because they make housing development more difficult.

"It's a subtle way, a different form . . . of red-lining," Carter said. "If anyone is downzoning in a changing neighborhood, they're doing it to protect themselves."

Richard Cartwright, owner of a radiator repair shop in Madrzyk's ward, said the alderman has told him and other businessmen that he wants to control development to maintain the racial balance of his Southwest Side ward.

Cartwright recalled his 1984 battle to keep Madrzyk from downzoning his property at 6132 S. Central Ave.

"We got together to fight it after we knew what he was doing, but it was too late," Cartwright said. "If I want to put an addition on, I have to see him. If we have a fire, I'm out of business."

Said Armon Schmidt, president of the Midway Business Association in Madrzyk's ward: "There's a cloud out here through the whole neighborhood. You can't really measure it, you can't take a picture of it, but the threat of downzoning is there."

Attorney Daniel Houlihan gave $500 to Ald. Burton Natarus's campaign fund five weeks after one of his clients received a zoning change in Natarus's Near North Side 42d Ward.

The Monroe Center Venture contributed $1,000 to then-Ald. Wallace Davis four months before its plan for a West Side real estate development was approved by the Committee on Zoning.

Prudential Insurance Co. gave Ald. Roti a $1,000 contribution two months before the zoning committee approved the company's new downtown office building.

In each case, the alderman's support was crucial, a first step before developers could get zoning changes and break ground for multimillion-dollar projects.

And while executives of all three companies said they felt no pressure to contribute, they acknowledged that making such well-timed contributions is routine in Chicago.

"It's as simple as this," said Theodore Novak, Chicago attorney for Prudential. "Fred Roti is the 1st Ward alderman, and the building is in the 1st Ward. All of their interaction with government is through Fred Roti. He is their liaison to all levels of government."

Aldermen representing the most development-heavy wards have received thousands of dollars in campaign contributions from zoning applicants, often within weeks of zoning changes.

Roti, whose ward includes downtown and the expanding South Loop, raised $16,900 from zoning applicants in the three years studied by The Tribune. Natarus, representing the Near North Side, received at least $2,450 from persons seeking zoning changes. And Wallace Davis, then representing the Near West Side, was given $1,300 in the last two months of 1985, when several developments were proposed for his ward.

These figures are probably conservative; campaign contributions often are made in the names of company executives or by lawyers who represent developers.

Houlihan, for instance, is one of the most successful real estate lawyers in Chicago. He said he contributes several thousand dollars to aldermen and other officials each year.

Ald. Joseph Kotlarz (35th) received at least $2,850 from lawyers and businesses seeking zoning changes in his ward.

The 33d Ward Democratic Organization, whose committeeman is Ald. Richard Mell, was given $1,200 by a development company that won zoning approvals for a 12-story apartment building in the ward.

Ald. Dorothy Tillman (3d) received $500 from a real estate firm four months after she helped it get zoning for a shopping center in her South Side ward.

Developers said they contribute to local aldermen because the council members can make or break their projects.

Ted Peterson, senior vice president of U.S. Equities Inc., which gave $300 to Wallace Davis one month before receiving a zoning change, said: "I don't have to tell you how things work in City Hall. The alderman in whose ward the zoning question is in is the one who technically stands up and can say, 'I support this, or I don't support this.'"

The Tribune's review of zoning records underscores the autonomy local aldermen have in zoning matters.

At a Jan. 31, 1984, committee meeting, James R. Sneider, a lawyer for an investment company building a Handy Andy store in the 8th Ward, then represented by Ald. Marian Humes, announced that he had a long line of witnesses ready to testify in favor of the project.

Gabinski stopped him, saying: "I have Ald. Humes here, who will be your best witness, and I would suggest that maybe we ask the alderman to make a comment."

Humes, now under indictment for allegedly taking bribes from a city contractor, told the committee that she favored the project. Gabinski pushed it through without debate.

At a meeting on Jan. 31, 1984, Ald. Roman Pucinski (41st) upset Natarus when he questioned developers of a proposed hotel and office building on North Michigan Avenue.

Natarus said Pucinski should stick to his own ward, and Pucinski shot back: "It's in Chicago. Is the ward in Chicago?"

Natarus ended the exchange by saying, "You stick to your ward, and I will stick to mine."

The zoning committee concurred, and with Natarus's support approved the project without further debate.

In December, 1984, Ald. Bernard Stone (50th) changed an entire section of the city's zoning law so a friend could add two bedrooms to his house.

The friend, Rabbi Erwin J. Giffin, had a seventh child on the way; his two-story house on North Mozart Street was getting crowded.

Giffin had tried to get a building permit, but the city's building department turned him down, he said. Under the zoning code, it was illegal to have a house that big on a lot his size.

To solve Giffin's problem, the alderman offered a major alteration to a zoning formula that governs the size of a house on a lot.

Before Stone's change, the square footage of a house could not total more than 50 percent of the lot.

After Stone's revision was passed by the Committee on Zoning and the full council, the ratio of house to lot size jumped to 65 percent. Stone said he asked for 70 percent, but fellow aldermen persuaded him to scale back his request.

With Stone's change, developers could come in and get permits to build enormous houses on relatively small lots. Hollander and other city officials envisioned lines of homeowners applying to expand their houses, and the over-building that might ensue.

"The potential was there for people who had houses on small lots to start crowding," said Maurice Parrish, the city's zoning administrator.

Stone admitted that Giffin's plea was the main reason he sought the change. But he said other residents of his ward later approached him about the same problem. He said he wanted to encourage people to expand their houses so they wouldn't have to move to the suburbs.

Hollander said this was no reason to rewrite the entire law.

"I don't think there is ever a need to change the law for an individual problem," she said. "There must be some other way to handle the problem instead of changing the law for the entire city."

In 1986, Hollander and other planning officials were able to convince the city council that anyone wanting to take advantage of Stone's law would first have to get city approval.

Despite the concern about Stone's zoning revision, only a single alderman, Pucinski, voted against the change.

"My ward is 95 percent single-family houses, which gives it an atmosphere of open space," Pucinski said. "That is what gives the area charm and beauty."

Ann Marie Lipinski, R. Bruce Dold, Joel Kaplan and Sandy Slater contributed to this report.

READY FOR REFORM?

CLEANING UP CITY COUNCIL MAY BE UPHILL BATTLE

SUNDAY, OCTOBER 18, 1987

BY DEAN BAQUET AND ANN MARIE LIPINSKI

Last Tuesday morning Ald. Timothy Evans (4th) talked of his plans for reform of the Chicago City Council.

As chairman of the Committee on Finance and Mayor Harold Washington's council floor leader, Evans is the most influential member of the 50-member council—an alderman whom Washington had singled out five days earlier as one who should "get about the business of resolving" the embarrassment that is the nation's largest municipal lawmaking body.

Evans told a reporter that in response to a series in The Tribune on council corruption he would review other city councils to arrive at a model for change.

"We are prepared to clean up our own house as a city council," he added.

What Evans did not say was that two hours earlier he had quietly dispatched a member of his Finance Committee to meet with Ald. Lawrence Bloom (5th), chairman of the council's Budget Committee, and submit a last-minute addition to Bloom's committee meeting agenda. That addition asked Budget Committee members to slice $61,000 out of the city's fund for worker's compensation claims and bestow it upon six council committees.

Among the committees slated for the year-end windfall was one that, until Friday, had not met since July. Another is run by an alderman who had used the committee payroll to hire the daughter of his political mentor and ward committeeman.

The reason for the hasty transfer of funds? The committees' vice chairmen were upset that they hadn't been able to add their own workers to the patronage-packed committee payrolls and they wanted amends before year's end.

In light of another tremor on Chicago's political landscape last week —the trial and bribery conviction of former Ald. Wallace Davis Jr. (27th), accused by a prosecutor of running his office "like a toll booth" —Evans's action and the Budget Committee's approval of the transfer was a trifle.

But its timing illustrates the arrogance and duplicity that have prevented reform of a council that has seen 13 of its members convicted of crimes related to their offices in the last 15 years.

A six-month investigation by The Tribune uncovered widespread waste, patronage and conflicts of interest in the council. Thousands of documents and hundreds of interviews depicted a council whose members routinely place their interests before that of the public.

If Evans's actions are any measure, reform of the council may be an uphill battle that hinges on how much pressure Washington and his allies receive to revive a series of dormant legislative proposals. And it may provide the most crucial test of just how serious the mayor is about backing up the reform rhetoric he has spouted since his election, rhetoric that so far has been called into question by a major federal investigation and the mayor's failure to clean up the abuses it highlighted.

"There are members of the city council who are embarrassed by what was in The Tribune," Washington told a luncheon of television reporters Thursday. "I will guarantee I will be a partner in cleaning up those problems.

"I didn't vote for them," he said of the aldermen. "The only one I voted for was my own. I didn't vote for the other 49. I will not take the jacket for that."

When Washington and his council allies were struggling to wrest control of Chicago's government from a powerful cadre of aldermen, the mayor often criticized council leadership as wasteful, even corrupt.

Now that Washington's supporters run the council, the mayor, like his predecessors, appears more than willing to use expensive patronage to win the support of aldermen. Though Washington blustered that he would investigate the committees, his 1988 budget includes an additional $646,814 in spending for many do-nothing committees.

For Washington's council allies, winning control, it seems, is less an opportunity for reform than a chance to share in the spoils of government.

The historic cynicism of city officials and the public has permitted flagrant abuses to flourish in the council. In Chicago, a legendary haven for municipal corruption, even some segments of the press yawn at the newest scandal.

Last week, following disclosures that aldermen have routinely diverted city money to themselves and their friends and often vote on measures that affect their business clients, one radio talk show host asked: "So is this news?"

An editorial commentator on another radio station sadly noted that the biggest tragedy was not the disclosure of greed and profiteering, but the depressing chances for reform.

And in the City Hall press room, where some members of the Chicago media cover daily government proceedings but rarely get the opportunity to delve beyond, a radio station recorded that the typical response was: We knew this all along, even though we've reported little about it.

Indeed, Vivian Weil, who teaches business ethics at the Illinois Institute of Technology and has conducted ethics seminars for city officials, said this sneering attitude may be the biggest stumbling block to reform in Chicago.

"One of the things that is important to remember is that there is a long-entrenched way of doing things in the city," she said. "It's very hard to get out from under such revered practices."

But judging from the letters that came in as a result of the newspaper's series, some Chicagoans are getting impatient with bloated government financed by rising taxes, and they are struggling to find a blueprint for change.

"I think it's time that me, and people like me, stop reading such articles as yours on the criminal handling of our city council and saying 'tsk, tsk' and turning the pages," wrote one North Side resident. "How can I effect a change? Tell me what to do to arouse people like me. And can we make a difference? Maybe now is a good time."

How to revamp a council that by all accounts is wallowing in self-interest, patronage and parochial politics?

Reform-minded aldermen and other officials say that beyond the difficult task of eliminating attitudes that have perpetuated a corrupt city council, there are some specific measures that would make it harder for aldermen to abuse their positions.

For one thing, they say, the city's much-heralded new ethics law must not only be defended against the aldermen who want to scuttle it, it must be made stronger to impose penalties on council members who violate it.

"I'm intensely aware of the desire on the part of some aldermen who want to weaken the ethics ordinance," said Harriet McCullough, executive director of the mayor's Board of Ethics, which reviews allegations of wrongdoing by city officials. "They have not been discreet."

A handful of aldermen, including Fred Roti (1st), who sells insurance to the city in a clear but long-ignored conflict of interest, have been lobbying to repeal or limit the ordinance. Roti, for one, has tried to convince his colleagues that a provision of the ordinance requiring extensive economic disclosure just gives the press fodder to criticize aldermen.

This effort by Roti and other aldermen is particularly hypocritical, given that the council unanimously approved the ethics ordinance on the eve of the last council election.

The ordinance's defenders take heart in their belief that the publicity generated by disclosure of widespread conflicts in the council will make it difficult for aldermen to gut the ordinance, said Michael Holewinski, a top mayoral aide who was instrumental in the drafting of the ethics law.

But the fight to protect the ethics ordinance should not overshadow the fact that it does not even address most of the abuses that plague the council. Once the ordinance is saved, it must be broadened to get at the kind of corruption that has come to rule the council.

For example, while the ordinance set up an agency to investigate violations by city workers, it decreed that only one body could investigate aldermen—the council itself.

The ordinance lists various penalties for wayward government workers, from firings to criminal prosecution. But it does not address specific penalties for aldermen, except to say punishment should be set by the council's Committee on Rules.

Aldermen have traditionally used this committee to bury controversial legislation, including a handful of still-languishing reform laws. As one measure of this committee's ability to police the council, consider that former Ald. Clifford Kelley (20th), chairman of the committee when the ethics law was passed, pleaded guilty several months ago to taking bribes from city contractors.

Former U.S. Atty. Thomas Sullivan, whose landmark 1986–87 study of corruption in government was heralded by Mayor Washington as a necessary first step for reform, said he is stung by the fact that his toughest suggestions were rejected in debate over the ordinance.

"No present elected city official has supported my recommendations," Sullivan said in an interview Thursday. Recalling the praise Washington heaped on his $600,000 taxpayer-financed report when it was completed last spring, Sullivan said, "It was all very nice, and he was going to have people look at it. As far as I know they're still looking at it. Nobody enacted anything from a report they spent a lot of money to get."

Sullivan's report was commissioned shortly after disclosure of allegations that a high-flying New York company vying for city bill-collection contracts had paid off high-ranking city officials, including at least four aldermen.

For one thing, Sullivan recommended that the ethics board be permitted to investigate aldermen as well as other officials. He also said that the city's Office of Municipal Investigations, which investigates charges of corruption in the executive branch of the city government, should be permitted to look into the legislative branch as well.

Otherwise, Sullivan and McCullough said, there is no system to conduct an independent investigation of an alderman.

"The only recourse is the citizenry who elects them and the media," said McCullough. "But ultimately it comes back to the citizens."

She added, "Citizens get what they deserve."

McCullough's comments seem to offer little hope, given that former Ald. Kelley received 46.6 percent of the vote in his last election, despite an indictment that accused him of taking bribes from a waste hauler that runs a giant dump near his ward.

Another reform that has been foundering in council committees for two years is a proposal by Ald. David Orr (49th) that would force council members to account for how they spend their $1,500 monthly office expense accounts.

That money is supposed to be used to rent, furnish and staff satellite offices in aldermanic ward headquarters across the city. But the investigation found that at least six aldermen pocket the money, while others pay rent to themselves and political associates. None of the aldermen returned any of the expense money, even though many said they really didn't need it to run their offices.

Following the report on the office expense accounts, Ald. Evans introduced a council resolution calling for hearings to set "guidelines" on how aldermen may spend their expense allowances and committee budgets. However, interviews with aldermen indicate the measure may be in for a fight.

Even Ald. Marlene Carter (15th), who does not pocket any of the city money, said, "I think it's your personal business" how the expense money is spent.

Orr, who two years ago watched his ordinance calling for public accounting of expense accounts go down to defeat, has won nothing but derision from his colleagues for his persistent efforts to push council reforms. Some of his allies recently threatened to take his name off legislation calling for apartment security locks because of his public cries for stringent ethics laws.

If Washington's proposed 1988 budget is any measure, the one reform that the city's self-professed reform mayor will not push is a revamping of the expensive network of council committees. The 28 committees—many of them patronage havens that rarely meet and that do little work—spent much of their budgets on items such as beepers, car phones, gifts, travel, computers, video equipment and office furniture.

If Washington's budget passes, they will be able to buy even more of these luxury items. The new budget includes a 12.5 percent increase for the council's 28 committees, which would raise their budget from the $5.2 million appropriated in 1987 to $5.82 million.

Washington had proclaimed that he would investigate the committees and that there should be fewer of them.

One reform effort that is winning some support is a plan to eliminate potential corruption in the council's stranglehold over zoning.

Last week, The Tribune reported that aldermen routinely sponsor zoning changes for unidentified businesses. For example, Ald. Sheneather Butler (27th) supported a change that benefitted a liquor store in which her father has a secret interest.

Following that report, Ald. Danny Davis (29th), the newly appointed chairman of the council's Committee on Zoning, said he would push legislation to eliminate such anonymous zoning changes.

Meanwhile, Davis and other Zoning Committee members would do well to study a growing trend in big city zoning: the establishment of independent hearing boards that weigh zoning changes on the merits, as opposed to political connections.

Even if some of these specific reforms are implemented, the key obstacle remains a cynical city government that for generations has been unwilling to let go of the spoils of its power.

Indeed, the abuses are regarded as every day occurrences in city business.

For example, one of the disclosures in the series was that Ald. William Henry (24th) had used his position to push his soft drink, Soul Cola. Henry tried to get it sold at city festivals, and he lobbied the city to lend $1.3 million to the one supermarket chain that carries the drink.

Some aldermen observed that the Henry story was actually great publicity for the West Side alderman, a view apparently shared by Henry. At the last council meeting, the burly alderman approached a reporter and smiled broadly.

"Thank you," he said. "I'm going to send you guys a case of Soul Cola every day."

FOUR

REBELLIOUS GENES

1988 WINNER IN THE EDITORIAL CARTOONING CATEGORY

"For a distinguished example of a cartoonist's work, the determining qualities being that a cartoon shall embody an idea made clearly apparent, shall show good drawing and striking pictorial effect, and shall be intended to be helpful to some commendable cause of public importance . . ."

The Atlanta Constitution
and The Charlotte Observer
Doug Marlette

Even before Jim Bakker shattered his pious image by confessing to moral transgressions, cartoonist Doug Marlette had found a ready target to lampoon. His cutting humor has also brought other public figures down a notch or two.

I have rebellious genes floating around inside of me. That is the only way I can explain my willingness to challenge authority and question power. Editorial cartoons, by their very nature, challenge conventional thought. For instance, you will never see a good cartoon that says, "Three cheers for the status quo," or "Hooray for the way things are!"

Cartoons are a vehicle of attack, so the best ones possess a certain fury. The best satirists—Jonathan Swift, Mark Twain, Joseph Heller, Walker Percy—were disappointed with the way things turned out, and they expressed a basic rage in their work. The trick is to channel that rage in a constructive way. Satirists use their rage to clarify and illuminate values.

That's one of the things I like most about my work—confronting contradictions, pointing out the ironies and holding my own prism up to the light and looking at issues from my own perspective. I like showing the banality of evil. I like to show that goofy, mundane people sometimes do horrible things.

I like turning symbols upside down and inside out and playing with images so that they are not so predictable. I enjoy taking familiar symbols and clichés that have been trivialized and denuded of meaning and retooling their content and restoring their meaning by looking at them with new eyes.

Every artist looks at things in a certain way—whether it is Cezanne seeing trees in his way or Picasso seeing human beings in his. Cartoonists also see things in their particular way. There is no "correct" way, as long as we are effective, evocative and say something worth saying.

—Doug Marlette
The Atlanta Constitution

" RELAX—IT'S JUST JIM AND TAMMY COMING AGAIN! "

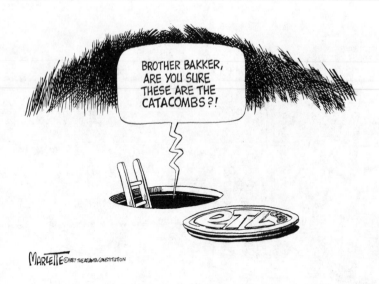

"PRESIDENT?...NO, CHILD, BUT YOU CAN GROW UP TO BE FRONT-RUNNER!"

"WE STARTED OUT REFLAGGING KUWAITI TANKERS!..."

"COLONEL NORTH COULDN'T MAKE IT TO THE HEARINGS TODAY, BUT HE SENT ALONG HIS UNIFORM FOR QUESTIONING!"

"... AND FILLING IN FOR JOHNNY THIS WEEK IS *MIKHAIL GORBACHEV!...*"

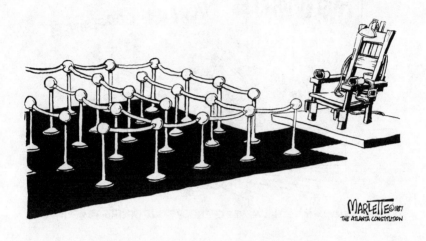

JIM AND TAMMY DRIVING THE MONEY CHANGERS OUT OF THE TEMPLE

"I'M GONNA PASS THE TOYOTA, HONEY— COVER ME!"

FIVE

THE PENTAGON'S SECRET CACHE

1988 WINNER IN THE NATIONAL REPORTING CATEGORY

"For a distinguished example of reporting on national affairs . . ."

The Philadelphia Inquirer
Tim Weiner

A growing part of the United States defense budget is being shunted to what the Pentagon calls its "black budget." But national security laws prevent public debate on this budget, much to the chagrin of critics. Tim Weiner reveals some of the questionable projects that are being carried out under the veil of secrecy.

In a sense, this series began five years ago in a dusty file room at the county courthouse in Camden, New Jersey. I was beginning to get my hands on a story that involved scores of real-estate hustlers, sleazy state and federal officials, crooked mortgage bankers and the like. I knew I was on to something, but I wasn't sure of what.

I went to see one of the old-time courthouse apparatchiks, a cigar-chomping gnome named Sal. I told Sal what I was looking at and what I thought the scam might entail.

"Listen, sweetheart," he said. "You are opening up a real Panorama box here."

Sal's malaprop expressed perfectly the way I think of the complicated assignments my newspaper, *The Philadelphia Inquirer,* loves its reporters to undertake. Inside the "Panorama box" is a broad vista filled with extraordinary details, encompassing a vision few people ordinarily see. Ideally, *The Inquirer*'s investigations take the lid off the box and let people look inside at the works.

My training was as a federal courthouse and white-collar crime reporter. Dig up the documents. Follow the dollars. Get the records and see what they say. The people you talk to may equivocate. The document, as the lawyers say, speaks for itself.

So when *The Inquirer* decided it wanted a long look at what was happening to the Pentagon's budget under the Reagan administration, there wasn't much question of where to start, or how to go about the work. Welcome back, I thought, to the box.

I returned from four months in the Philippines in April 1986. I rented a tiny apartment in Washington, plugged in a portable computer and hauled in scores of Pentagon budgets and budget-briefing books from 1981 through 1987. Many had to be purchased from the National Technical Information Service at hundreds of dollars per armful. For the better part of three months, I read through those technical papers on nuclear war-fighting strategies and the state of the military arts in the 1980s.

I interviewed members of Congress who had never even heard of the black budget. But they were learning. A small stink was being raised in Congress over waste and fraud on so-called black projects. I traveled to California to interview workers at companies deeply involved in black military programs. They (and their past and present colleagues at other companies in other states) painted a far more frightening picture than did the congressional investigators.

All demanded anonymity, and I was uncomfortable using unnamed sources, so three weeks' work essentially resulted in three paragraphs' worth of print. But the interviews strongly reinforced my sense of what underlay the numbers on the Pentagon computer printouts.

A picture began to emerge.

The Reagan administration's passion for secrecy had profoundly altered the size and scope of classified spending within the Pentagon, for the black budget was growing some six times faster than overall Pentagon outlays. The nature of the secret spending was something new, as well: two dominant themes within the black budget were the administration's vision of winning a prolonged nuclear war, and of creating secret Pentagon units that would function as a high-tech hybrid of the Central Intelligence Agency and the Green Berets.

Something was coming unraveled in Washington in the summer and fall of 1986. Members of Congress and congressional staffers I talked to had a strong feeling that they were being lied to about even mundane military and intelligence matters. Many felt that, in the constant tug-of-war between secrecy and democracy in such matters, secrecy was winning, and winning ugly. They felt the administration regarded them as a threat, as the enemy, and that disinformation and misinformation were being used as weapons in this struggle.

In late November, in the Philippines, it looked as if Corazon C. Aquino's government might fall, and *The Inquirer* sent me back to Manila. A few days later, in a small town on the island of Mindanao, I heard an unbelievable story on the BBC's World Service report about

Oliver L. North, Iran, the contras and a whole lot of money. I came back to Washington the next week.

Ultimately, as former CIA director Stansfield Turner said in one of our telephone conversations, it all boils down to truth-telling. Many stories had been written before about the black budget and related topics. Many, I hope, will be written in the future, because governments lie, and lie with zest and impunity. I tried in this series to tell our readers, in the simplest and most direct way I could, that secrecy within President Reagan's Pentagon was spinning out of control, with scary consequences for years to come.

—Tim Weiner
The Philadelphia Inquirer

A GROWING 'BLACK BUDGET' PAYS FOR SECRET WEAPONS, COVERT WARS

SUNDAY, FEBRUARY 8, 1987

BY TIM WEINER

Two years ago, a startling item appeared in President Reagan's budget. It was a military project code-named Aurora, and no further description or explanation was given. But Aurora caught people's attention anyway. That's because the projected budget showed its cost soaring from $80 million in 1986 to $2.3 billion in 1987.

What sort of project grows like that?

Not one the Pentagon wants to talk about.

In the administration's defense budget this year, there is no mention of Aurora. The project and its billions have "gone black"—vanished into the vast cache of secret accounts that the Pentagon calls its "black budget."

Since President Reagan took office in 1981, his administration has more than tripled the black budget. This secret spending for classified programs now totals at least $35 billion a year, according to an Inquirer investigation of Defense Department records, corroborated by Pentagon and congressional sources. It now accounts for 11 percent of the Pentagon's current $312 billion spending request, and that number is bound to swell, for the black budget is growing faster than any other major sector of the federal government.

The Pentagon says nothing publicly about the black budget, and most members of Congress have no access to details about it.

Under the cloak of black-budget secrecy, the Reagan administration is spending billions on nuclear bombers and millions to train dolphins as underwater saboteurs. It has developed elaborate plans for winning a months-long nuclear war—World War III—and preparing for World War IV. The plans include robots stalking radioactive battlegrounds, satellites orchestrating nuclear attacks and generals speeding along interstates in lead-lined trucks, ordering warheads fired from faraway silos.

The black budget also funds a host of secret weapons, covert military units, one-quarter of all military research and development and at least three-quarters of the U.S. intelligence community's espionage and covert activities.

The black budget is split about evenly between funds for secret weapons and funds for intelligence agencies. The military's portion alone has grown eightfold, to at least $17 billion, since Reagan took office.

The portion of the U.S. intelligence budget hidden away in the Pentagon's secret accounts has doubled to at least $18 billion under the Reagan administration. And no part of the intelligence budget has grown faster than funds for covert operations—currently more than $600 million a year, according to intelligence analysts.

The controversy swirling in Washington over the covert sale of weapons to Iran and the diversion of millions of dollars in profit to contra forces in Nicaragua shows how the secret use of secret funds can undermine trust in government, warp foreign policy and damage a presidency—when it is detected.

The spending of those millions to finance secret wars has now raised congressional hackles, but the spending of billions to finance secret weapons continues to grow largely unchecked.

The black budget now is nearly as big as the entire federal budget for health care. It is far bigger than the federal budget for education or transportation or agriculture or the environment.

The black budget's fastest-growing component is secret spending on military research and development. Now approaching $11 billion, it has increased 1,357 percent under Reagan. It is three times bigger than the entire budget for the State Department. And no end is in sight.

This is growth that foreshadows huge future increases in the overall black budget, for research and development is the acorn from which the defense oak grows. So the secret spending will only accelerate as such projects as Aurora—which was a code name for the $60 billion Stealth bomber project—go from the drawing board to the assembly line.

National-security laws forbid any public debate in Congress that would reveal specific weapons or specific dollars or, for that matter, specific foul-ups in the black budget.

Thomas Amlie, a Pentagon missile expert with security clearances high enough to know about some black programs, says the military has "three basic reasons for having them. One, you're doing something that should genuinely be secret. There's only a couple of those, and Stealth ain't one of them.

"Two, you're doing something so damn stupid you don't want anybody to know about it.

"And three, you want to rip the moneybag open and get out a shovel, because there is no accountability whatsoever."

As a consequence, critics say, the black budget is far more vulnerable than the rest of the defense budget to shoddy work, inflated bills and outright fraud by contractors and subcontractors. Rep. John D. Dingell (D., Mich), whose House Energy and Commerce Committee is trying to penetrate the secrecy surrounding Pentagon spending, said flatly that the black budget "conceals outright illegal activities.

"The Pentagon keeps these programs of almost unbelievable size secret from Congress, from the General Accounting Office, from its own auditing agencies," Dingell said. "And every time they have kept secrets from us, the facts, when they come out, have been surrounded by a bodyguard of lies.

Although the few members of Congress who are briefed on the black budget, and the larger number who are not, are growing increasingly unhappy with the system, they have been unable to pierce the Pentagon's shield of secrecy.

In the U.S. House of Representatives, the chairmen and ranking minority members of committees dealing with military matters receive briefings on black projects. In all, about 30 House members are given limited information about some black programs, according to congressional staff members. Senators overseeing military and intelligence affairs have greater access.

Two of those in the know, House Armed Services Committee Chairman Les Aspin (D., Wis.) and ranking minority member William Dickinson (R., Ala.), think the Pentagon's secrecy is unjustified. They have said 70 percent of the black budget could be declassified at no risk to national security.

Black budget is the Pentagon's own term for projects it hides from public view by classifying their titles, their costs or their objectives. (It does not include the Strategic Defense Initiative, or "Star Wars," which has been kept out of the black budget so that it can be promoted openly in the political marketplace.)

Black projects are concealed in several ways. In many cases, their costs simply are deleted from the unclassified budget. Some are given code names, such as Bernie, Tacit Rainbow and Elegant Lady, or hidden under innocuous headings such as "special activities" and "advanced concepts."

For example, the fiscal 1988 Air Force procurement budget includes a line item of $4.7 billion for "selected activities," $3.1 billion for "other production charges" and $2.3 billion for "special programs." That is all that Congress as a whole knows about these three black programs and the $10.1 billion they will consume.

All told, more than $25 billion—nearly one-fifth of all Pentagon spending for developing and producing weapons and materiel—is hidden in the black budgets for research, development and procurement.

These secret programs are financing aircraft, weaponry and military satellites whose final cost will far exceed $100 billion.

"A fair question would be: What the hell's going on here? This is a tremendous amount of money to be spending with no oversight," said John Steinbruner, an expert on nuclear-war strategy who directs foreign-policy studies at the Brookings Institution in Washington. "Somebody's got to say: 'Hey, are we running a democracy or not? Is the fetish for secrecy undermining the political process?' "

"This is a problem that Congress persistently refuses to face, and the consequences could be very, very serious," said William W. Kauffman, a top defense-budget adviser to Presidents Kennedy, Johnson, Nixon, Ford and Carter. "I think people in Congress don't realize that with the black budget increasing as it is, they've really got an explosive situation on their hands. Either the Pentagon is going to have to give some of these projects up or we're going to see an explosion in budget authority and outlays."

But few members of Congress have the time or energy to fight the Pentagon for information on black projects. Several spent more than a year trying to obtain accurate budget data on the Stealth bomber. The Pentagon finally released five-year-old classified cost figures that many in Congress suspected were misleading.

"They control what the Congress gets and sees," said Rep. Denny Smith (R., Ore.), who calls himself a "cheap hawk," a cost-conscious conservative, on defense issues. "As as congressman, I can't get information. . . . They don't want to have us mucking around in their budget.

"There's a real question here," Smith said. "Will the military accept civilian leadership when it comes to choosing weapons?"

A senior staff member of the House Government Operations Committee said that even what little congressional oversight exists has been weakened by the Pentagon's budgetary sleight-of-hand. He said the Pentagon uses a double-ledger system of accounting for black projects in which "brooms become computers" and computers become bombs.

"The Pentagon gets tremendous benefits from misleading Congress, and very few risks," he said. "As more and more money disappears into these ultrasecret programs, the checks and balances are basically being eroded. . . . Congress has become less and less alert to this. It is abdicating power."

The black budget, Defense Secretary Caspar W. Weinberger said at a Jan. 6 news conference, is made up of "funding which we believe it is better for us not to publicize, on the very sound premise that we don't see the purpose of giving additional information to the enemy."

Weinberger, of course, was referring to the Soviet Union. However, many members of Congress believe he had another adversary in mind.

"The attitude of this administration is that Congress is the enemy," said Rep. William H. Gray 3d (D., Pa.), chairman of the House Budget Committee. "So we simply do not get nearly enough information to keep track of these secret accounts. The administration has run wild in this area. They are trying to end-run Congress as if there were no checks and balances in the Constitution. It is a very dangerous policy."

And even the staunchest supporters of national security now are questioning the black budget's growth.

"I know quite a lot of black programs, and many of them are well-managed," said Richard Garwin, a longtime defense consultant and presidential adviser who helped develop the hydrogen bomb. "But the proliferation of these programs is very bad. It is primarily to avert criticism and evaluation. It is part of a general trend of this administration to block information on its programs, whether they be classified or unclassified. And that is profoundly anti-democratic."

Increasingly, the Pentagon is pushing previously unclassified programs into the black budget. About $4.5 billion in once-public Pentagon spending, such as funds for the Milstar space satellites designed to help fight nuclear wars, has vanished into the black budget in the past two years.

"Huge areas have been removed from public debate," said Jeffrey Richelson, a professor at American University in Washington who has written several acclaimed studies on U.S. and Soviet intelligence. "Whole programs have gone black without questions being asked, such as: Do we need these weapons? Will they be destabilizing?"

Richelson said, "The secrecy once reserved for extraordinary programs"—such as the Manhattan Project to build an atomic bomb during World War II—"now has become an everyday, every-time affair."

Why are more and more projects becoming black? The foremost reason is the Reagan administration's desire for secrecy. That has driven the black budget upward more forcefully than any weapon in the Pentagon's plans.

In 1982, President Reagan signed an executive order revising the procedures for keeping secrets. The order said, in effect, that in balancing the public's right to know against the government's power to keep secrets, secrecy would carry more weight.

The order allows bureaucrats to "reclassify information previously declassified" and forbids them to consider the public's interest in access to government information when deciding to classify a document. Since then, the government has been classifying more documents and declassifying fewer than in previous administrations, according to the federal Information Security Oversight Organization, which monitors classification orders.

But there may be reasons other than secrecy that are driving the black budget higher.

A recent report by a presidential commission on defense-security practices warned that black programs "could be established . . . to avoid competitive procurement processes, normal inspections and oversight." And a senior House Armed Services Committee staffer, Anthony Battista, noted in a 1985 briefing that a multimillion-dollar radar-jamming system was classified to hide the Pentagon's violation of competitive bidding rules in awarding the contract.

Battista told the Armed Services subcommittee on research and development that the Pentagon "is putting more and more into . . . the black programs, not because of national security, but simply to skirt the normal acquisition process."

Very few federal investigators have the security clearances necessary to audit black programs, which usually are classified as "sensitive compartmented information," a classification above top secret. There are more than 10,000 such security "compartments," and it is illegal for anyone without that specific clearance to possess knowledge of the program.

That raises the question whether the fiscal abuses revealed in unclassified Pentagon procurement programs—the $7,000 coffee-pots and $600 screws—also are occurring in secret.

"In a black project, people don't worry about money," says a systems engineer who has worked on four black projects at the space systems division of Lockheed Missile and Space Co. in Sunnyvale, Calif.

"If you need money, you got it. If you screw up and you need more, you got it," said the engineer, who asked that his name not be published. "You're just pouring money into the thing until you get it right. The incentive isn't there to do it right the first time. Who's going to question it?"

Questioning the black budget is difficult for a Congress lacking information. But limits in future defense spending required by the Gramm-Rudman budget-cutting law may force the issue. The law, which is designed to phase out the federal deficit by 1991, says 50 percent of the budget cuts should come from defense spending. And the federal deficit this year will be $174.5 billion, according to the nonpartisan Congressional Budget Office.

Those seeking more bang for the defense buck are concerned that the growing black budget will crowd out defense spending for mundane but crucial things such as boots and bullets.

"What we see in three to four years is a train wreck coming," said

Gordon Adams of the Defense Budget Project, a Washington research organization that analyzes Pentagon spending. The crash he envisions: rushing headlong in one direction, tens of billions of dollars in immovable black weapons projects; coming the other way on the same track, tens of billions in unstoppable budget cuts mandated by the Gramm-Rudman law.

"The consequences of that train wreck for national security are enormous," Adams said. "What piece of flesh do we cut? Do we mothball part of the Navy? Cut personnel? We will have to make those choices, and all for a black budget we know nothing about."

But something can be learned about the black budget. The Inquirer reviewed more than 10,000 pages of Defense Department budget documents, studied the congressional testimony of Pentagon officials and interviewed military and intelligence experts inside and outside of the Pentagon for this series.

Within the military's black budget, no subject is more controversial or costly than Stealth technology, which is designed to enable aircraft and missiles to elude enemy radar.

Although the technology is a relatively open book—an informative volume on the subject can be bought in the Pentagon bookstore and accurate models of Stealth fighters can be purchased in toy stores—its true cost remains a state secret. Defense analysts place the combined costs of Stealth projects for Air Force fighters and bombers, nuclear cruise missiles, pilotless drones and Navy attack planes at $100 billion.

The most costly by far is the Stealth bomber, which is becoming the most expensive weapon in American history. The Air Force wants 132 of the planes delivered by the early 1990s. Most military experts place the bomber's ultimate price at about $450 million apiece. If that estimate is accurate, the Stealth bombers' total cost will be $60 billion —a sum equal to the combined annual budgets of New York, New Jersey and Pennsylvania.

Stealth-bomber spending may be spread out over several programs to hide its immense size. Now that Aurora has vanished, some analysts say Stealth money is cached in two Air Force line items: "other production charges—$3.1 billion" and "special programs—$2.3 billion." Some say it is hidden within the Department of Energy's $8 billion budget for military programs.

The Pentagon refuses to disclose the price tag on Stealth technology, saying the Soviets could deduce the status of the projects by tracking the spending. Top Pentagon officials decline to respond to reports that the Stealth aircraft's heralded radar-evading ability already has been outstripped by advances in radar technology. They have denied in a public hearing before a congressional oversight committee that Stealth aircraft exist.

The hearings stemmed from a series of security lapses and frauds on Stealth projects. The Stealth-related criminal cases are only "the tip of the iceberg" of illegal conduct on black projects, said Robert C. Bonner, the U.S. Attorney in Los Angeles, a hub of secret military contracting.

One engineer hired by Northrop Corp., the lead contractor on the Stealth bomber, was a Florida chain-gang alumnus named William Reinke. He was convicted of defrauding the company of more than $600,000 by channeling Stealth subcontracts to a company he secretly owned. In another case, a Northrop purchasing agent, Ronald Brousseau, was convicted of rigging contracts in exchange for kickbacks from subcontractors. He described the ease of defrauding black programs to a government informant wearing a concealed tape recorder: "We don't have any heads, we don't have any supervisory people. . . . Nobody questions dollars or anything like that."

Few in Congress can adequately question dollars invested in Stealth technology, or expect satisfactory answers about Stealth's capabilities, said Rep. Mike Synar (D., Okla.), because of "the absolutely adamant refusal by the Pentagon to release information on Stealth," a refusal Synar called "an insult to Congress."

Synar said his experience in trying to obtain accurate cost figures on the bomber taught him this lesson: "It's obvious that Defense [Department officials] will not be truthful with Congress and the American public when they think it's in their interest."

Stealth is the biggest of the black programs, but other secret military projects absorb billions of defense dollars, Pentagon documents show. Sophisticated Army and Air Force electronic-warfare systems; Navy programs aimed at disguising U.S. submarines' movements and detecting enemy subs with underwater sensors, and advanced computer, radar, communications and jamming systems are among the projects driving up the black budget.

All are cloaked in the secrecy that traditionally has been reserved for the nation's espionage agencies.

The intelligence community receives more than 75 percent of its funds from the Pentagon's black budget. The intelligence community's share of the black budget funds the CIA, the National Security Agency and the National Reconnaissance Office, as well as the military's intelligence branches. Their budgets appear in no public document.

The CIA's budget, an estimated $2.5 billion, has more than doubled under the Reagan administration. And no part of it has grown faster than funds for covert operations, now $600 million or more a year.

But the CIA's budget remains the smallest of those of the three major intelligence agencies. It is dwarfed by the National Security Agency's, which has been placed at $10 billion.

The NSA is a global vacuum cleaner of intelligence. Its listening posts include ground stations around the world and KH-11 spy satellites orbiting the earth. The satellites and ground stations intercept information from telephones, telexes, microwave transmitters, missiles and satellites. NSA computers can pick out specific conversations from the babble of international telecommunications traffic.

The NSA also conducts surveillance within the United States. A secret court of federal judges, which meets periodically in a secure chamber within the Justice Department, grants the NSA license for domestic operations. Under a secret directive signed by President Reagan, the NSA has access to the computer systems of the IRS, the Social Security Administration and every other civilian government agency.

No law establishes or limits the powers and responsibilities of the NSA, which was created by a secret, seven-page order signed by President Harry S. Truman in 1952. The NSA regularly spied on American citizens until 1973, when revelations in the Watergate affair ended that practice. The only known mention of the agency in the public laws of the United States is a 1959 statute that states: "Nothing in this act or any other law . . . shall be construed to require the disclosure of the organization or any function of the National Security Agency."

Employing at least 60,000 civilians, and working closely with the Pentagon from its Fort Meade, Md., headquarters midway between Washington and Baltimore, the NSA also controls the nation's cryptography program, making the codes for U.S. forces and breaking the codes of foreign nations.

The third major espionage agency is the National Reconnaissance Office. Its existence never has been openly acknowledged by the United States. It is an agency so secret that its letterhead is classified. It is known to operate satellite reconnaissance systems under the direction of the Air Force, and it provides photographic data to the intelligence community through a system of space platforms disguised as weather and research satellites. Its budget is estimated at $4 billion.

All three major espionage agencies overlap with the Pentagon in their missions. For example, the Army provides cover and personnel for CIA operations, such as the training of the Nicaraguan counter-revolutionaries, the contras. The Pentagon controls a variety of intelligence programs, including the entire National Reconnaissance Office, the NSA's spy satellites and code-breaking, research and development of espionage equipment, and submarine surveillance of the Soviet Union.

Most congressional critics of the black budget make a practical distinction between the rapid growth of secret military spending, which they see as largely unjustified, and the black budget for espionage. Few have argued that intelligence programs should suffer public scrutiny.

But even this consensus has been strained by revelations that the CIA has kept Congress in the dark about covert operations of questionable legality, ranging from the mining of Nicaragua's harbors to the arms-for-Iran and cash-for-the-contras deals.

"I'm not against black programs," said Stansfield Turner, who served as CIA director from 1977 to 1981. "But is Congress willing to let these programs go through without knowing what's in them? It's clearly become much more difficult for Congress to get information, and it's clear that congressional oversight has been narrowed. I don't know whether that's a good thing."

PLANNING FOR WORLD WAR IV

MONDAY, FEBRUARY 9, 1987

BY TIM WEINER

On Dec. 4, an Atlas-Centaur rocket blasted off from Cape Canaveral. It carried the first space test of Milstar, a multibillion-dollar satellite system funded by the Pentagon's secret "black budget."

Milstar is the centerpiece of a $40 billion plan to prepare for World War IV.

Four?

Four. Since 1981, shortly after President Reagan took office, the fundamental U.S. defense strategy has been to be able to fight and win a six-month nuclear conflict—World War III—and remain strong enough afterward to strike again.

Long after the White House and Pentagon are reduced to rubble and much of civilization is destroyed, the strategy would call for computers to run a war no human mind could control, orchestrating space satellites and nuclear weapons over a global battlefield.

The strategy envisions generals huddled in underground bunkers, aloft in converted 747s and speeding down interstate highways in lead-lined tractor-trailers. These nuclear-war command posts would harbor computer terminals linked to space satellites that would help direct nuclear missiles from silos and submarines.

The key to this strategy, the Pentagon maintains, is to build a computerized communications network that can command and control the nation's nuclear forces during and after World War III.

The Pentagon calls this network "C^{3}I" (pronounced see-cubed-eye), shorthand for command, control, communications and intelligence. Part of a $222 billion plan to modernize the nation's nuclear forces, C^{3}I would become America's central nervous system for nuclear war, the brain that controls the brawn of missiles, bombers and submarines.

Increasingly, major components of the nuclear C^{3}I system, such as Milstar, have been hidden in the black budget, the Pentagon's secret funds for classified projects. Naturally, this has severely limited congressional oversight and public awareness of the new network.

And as billions and billions for C³I disappear into the black budget, less and less is known about the ultimate cost and structure of the nation's nuclear strategy.

New C³I systems hidden in the black budget include:

• The Milstar system of satellites, orbiting 70,000 miles above the earth, receiving and relaying commands to launch nuclear weapons.

• Satellite sensors designed to guide nuclear missiles in flight, track their progress and report back on the damage they inflict.

• Tractor-trailers hauling nuclear command posts, dodging Soviet attacks on the open road.

The ultimate cost of these three black programs alone may exceed $30 billion.

C³I projects still in the unclassified Pentagon budget include:

• Robots that can gallop like horses and walk like men, carrying out computerized orders as they roam the radioactive battlefront.

• A nationwide network of 500 radio stations that could broadcast orders to nuclear-missile silos and underground bunkers.

• A search for ways to protect crucial computers from the effects of nuclear weapons.

Take Milstar, just one component, although a crucial one, of C³I. For years, the Milstar project gathered dust in the Pentagon's files. It was considered impossibly expensive.

But the Reagan administration's military buildup has brought it from the drawing board to the launching pad.

Since 1984, the administration has spent at least $1.5 billion to develop the space satellites and other communications equipment for Milstar. Military analysts estimate the ultimate cost of Milstar at between $15 billion and $20 billion.

The true cost will remain a secret. Last year, the Milstar satellites disappeared in the Pentagon's black budget, where they are less likely to face scrutiny from Congress and critics.

Milstar would work like this, if it works at all, in a nuclear war:

Imagine two networks, one in space, one on earth. The first is a constellation of eight satellites, strategically placed in orbits around the earth, 70,000 miles or more in space. The satellites connect with the second network, thousands of radios and computer terminals in underground bunkers, missile silos, submarines, tractor-trailers and airborne command posts.

Milstar would be the global nuclear-communications switchboard, connecting all the command stations during and after World War III, receiving and relaying the launch orders for nuclear weapons.

This concept—"connectivity"—is the buzzword for the 1980s at the Pentagon and the basis for the C^{3}I network.

All commanders dream of ways to pierce the fog of war, to obtain intelligence fresh from the battlefield, to give orders that will be carried out instantly, to communicate with fellow officers. To command. As Gen. Thomas Power, the legendary head of the Strategic Air Command in the 1950s, put it: "Without communications, all I command is my desk."

Pentagon officials have told Congress that Milstar's satellites and terminals will provide "connectivity" for months after nuclear war erupts.

Milstar would connect the nation's military leaders with the commander-in-chief. If the president escapes from Washington in the "doomsday plane," a converted 747 intended to evacuate the president from Washington, he could use Milstar to order nuclear-submarine commanders thousands of miles away to hit Soviet targets in Moscow or Vladivostok.

If Washington is destroyed and the president, vice president and secretary of defense are killed, the new nuclear commander-in-chief will be an Air Force general already aloft in a modified 707. (Continuously, in peacetime or in conflict, a general and battle staff from the Strategic Air Command are in flight over the Midwest in one of several planes code-named Looking Glass.)

Messages sent through Milstar would tell the Looking Glass commander if Washington was gone. He would then use Milstar to coordinate the nation's nuclear missiles and bombers.

The Pentagon still has not solved one problem that might prevent the "doomsday" and Looking Glass planes from playing their crucial roles throughout a six-month nuclear war: The planes cannot remain aloft for more than 72 hours before their lubricants run out and their engines die.

If the airborne command posts fail, Milstar would transmit that information to generals in the Pentagon's alternative command center, deep underground in the Catoctin Mountains near Raven Rock, Pa. Then these generals could take control, using the satellites to transmit orders telling troops to evacuate cities, or to fire MX warheads from silos in Wyoming.

When it is completed, Milstar will join two other nuclear-war-fighting systems in space.

Navstar, also known as the Global Positioning System, was canceled by the Carter administration but resurrected in 1982. It is expected to be completed by 1990 at an estimated final cost of $8 billion to $12 billion.

Navstar's 18 satellites will play a crucial role in a nuclear war. Their computer systems will help nuclear weapons hit bull's-eyes. According to congressional testimony, the satellites can guide nuclear missiles and fix them on their targets with accuracies of 50 feet or closer.

How will the U.S. military commanders know if the missiles have accomplished their missions? A set of sensors that will ride piggyback on Navstar satellites will tell them.

The sensors are called IONDS, for Integrated Operational Nuclear Detection System. Pentagon officials have told Congress that the sensors are designed to survey the global battlefield, pinpoint nuclear explosions, assess the damage and report the results back to commanders in airborne posts and underground bunkers.

Like Milstar satellites, the nuclear-detection technology for IONDS is being developed mostly under black-budget financing. Its ultimate cost is unknown.

While much about the C^3I technology's role in nuclear policy remains classified, several aspects seem clear:

The new generation of C^3I satellites is a step toward the militarization of space. The C^3I network gives computers an ever-growing power over nuclear forces. The technology remains uncertain until tested in nuclear war. And the multibillion-dollar projects hidden in the black budget still represent only a small down payment on a C^3I system that can endure a long nuclear war.

"One reason the black budget is growing so fast is the Reagan administration believes it can win a nuclear war," said Gene La-Rocque, the retired Navy admiral who directs the watchdog group Center for Defense Information in Washington. "We've moved away from a policy of deterrence, where you *want* your enemy to know what you've got. If you want to win a nuclear war, you've got to keep your capabilities a secret."

Defense Secretary Caspar W. Weinberger has told Congress that the C³I network is "perhaps the most urgently needed element" in the Reagan administration's trillion-dollar military buildup. This urgency stems from a shift in the nation's nuclear-war-fighting strategy.

Shortly after President Reagan took office, in October 1981, he signed a secret "finding" called National Security Decision Directive 13. While the text of NSDD-13 remains a secret, its meaning is not. The strategy it proclaimed has been repeated in the testimony of Pentagon officials before Congress and in scores of published works by military analysts.

That strategy says the idea of a one-day nuclear war is outmoded. It says that 20 million or more Americans can die in World War III, and the United States will still survive as a nation. It says the United States should have the power to control the escalation of a long-drawn-out nuclear war and force a Soviet surrender. And it says the new C³I network must then control a reserve of nuclear forces large enough to allow the nation to fight again.

The strategy relies heavily on space-based C³I platforms such as Milstar and Navstar. International treaties forbid the military use of space. Congress has asked Pentagon officials whether their plans violate these agreements. The Pentagon has replied, in a statement with Orwellian overtones, that the United States interprets "the right to use space for peaceful purposes to include military uses of space to promote peace in the world." And Congress has funded the satellites.

Back on earth, the Pentagon's C³I plans depend on ways to keep commanders alive.

In an all-out nuclear war, Pentagon planners realize, few major command posts would avoid direct nuclear hits. The Soviet Union knows where to find crucial nerve centers such as the Pentagon and the Strategic Air Command headquarters in Nebraska.

Figuring that a moving target is harder to hit, the Pentagon has a $3 billion investment in mobile command posts under way. The idea, the Pentagon has told Congress, is to have a large number of C^3I centers that the Soviets cannot target. This is the thinking behind a project code-named Island Sun.

It is a plan to create convoys of tractor-trailers in which generals could operate computerized command posts after nuclear war begins, according to congressional testimony by Defense Secretary Weinberger. Just how the trucks would operate—for example, where they might refuel or change a flat tire—is unknown, because the project is classified. However, the Pentagon budget shows that Island Sun has absorbed $165 million in research-and-development funds over the past four years.

Island Sun is one of many related C^3I projects to create mobile ground terminals, linked through Milstar, that in effect would be tiny Pentagons coordinating the nation's nuclear forces as they dodge Soviet intercontinental ballistic missiles on the highways, on freight trains and aboard merchant ships at sea.

But Milstar and its ground terminals are not the only way to coordinate the nuclear arsenal. The Pentagon plans to spend nearly $1 billion on creating an enduring conventional communications system, one so large and containing so many parts that the Soviet Union could never eliminate it.

The system is called GWEN, the Ground Wave Emergency Network. GWEN is planned as a network of up to 500 unmanned radio towers. At least 50 are already in place near towns and cities including Aurora, Colo.; Manhattan, Kan.; Fayetteville, Ark., and Gettysburg, Pa. Each station has a range of several hundred miles and can relay messages to sister stations, creating a national network, Radio GWEN.

GWEN's programming would include orders to launch nuclear weapons. It would link early-warning radars, missile silos, air bases, submarines, underground bunkers, Strategic Air Command headquarters and the Pentagon.

The genius of GWEN, according to Pentagon planners, is that the Soviets cannot possibly destroy all 500 towers. There will be so many GWEN relay stations and switching routes that the system should endure during and after a nuclear attack. And if it falters, balloons carrying compatible radio antennas could be inflated and sent aloft.

•

Another question the Pentagon is grappling with as it tries to create a nuclear-war-fighting network is the human factor. Would soldiers carry out their roles in the heat of nuclear battle? The Pentagon is researching ways to educate soldiers to "understand the impact of enemy nuclear firepower" and to "prepare them to cope with operations on the nuclear battlefield," according to congressional testimony.

And where the human mind and body cannot cope with nuclear war, the Pentagon's planners tell Congress, computers will. They will play a very large role in the command and control of nuclear forces.

Thinking machines can supplant privates and generals alike in wartime, according to the Pentagon's Defense Advanced Research Projects Agency (DARPA), which notes in its 1987 budget that "computers can assist, advise and/or relieve military personnel in complex decision-making tasks [which are] dangerous or rapidly changing."

"Computers are extremely important," the Pentagon's former director of ballistic missile defense, Jacob Gilstein, has told Congress. "No human being can enter the real-time decision-making loop and control the system. It has to be preprogrammed with logic so the computer can make the decision and run the game."

Just as computers will have to do the thinking in nuclear war, computer-controlled robot soldiers may have to do the grunt work in the nuclear battlefield.

DARPA is working on a variety of robots—"hexapods" that move with a tank's agility and speed, "quadrupeds" that gallop and trot, "walking vehicles," and robot hands and fingers. It is using increasing amounts of money and manpower to develop robot intelligence, focusing on "flexible software systems that show unique promise for solving complex military problems." Commanders will communicate with robots through "a state-of-the-art man-machine interface called IRUS," according to DARPA's budget.

DARPA envisions a robot soldier of the future that takes orders "but does not generate discourse"—no back talk or balking. The new generation of robot soldiers eventually will give commanders the ability to have their commands carried out in "an enhanced nuclear environment"—the Pentagon's language for a lethally radioactive battle-field.

A multibillion-dollar effort is under way to protect everything from underground bunkers to airborne command posts against the varied effects of nuclear explosions. But the most immediate danger to C³I is not the radiation of nuclear weapons, or the blast, or the firestorm. It is a much-discussed, little-understood phenomenon called the electro-magnetic pulse, or EMP.

Nuclear experts disagree emphatically on the effects of EMP, and the possibility of defending against it. They only agree that it is a real phenomenon.

A nuclear blast high in the atmosphere creates an enormous electro-magnetic charge, a wave of intense lightning bathing the land below in an electric storm. This pulse was experienced in Hawaii in 1962, when the U.S. exploded three high-altitude nuclear weapons over the Pacific. Although the test took place 800 miles away, street lights went off across Oahu and burglar alarms went haywire in Honolulu.

The implications for C³I are far more serious. The entire structure of C³I rests on computers. If the computers cannot function during nuclear war, almost nothing will. Those who consider EMP a grave threat say it could disrupt every computer chip in the system, over-loading low-voltage circuits with a tremendous burst of high-voltage energy. In theory, the network could be undone by a single nuclear bomb.

Realizing that every minute counts in nuclear war, the Pentagon is seeking ways to prevent C³I from being temporarily disconnected by the electromagnetic pulse.

The cables that connect Minuteman missile silos to their launch centers are encased in six inches of lead. At Kirtland Air Force Base in New Mexico, Pentagon scientists shoot 10 million volts of electricity through aircraft and electronic equipment, testing ways to protect them. The president's "doomsday plane" has $100 million worth of EMP shielding. Every C³I satellite will have some form of EMP armor.

All the parts of C³I—the computers, the Milstar satellites, the mobile ground stations and the rest—appear technologically feasible to the Pentagon. The trick will be in weaving them all together into one durable war machine.

As of now, the Pentagon has told Congress it has "high confidence" that the C³I network will "endure through trans- and post-attack phases of a Soviet nuclear strike."

But nobody really knows if the C³I system will work. And no one will, until a full-scale nuclear war erupts.

Skeptics inside and outside the military say neither the tens of billions already spent nor the tens of billions needed to complete what has begun will buy the C³I network the Pentagon wants.

They say the Pentagon's vision of the ultimate nuclear-war machine is an illusion.

The goal of a durable C³I system—one that would last for weeks and months during a long nuclear war—"will cost tens of billions of dollars over and beyond what we are spending today . . . and it is not clear how long such a system would endure," warned Charles A. Zraket, executive vice president of the Mitre Corp., the nation's premier C³I think tank.

The Pentagon is undaunted. "They've consistently sent the signal: They want an enduring system. They've told the weapons and systems designers to do it. And they've driven the designers crazy," said John Steinbruner, a C³I expert at the Brookings Institution in Washington.

"The designers don't know how to do it, even spending tens or hundreds of billions of dollars," Steinbruner said. "We do not know how to build a system that could endure a large-scale attack. But the money's being spent, no question about it."

Upon his retirement in 1982, the chairman of the Joint Chiefs of Staff, Gen. David Jones, told Congress that the military was throwing money into "a bottomless pit" by planning for a nuclear war of controlled scale and duration.

"I don't see much chance of nuclear war being limited or protracted," he said.

Very little unclassified information exists about the Pentagon's post-World War III plans. But the question was addressed many years ago by the man who discovered the power of the atom. Albert Einstein once was asked what weapons would be used to fight a third world war. Einstein replied that he really didn't know, but he had an idea what weapons would be used in World War IV.

"Sticks and stones," Einstein said.

COVERT FORCES MULTIPLY, AND SOME RUN AMOK

TUESDAY, FEBRUARY 10, 1987

BY TIM WEINER

A dashing and much-decorated lieutenant colonel found himself in deep trouble in November.

His superiors had called him to account for millions of dollars drawn from the Pentagon's "black budget." The funds were for covert operations. He had used front companies, secret bank accounts, laundered money. Unconventional ways of doing business. His superiors pressed him for answers. His explanations didn't add up.

The dashing lieutenant colonel in question was not running arms to Iran. But his troubles foreshadowed that foreign-policy snafu.

Lt. Col. Dale C. Duncan of the Army's Special Operations Division ran a mission code-named Yellow Fruit. Housed in an ordinary-looking business office in the Washington suburbs, it was to provide undercover financing and security for covert Army units operating overseas.

The mission had run amok. Duncan stood before a secret court-martial Nov. 10 in a tiny, tightly guarded room at the Army's Intelligence and Security Command in Virginia. The charges against him were serious: forgery, theft and obstruction of justice. And military justice was severe: 10 years in prison and a $50,000 fine.

Duncan's case was only one in a series of Pentagon investigations into how secret military forces had spent hundreds of millions of dollars over the last six years. The investigations revealed abuses of money and power in covert Pentagon operations at home and abroad.

Now, after the revelations of back-channel deals to deliver Pentagon arms to Iran, and high-profile CIA support for the Nicaraguan rebels in Central America, the work of Duncan and his covert cohorts appears to be part of a larger pattern.

For the secret inquests at the Pentagon and the public controversy over the CIA's operations have a common root: All were part of a surge in covert action undertaken by the Reagan administration, action often concealed from Congress—and all were funded through the black budget, the Pentagon's cache of secret funds shielded from public scrutiny.

"This administration has overstressed covert action. They have tried to do too much," said former CIA director Stansfield Turner, a firm believer in the uses of secret operations.

"They have not limited covert action to situations where you have some chance of succeeding. They have undertaken covert actions so large and so controversial that they leaked out, they became overt," Turner said. "It has done some damage."

Today, Pentagon spending for covert operations around the world totals at least $2 billion, the most since the height of the Vietnam War, according to congressional overseers and military analysts. The money is split among the CIA and a host of secret Pentagon forces skilled in espionage, sabotage, psychological warfare and even the use of tactical nuclear weapons.

The Pentagon's black budget finances the CIA's covert actions and the CIA director's contingency fund to support such operations. Together, these hidden accounts have more than doubled since 1981. The CIA's share of the $2 billion for covert action has reached at least $750 million a year, according to congressional sources who oversee the intelligence community. From El Salvador to Ethiopia, from Afghanistan to Angola, the black budget has supported more than 50 CIA covert operations around the globe over the last six years.

Beyond the CIA, black-budget funds for Pentagon covert operations and personnel have skyrocketed under the Reagan administration and now exceed $1.25 billion a year, according to congressional sources. The bulk of these missions are handled by the Special Operations Forces, whose members include Army Green Berets and Rangers, Navy SEAL commandos and an Air Force wing.

The Special Operations Forces are America's secret soldiers. In peacetime, their main mission is to carry out clandestine operations against foreign powers. Their motto is "Anything, Anytime, Anywhere, Anyhow." And their critics say that about sums up the problem.

In Central America, they have helped counterrevolutionaries who are trying to overthrow the Nicaraguan government.

In the United States, they have worked with the FBI, bugging and wiretapping the hotel rooms of visiting Soviet officials, according to congressional sources.

In West Germany and South Korea, they are trained to use small nuclear land mines called "backpack nukes" for sabotage, according to congressional records.

Hundreds of millions of dollars are being spent to buy weapons and equipment designed expressly for them: Polaris nuclear-powered ballistic-missile submarines converted to carry commandos, laser-guided weapons, sophisticated intelligence-gathering equipment, and the like.

Defense Secretary Caspar W. Weinberger has told Congress that building up Special Operations Forces is "one of this administration's highest priorities," and the Pentagon and Congress have spent the money to fulfill that desire. The Pentagon plans to have 20,000 covert soldiers by 1989. The forces' unclassified budget has risen from $440 million in 1981 to a requested $2.5 billion this year.

Part of this unclassified budget is channeled into covert activities undertaken by the Special Operations Forces. Separate black-budget funding also supports secret Special Operations missions, according to staff members of congressional oversight committees who spoke on condition of anonymity.

As the special forces' budgets have grown, so has their power. Today they are the American forces used most often around the world. They are "the only force we are actively using today to meet the Soviet challenge," Deputy Assistant Defense Secretary Noel C. Koch has told Congress.

Ties between the Pentagon's Special Operations Forces and the CIA appear to have grown stronger than at any time since the incursions of U.S. forces into Laos and Cambodia during the Vietnam War. In the eyes of some members of Congress, the close ties are calculated to allow the CIA to evade congressional oversight.

That is because the Special Operations Forces have one freedom the CIA does not: They are not required to report their covert activities to Congress. "There's a real danger that these special forces could be used by CIA programs and thus skirt congressional review," said Sen. Jim Sasser (D., Tenn.).

And, although the CIA is supposed to inform Congress of its covert operations, the CIA, under director William J. Casey, interpreted that requirement loosely. Working to overthrow the Nicaraguan government, mining the Nicaraguan port of Corinto, supporting the Nicaraguan contra rebels, the CIA has consistently acted without informing Congress, straining the bounds of its charter.

As just one example of that strain, the CIA last week forced its station chief in Costa Rica to retire. The agency decided that the station chief had lied about the depth of his involvement with Lt. Col. Oliver L. North, the National Security Council aide who was fired in November for shipping arms to Iran and then reportedly diverting funds to the contras. The CIA station chief apparently worked closely with North to funnel aid to the contras when such military assistance was forbidden by Congress.

The investigations of how military men and CIA agents have collaborated on ill-fated and possibly illegal foreign-policy initiatives are continuing. Already they have put a spotlight on the CIA, and have suggested that its operations have grown beyond the laws intended to control them.

But little attention has focused on the Pentagon investigations into the use and abuse of covert military operations. Those internal inquiries have found financial or political wrongdoing in four secret military units, including Duncan's, detachments of highly motivated soldiers whose influence grew strong in the Reagan years, nurtured by hundreds of millions of dollars from secret Pentagon accounts.

'THE CRAZIES IN THE BASEMENT'

Ronald Reagan came to office in 1981 on the day Iran released Americans held hostage for more than a year. He vowed repeatedly to strengthen American forces so that the United States never again would be humiliated by a hostile nation.

Out of this vow sprang a host of new military and intelligence initiatives. The CIA would be given new freedom and new vigor. The armed forces would have billions upon billions of dollars in new funds. There would be new faces, new missions, new forces.

One of them was a new Army Special Operations Division, which began with an annual budget of at least $100 million a year. The officers attached to the division had headquarters in a subterranean

Pentagon office. Their methods were unconventional and their projects were ambitious. They quickly became known at the Pentagon as "the crazies in the basement."

Among them was Lt. Col. Dale C. Duncan. In 1981, when the Special Operations Division took shape, he was only 35 years old. But he rose to command a domestic Special Operations mission, code-named Yellow Fruit.

Sometime in 1983, one of the men assigned to Yellow Fruit blew the whistle on Duncan. He reported allegations of gross financial misconduct, and worse. Thus began a slow, painful, three-year internal investigation by Pentagon officers who were forced to apply standard accounting practices and military regulations to a freewheeling covert operation.

The unclassified court record in the Duncan case suggests that the main mission of Yellow Fruit was to disguise the activities and finances of Special Operations Forces operating in Central America and elsewhere overseas.

Much of the stenographic record of Duncan's court-martial is classified and most of the court-martial's sessions were closed to civilians, so the public record in the Duncan case is scant.

But the public record strongly suggests that large sums of money disappeared into a company called Business Security International, based in the Washington suburb of Annandale, Va., and intended to disguise the existence of Yellow Fruit and related missions.

In law-enforcement terms, Business Security International was a front. It was created as an instrument to finance and conceal Special Operations Division activities.

Yellow Fruit funds were laundered—their source disguised by paper transactions—to give the secret unit the ability to deny its financial ties to the Army, according to the court record. Nor could some of the funds be traced once they were spent. The Special Operations Division's accountant, Maj. Ronald Lee, testified at the court-martial that "there were no controls [over] an organization that was spending hundreds of thousands, millions of dollars."

One of the signs of the struggle to rein in the mission lies in the case against Duncan's commanding officer, Col. James E. Longhofer, the former head of the Army's Special Operations Division. Longhofer was the division's liaison with the CIA. He was not accused of financial wrongdoing, but he was charged and convicted of dereliction of duty, disobeying a lawful order and conduct unbecoming an officer, and he received a two-year prison sentence. The record suggests that Longhofer failed to report allegations of Duncan's misconduct to his superiors.

The case was not an isolated incident involving a single runaway unit. It sparked a series of Pentagon investigations into the books and records of the Special Operations Forces.

Congressional investigators say these internal audits disclosed financial abuses by at least two other units. They said 80 members of the Delta Force—representing one-fourth of the super-secret guerrilla unit based at Fort Bragg, N.C.—were disciplined for financial reasons. And, they said, there were similar problems in a Special Operations unit code-named Seaspray, which flew aerial reconnaissance missions in Central America for the CIA and the National Security Agency.

No public record of these investigations is known to exist. What is known is that Yellow Fruit, Seaspray and the Delta Force all reported to a group called the Intelligence Support Activity.

THE ACTIVITY

The Intelligence Support Activity was a secret spy squad, with a corps of at least 250 officers, that the Pentagon created in 1981 behind Congress' back, according to interviews with several congressional investigators.

The group rose from the ashes of the failed attempt to rescue Americans held hostage in Iran in 1979 and 1980.

During the hostage crisis, according to congressional sources and military analysts, the CIA had almost no one in Iran to provide what it calls "human intelligence," the kind of information that satellites and other high-tech sources cannot gather. Its ability to spy on Iran was crippled. The military was being asked to mount a dangerous assault in a strange country without crucial information.

So the Pentagon formed an ad hoc unit to gather intelligence for Operation Eagle Claw, the Iran hostage-rescue mission.

Eagle Claw was a disaster. The mission aborted in death and destruction as aircraft collided in the Iranian desert. Among the lessons the Pentagon decided it had learned from the failure was this: Never improvise espionage for such a mission. The military concluded that it needed a permanent, unified, covert group to coordinate paramilitary actions and intelligence-gathering.

Thus the Intelligence Support Activity was born.

Its members simply called it "the Activity." It was formed shortly after Reagan took office in 1981, according to one congressional source, with at least $10 million in seed money from the Special Operations Forces budget.

Two officers who are said to have participated in the Activity were Lt. Col. Oliver L. North and Maj. Gen. Richard V. Secord.

North was the National Security Council's point man on covert operations. His energies helped convert the NSC from a body that assisted in making policy through painstaking analysis into an operational wing of the CIA and the Pentagon. Secord would emerge as a central figure in the Iran arms deal, sharing a secret Swiss bank account with North. He was an Air Force commander with a rich background in covert actions dating back to the 1960s, when he worked with the CIA in directing a secret air war in Laos.

In the first months of the Reagan administration, North and Secord began working together on the controversial $8 billion sale of Airborne Warning and Control System (AWACS) radar planes to Saudi Arabia. The sale apparently generated several hundred million in extra Saudi funds to support U.S.-backed guerrillas in Afghanistan and Central America.

In December 1981 and January 1982, North worked with the Activity on attempts to free Brig. Gen. James L. Dozier, a senior American NATO officer kidnapped for six weeks by Red Brigades terrorists in Italy.

The Activity worked on many of the Pentagon's most sensitive missions, first and foremost of which was to support the Nicaraguan contras. There also were covert actions undertaken in Europe, Africa, Southeast Asia and the Middle East, according to intelligence analysts.

Then, in March 1983, the Activity's cover was inadvertently blown by a former special forces lieutenant colonel testifying before a House Foreign Affairs subcommittee.

Retired Lt. Col. James "Bo" Gritz told the subcommittee an amazing story. Gritz had long contended that some American soldiers missing in action were still alive in Laos. He told Congress that he had worked with the Activity on plans for a secret mission to find these Americans, if they existed.

"The Activity was a field unit and would have put an American across into Laos to verify, using various recording means, the presence of Americans thought to be at specified locations," Gritz testified.

There was a problem with Gritz's testimony. Congress never had heard of anything called "the Activity" and was disturbed to learn that the Pentagon had a secret detachment of spies and Rambo prototypes running around the world.

Congress was not opposed to such missions—far from it. Congress during the Reagan years has supported them with hundreds of millions of dollars. But Congress said it wanted to be told about espionage activities, preferably in advance. That is the law.

A subsequent investigation by Lt. Gen. William Odom, now the head of the National Security Agency, apparently determined that the Intelligence Support Activity was out of control. There was little or no oversight, and there were some bizarre financial doings. For example, the investigation found that, for reasons unknown, Special Forces officers bought a Rolls-Royce and a hot-air balloon from federal Drug Enforcement Administration agents.

There followed something of a purge of officers associated with the Activity, according to military and intelligence observers.

Secord left the Pentagon in May 1983 to become a private arms dealer and consultant. He quickly secured a $1,260-a-week consulting job with the Pentagon's Office of Special Operations. In the fall of 1983, the Pentagon hired him as a member of the Special Operations Policy Advisory Group, a group of retired generals who were asked to provide "disinterested, expert advice" on covert actions. While he advised the Pentagon, he dealt in the international arms market and secretly worked with North on supplying the contras.

No one seems to know exactly what became of the Activity. Did it cease to exist after its cover was blown? Was it renamed and reshuffled? Were its members swallowed up by the revitalized Special Operations Forces? Pentagon officials deny anything called "the Activity" existed in the first place, so they cannot confirm or deny its continued existence. Congressional overseers don't know or can't say.

SECRET WEAPONS, SECRET WARS

The embarrassing realization that Congress didn't know of the Activity opened an old wound. Salved and partly healed, it was ripped open again and again by other revelations that caught Congress by surprise—the administration's secret mining of Nicaraguan harbors in 1984, the secret arms deals with Iran, the secret flow of aid to the contras in apparent defiance of a congressional ban.

Old questions without clear answers are being asked again. How does an espionage agency function in an open society? How much control should Congress have over covert operations? Who decides what should be kept secret?

In William J. Casey's CIA, the answers were clear.

The now-retired CIA director said he did not want a low-profile agency, he wanted "a no-profile agency," as he told an interviewer in 1983. But the sweep of the CIA's missions under Casey may have sabotaged that desire, according to Turner and other intelligence professionals.

Sen. Patrick Leahy (D., Vt.) of the Senate Intelligence Committee said Casey's flaw as CIA director was that "he so strongly supported covert actions—in fact, substituted covert-action policies for foreign policy—in a way that built up a layer of distrust."

Casey's mandate was to rebuild a CIA that had been damaged by discoveries of misconduct and repeatedly reined in during the 1970s. The resurgence of the CIA began the day Reagan was inaugurated as President. The director of central intelligence was given a new status: the rank of cabinet member. Under Casey's leadership, the CIA's budget doubled since 1981. Funds for covert actions grew even faster than the overall CIA budget.

And the mumbling, oblique testimony Casey gave Congress kept legislators in the dark about some of the CIA's biggest and most controversial missions.

"It's important to understand the contempt Casey has for Congress and the whole oversight process," a former high-ranking intelligence official said in an interview before Casey's resignation last week.

Covert operations, cut back to a bare minimum under Presidents Gerald R. Ford and Jimmy Carter, soared in number and scope: Iran, Nicaragua, El Salvador, Ethiopia, Chad, Cambodia and Lebanon were some of the sites for the more than 50 covert operations launched under Casey, the most since the days of Vietnam.

Congress has limited powers to oversee covert action. Since 1974, the law is that the president must "find" the action "important to the national security of the United States," and that certain members of Congress must be informed of his finding "in a timely manner." The president legally can restrict knowledge of covert action to eight members of the Senate and the House: the chairmen and vice chairmen of the intelligence committees, and the majority and minority leaders.

Of course, he also can violate this understanding, as many in Congress contend President Reagan did in authorizing arms shipments to Iran.

"It's a process that allows the executive branch to make law," said a senior congressional overseer of the intelligence community. "At its worst, it is an erosion of democracy."

Now Casey has retired and lies gravely ill in a Washington hospital while a firestorm of criticism grows over the CIA's role in swapping weapons for hostages with Iran.

And Congress once again is struggling to define its power to oversee the uses and abuses of secret funds, secret weapons and secret wars.

SIX

BITTER POLITICS IN THE MIDDLE EAST

1988 WINNER IN THE INTERNATIONAL REPORTING CATEGORY

"For a distinguished example of reporting on international affairs, including United Nations correspondence . . ."

The New York Times
Thomas L. Friedman

Thomas L. Friedman, who had previously witnessed a rising fundamentalist movement in Lebanon, discovered fundamentalism is also gaining among some Jews in Israel. He spotlights other changes, including a demographics war and a growing militancy among Arab youths, that are challenging Israel from within its own borders.

Barring extraordinary achievement, it seldom happens that a reporter wins more than one Pulitzer Prize. The body of Tom Friedman's work in Israel, we believe, represents just such an achievement.

Mr. Friedman earned his first Pulitzer in 1983, at the age of 29, for his brilliant and courageous coverage of the massacre of Palestinians in Beirut's Sabra and Shatila districts. The next year, continuing what is plainly the most searching exploration of the Middle East that any American journalist has made in this decade, he drove out of ruined Beirut and across military barriers and frontiers to Jerusalem. Politically he was now on the other side of the moon, covering what was essentially the same story in circumstances that demanded a different kind of discipline and skill.

In Israel the risk he faced—and overcame—was not physical but cerebral: the risk of being trapped by the familiar and awful stereotypes of the Arab-Israeli conflict. Having experienced that conflict at its worst for several years in Beirut, it might have been expected that his reporting from Israel would dwell on the confrontation between Israel's organized military might and Palestinian resistance.

In Israel, with an authority and independence of mind unusual in daily journalism, this superbly prepared correspondent, fluent in Arabic and Hebrew, delved far beneath the surface of everyday challenge-and-response reporting. His deeper subject became the struggle taking place inside the minds of the antagonists.

Israel, he recognized, was not just a Jewish state that had survived four decades of hostility from its neighbors, but a state that, for all its military invincibility, was painfully at odds with itself. As their occupation of the overwhelmingly Palestinian West Bank stretched into its third decade, Israelis were finding that their dream of life in a Jewish national state was being supplanted by the reality of life in what was swiftly becoming a binational Arab-Jewish territory. Arabs, meanwhile, faced the rise of Islamic fundamentalism in their own communities. And with this, some faced as well a paradoxical recognition that the enemy within might be more of a threat to their aspirations than were the familiar Zionist antagonists.

On both sides, ambiguity and ambivalence began to undermine nationalist certitudes, a process that Mr. Friedman recognized early and charted more sensitively and doggedly than any other correspondent.

On both sides, too, he recognized that religious zealotry was on the rise and with it a basic antagonism to the very idea of common ground. There was a telling and depressing symmetry between Mr. Friedman's reporting in 1987 on the rise of Islamic fundamentalism among Israel's Arab minority and the rising influence and political power among Jews of a non-Zionist ultra-orthodox minority who regard the modern Jewish state as an unfortunate aberration. Israel was becoming a less comfortable place for secular Jews as well as for secular Arabs.

Studying the portents, including the demographic trends that seemed bound to produce an Arab majority within a generation, Mr. Friedman was sometimes reminded of Lebanon's tragic fate. Young Palestinians, he wrote, were dreaming less of the achievement of their own state and more of crude revenge. "At some point," he warned, "this conflict will stop being about its root causes and will just be about hatred. At some point it will no longer be a conflict on the way to a resolution but a way of life—or, more appropriately, a way of death."

Mr. Friedman began 1987 with a telling front-page article on the rage of young Palestinians. The year ended with the worst explosion yet of that rage. Israeli officials blamed the unrest on terrorist "agitators" and Western television crews. Our correspondent, more effectively than any other, pointed to its deeper causes.

—The editors
The New York Times

PALESTINIANS UNDER ISRAEL: BITTER POLITICS

MONDAY, JANUARY 12, 1987

BY THOMAS L. FRIEDMAN

RAMALLAH, Israeli-Occupied West Bank—In December, on a quiet morning in this Christian Arab town north of Jerusalem, a 16-year-old Palestinian schoolboy walked up behind an Israeli soldier, pulled an ax out of his blue schoolbag, started shouting something about "Palestine" and began striking the soldier on the head.

The wounded soldier was taken to a hospital with severe cuts. The youth was taken to prison. All the army spokesmen would say about the young Palestinian was that he was acting on his "own initiative" —that is, no one ordered or paid him to do it; he just did it on his own accord.

This scene has been repeated several times in the last year, with young Palestinians using kitchen knives or sharpened screwdrivers to attack Israeli soldiers or civilians in broad daylight. And at Bir Zeit University north of Jerusalem in December, Palestinian students threw stones at heavily armed Israeli troops, who responded with live ammunition. Two students were shot to death, but the stone throwing continued for another week at schools all over the West Bank.

THE POST-1967 GENERATION

These young Palestinians are members of the post-1967 generation, who have spent all their lives under Israeli rule in the occupied West Bank and Gaza Strip and are increasingly making their political views felt. Their views are important for many reasons, most notably that in the years to come, they will be the Palestinian leaders and, perhaps, negotiators.

Judging from a wide range of discussions with West Bank Palestinian high school students and teachers, as well as with college students and professors, two themes in the thinking of this new Palestinian generation are striking.

First, although only a tiny number of the young Palestinians would ever think of wielding an ax, many seem to identify clearly with the blind rage of the ax wielders. They no longer seem to view violence as serving as a means toward a particular political objective; most say that they have given up hope for any solutions. Theirs is simply a politics of revenge.

VIOLENCE 'JUST OCCURS'

"I think that our generation of Palestinians have reached a point psychologically where we want any means of getting back at the Jews," said Meral, an 18-year-old Palestinian student at Bir Zeit University who did not want to give her last name, in order to avoid repercussions. "You just get the feeling the Jews want to aggravate us. Palestinian violence now is something that just happens. It's not planned; it just occurs."

Sara Salah, principal of the girls' high school in the Aida refugee district near Bethlehem, said, "My students' main problem is that they don't like their lives with the Jews."

The second striking feature about the new generation of Palestinians is that although they have had more direct contact with Israel and Israelis than previous generations of Palestinians, the experience in the occupied territories has done nothing to moderate their feelings. If anything, it has radicalized them.

This Palestinian generation seems to belie the conventional wisdom that the problem with the Arabs and the Israelis is that they do not know each other. Many of the young Palestinians say they believe the problem is that they and the Israelis do know each other, and that each wants the same land free of the other.

"We are two generations that are basically brought up the same way," said Serene, a 20-year-old Bir Zeit student who is studying literature, speaking of her Israeli and Palestinian peers. "They are a generation brought up to hate the Palestinians, and we were brought up to think the same about them. We don't need to talk to them to know what they are thinking because we know that they were brought up to think the same way as we do—only opposite."

"I was driving on the road from Jerusalem to Jericho one day last year and was stopped at an army checkpoint," she added. "We were there for a while, and at one point an Israeli soldier started trying to talk to me. I wasn't very friendly. Finally, he said to me, 'You hate us, don't you?' I said, 'What do you think?' "

'NOT GOING TO CONDEMN HIM'

"I would not go out and kill an Israeli civilian myself, but I also would not condemn someone who does," Serene said. "They are killing so many of our civilians here and in Lebanon. If someone has the guts to go out and stab one of theirs, I am not going to condemn him."

Another indication of how little living together has led to any deeper appreciation of the other's point of view is that these young Palestinians almost never refer to Israelis as Israelis. Instead, they call them the "Jews."

It appears from discussions that they believe that referring to Israelis as Israelis would be to acknowledge that there is another legitimate national collective on the land. So instead, they refer to them only as Jews, with no national connotations.

When this is pointed out to them, they quickly note that many Israelis do the equivalent to them, referring to them not as Palestinians but as "the Arabs of the land of Israel," an amorphous ethnic group living in someone else's country.

It seems that neither side can stand the symmetry of acknowledging that there is another legitimate collective on the land, because to do that would be to relinquish some of the exclusivity of their own claim and make their own "rights" relative instead of absolute.

LOSING CONTROL OF FUTURE

The most important factor shaping the attitudes of the new generation seems to be the feeling that they have lost control over their own future, as individuals and as a collective.

Because of the Israeli occupation, their opportunities as individuals are highly restricted. After they graduate, they cannot obtain a license to start a new business if it competes with an existing Israeli industry. There are few interesting Government jobs available to them, because virtually all are controlled by Israelis. They can leave to look for work in Jordan or the Persian Gulf, but under Israeli regulations any male between the ages of 16 and 26 who leaves cannot come back for at least nine months. The regulation was imposed to prevent gun-running and to encourage settlement abroad.

One of the paradoxes of the last 20 years is that it was the Israelis who, by offering many employment opportunities to West Bank Palestinians in manual labor inside Israel, created a huge Palestinian middle class that could afford to send its children to colleges and technical schools.

When the West Bank was under Jordan, there was only a tiny middle class, and the mass of the population was composed either of peasant farmers or landed gentry. Historically, it has been the middle classes who have most often had the sophistication and the motivation for serious upheavals.

Today, according to the Center for Palestinian Studies, an Arab research organization in Jerusalem, there are 17,000 Arab youths in the West Bank and Gaza studying at 20 post-high-school institutions. Many of those who graduate from these institutions, however, never end up working at what they were trained for.

Their frustrations derive from the Palestinian identity that has been shaped in the West Bank in the last 20 years of Israeli occupation.

Under the Jordanian occupation, Palestinians were never quite sure what their identity was. Their passports were issued by Jordan, and they were represented in the Jordanian Parliament; but although some thought of themselves as Jordanian nationals and assimilated into Jordanian society, many others viewed themselves as Palestinians and resented the Jordanian attempts to play down their separate identity.

Under the Israeli occupation, by contrast, they no longer had an option of assimilating. The challenge of the Israeli occupation, coupled with the rise of the Palestine Liberation Organization and the collapse of Pan-Arabism as a predominant ideology after the 1967 war, all combined to forge a Palestinian national consciousness among West Bank youth.

"Between 1949 and 1967, whenever anyone asked me what I was, I always hesitated," said Munir Fasheh, Dean of Students at Bir Zeit University, who grew up in Ramallah. "Legally, I was Jordanian, but emotionally I was Palestinian. Now, there is no kid on the West Bank under the age of 25 who has ever experienced anything other than being a Palestinian. When you consider that 60 percent of the West Bank population is under the age of 20, it means that for three-quarters of them Jordan is something that doesn't exist."

But under the Israeli occupation, this Palestinian political identity is not allowed to find expression in political parties, political assembly or self-rule.

Israel, Jordan and the United States are trying to help King Hussein reassert his traditional influence over the West Bank and to undermine the P.L.O.'s popularity there, in hopes of being able one day to arrange a Jordanian-Israeli solution.

'60 OR 70 YEARS BEFORE VICTORY'

This policy, however, seems to be in contradiction with the mood among the young generation, whose attitudes about peace have been shaped almost entirely by the P.L.O.

"For tomorrow, we want the West Bank and Gaza, with the P.L.O. in charge," said Abdullah, a 23-year-old engineering student at Bir Zeit. "For the day after tomorrow, we want a democratic, secular state in all of Palestine, so that the Palestinians from Haifa and Jaffa can go back home. I estimate 60 or 70 years before victory."

Zuhad, a veiled 20-year-old Moslem fundamentalist who is majoring in linguistics, said: "I want an independent state in all of Palestine by armed struggle. Why not all tomorrow? They took it with armed struggle, so we'll get it back with armed struggle."

As for the future of the Israelis, Serene said: "Don't worry—we are not going to throw the Jews into the sea. It is just that Jews are a religion, not a nationality. All those Jews who were here before 1917 can stay. Those who came later will have to return to the countries they came from."

But what if they cannot?

"I think they can," she said.

The Israeli authorities are not unaware of the hard-line views of many educated Palestinian youths. They tend, however, to view the hard-liners as a minority elite that has intimidated, or out-talked, a majority who only want to be left in peace and accommodate with the status quo.

"Maybe we are talking about 12,000 students who are now intensely pro-P.L.O.," said a top Israeli Army officer in the West Bank administration. "We assume that whatever solution will be achieved here, this group will be out in the streets opposing it."

ARAFAT IS STILL A HERO

Moreover, the officer said, when these youths grow up and have to get jobs they will moderate their views, both because they have matured and because Jordan and Israel together control most of the employment opportunities in the area.

But others say this could lead to more frustration rather than more stability.

It is hard to sit with young people anywhere in the West Bank today and not find them expressing support for Yasir Arafat, the P.L.O. chairman.

This may seem incomprehensible, in that Mr. Arafat has only losses to show. But it seems that the more he loses, the more the young Palestinians identify with him as someone who, like themselves, is caught in a vise between Israel and the Arabs.

"Arafat is like the stones we throw in demonstrations," Meral said. "When we stand against the Jews, all we have is this stone. He may be weak in what he can do, but he is the symbol of the Palestinians. He is the stone we throw against the world."

AN ISLAMIC REVIVAL IS QUICKLY GAINING GROUND IN AN UNLIKELY PLACE: ISRAEL

THURSDAY, APRIL 30, 1987

BY THOMAS L. FRIEDMAN

UMM AL-FAHIM, Israel—In this Israeli Arab village about an hour's drive north of downtown Tel Aviv, Israeli Moslem fundamentalists have just erected new bus stops with separate seating areas for men and women, in strict observance of Islamic piety.

Down the road a few miles, at Yunis's Restaurant, once a favorite Arabic dining spot and watering hole for Israeli Jews, Yunis recently stopped serving hard liquor and beer in deference to the surge in Islamic fundamentalism in the nearby Israeli Arab villages.

But perhaps it is the new style of soccer games that really leaves the visitor feeling at times that he is in Saudi Arabia, not Israel. Last September, a group of observant Israeli Arab Moslems withdrew from the Jewish-run league and formed their own 38-team soccer league, representing Arab villages from across Israel.

Their games look like any other, except that it is not only the referee's whistle that brings play to a halt. When the muezzin's wail carries across the field from a nearby mosque, both teams stop, line up, face Mecca to the southeast and kneel in prayer, with their white tennis shoes forming a neat, if incongruous, row behind them. When prayers are over, play resumes.

STIRRING IN THE LAND, HOME-GROWN FERVOR

The Islamic revolution has come to Israel.

From Israeli Arab villages in the northern Galilee, to the turbulent Palestinian universities in the Israeli-occupied West Bank, to the teeming refugee districts of the Israeli-occupied Gaza Strip, an Islamic revival is taking place among Moslems living under Israeli control.

The revival was inspired in part by the Iranian revolution led by Ayatollah Ruhollah Khomeini. But it is also a home-grown movement of Palestinian Moslems seeking strength to confront Israel by returning to their classic Islamic identities that once brought them grandeur.

The Islamic movement is bringing some Israeli Arabs and some West Bank and Gaza Palestinians much closer through the common bond of a resurgent faith. At the same time, Moslem associations are attracting many adherents among Palestinian youths, and they are becoming a major challenge to the secular Palestine Liberation Organization, led by Yasir Arafat.

Most important, the Islamic revival in Israel, coupled with the religious-nationalist upsurge among some Israeli Jews since the 1967 war, is beginning to transform the nature of the Arab-Israeli conflict. The Israeli claims to a "Greater Israel" are now increasingly met by Moslem demands for an "Islamic Palestine."

What this means for the already intractable Arab-Israeli conflict, said Eli Rekhess, a Tel Aviv University expert on Israeli Arabs, is that future "coexistence will be that much more difficult and the lines of differences between the two communities that much sharper."

GENESIS OF REVIVAL: THE '67 ISRAELI VICTORY

About 600,000 Palestinian Arabs live in Israel and 1.3 million in the occupied territories; 92 percent of them are Sunni Moslems, and 8 percent are Christians. There are virtually no Shiite Moslems, who predominate in Iran.

Although the Islamic revival is still a minority phenomenon among these Palestinian Moslems, it touches very deep chords in the wider secular Moslem population, and its leaders have the credibility and potential power to exercise disproportionate influence over Palestinian politics.

Most Israeli Jews have no idea that in the quaint and seemingly sleepy hilltop Arab villages of the Galilee, which they drive past every day on visits to kibbutzim, an Islamic fundamentalist movement has been building since 1967.

Before 1967, there was no advanced Islamic teaching center in Israel. But, paradoxically, through the victory of the Israeli Army in 1967, Israeli Arabs found themselves back in contact with the Moslem holy places in Jerusalem and the centers of Islamic learning in Hebron, Jerusalem, Nablus and Gaza.

Seated in the spartan office of the Islamic Association of Umm al-Fahim, an Israeli Arab village in the lower Galilee at the center of the Islamic revival, Sheik Hashem Abdel Rahman Mahajani, 27 years old, explained its origins. On the wall was a map of Israel, marked "Islamic Palestine 1948," which did not show Jewish settlements.

"Before 1967, we were cut off from all Arab and Islamic culture—we almost became Jews," he said. "There was nowhere to study religion. When the West Bank was opened, we learned a lot about Islam. All our religious books came from the West Bank and Gaza, and many lecturers."

In mid-April, the senior Moslem cleric of Jerusalem, Sheik Saad e-Din al-Alami, the Mufti, who before 1967 could not contact Israeli Moslems, went to the Israeli town of Beersheba, unfolded woven prayer rugs outside the municipal museum and led some 20 Israeli Arabs and Bedouins in prayer. The Beersheba museum was, until 1948, a Turkish-built mosque, and the local Moslems have enlisted Sheik Alami to help them get it back.

Sheik Mahajani said he himself grew up in a traditional but not overly religious household. When he graduated from high school a decade ago, one of his teachers suggested he go to Hebron Islamic College in the West Bank. There, he earned a bachelor's degree in Islamic religious studies, then returned to his village in Israel to teach others.

He said another important external fillip for the Israeli Moslem revival had come, unexpectedly, from the peace treaty with Egypt, which opened Israeli Arabs to influences from Islamic centers in Cairo.

"Today," Sheik Mahajani said, "I know all of the developments of the Islamic world by reading the Egyptian newspapers and magazines."

A NEW GENERATION TRIES A NEW PATH

The Islamic revival in Israel turned from a cultural to a political phenomenon with the Iranian Islamic revolution of 1979 and the coming of age of a new post-1967 generation of Israeli Arabs, who sought to express their awakening Palestinian Arab identities and distinguish themselves from Israeli Jews and the Westernized culture epitomized by Tel Aviv.

"Within Israel, the Islamic revival is not a movement of the up-rooted," said a Hebrew University expert on Islam, Emanuel Sivan. "Rather, it is middle-class people and their children reaffirming their identity as Moslems, above all else, and aspiring to liberate Palestine as a Moslem land."

This potent mix of cultural, religious and nationalist elements was clearly behind the first serious Islamic revolutionary movement in Israel, known as Usrat al-Jihad, or the Family of Holy War, led by a dynamic young sheik named Abdullah Nimr Darwish from the Israeli Arab village of Kfar Qasem, near Tel Aviv.

Organized in the late 1970's, Usrat al-Jihad reportedly advocated sabotage and violence against Israeli and secular targets. It was uncovered by the police before it had done much damage, and in 1981 Sheik Darwish and 56 followers were imprisoned.

Upon his release in 1984, he and his followers in the Arab villages of Israel organized themselves into a loosely connected Islamic Association to work for peaceful change in Islamic society in Israel.

Sheik Darwish was recently interviewed in his office in Kfar Qasem, where the Israeli authorities have him temporarily under town arrest.

"After I got out of prison, I tried to find a new way," he said, trying to explain how he now justifies working peacefully to advance Islam in a nation under Jewish control. "I found the answer in Islamic history in the story about the Moslems who lived a Moslem way of life in Ethiopia under the Christian emperor. The Prophet Mohammed approved their conduct. We consider ourselves like them."

The sheik repeated over and over again, as if for hidden ears, that his organization works "only through education, culture and social reform to give every Moslem here back his identity."

NONVIOLENT APPROACH: MOSQUES SPRING UP

Motivated in part by Sheik Darwish, and in part by other dynamic local village preachers, the Islamic revival in Israel has adopted this nonviolent approach.

The fruits of their labor can be seen in the Arab villages of northern Israel where spanking new white-stone mosques are sprouting across the horizon. In Umm al-Fahim, a village of about 5,000 people, seven mosques have been built in the last 10 years, after decades in which there were only four.

Moslem fundamentalists have also won control or influence in the local councils of several Israeli Arab villages, such as Fureidis, Kfar Bara and Kfar Qasem, in local parties with names like Al Huda (Guidance) or Islah (Islamic Reform).

The Islamic Association in Umm al-Fahim, as in other villages, has organized Moslem youths into work brigades, which build roads, mosques, clinics and Islamic-style bus stops.

In Kfar Qasem recently, Sheik Darwish organized the building of a three-story kindergarten in three days. Villagers worked in shifts around the clock in a festival-like atmosphere, while a microphone blared out from the top of a mosque the donations of various families. These included truckloads of sand, $50, a gold ring and even one shekel (65 cents) from a young boy who donated his "ice cream money."

In many Israeli Arab Moslem villages, the Parent-Teacher Associations have been taken over by orthodox Moslems, who have arranged for the schools to give greater emphasis to Islamic history, and even to run competitions for knowledge of the Koran, Sheik Hashem said.

Today, about 25 percent of each girl's high school class in Umm al-Fahim and nearby villages wear head coverings and conservative dress, "and there is a steady increase every year, praise be to Allah," Sheik Mahajani said. A decade ago, there were virtually none.

NO PICTURES OF ARAFAT, NO USE FOR KHOMEINI

Although they insist they are apolitical and only religiously and culturally oriented, the literature of the Israeli Moslem revivalists says otherwise. Their main journal, Al Serat, edited by Sheik Darwish, has a heavy dose of Palestinian nationalist slogans and stories about sheiks who were "martyred" for Palestine. Nowhere does Mr. Arafat's picture appear.

Ayatollah Khomeini, who was initially looked upon as a role model, now appears to be totally discredited in the eyes of Israeli Moslems—

not because he is a Shiite and they are Sunnis, but because of the way they view the Iranian revolution as having devoured its own children and divided the Islamic world.

"In the beginning, when Khomeini first appeared, we saw him as a rising sun in the sky," Sheik Darwish said. "But today, he is not a sun, not even a moon. He is just a darkness."

In the Gaza Strip, the Islamic revival has also been building strength since 1967. The number of mosques has grown in 20 years from 75 to 150. Many religious young men in the Gaza Strip now play soccer in long pants and swim on the segregated beaches in conservative knee-length shorts. And there has been a return to such traditional practices as the use of the suwak, a small wooden peg with a serrated edge made from a palm branch that the Prophet Mohammed was said to use to brush his teeth.

On several occasions recently, Islamic militants in Gaza have tossed nitric acid on secular women who were thought to be exposing too much skin. When The Jerusalem Post asked an observant student at Gaza Islamic University whether her long dark robe and head covering were not terribly hot, she said, "It's hotter in hell."

It was in trying to explain the Arab world's defeat in the 1967 war, said Mohammed Siam, the president of Gaza Islamic University, that many Gaza Palestinians, like many Egyptians, turned back to religion, interpreting the 1967 loss as a result of deviations from Islam.

Dressed in a traditional red-checked Arab headdress and twirling a strand of red worry beads around his thumb, Mr. Siam said: "The 1967 defeat pushed people to ask themselves: 'Why were we conquered? We are many and the Jews are few.' One answer was that we were empty—no faith in the heart. To be strong is to have courage. The Arabs did not have enough faith to stand on their feet."

WHAT COMES FIRST: BULLETS OR BELIEF?

Opened in 1978 with the help of Al Azhar Islamic University in Cairo, the Gaza Islamic University now has 5,000 students, including six Israeli Arabs, learning religious and secular subjects with every lecture repeated twice—once for women in their separate classrooms and once for the men. It is the only institution of higher education in Gaza.

For years the Israeli authorities were believed to be giving the Moslem Palestinian organizations in Gaza a wide berth to organize, hoping that this would promote fighting among Palestinians and help the Israelis gain strength at the expense of the Palestine Liberation Organization under Mr. Arafat.

An angry pro-P.L.O. Palestinian educator from Gaza said: "For the fundamentalist, the Land of Palestine is not an end in itself. We say first the home, then the religion. They say first religion and then the home."

The fundamentalists, with ample money from Saudi Arabia and other Persian Gulf countries, are now almost as strong a political force in Gaza as the P.L.O., regularly prompting street fights and campus brawls between the two groups. Israel may soon regret having shown them any leniency.

"First you have to build belief," a Gaza University professor said. "Once that is strong enough, the gun can be carried and no power on earth can stop you. Empty people will always turn their backs to the gun. Full people will face it with their chests because they know that if they die, they go to paradise and if they live they will have victory —but either way they win."

But what would Palestine look like the morning after such a victory? Neya, a 20-year-old Gaza Islamic University student council leader, explained, beginning his remarks with the Koranic introduction, "In the name of God the Merciful and the Compassionate."

"In Islamic history there is a grandeur," he said. "Palestine will be like the other Islamic states in history. And because it will be run by the teachings of Islam, it will have room for every faith, Jews or Christians. Islam is known for its tolerance."

Some more secular residents of the Gaza Strip find this revival oppressive. A Palestinian educator from Khan Yunis said: "Two years ago I had a wedding in my home for my eldest son. We had a traditional Palestinian band from the West Bank and served alcohol. I needed to call 21 of my cousins to come and stand outside the apartment to protect the wedding party from the sheiks who wanted to come and break it up."

WHERE IT ALL BEGAN: STUDENTS AND THE POOR

No one has any doubts about when the Islamic revival began in the West Bank among students, young villagers and poor refugees.

In the 1978 student elections at Bir Zeit University in the West Bank, the Islamic fundamentalist bloc won about 3 percent of the votes, with P.L.O. groups taking virtually all the rest. In the 1979 student elections, soon after Ayatollah Khomeini's revolution in Iran, the Islamic bloc won 43 percent of the votes.

"Students looked at the Iranian revolution and said, 'Wow, Islam works,'" a Bir Zeit professor said. They asked themselves why, if Iranian Moslems armed only with faith could overthrow the American-supported Shah, they could not prevail over Israel.

At a recent rally by the Islamic student bloc at Bir Zeit, 400 students gathered in the parking lot to chant in unison verses from the Koran. The rally ended with everyone shouting, "I am a Moslem! An Arab! A Palestinian!"

A secular student observing the scene remarked, "It is kind of scary."

The Bir Zeit professor, a graduate of an Ivy League college, said: "If I were younger, I would go fundamentalist. When I was growing up, Nasser was the symbol of hope for ordinary people. But the 1967 war broke him. Then the P.L.O. came along, and it captured the imagination of the youth. But the Lebanon war broke it, at least for some."

"So now young people have turned to something that the Israelis can never break," he continued. "Islam cannot be broken. The Israelis can uproot my trees or burn my house, but they can't take Islam away from me. I am right. They are wrong. God is on our side."

A young black-bearded Islamic student leader, when asked by an Israeli about the future of the Jewish presence in this land, said: "You will not be here. We will fight until you leave the land which you defiled. Then we will cleanse the Temple Mount with rose water, just as we did after the Crusades."

One of the most senior Israeli officers in the West Bank was talking recently about how the chant "God is great!" now increasingly competes in Palestinian demonstrations with P.L.O. slogans and what this renewed devotion to the religion of the Prophet Mohammed portends.

"When I go into Palestinian homes," the Israeli officer said, "I always look to see what they have on the walls. Often it is a picture of Yasir Arafat and then some Islamic sayings. So I ask myself, what happens when Arafat goes? Who replaces him? I don't think it is going to be one of his deputies. Arafat is a symbol. I am afraid it is going to be Mohammed, and you can't bring Mohammed to a Geneva peace conference."

There was a striking incident in the West Bank recently that may have been just an accident, or may have been a glimpse of the future.

Late at night, a young Palestinian was coming toward the Jewish settlement of Qiryat Arba, outside the West Bank town of Hebron. The Palestinian was carrying a small dark object in his hand. The guard thought the youth was carrying a grenade, and when he failed to heed a warning to halt, the guard shot and wounded him.

As the guard carefully approached the wounded youth, he discovered what was in his hand.

It was a Koran.

ARIEL JOURNAL
ONE WEST BANK PLAN:
MIX CONCRETE AND YUPPIES

TUESDAY, JUNE 2, 1987

BY THOMAS L. FRIEDMAN

ARIEL, Israeli-Occupied West Bank—Ron Nachman's critics call him a one-man obstacle to peace. His neighbors just call him Mayor, friend and "hey, you." He calls himself a simple pioneer for the Likud bloc, Israel's large nationalist party.

Mr. Nachman is the Mayor of one of the fastest-growing Israeli towns in the West Bank. With all the discussion these days about an international peace conference on the Middle East, and Israel's possibly ceding part of the West Bank to Jordan, Mr. Nachman recently invited an American for a tour and what he called "a dose of reality."

Whatever foreigners may think of Mr. Nachman's version of reality, it is widely shared among the 65,000 Jews in the West Bank, and it will be widely aired in Israel if an international conference is ever held.

The Mayor began his tour by rolling out huge color aerial photographs of Ariel, in the heart of the West Bank about an hour's drive north of Jerusalem. Brimming with enthusiasm, his voice constantly had to compete with the din of jackhammers and earth-moving equipment outside his door.

"Do you have any idea how big Ariel is?" asked Mr. Nachman, one of the founders of the nine-year-old town. "It is 12 kilometers wide," or about seven and a half miles. "That is almost the same width of the state of Israel at its narrowest point before the 1967 war. Did anyone ever tell you that?"

PLAN FOR 100,000 PEOPLE

Actually, that 7.5-mile span refers to the total area zoned for Ariel's projected 100,000 residents. Only the core of it is settled now, with 6,000 Jewish residents, 3,000 of them under 18.

On the eastern boundary, though, a high-tech industrial park is rising, and on the western edge an industrial zone employing several thousand people is already in operation. For now, most of Ariel's residents work in Tel Aviv.

"Everyone is speaking about an international conference and territorial solutions but they don't know the reality," Mr. Nachman said in a voice laced with contempt. "Abba Eban? He's never been here. Shimon Peres? I think he was here three years ago. Yitzhak Rabin? I don't know when he was here last."

"They have no feel for what is happening here," he said, hopping into his car for a tour. "Action, action, action, all the time. Peres can speak and speak and speak, but we do."

The first stop was the shopping center—about 20 businesses ranging from high fashion to hamburgers. Down the road was a tastefully designed swimming club, where the bright grass and the blue Olympic-size pool contrasted sharply with the sand-colored houses and rocky hills in the background.

'WE'RE A TOWN AND I'M A MAYOR'

"In the Western media they are always calling us 'settlements,' " complained Mr. Nachman, a 44-year-old industrial engineer and fourth-generation Israeli. "We're not a settlement. That has a negative stigma. Sounds like a bunch of fanatics. We're a town and I'm a Mayor. We're normal. We're Yuppies. We have four schools and nine day-care centers. You call that a settlement?"

"We are a liberal, non-fanatical, pluralistic community—90 percent secular and 10 percent religious, 60 percent Sephardim, 40 percent Ashkenazim," he added. "We are just a cross-section of average Israel, a real melting pot."

Part of the high-tech park is already leased to Israeli software and computer research and development companies, who will get tax breaks from the Government for setting up shop here. Along the boundary of the park, Mr. Nachman pointed out rows of neatly planted young olive trees growing in steel barrels.

"If land is cultivated, then it is private property and not state land and it cannot be expropriated," he said. "If we try to move left or right, they block us with olive trees."

Mr. Nachman swung his car down a narrow asphalt road to the Arab village of Salfit, Ariel's sister city, so to speak. Young women and a few old men milled about in the quiet streets, amid the old stone houses built along the contours of terraced slopes—in stark contrast with Ariel, which is built on a bulldozer-flattened hilltop.

A WAVE FROM THE BARBER

"It is empty here during the day—all the men are working in Tel Aviv," Mr. Nachman said.

At one point he brought his car to a halt in front of the village barber shop, tooting his horn twice. The barber lifted his razor from a man's lathered chin and gave a friendly wave.

"This is my barber," Mr. Nachman said. "I'm not afraid to risk my neck putting it under his razor.

"We don't have problems with the Arabs; we have problems with the Jews. Some Israeli leftists call us an 'obstacle to peace.' They don't understand that the more Ariel grows the sooner peace will come, because the sooner the Arabs will realize that they better move fast and settle with us before they lose their chance."

The tour swung west to the industrial park, where large factories, including one from the Government-owned Israel Military Industries, are already up and others are being put together in prefabricated pieces.

Admiring the cranes lifting a prefabricated slab into place, he said: "Look at that roof. It wasn't there yesterday. Working. Working. Another 30 more factories coming. All private enterprise. Who said there is no pioneering in Israel today?"

As he headed back to his office, the tour over, a cement-mixer truck almost squeezed his car off the road. Mr. Nachman barely flinched.

"I love those big trucks," he said. "I love that concrete."

FIGHT BUILDS OVER THE SHAPE OF RELIGIOUS FUTURE IN ISRAEL

MONDAY, JUNE 29, 1987

BY THOMAS L. FRIEDMAN

BNEI BRAK, Israel—Until six months ago, Shimon Tsimhe had the hottest newsstand business in Bnei Brak—before the bombing. Now he ekes out a living selling falafel sandwiches.

"I used to sell lots of newspapers—lots," Mr. Tsimhe said nervously, looking over his shoulder. "But there were threats."

"They told me it would be better if I didn't sell newspapers," he added. "They said it would be better if I sold falafels."

CENTER OF 'ULTRA-ORTHODOX'

Down the street in this Tel Aviv suburb, a center for the deeply religious Jews generally referred to here as the "ultra-Orthodox," Leah and David Green's newspaper kiosk also did a brisk business selling daily Israeli newspapers—before the bombing.

They still sell secular papers, but quietly, through the back door, with the stealth that a small-town American drugstore might use to sell Playboy or Penthouse.

Mr. Tsimhe and the Greens, who are all Zionist religious Jews, had their shops damaged by a group of deeply Orthodox Jews who reject the modern state of Israel, from its army to its newspapers. They have either bombed or intimidated virtually every news seller in Bnei Brak into removing all daily Israeli papers from their shelves.

A RELIGIOUS POWER STRUGGLE

The Bnei Brak newspaper war is symptomatic of a national religious power struggle under way in Israel. At stake is who will determine the Jewish religious character of Israel.

Will it be the non-Zionist ultra-Orthodox, who do not see in the reborn state an event of major religious significance and who believe instead that a Jewish state will be worth celebrating only after the

Messiah comes and the rule of Jewish law is total? They make up about 5 percent of the population.

Or will it be those Zionist Orthodox Jews who see in Israel's creation an important religious event and believe that Judaism, when reinterpreted for the 20th century, can flourish in a modern state? These Jews make up about 15 percent of the population.

If recent trends are any indication, religious and political power among Israel's strictly observant Jews is gravitating to the non-Zionist minority, while the Zionists are increasingly on the defensive. If this trend continues, it will have a major effect on Israeli society and on Israel's relations with Jews overseas.

"American Jews, who have often been concerned about rising Christian or Moslem fundamentalism, must recognize that a serious Jewish fundamentalist revival is gaining strength in Israel as well," said Daniel J. Elazar, an expert on religious politics.

The nonreligious Israeli majority, represented largely by the Labor Party and the Likud bloc, is watching and waiting to make political deals with whatever religious parties emerge strongest and most able to deliver votes in exchange for concessions on religious issues.

Although there has been a strong ultra-Orthodox community in this land since before the Zionists immigrated, these people, who are known in Hebrew as Haredim or "those who are God-fearing," always lived secluded from the rest of the society. Until recently, they made little attempt to integrate or dominate.

But in the last few years, according to Menachem Friedman, a Hebrew University expert on Haredi society, "the Haredim have begun to feel confident enough to present themselves as a real alternative model to the 'evil' modern society of Israel."

The majority of Haredim in Israel, who include Hasidic sects related to those in the United States, do not engage in the violence that has taken place in Bnei Brak. Rather, their newfound active role is channeled through peaceful means.

'THE PAST IS OURS; THE FUTURE IS OURS'

One symbolic effort has been a recent attempt by Haredi yeshivas to "convert" Israeli fighter pilots, who are widely considered to be the elite of the Israeli military and society, into giving up their wings and taking up a life of Torah study. Nearly a dozen pilots are reported to have quit the air force under these conditions, and their pictures have quickly been put up on posters in religious neighborhoods as signs of success.

"Slowly, slowly I see every day more and more people in the land of Israel having the knowledge of God," said Rabbi Menachem Porush, a 72-year-old leader of the Haredi party Agudat Israel.

"When I look at my great-grandchild, I say to myself: In 20 years he will live in a real holy land, with a real holy people. It will be a different parliament from the one we have today. Remember, the past is ours; the future is ours. We just have to bridge the present."

What distinguishes the Haredim from other Israeli Jews is not only their dark black coats, long sideburns and black fur hats, which they wear just as their ancestors did in 17th-century Eastern Europe, but also their conviction that the Zionist revolution has not constituted any important change in Jewish life. That life, they feel, is ideally practiced today in its Orthodox form just as it was 100 or 1,000 years ago.

They do not celebrate Israel's Independence Day. For them, independence day is, as it always was, Passover, which marks the Jewish liberation from Egypt 3,000 years ago.

The Haredim believe that it was loyalty to the Torah and its religious code for living, not nationalism, that kept the Jews alive through the ages and gave meaning to Jewish communal life. They see Zionism, with its avowed aim of making the Jews "a nation like all other nations," as destroying the singular religious identity of the Jewish people.

The Haredim seek to justify not serving in the Israeli Army, while enjoying the security that it provides from hostile Arab neighbors, by arguing that they too are protecting the country by keeping the "authentic" Jewish heritage and spirituality alive.

ROOTS THAT PREDATE THE ISRAELI STATE

While nonreligious Israelis may feel their ways of life threatened by Haredi demands to close movie houses, remove pictures of bikini-clad women from bus-stop advertisements or ban soccer games on Saturdays, the Haredim see things differently.

Many have family roots in Israel that date long before the first Zionists arrived, when the only Jews who lived here were religious. In their view it is their way of life that has been besieged by modern Israeli society, said Rabbi Porush. His family has lived in Israel for eight generations.

When Israel was founded 39 years ago, the secular Zionist majority was ready to accept the Haredi groups because they reminded them of their grandfathers and because the Zionists felt certain that these people, speaking Yiddish and dressed in Eastern European attire, would wither away in a generation.

According to the Jerusalem Institute for Public Affairs, the average number of children in Haredi families is 8, compared with 3.5 for religious Zionists and 2.2 for secular Zionists. The majority of new immigrants today are deeply Orthodox Jews from North America and Western Europe, while Western liberal Jewish immigrants are a mere trickle.

"I just read that 250,000 Israelis are living in the United States," Rabbi Porush said. "I can tell you that none of those leaving are religious Jews. The Zionists say Israel should be a nation like all others. So if things don't work out here, they just go elsewhere. Our people are coming here and staying here because this is a holy land, and only here can you fulfill certain commandments of the Torah."

In the 1977 elections, the Zionist National Religious Party won 12 seats in Parliament; today it has four and in the next election could hold even fewer. The ultra-Orthodox party Shas, which did not exist in 1977, has four seats today, and Agudat Israel has two.

GAINING GROUND AS RELIGIOUS LEADERS

The Haredi communities have been gaining strength not only through numbers, but also through religious leadership.

What they have done is to establish their own rabbinical courts and religious authorities, believing them more observant and knowledge-able about religious affairs than the state-appointed Chief Rabbis or Zionist religious parties.

In their view, the notion of a chief rabbinate appointed and paid by a secular state is repugnant to the traditional Jewish notion of the rabbi whose authority grows from his own piety and knowledge.

For example, the Chief Rabbi's office is responsible for deciding what food is kosher, but the Haredim will eat food only if their own rabbis have stamped it "strictly kosher." The Israeli press recently reported about a salt factory that has five rabbis at the end of its production line, some from the Chief Rabbi's office and some from the Haredi community.

The Haredi rabbis have told the management of some luxury hotels that they will hold bar mitzvah and wedding celebrations there only if the hotels hire Haredi rabbis to supervise their kosher kitchens. The hotels have generally agreed, because by hiring such a rabbi they can open up a new, growing market and not lose the other more moderate religious markets, whose members also recognize Haredi kosher supervision.

Once a hotel is signed up, the Haredi rabbis go to their suppliers and explain to the butchers and bakers that if they want to continue selling to the hotels, they will have to adopt Haredi kashrut supervision. This process goes on down the line of suppliers.

'WE HAVE ONE FLAG: THE TORAH'

The Haredim have also used their influence to affect how Israelis study their traditions and educate their children.

As a result of the Haredim's devotion to Jewish learning and the building of new yeshivas, they and their rabbis, not the religious Zionists, now set the standards for what it means to be a "talmid hacham," or learned Jewish scholar.

The religious Zionists have "lost their way," Rabbi Porush said. "They carried two flags, one of nationalism and another of Torah. They were always torn between the two. We have one flag: the Torah. That is why the power is in our hands now."

The Israeli Government runs a network of Zionist religious schools, which educate about 30 percent of the country's youth, conduct prayers in the classroom and teach religious and secular subjects.

But in recent years these high schools have found themselves short of religious Zionist faculty and have sought help from the growing number of learned Haredim to teach their children religious subjects. As a result, the state religious schools today have many faculty members who do not believe in the state of Israel or the possibility of integrating Jewish tradition with modernity.

"In the old days, the principals of the state religious schools looked to the Zionist National Religious Party for spiritual guidance," said Eliezer Shmueli, former director general of the Ministry of Education. "Now many of them look to the Haredi rabbis."

"For a long time we watched this happening very passively," said Yehuda Ben-Meir, a leader of the religious Zionist camp. "We tolerated it because we may have had a hidden inferiority complex that the Haredim really were more religious than us. When they were proselytizing secular Jews, we thought it was fine, but when they started taking our own children and questioning the religious legitimacy of our own yeshivas, it was too much. We have started to fight back."

ONE ISSUE ONLY: A RELIGIOUS AGENDA

Because the Haredim now dominate the religious bloc and because the religious bloc in Parliament holds the balance between Labor and Likud, it is the Haredim whom the secular politicians are increasingly seeking to placate.

"The Haredi politicians know how to play the political game very well," Mr. Elazar said. "They know how to work the halls, build alliances and to use the system to their advantage. While they take an interest in secular issues, they mainly focus on their own religious bread and butter."

Unlike the Zionist National Religious Party, which was ready to compromise with the secular majority on some issues of synagogue and state, the Haredim used their power in Parliament for one purpose only—to get the Israeli democratic state to accept their religious agenda.

"The Haredim live in ghettos," Mr. Ben-Meir of the National Religious Party said. "They don't come in contact with the secular population and they don't care about them. All they care about is keeping their own people happy, and the more extreme they are, the happier they are.

"The religious Zionists like us come in contact with the rest of the public—at the university, at work and in the army. So while we never compromise on basic religious values, we are ready to make political compromises in order to live together."

A BITTER FIGHT OVER FARMING'S SABBATH

This was illustrated during the recent debate over the issue of shmitta, or the sabbatical year.

The Torah enjoins that every seventh year Jewish farmers in Israel let their land lie fallow as a sabbath. When the Zionists returned to Israel in the 20th century, however, observance of the sabbatical was not economically feasible. So the religious Zionists, led by Rabbi Abraham Kook, ruled that a Jewish farmer could "sell" his land for the year to an Arab, with a fictional contract, and his land would then not be Jewish-owned. That would allow him to eat of its harvest.

But this year when the Chief Rabbis, following on Rabbi Kook, advised Israelis to "sell" their land to the Arabs, the Haredim denounced this as a religious fraud. They insisted that the state instead sell the entire crop of Israeli-grown wheat abroad and import American-grown wheat in its place.

The Minister of Industry, Ariel Sharon of Likud, bowed to the increasing electoral power of the Haredim and agreed to try to work out a solution along the lines they stipulated, thereby enraging religious Zionists.

During the Cabinet debate on the subject, the Minister of Religion, Zevulun Hammer of the National Religious Party, was quoted as saying, "The Haredim deserve support, but there is no justification for all the arrangements regarding shmitta to be carried out in opposition to the Chief Rabbis."

Mr. Sharon reportedly said, "I respect religion and the rabbis."

This prompted Minister of Absorption Yaacov Tzur, a member of the Labor Party, to retort about the Haredim: "I also respect them, but there are other questions. This is a group of people for whom our national anthem, the flag, Independence Day and serving in the Israel Army mean nothing. It is not a problem of shmitta, or wheat, but of blackmail."

BARGAINING FOR CONTROL ON DEFINING A JEW

In a few weeks Parliament is again scheduled to debate the issue of who is considered a Jew. The Haredi parties want Parliament to reactivate a pre-1948 law governing changes in religious status that would empower the rabbinate to determine the religious status of any convert to Judaism who immigrates to Israel.

Since the Haredi parties do not recognize American-style Reform or Conservative Judaism, anyone converted by a Reform or Conservative rabbi would not be considered Jewish or eligible for automatic Israeli citizenship.

In a deal struck in May between Shas and the Likud bloc, Likud, which is led by Prime Minister Yitzhak Shamir, agreed in principle to back such an amendment.

"If this bill passes, it will mean that a person who was converted by a Reform or Conservative rabbi, who may have been living as a good Jew all his life, will be considered a non-Jew the minute he fulfills the Zionist dream and comes to Israel," said Rabbi Richard Hirsch, representative of the Reform movement in Israel.

The Likud accepted such a bill as part of a deal in which Shas agreed not to throw its support behind efforts by Foreign Minister Shimon Peres, leader of the Labor Party, to call an international peace conference on the Middle East. Had Mr. Peres offered Shas the same deal on the Jewish identity issue that Likud did, Shas would have supported an international conference.

"The only interest Labor and Likud have in religion is which rabbi can deliver to them the most votes to stay in power," said David Hartman, the modern Orthodox Israeli philosopher.

"But once these ultra-Orthodox have finished off the religious Zionists, they are going to take on the non-religious Zionists—that is, Labor and Likud—and make this state an uninhabitable place," he added.

"Unless the modern Zionists wake up and assume responsibility for articulating a view of Judaism that can live with the modern world, they will be digging their own grave," Mr. Hartman said. "They will be left with a Judaism that repudiates modernity and will, in the end, undermine the whole Zionist structure that has been built here."

A FORECAST FOR ISRAEL: MORE ARABS THAN JEWS

MONDAY, OCTOBER 19, 1987

BY THOMAS L. FRIEDMAN

GAZA, Oct. 12—Forty-two-year-old Suad al-Hadidi is a symbol of what Yasir Arafat calls the Palestinian "demographic bomb."

Sitting up in her bed in the maternity ward of the Remal Health Center in Gaza, Mrs. Hadidi proudly folded back some thin white sheets to show off her 10th child, a handsome girl named Ayat, who was born the night before.

Ten children is nothing unusual for Palestinians in the occupied Gaza Strip, said Dr. Zuhni Yusef al-Zahidi, head of maternal health care at the clinic. He said he knows several mothers who have up to 15 pregnancies and one man whose three wives bore a total of 25 children.

PRESSURE ON THE ISRAELIS

"Many people here say, 'We must have more babies to compensate for our losses in Lebanon and to put pressure on the Jews to come to the negotiating table,' " Dr. Zahidi said in Arabic, as Mrs. Hadidi and other women in the maternity ward nodded approval.

Because of families the size of Mrs. Hadidi's, in 12 years Israel and the occupied territories will be, in demographic terms, a binational state. In 1985, for the first time, the total number of Arab children under the age of 4 in Israel, the West Bank and Gaza Strip was greater than the total number of Jewish children under 4—370,000 Arabs to 365,000 Jews.

The problems that the rise in Arab population pose for Israeli Jews is rapidly becoming the central issue in the political debate here about the future of the occupied territories and the character of the nation in the 21st century.

"We are heading for a binational state, not a Jewish state—no question about it," said Prof. Arnon Sofer, a leading expert on the demographic question and dean of the Faculty of Social Sciences at Haifa University.

Unless Israel withdraws soon from the West Bank and Gaza Strip, he said, Israelis will eventually be faced with the "calamity" of an Arab majority.

In such a situation, Israeli Jews will either have to extend voting rights to the Arabs in the occupied territories and risk their taking over the state, or systematically deprive them of their rights and turn Israel into a South Africa-like nation.

But not everyone here believes the future is so bleak.

"Everything we have accomplished here was against the statistics, so why should things change now?" asked Geula Cohen, leader of the rightist nationalist Tehiya party, which favors annexation of the entire biblical "Land of Israel"—that is, pre-1967 Israel, the West Bank, Gaza and all of their inhabitants.

"If we would have paid attention to demographic forecasts in 1948 we never would have declared a state," Mrs. Cohen said. "Just because you get a headache, doesn't mean you should go out and chop off your head. I don't deny that there is a problem, but we can live with it."

The most recent Central Bureau of Statistics figures, in 1985 recorded 3.52 million Jews living in Israel and the occupied territories, or 62.8 percent of the population. There were 749,000 Israeli Arabs, 813,000 West Bank Arabs and 526,000 Gaza Arabs for a total of 2.08 million Arabs, or 37.2 percent of the population.

That picture is rapidly changing. According to bureau figures, in 1985 Israeli Jews had an average birth rate of 21.6 per 1,000 people, while Israeli Arabs had a birth rate of 34.9, Arabs of the West Bank 41.0 and Arabs of the Gaza Strip 46.6—more than double that of Israeli Jews.

Given these rates of growth, the bureau has prepared various low and high demographic forecasts for the 21st century. The low population forecasts assume decreasing rates of natural growth—that is, births over deaths—in each group and high rates of emigration. The high forecasts assume the opposite.

Professor Sofer has averaged all of the high and low forecasts and adjusted them for the year 2000. A bureau official verified his figures.

THE NUMBERS ARE CLEAR: 4 OUT OF 10 WILL BE ARAB

In the low average forecasts, in 12 years Israeli Jews will number 4.2 million, or 58 percent of the population, and Arabs in Israel, the West Bank and Gaza 3.1 million, or 42 percent.

In the high average forecasts, Israeli Jews will number 4.3 million, or 54 percent, and the Arabs 3.7 million, or 46 percent.

In either forecast, Arabs will soon be almost half the population.

The bureau, which has been doing long-range population forecasts since the early 1950's, has consistently been highly accurate.

When the changing settlement patterns of these growing Arab and Jewish populations is used as a factor, another picture emerges.

In the Golan Heights, the Jews are still a minority, 38 percent to 62 percent. In the Galilee region of northern Israel, Arabs make up 52 percent of the population and Jews 48 percent. The Negev holds what Professor Sofer called "a kingdom of the Bedouin"—a large Arab Bedouin majority, except in the major towns.

In the West Bank, Arabs outnumber Jews 813,000 to 60,000, and in the Gaza Strip, 526,000 to 2,000. There are clear Jewish majorities only in the large cities, like Tel Aviv, Haifa, Jerusalem, Tiberias, Hadera, Nahariya and Netanya, and their metropolitan areas.

But for how long? According to a study done by Haifa University, the number of Jews in Haifa increased by five-tenths of 1 percent between the censuses of 1972 and 1983, while the number of Arabs there increased by 40 percent during the same period.

This is largely because the young, better-educated generation of Hebrew-speaking Israeli Arabs are leaving their villages and moving to Jewish big city neighborhoods to find better jobs, although not without problems.

Last June, the apartments of six Arab workers, who had moved from their villages to the Jewish Tel Aviv suburbs of Ramat Amidar and Ganei Yehuda, were set afire by Jewish youths. The Israeli police described the attack as a pogrom.

"We don't want Arabs living in our neighborhood," a Ramat Amidar resident told The Jerusalem Post. "Let them live in their areas in the Galilee and West Bank, where they belong, but not here. This is a Jewish neighborhood. We won't stop until the last Arab gets out."

Professor Sofer sees a security issue. "If the present Arab population creates such problems," he said, "imagine what it is going to be like in 12 years when their numbers will have almost doubled. We will be busy with internal security all the day."

More and more Israelis are concerned about the increase in the Arab population. One 24-year-old Israeli college student said she has encountered increasing talk among her Jewish friends about the need to have at least five children to keep up with the Arabs.

"I spoke to an old friend of mine from the army who just had his fourth son," she said. "When I congratulated him, he said, 'Well, this is my contribution to the demographic war.' "

WAY TO A COMPROMISE: STRESS DEMOGRAPHICS

The issue is also beginning to have a profound effect on both Israeli and Palestinian politics.

For example, Foreign Minister Shimon Peres, of the Labor Party, has used a new strategy in recent public remarks about his Likud bloc rival, Prime Minister Yitzhak Shamir.

Labor officials say that because the status quo still seems tolerable for most Israelis, they believe that the only ways to induce Israelis to seriously consider a territorial compromise with the Arabs are either under the pressure of a war begun by the Arabs, or through the recognition by enough Israelis of the demographic dangers.

Since a war is neither desirable nor likely, Mr. Peres has begun to emphasize the demographics.

The Likud bloc has traditionally referred to itself as the "national party." But Mr. Peres has been telling Israelis lately that "the Likud is not the national party but rather the binational party." By insisting on holding onto the West Bank and Gaza Strip indefinitely, he argues, the Likud bloc, in effect, insists on turning Israel from a Jewish state into a binational state.

The right-of-center Likud bloc has countered by saying that the Labor Party and its allies are "defeatists," who have lost faith in Israel's ability to attract large numbers of Jewish immigrants.

THE IMMIGRATION DREAM AND CALL FOR EXPULSIONS

In a speech June 25, Prime Minister Shamir declared that "from its inception, our nation was 'the smallest of all nations,' and it always faced demographic problems."

"Yet never did our people resort to the solution of escapism," he added. "That is no solution."

"If we can now reinvigorate the economy in order to provide appropriate employment," he said, "we can aspire to a resurgence of immigration."

Until recently only Rabbi Meir Kahane, an extremist, dared call publicly for the expulsion of Arabs from Israel and the occupied territories. Their continued presence in Israel, he argued, threatened the nation's Jewish character.

But in the last two years, the Deputy Minister of Defense, Michael Dekel of the Likud bloc, and Rehavam Zeevi, a retired Major General who commanded Israel's central front, the most important in the country, have suggested a transfer of some or all of the Arabs in the occupied territories to neighboring Arab states. This, they say, may be the only way of avoiding what Mr. Dekel called "having this area turn into a powder keg."

Among West Bank Palestinians there is a growing school of thought, though still a minority, that believes the "demographic struggle"—not the "armed struggle"—is the best strategy for pressing Israel to grant the Palestinians a state in the occupied territories.

A leading proponent of "demographic struggle" is Hana Siniora, a Palestinian newspaper editor from Arab East Jerusalem, who announced last June that he was considering running for the Jerusalem City Council next year.

No Palestinian from the annexed half of Jerusalem has ever run in an Israeli election out of a concern that it somehow connote acceptance, or recognition, of the occupation of Jerusalem and the West Bank.

Mr. Siniora said, however, that since the Arabs of Jerusalem pay full taxes to Israel, they might as well be represented on the city council. Many Palestinians are quietly urging him to run.

"Just making more babies is not enough," said a Palestinian intellectual, Sari Nusseibeh. "No one in Israel will be concerned by that alone. We have to put Israel on the spot. The demographic bomb will never explode without a fuse. The fuse will be our demand for equal rights."

But even if the Palestinians in the occupied territories did one day demand equal rights, it is doubtful that Israel would accommodate them, since this would be political suicide.

More likely, said an Israeli Middle East expert, Meron Benvenisti, the Israelis will adopt the solution that the ruling Maronite Christians did in Lebanon after it was clear they were becoming a minority in their own country.

They simply stopped taking a census.

ISRAEL'S ARAB ARMY OF MIGRANT WORKERS

S U N D A Y ,   D E C E M B E R   6 ,   1 9 8 7

B Y   T H O M A S   L .   F R I E D M A N

TEL AVIV—Israeli writer Dahn Ben-Amotz was standing on his second-floor balcony recently, repairing cracks in his stone wall with plaster. As he worked away, an Israeli couple came walking down the street. The Israeli man looked up at Mr. Ben-Amotz and shouted at him in Hebrew, "Hey, Ahmed, what time is it?"

"It was immediately clear to me that they thought I was an Arab simply because I was holding the tools of a construction worker," recalled Mr. Ben-Amotz. "You just don't see Jews in that position here anymore."

Indeed, Arab workers from the Israeli-occupied West Bank and Gaza Strip today form the backbone of the manual labor force in Israel —so much so that Jewish Israelis who still do blue-collar manual labor often wear yarmulkas or Jewish stars around their necks, whether they are religious or not, so that no one will confuse them with Arabs.

It is a common mistake, since each morning roughly 45,000 Palestinian workers from the Gaza Strip, or about half of the work force there, and 55,000 from the West Bank, or one-third of the work force there, come to work in Israel, transported by long caravans of buses and cars. Still thousands more, mostly Arab women, work in the West Bank as seamstresses in Arab-owned sewing shops, which produce clothes for the leading Israeli fashion houses.

Although they account for only 7 percent of the Israeli work force, these Palestinian laborers from the occupied territories dominate whole sectors of the Israeli economy, namely construction and agricultural field work and low-level municipal services along with the occupations of waiters, cooks and cleaners.

Their employment can be traced to the 1967 war, when Israel took control of the West Bank from Jordan and Gaza from Egypt. Unemployment in these occupied territories, already high, soared because

Palestinian businesses and farmers were cut off from their traditional markets. At the same time, following the war, Israel experienced an unprecedented building boom and economic expansion.

The market forces gradually drew the Arab workers from the occupied territories into Israel, which had a somewhat higher wage structure. But rather than displacing the Israeli Jews or Arabs who held manual jobs before 1967, the Palestinians from the territories tended to push the Israelis up the labor ladder of a growing economy. These Israelis tended to become foremen, engineers or bureaucrats, and Israeli waiters became maitres d'hôtel.

This phenomenon of a modern, Westernized economy using low-cost nomadic labor is hardly exclusive to Israel. Turkish workers in West Germany and Switzerland, Mexican workers in Los Angeles, and Egyptian, Syrian and Palestinian workers in the Persian Gulf play similar, if not much larger, roles as a cheap source of labor.

But what gives the phenomenon its unusual character here is that the "guest workers" and their bosses are also political enemies. The Palestinian bricklayer by day may be a bomb thrower by night. An Israeli contractor may be hiring Arabs one day and, as a reserve soldier, arresting them the next.

This creates a relationship full of paradoxes. Some 800 West Bank and Gaza Palestinians who have worked in Israel for more than 10 years and have turned 65 years of age are now receiving old-age pensions from a Jewish state they do not recognize. A Palestinian-owned pasta factory in the West Bank Arab village of Beit Zahur, which produces noodles for Israeli retailers, has its products stamped "kosher" by rabbis from the nearby West Bank Jewish settlement of Tekoah—which was partly built by Palestinian labor. A West Bank Jewish settler magazine, Nekuda, carries advertisements on one page from Arabs looking for work and editorials on another page assailing Jewish settlers who employ Arab labor.

Summing up the relationship, Yuval Portugali, a Tel Aviv University geographer, observed, "Both communities need each other and both communities fear each other."

At about 5:30 A.M., just as the sun curls up over the mountains of Moab and erases the crescent moon, Arab workers begin their morning ritual in Jerusalem. Still bleary-eyed from having left their West Bank villages as early as 4 A.M., they line up on the sidewalk leading out from the Damascus Gate of the Old City, clutching their lunch bags in one hand and warming their lungs with cheap cigarettes in the other.

There they will stand for hours in front of the Ali Baba Hotel, forming a human labor market, waiting for Israeli builders and other employers to drive by and pluck up the lucky ones for a day's work.

An Israeli contractor cruises up in a green Volvo. His car draws a dozen Palestinian workers off the sidewalk, each elbowing the other for the chance to cram his head into the car's open front windows. The contractor is nervous. He does not like being surrounded.

"How much? How much?" the workers shout at the driver.

"Twenty-five shekels for the day," he says in Arabic, holding a walkie-talkie in one hand.

"What is the work?" the men ask.

"Asphalting," says the contractor.

For 25 shekels ($14.50) there are few takers. Most of these men have come by bus or taxi from Hebron, which cost them almost 10 shekels round-trip. After a day's work they would be left with about $9. Most of them shake their heads and drift away from the Volvo, except a few youths who hop in the back seat. The contractor speeds off.

A mini-van approaches, the driver slows, the workers swarm toward the vehicle but the driver suddenly speeds away. Someone spits at the van.

How do they decide who gets the work when it is offered?

"We just attack the car," explains Muhammed, a 40-year-old father of 10 from Yatta, a village near Hebron. "Whoever gets there first wins. It is like 50 dogs chasing a bone. I would work in Hebron for half the price, but there is no work there."

How does he get along with his Jewish bosses?

"Some of them are better than friends and others are worse than enemies," explains Muhammed, his black-checked Arab headdress drawn tightly around his head to fend off the morning chill. "You just hope you'll get a good one."

The workers seem to know the contractors by their cars. Some have steady, loyal employers for weeks, months or even years. When the boss's car drives up to the curb, these workers silently climb into the back for the ride to a building site. Others who must look for a new boss each day watch them with envy.

"Stay away from the one in the white Mercedes," someone shouts. "He doesn't pay."

A group of young men from Bethlehem are asked whether they have helped to build Jewish settlements on the West Bank and how they feel about it.

"You don't go to your own funeral," says one, explaining why he would never work on Jewish settlements, most of which are built with Arab labor. But most of his friends disagree.

"Don't you think we know we are helping them build their state?" said Muhammed Nawaf, a 24-year-old from a village near Bethlehem.

"I helped build Efrat," he adds, referring to the Jewish town near Bethlehem. "It is a real humiliation. Neither side is happy with you, and you know you are doing something against your own people, but you need the food."

Someone in the back shouts: "Let Arafat do something for us and we would not need to work for the Jews."

But the debate is cut short by another car driving up, offering work for the day, drawing them all like metal filings to a magnet.

Fourteen similar streetside Arab labor markets exist in Tel Aviv, Haifa and other cities. Many other Palestinians will be recruited directly from their villages or refugee camps by a ra'is—an Arab, or sometimes Jewish, labor boss who works as a middleman between the Arab labor pool and the Jewish marketplace. Both those recruited by a ra'is and those hired on the street are paid by the day and do not get any social, retirement or unemployment benefits, a practice that is technically legal.

The rest of the Palestinian migrant labor force, about 40 percent of the total, enters Israel officially through 39 employment offices run by the Ministry of Labor in the West Bank.

PALESTINIAN CAUSE TURNS TO FURY AS IT PASSES FROM FATHERS TO SONS

MONDAY, DECEMBER 28, 1987

BY THOMAS L. FRIEDMAN

JERUSALEM, Dec. 27—Behind the Palestinian riots of the last few weeks is a story about fathers and sons—Palestinian fathers and the sons over whom they may have lost control.

The recent Palestinian demonstrations against Israel, which left at least 21 Palestinian youths dead, may one day be remembered as the changing of the guard among the Palestinians.

The Palestinian fathers grew up in the West Bank under Jordanian rule, or in Gaza under Egyptian rule. After Israel captured those territories in 1967, they more or less came to terms with the situation, got to know a few Jews, worked in their factories, even learned some Hebrew and were, at least until last month, ready for a peaceful settlement with a Jewish state provided a Palestinian state was created alongside it.

FEW HAVE A JEWISH FRIEND

But the sons, the stone-throwers, those who were ready to bare their chests at Israeli soldiers, had their temperaments forged in a different furnace. They have known only a dead-end life under the Israeli occupation. Few have ever had a Jewish friend. Few have not been interrogated by Israeli security men.

The Israeli soldiers their fathers feared and their grandfathers fled do not frighten the sons anymore. The sons wear their arrests, their prison records and their wounds with the same bravado that American teenagers wear their high school letter jackets.

Where their fathers were ready to soften their political edges, maybe even make compromises with the Israelis, the sons only seem to know the dialogue of the stone and the politics of rage. Where their fathers were a moderating influence on the Palestine Liberation Organization, their sons are not afraid to mock the P.L.O. as a "Cadillac revolution" gone fat.

AN EXCHANGE OF HATRED

In the Balata refugee camp outside Nablus, in the Israeli occupied West Bank, a knot of 15- and 16-year-old boys, black-checked Arab headdresses wrapped around their necks, were gathered today outside a butcher shop. Many of them had friends or brothers taken away in the security roundups. All of them took part in the recent disturbances. Rawhi, 15, flashed a bruise above his eye to prove it.

As they gossiped, an eight-man Israeli Army patrol walked by, its soldiers darting their eyes in all directions. The Israelis locked gazes with the Palestinian youths for a moment. It was hard to tell who was more frightened, but the hatred they exchanged was electric.

"While the soldiers are inside the camp, we won't rise up," one of the youths said quietly. "But as soon as they leave, we will rise again."

"Yesterday was bad," said another. "Today was very very bad, and tomorrow will be very, very, very bad."

Talking with Palestinians in recent days, it has become clear that the riots have changed something: The fathers, who once had a common language with the Israelis, however limited, seem to have yielded the field to their sons, who know only the stone against the bullet.

Ilan Kfir, a reporter for the Israeli newspaper Hadashot, caught the mood when he wrote that after the riots in the West Bank and Gaza "it is doubtful whether any of the notables in the territories described as moderate and candidates for a Jordanian-Palestinian delegation will dare stand up now: not Faez Abu Rahme, not Hanna Siniora and certainly not veterans such as Elias Friej and Rashad as-Shawwa.

"If the political process is ever renewed, the rules of the game will be different," he added. "The P.L.O. and leaders of the uprising in the territories—new names on the political map—will determine who will be the representatives to negotiations. It is doubtful whether a political consensus will be created in Israel in favor of negotiating with them."

STUDYING IN AMMAN

Ibrahim Karaeen, a Palestinian journalist and nationalist in East Jerusalem, knows about the eclipse of the fathers. He has boys 7 and 5 years old and a girl of 3.

Mr. Karaeen was 19 when the June 1967 war broke out and was studying English at the University of Amman in Jordan. Israel sealed the border after the war, so he returned illegally with some friends by fording the Jordan River. On the other side, a patrol of soldiers arrested him.

"I had never met a Jew growing up," he recalled. "I had no idea how they even looked. We were brought up to believe that they were all monsters. When the Israeli soldiers arrested me, I saw the monster for the first time and I was sure the monster would kill me.

"But then they took us to Nablus jail, and there I saw that there were some Israelis who would shout and curse at us all the time and others who would treat us decently," he said. "I paid a fine, and they let me go to my home in Jerusalem."

In 1972 he became one of the first Palestinians from the occupied territories to enroll at the Hebrew University of Jerusalem, from which he graduated in 1975 with a degree in English literature. Along the way he formed many friendships with Israelis.

"At the time, most of us never thought the occupation would continue for 20 years, so we thought we should use the opportunity to get to know each other," he mused. "I was often invited to Jewish homes, and I would invite them to my home."

A staunch advocate of a Palestinian state, alongside a Jewish state, Mr. Karaeen feels certain most of his generation shares his views.

ISRAELIS MISS A CHANCE

"I learned through my experiences to look at human beings as human beings and to treat them accordingly," he said. "But the opportunity for interaction that was given to me will probably not be given to my children."

Why? As the occupation stretched into 20 years, Mr. Karaeen found his dialogue with Israelis dwindling away. Palestinians were either dealt with as quislings who cooperated with the occupation or they were banished to the margins, he said. Israel's category of Israeli "enemies" came to include even the moderate Palestinian nationalists ready to settle for a Palestinian state in the West Bank, Gaza and Jerusalem.

Jamil Hammad, a 47-year-old Palestinian writer from Bethlehem, is the father of three sons between the ages of 20 and 24. His middle son received a severe head wound in 1982 when Israeli troops fired a tear-gas cannister at him at close range during a demonstration.

The elder Mr. Hammad has no doubts that in the fading of his generation of Palestinian nationalists the Israelis have missed their best chance for a peaceful settlement with the Palestinians.

"My sons are very different from my generation," he said. "They did not witness the Arab defeat of 1967, so they don't have any inferiority complexes. But most important, my sons believe that they can, by their actions, change the world. They are full of confidence. They are not smashed and frustrated like my generation."

FATHERS ARE 'RADICALIZED'

"When you talk about frustration in the West Bank," Mr. Hammad said, "don't include the young people. It is we, the over-40 crowd, who are the frustrated ones. But I tell you, if the Israelis are going to negotiate, they should do it with the Jamil Hammads. Otherwise they will have their hands full with my boys Haitham, Suhail and Sadir—they don't believe in the language of concessions."

But while the young generation has indeed taken to the streets in a way many of their fathers never did, one should not think that their fathers are not rooting them on, said Sari Nusseibeh, a philosopher in Bir Zeit University on the West Bank and the father of two boys, 11 and 8.

"What you have today," Mr. Nusseibeh said, "is fathers being radicalized by their sons. I could not help but watch the scenes by our house of young boys burning tires in the road without thinking of a Phoenix rising from the ashes."

"As soon as the clashes began around our house, my sons ran up to the roof with binoculars and reported on the 'battle,' " he added. "Every time the Israelis pulled back, they shouted 'The Palestinians are winning, the Palestinians are winning.' Suddenly I saw them both with one foot out the door. Once they get out there, they will definitely be more radical than me. We are entering a whole new country-side. This is only the beginning."

Indeed, Mr. Karaeen said, fewer Israelis come by the house these days. His children have no friends on the other side.

A CONTAMINATED ATMOSPHERE

"With all of this uprising going on, it is hard to tell a 7-year-old the whole story—that there are good and there are bad and that we have some Jewish friends," Mr. Karaeen said. "Even if I did, he hears other things at school now. He will never have the same experience as me. The atmosphere now is so contaminated. But to know a different reality and not be able to impart it to your own son, that is very painful.

"If this continues, in a few years there will be no dialogue at all," he predicted. "We, the fathers, are all asking ourselves, 'How will our children judge us—as cowards, as nationalists, as realists?'

"If they judge me according to their experience, then I am afraid they will judge me negatively. Did my way of life bring anything positive for them? The answer will be no, and they will judge me as having been mistaken. Nothing could be more embarrassing for a father."

When the moderate nationalists of his generation were still ruling the West Bank as mayors or in other leadership positions, Mr. Karaeen said, they were a buffer between Israel and the more extremist and religious fundamentalists among the Palestinians. When a disturbance happened, they would mediate between the Israeli authorities and the youths to calm things down.

But now this buffer group has been expelled or dismissed. In the last two weeks when the Israeli Army called in the Palestinian leaders they appointed in place of the moderate nationalists in the West Bank and told them to cool things down, these "leaders" were not able to exert any influence.

NO PEACE IN OWN HOMES

"Now all the Israelis have to talk to are people who cannot even bring peace to their own homes," Mr. Karaeen said. "They talk with fathers who have no connections with their sons."

"To talk politics, you need politicians, but they have not left any," he said. "When they arrested all these people last week, they said they were just arresting the 'organizers.' One thousand organizers? In 10 years they will just have to put a wall up around the whole West Bank and Gaza Strip to arrest all of the organizers."

So what is left? For his generation, too old to fight and too wise not to appreciate the shades of gray, only cynicism is left, Mr. Karaeen said.

"The process my generation went through has left us cynics," he said. "The process our sons are going through has left them as radicals. The end result in both cases is dangerous."

"My way of life at least had a ray of hope in it—a hope that was aborted," he added. "Our sons' way of life leads only to explosions."

SEVEN

THE RESCUE OF BABY JESSICA

Photographs to follow after page 318

1988 WINNER IN THE SPOT NEWS PHOTOGRAPHY CATEGORY

"For a distinguished example of spot news photography in black and white or color . . ."

The Odessa American
Scott Shaw

Sometimes, the cliché holds true. One photograph can tell it all. Dozens of photographers waited impatiently in Midland, Texas, where Jessica McClure was trapped in a well shaft. They knew they would have only one chance to capture the moment when she was brought to the surface. For Scott Shaw it was a prize instant.

When 18-month-old Jessica McClure fell into an abandoned water well, no one expected it to be an event that would capture the world's attention. The same week, a plunging stock market, gunfire in the Persian Gulf and Nancy Reagan's cancer surgery took a backseat to Jessica's plight.

At first my editors thought it was a fairly routine story that would probably be resolved quickly. No one dreamed that the ordeal would last 58½ hours.

In fact, when I arrived at work that Wednesday morning on October 14, no mention was made of the girl trapped 22 feet down in the well in Midland, Texas. After two hours at work, I asked the city editor, Gail Burke-Frandsen, what Mark Rogers, the paper's chief photographer, was doing. She said he was covering the rescue of a child stuck in a well and would probably be back soon.

I left for some assignments in Odessa. Later I was told to relieve Rogers at 4 p.m. When I arrived, Jessica had been trapped for 6½ hours. Rogers said that workers were confident she would be out in a few hours.

I had to stand on a ladder to watch the rescue efforts. The well Jessica tumbled into was just inside a four-foot fence in the backyard of a house where Jessica was being cared for.

A drilling rig was being used to dig a tunnel parallel to the well. The plan was to make another tunnel to the well to bring Jessica up.

Rescue workers monitored Jessica's condition with binoculars and a microphone. They could hear Jessica occasionally singing "Winnie-the-Pooh" and getting angry when the drilling was too loud. Her fighting spirit urged the workers on as they continued to work to free her.

As night approached, it looked as though Jessica wouldn't be rescued before daybreak. Lights were set up as workers continued to dig. A large tube pumping heat and oxygen was placed over the well as the temperature dropped.

The weather forecast called for rain. A heavy rain could flood the well and rescue tunnel. The rain did come, Thursday morning, but, luckily, it was brief enough that it didn't hamper the rescue effort.

Newspaper, magazine, television and radio personnel set up camp in the adjacent backyard while waiting for the rescue. Everyone tried to stay warm. Some slept and others talked to pass the time. I stayed at the scene until 8 a.m. when I was relieved by another photographer, David Sams. I had been there 16 hours.

I left my film at the paper and went home to sleep for four hours. I then went back to the paper to shoot more assignments in Odessa for the next 10 hours. Throughout the day workers kept promising she would be out in "two more hours, two more hours."

At 11 p.m. I was back at the rescue sight. Rescuers had worked 37½ hours, but not much progress had been made since I left earlier that day.

The importance of the story had grown immensely, as had the number of media people on the scene. When I had left that morning, there were four photographers and four television crews sharing three ladders. Now there were about 20 photographers and 12 television crews on at least 25 ladders. Reporters from a number of newspapers and magazines were also roaming the yard.

Drilling experts from across the country were flying in with different suggestions on how to cut through the hard caliche rock that separated the rescuers and Jessica.

Shortly after noon workers had broken into the well shaft. They just had to enlarge the hole and said she would be out in one hour. Everyone readied for Jessica's appearance. After a few more hours they decided they still didn't have enough room to bring her out unharmed.

The failed attempt brought disappointment to many exhausted people, some of whom had been there for more than 50 hours. I was beginning to wonder if it would ever end. Doctors were saying that she might not survive much longer.

A few hours later, workers were again confident that she would be rescued soon. This time they were right. Their determination and hard work were about to pay off.

I checked my camera equipment to make sure everything was set right and working properly. I thought about what lens I should use when she was brought up and subsequently taken to the ambulance.

By now it was dark. I decided to use a flash to supplement the rescue lights. This would allow me to use a slower speed film for a better quality image.

I had been at the scene for almost 22 hours and had slept only four of the last 60 hours. My eyes were so tired that I worried I might have trouble focusing as they rushed her to the ambulance.

Suddenly, a paramedic brought her up from the well. She was all right. By the time I had shot 11 frames, another paramedic was carrying her to the ambulance. I shot my 12th frame as they passed, running, by me. Her parents, Chip and Reba McClure, were waiting in the ambulance. While Jessica was rushed to the hospital, everyone at the scene cheered.

I ran back to my car for the 30-minute drive to Odessa. Speaking to editors via my car radio, I was told I needed two shots for the front page, plus enough for a photo page inside the front section.

Managing editor Olaf Frandsen decided to devote the top half of the front page to a close-up photo of Jessica being rushed to the ambulance. The shot that won the Pulitzer Prize was the dominant image on the photo page, showing the rescue workers surrounding Jessica.

—Scott Shaw
The Odessa American

EIGHT

THE GRAVEYARD

Photographs to follow after page 318

1988 WINNER IN THE FEATURE PHOTOGRAPHY CATEGORY

"For a distinguished example of feature photography in black and white or color . . ."

The Miami Herald
Michel duCille

The cocaine trade moves in the shadows, but evidence of its pervasiveness is revealed daily in deaths, violence and decay in our communities. Michel duCille ventured to the Graveyard, a cocaine nerve center in Miami, and gave dimension to the statistics.

"Design a drug for maximum destruction: It should be highly addictive, plentiful and cheap enough so even the impoverished can get hooked. It should have only a short high, followed by an intense craving for more. It should have dangerous side effects and debilitating long-term consequences. Design a community with maximum vulnerability: fill it with bleak apartments badly maintained. Populate it with people deprived since birth who have little to look forward to and few, if any, successful role models. Create an atmosphere in which criminal activity can flourish unchecked. Put it all together, and call it The Graveyard."

Every once in a while a piece of journalism exposes a failing of society with such vivid force that continuing to ignore the problem becomes unthinkable. Such was the case with the stunning story and photo essay on crack cocaine that dominated *The Miami Herald*'s *Tropic* magazine on April 5, 1987. It all began as the obsession of one photographer, but quickly became the center of a reporter's life as well.

The photographer, Pulitzer Prize winner Michel duCille, felt that *The Herald*'s coverage of cocaine abuse had been far too limited: that it most often dealt with the aberration, the white professional whose career and home life were destroyed by the drug. What he saw as he canvassed the black areas of Miami was far more frightening: entire neighborhoods given over to crack cocaine and its profiteers: whole communities dying in a haze of sweet smoke.

He decided, at last, to focus not on one section of town, or one neighborhood, but on one public housing project: a bleak compound of once hopeful apartments now called The Graveyard.

So duCille moved into The Graveyard, accompanied by a *Herald* reporter, Lynne Duke, hanging out among the garbage and the broken glass until they were just other black faces, until no one noticed them anymore. That was when duCille began taking pictures, for a week, then two, then five and six. The world of The Graveyard opened to them in all its horror and mundanity.

The day after duCille's pictures and *The Herald*'s story appeared, county administrators and housing officials held an early morning meeting. It was the beginning of a community reaction that would completely rewrite the reality of The Graveyard, and even erase the name:

• April 10: Dade County's Housing and Urban Development Department installs an 8-foot fence around the perimeter of The Graveyard to keep nonresidents out. County workers also replace missing light bulbs in and outside the housing project and issue parking decals to residents. Vacant apartments that have been used as "get-off houses" are boarded up.

• April 13: A special county task force unveils a plan to combat the sale and use of crack at 16 county housing projects.

• April 22: Twelve private security guards hired by the county at a cost of $6,000 a week begin patrolling The Graveyard 24 hours a day. Parking lot security gates are installed.

• April 30: The Florida Senate approves legislation empowering Florida counties to evict from county-run housing projects any resident convicted of using or selling narcotics.

• Aug. 8: The Graveyard's tenants' council reports that some apartments in the project have been renovated and that the open sale of crack has all but disappeared. The tenant council christens the project New Haven Gardens.

• Nov. 8: Judy Williams, a crack addict featured in *Tropic*'s cover story, "The Graveyard," graduates from a 6-month drug rehabilitation program.

"The Graveyard" is an astounding piece of photojournalism, the work of one man with the vision to see a compelling and important story, and the courage to carry it through.

—Pete Weitzel, Managing Editor
The Miami Herald

NINE

FLORIDA'S SHAME

1988 WINNER IN THE EDITORIAL WRITING CATEGORY

"For distinguished editorial writing, the test of excellence being clearness of style, moral purpose, sound reasoning, and power to influence public opinion in what the writer conceives to be the right direction . . ."

The Orlando Sentinel
Jane Healy

Residents of Orange County, Florida, have been struggling with traffic jams, adapting to overcrowded schools and watching their park land disappear as developers have gotten rich off the Great Land Grab. Jane Healy of *The Orlando Sentinel* doesn't mince words in identifying who is to blame.

Things were supposed to have gotten better in Florida.

The state Legislature had passed tough laws to manage its incredible growth; the Orange County Commission had even approved a tough plan to say where and when growth in the Orlando area should be allowed. Everything was just jim-dandy—until you looked closely at what was happening.

In reality, the grub for growth at any price hadn't stopped. Not for a second. The developers were whipping their political cronies around just as they always had. As usual in Florida, the politicians were obeying the developers' orders at everyone else's expense.

That is why I wrote these "Florida's Shame" editorials. I saw Orange County and its neighbor, Seminole County, headed for a disaster of clogged roads, ruined rivers and jammed schools if they didn't get a hold on their growth. I saw that commissioners still were making piecemeal decisions with no thought of their county's future.

Had I looked at things piecemeal, I also might not have seen the county as Florida's next disaster-in-the-making. After all, the new developments were better planned and more attractive than before. "Quality development" was the buzzword of the New Florida.

Instead, I chose to step back and look at all these decisions together. *The Sentinel*, of course, had been regularly writing editorials on the commission's daily planning and zoning decisions. But I thought a series would allow us to take a broader and deeper look at where the county was headed.

I could see from the jammed roads that growth wasn't being managed properly. That much was obvious. But in doing my research for the editorials, I found that the jammed roads were only one sign of the mismanaged growth. Lousy decisions by the commission were also forcing elementary school students to eat lunch at 10:30 in the morning; forcing students in a just-opened high school to take courses in the physical education storage room and forcing residents to drive miles and miles to enjoy a park.

The commission wasn't planning at all for its growth; it was simply reacting.

I went about these editorials in a rather unconventional way—for many editorial pages, anyway. Instead of reading stories and basing my opinions on them, I interviewed dozens of people—politicians, developers, planners and ordinary residents—to gather original material. I pored over dozens of planning documents and developers' plans as well. A touch of investigative reporting applied to the editorial page.

This reporter's approach to editorial writing—something we practice routinely on *The Sentinel* editorial page—is what made the difference. It gave me an enormous amount of authority on the subject, which I wouldn't have had if I had simply read news stories. In other words, I knew what I was talking about.

This expertise also made it easier for me to raise hell about the situation. As strong as the editorials were, I knew I would feel comfortable defending them.

Then I put the material together for a series that ran for six days straight.

The reaction from the readers was instantaneous and gratifying. It showed that we had struck a nerve about runaway growth in the Orlando area. *The Sentinel* received more than 200 letters from readers demanding that the county commission do something about the mess. And the commission responded: Two weeks later it halted for two years big projects in the rural areas.

Reaction from the developers was, well, a bit less supportive.

Three major development companies pulled $55,000 in ads from the newspaper in the few weeks following the series. They accused us of being antigrowth—which was not true. We are for growth, but for managed growth. The lost revenue now is believed to be several times what was pulled in those first few weeks.

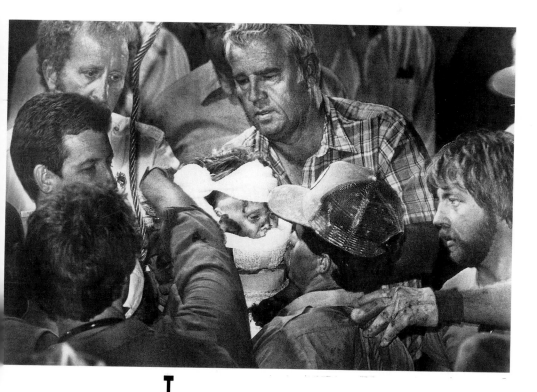

Their concern written on their faces, rescue workers crowd around 18-month-old Jessica McClure as she reaches the surface following her 58½-hour ordeal in the water well shaft in Midland, Texas.

Making crack is easy. It doesn't take a chemist. Powdered cocaine is mixed with water and baking soda and then heated until solid. It is then broken into small chunks that look like soap pebbles.

A crack addict holds a pipe that is still smoldering with cocaine vapors from a piece of crack she just smoked. The pipe is made from a miniature liquor bottle—the type served on airliners.

Night time at The Graveyard is especially scary. While drugs are sold in front of small children, random violence often erupts between drug dealers and addicts.

A woman named **Pat** slumps on a milk crate in an abandoned apartment that has been converted into a crack den. Smoke hangs heavy in the air. She is talking about a man who is supposed to love her but doesn't. "That's why they gave this damn hellhole the name Graveyard, because these folks ain't nothing but zombies, the living dead, don't have no feelings."

A man smokes the last of three rocks he bought. He'd planned to take them home but couldn't wait that long, so he scavenged a beer can, turned it into a pipe and smoked right out in the open.

A homeless prostitute sleeps at midday under a filthy blanket in a crack house. As she sleeps, people wander in, get high and leave. She never stirs. The Graveyard, a county-owned apartment complex, is used and taken over by the addicts and dealers. Officials board up the windows and doors, but the addicts and dealers simply unboard them almost as soon as they go up.

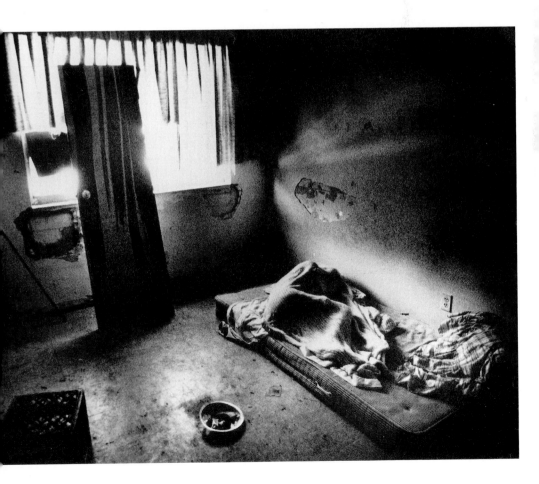

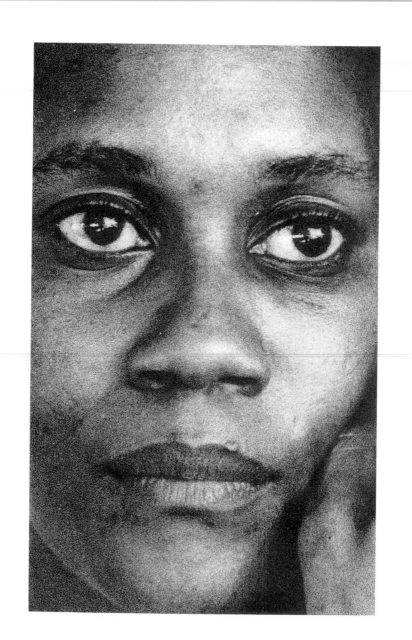

◄ **J**udy Williams, mother of five: "I feel like I'm a halfway good mother. I'll be a good mother when I get off crack, and I don't use my money for crack. But right now, I'm a halfway good mother."

▲ **T**his abandoned car is called the "base car," a place to do a deal or get high. This woman fell asleep one night. She was still there the next morning. She hadn't stirred a bit.

Fredrick Thompson is subdued by police after he resisted arrest during a police sting operation designed to catch buyers of crack at The Graveyard.

Mico, as dealer/addict, looks out the window of an abandoned apartment that he and others use as a basehouse; he often uses the window as a lookout spot for the police and potential buyers of his merchandise.

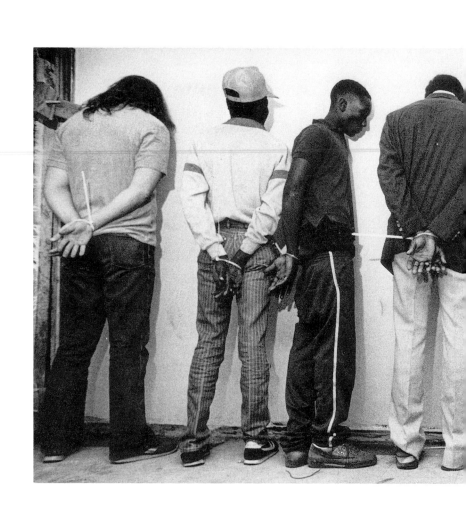

Whites, Latins and blacks were among 29 people arrested in one sting operation at The Graveyard. During a sting, police pose as drug dealers (sellers). After the sale, other police officers arrest the buyer for drug possession. It is meant as a deterrent.

A man weeps after his arrest in The Graveyard during a police sting operation. "Please let me go," he cries. "I don't want my kids to know what happened to me."

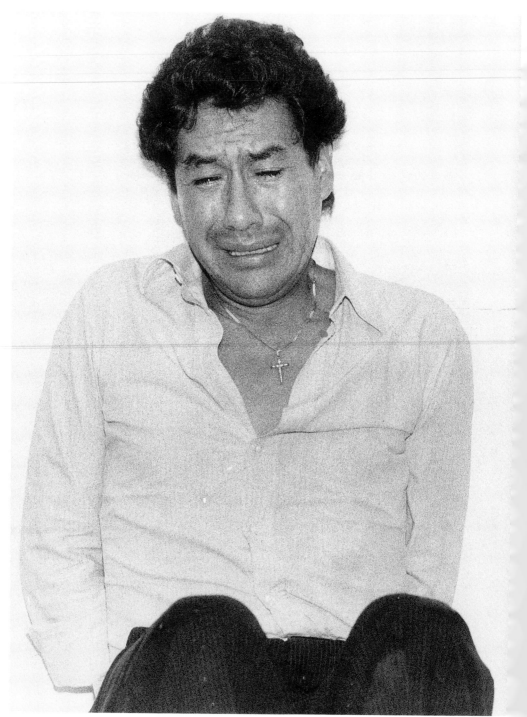

A month after these editorials ran, I followed with another "Florida's Shame" series. These editorials concentrated on a beautiful river in suburban Seminole County that was threatened by urban growth.

Again, I used the same approach of interviewing dozens of people, perusing documents and even canoeing the river. These editorials ran over four days straight and also produced gratifying results. The governor decided to champion the river, and regional governments moved to ban development along its banks.

These were not the readers' first taste of "Florida's Shame." I had been writing the series since 1984. Then the situation was somewhat different—the Legislature hadn't yet started to crack down on local governments allowing quick-buck developers to get rich at everyone else's expense. I wrote a series on that. In the 1984 and 1985 legislative sessions, legislators finally did crack down, though the law won't go into effect until next year.

In 1985, "Florida's Shame" concentrated on overbuilt coastal communities that were destroying our beaches. The Legislature finally did something about that, too, forcing new condos farther off the beach.

The "Florida's Shame" editorials had a common thread—that Florida was destroying the very things that have made life here so alluring.

The writing style of the editorials also had a common thread. In each editorial I tried to find powerful examples that, almost by themselves, would persuade the reader that things needed to change if we still were going to enjoy living in Florida in 10 to 15 years. In each editorial I also tried to use a different writing device to grab readers' attention.

Graphics—charts and maps—accompanied the editorials as well. I made sure that each graphic carried an argument of its own—something that would help persuade readers of our position even if they didn't want to read the text.

Finally, had it not been for a few other people at *The Sentinel*, "Florida's Shame" may never have existed.

Had special projects editor Jim Clark not launched the powerful "Florida's Shame" news project in 1984, I would never have been moved to write the "Florida's Shame" editorials at all.

Had my editor, John Haile, not taught me the most effective way to write these editorials, "Florida's Shame" never would have had the same effect on readers.

And had publisher Tip Lifvendahl not stood by these editorials so staunchly—in the face of lost advertising and angry developers—"Florida's Shame" never would have been published.

—Jane Healy
The Orlando Sentinel

AN ORANGE GOING SOUR

SUNDAY, NOVEMBER 1, 1987

BY JANE HEALY

How would you like to live in a place where:

(A) Some elementary school children must eat lunch at 10:30 a.m. because the cafeteria is too crowded to seat everyone during normal lunch hours?

(B) All but one high school is overcrowded. Some academic classes have to be held in the school gym or, worse, the gym's storage room?

(C) Cars jam up bumper to bumper on dozens and dozens of roads, and the worst is ahead. A place where in just seven years half of the major roads will be carrying more cars than the roads were built for?

(D) Parks rank so low on priority lists that total park acreage must increase by 60 percent just to meet state standards?

(E) All of the above?

Welcome to Orange County, Fla., the 13th fastest-growing area in the country, where you never have to choose between the rotten fruits of unmanaged growth. In Orange County, the answer is always (E), "All of the above."

The Sun Boom? No question, Orange County is right in the thick of it. The economic statistics look jim-dandy on paper, but kids don't go to school on paper. Nor do roads and parks get built on it. Beneath all those rosy data-bank projections, Orange County is being sold out for a quick buck. It's a county in crisis.

Mind you, Seminole, Osceola, Lake and Volusia counties have serious problems as well. But that's a subject for another day. In this series of editorials, we'll concentrate on Orange County, a place still hanging a "For Sale" sign at its border, a quick-buck, bottom-line piece of real estate that's selling its future for a pittance.

Is it the same tired Florida story? To some extent, sure. Taking the real-estate money and running may be the oldest profession in the Sunshine State. And elected officials here have been managed by quick-buck speculators, instead of managing them, since time immemorial, or so it often seems. But, no, the Great Florida Land Grab of the 1980s isn't the land boom of the 1920s.

Then, developers and land speculators used up Florida for their own purposes and headed back up North to enjoy life. Today's developers and land speculators use up Florida for their own purposes and head to North Carolina to retire.

Then, developers and land speculators stuck the communities they pillaged with all the bills for necessary services. Today's developers share in the cost of growth by helping build roads and sewer systems, but don't worry, they still can meet the Mercedes payments. Oh, yes, today's developments also look prettier, sit back farther from the road and might even have smaller signs.

But, face it, that's window dressing. The land grab continues. And when all is said and developed, the people who live here still are the ones left to fight the traffic, pay most of the bills and live with the eyesore.

Maybe worst of all, the all-consuming greed back in the 1920s was out in the open, where just about everyone who cared to look could see it for what it was. Today's greed gets to hide behind the illusion that Florida finally is serious about managing its growth.

The illusion? The tough new law the Legislature passed two years ago, the one that said services must go hand in hand with growth.

The reality? In the Orlando area, the law won't go into effect for at least three more years. That's a year later than originally scheduled. Too much paperwork for everyone, the state says. Let's wait just a little bit longer, it says. The rest of us can only wonder how many more times this deadline will be delayed.

This means at least three more years of business as usual in Orange County. Hold on to your steering wheel.

As for that thick, serious-sounding growth management plan Orange County has, yes, it exists. But try to get a majority of Orange County commissioners to treat it as anything other than an annoyance. Just look at the pitiful record:

August 1985—Orange County updates its 5-year-old plan for growth, leaving enough land in urban areas to accommodate developers for the next 20 to 30 years. In other words, the county says it won't be necessary to leapfrog out to rural areas and waste money building roads, utility lines and schools all over the place. Commissioners even agree that developers won't be able to ask for changes to the plan every time they walk in the door. They now can ask for changes only twice a year. Hallelujah, a new day.

Or perhaps we should say, it looked like a new day. Turns out most of these commissioners are leapfrogging fools.

Spring 1986—County commissioners grab at the first chance they can to leap 5 miles into the woods. They allow an industrial park in rural southeast Orange County that will employ 40,000 people. That's 5,000 more than work in downtown Orlando now.

Summer 1986—Commissioners allow 525 more rural acres to be developed at urban densities, this time on the west side.

Spring 1987—Commissioners open 3,790 acres southeast of Orlando International Airport to citylike development. They also open 1,200 acres near Windermere to such development.

Fall 1987—Commissioners say "go ahead" to urban development on another 300 rural acres east of Windermere.

By now you must be wondering how much of Orange County isn't on the verge of urban development. Good question. The answer is: not much.

Who benefits from this contempt for limiting urban densities to urban areas? Certainly not the typical Orange County resident. Such development only further strains the county's ability to provide adequate schools, roads and parks elsewhere.

No, the people who benefit from all this are the same folks who have been pillaging the Sunshine State for most of this century—the speculators and developers who get rich quick whenever land becomes urban overnight. How? Easy, land costs a lot less in the rural area, but once the county commission declares it urban, values skyrocket. A developer can build at least four times as many homes in urban areas because lots can be smaller.

Sadly, the county commission still refuses to say, "Enough. We won't be stomped on anymore for a quick buck." That is Florida's Shame.

MEAL FOR A MONSTER

MONDAY, NOVEMBER 2, 1987

BY JANE HEALY

Drive out the Bee Line Expressway east of Semoran Boulevard and you'll see woods, woods and more woods—pine, oak and wild wax myrtle. Now picture that same area in five or 10 years:

The woods? Forget 'em. Subdivisions now flank the expressway, and 10-story office buildings dot the landscape. Turn off at any of the many, many exits, and you'll run through the usual strip shopping center: an Exxon station, a McDonald's and Taco Tico and Kentucky Fried Chicken—the pine, oak and wild wax myrtle of the New Florida.

Drive through the housing developments, and you'll see the houses are new, but cars already jam the roads. Schools? When you finally do come across one, you can hardly see the main building through all the portable classrooms sitting outside. Parks for the kids to play in? Please, this is the Great Florida Land Boom. Who has time for parks? Come on back in another 10 years, and maybe someone will have gotten around to providing them.

A nice way to live? Hardly. Yet it might be the latest nightmare-come-true because Orange County commissioners have done nothing to insist that they, rather than developers, call the shots on growth for a big chunk of southeast Orange County. It's the latest chapter of the old Florida story, "Gimme, Gimme, Gimme."

To fill in this story go back to 1986 when a trio of commissioners approved International Corporate Park, a 2,900-acre office and industrial monster 8 miles east of the Orlando International Airport. It tells the story best of how Orange County still is being sold for a quick buck with no thought for tomorrow.

Not only will the corporate park have 20 million square feet of office and industrial space, but there will be 200,000 square feet of stores and restaurants. That's more stores and restaurants than serve downtown Orlando workers now. What makes all this even more absurd is that only six months earlier commissioners had agreed this area would stay rural. No more leapfrog development for this commission, no sir. That was the Florida of yesteryear.

So what happened? Yesteryear became today and tomorrow. A few influential people—including former County Attorney Charles Gray —did some fast talking, and pretty soon the commissioners were lapping it up. All the developers had to do was argue that there wasn't any other place to put this industrial park.

Sounds logical when you're talking real fast. But slow down for a minute, and you realize that there are 1,400 acres of industrial land just south of the airport at the Tradeport Park. And next to that sits Airport Industrial Park at Orlando, with 1,679 acres available. Does Orange County need another industrial park right now? Like it needs more traffic on Semoran Boulevard.

Don't misunderstand: Someone needs the industrial park—the developers. How could they make a huge profit without it? Yes, they'll have to pay for all the roads, sewers, water lines and drainage that go into International Corporate Park. The New Florida at least has that much sense. But hold your tears: These big boys can afford it. They paid about $2,000 an acre for this land. In April Lockheed Aircraft bought a 200-acre tract of the park for $20,000 an acre. You do the math.

Don't misunderstand, either: The industrial park itself isn't what's going to make it less enjoyable to live in Orange County. No, the big bust—the jammed roads and schools, the lack of parks—will come in the rural area west of the park. Even worse, everyone else in the county will get stuck with the bills for this mess.

County officials will tell you even now they won't let subdivisions, shopping centers and office buildings be built in the 20-square-mile pocket of woods between this industrial city and all the development around Orlando International Airport. But don't believe them for a minute.

The growth will come the same way the industrial park came— through fast talking. One property owner already has had engineers come up with a plan for offices, homes and stores on about 2 square miles of the land. It even has a name—"Bal-Bay." Don't think for a minute that other property owners aren't readying their own versions of "Bal-Bay."

Is there still any hope? It's hard to think why there might be. After all, why should the rules change now? Why should commissioners ever say no to anyone? Judging by their record, these commissioners take to unplanned, piecemeal development like a glutton to double chocolate cake.

For the moment, though, let us dare to dream. Let us dare to imagine that commissioners have the gumption to:

• **Ban development west of the industrial park until they know how much growth that area can handle.**

Is this too much to ask? Hardly. The commission's duty is to the voters, not to the developers and their smooth-talking lawyers. Without a ban, this land is going to get gobbled up for urban development.

We can just hear the lawyers arguing now: "Where did the commissioners expect the 40,000 people who will be working at the industrial park to live? Way on the other side of Orange County, so they can add to the already massive traffic jams? Ladies and gentlemen, get serious!"

Right now, the commission has no way to refute such arguments. It did, after all, approve the industrial park. Beyond that, commissioners must have some legal reason to turn down a development. The solution: Give itself a legal reason—a one-year ban, flat out and simple.

• **Decide soon what they will allow to happen to that area.**

Note, we say "soon," not "next year" or "in a couple of years." There has been far too much procrastination already.

The county has no idea how many roads it might need in this area, how many schools or parks. Will a school be built in southeast Orange at the expense of relieving overcrowding elsewhere? Will new roads be built there with precious county road dollars while traffic piles up elsewhere? Or will taxes simply be raised for everyone to pay for the commission's mistake? Sounds like the Three Stooges have taken over county government, doesn't it?

It's not as if someone didn't warn the commissioners. The commission's own staff said that by approving the industrial park the county was, in effect, giving up to urban development the 20 square miles between the industrial monster and the airport area. But the commission listens to its staff about as much as Lucy listened to Desi. More important, regional planners recommended 18 months ago that the county decide by now how much growth it can allow in that area. In other words, it should start *planning* for that area, rather than just reacting to fast talk.

Fast talk, that's what's running Orange County. That's also what's ruining Orange County.

PALM LAKE STRANGLER

TUESDAY, NOVEMBER 3, 1987

BY JANE HEALY

Students at Palm Lake Elementary might not be hungry for lunch at 10:30 in the morning, but for some of them that's just tough luck. That's when the school has to start shuffling children into the cafeteria. A new class follows every three minutes.

Absurd? Of course, but there's no other way to get the students fed. Take a look at the numbers:

Palm Lake Elementary School
Capacity: 600 students
Students: 900 plus
Date opened: August 1987

Too bad, also, for the students who enrolled at Dr. Phillips High School thinking they would get the best Orange County has to offer. Oh, the school is modern enough. That is, unless you're one of the students who has had to attend class in a physical education storage room.

Dr. Phillips High School
Capacity: 2,537 students
Students: 3,008
Date opened: August 1987

Pathetic? You bet it is, but not half so pathetic as what happened Sept. 21, just one month after Dr. Phillips High School and Palm Lake Elementary School first opened to overflow crowds.

The place: The Orange County Commission chambers. Developers stand before commissioners arguing that they should allow up to 4.4 homes on each of 300 acres in southwest Orange County just east of Windermere. Until now, no more than one home had been allowed on each acre. One developer's consultant boldly cites the availability of Dr. Phillips High School as reason why more houses should be allowed on the land.

The commission action: Approved.

The result: More houses per acre, more families per school district, and far more students than the schools in southwest Orange County were ever meant to handle.

Will Palm Lake Elementary School students find themselves eating lunch at 9 a.m. after those developments have opened? They could call it brunch. Will Dr. Phillips students have to start meeting in the parking lot for something other than drivers' ed classes? Dr. Phillips already has added 10 portable classrooms to the school. One woman who lives next door told County Commissioner Vera Carter that she feels as if she were living next to a "Georgia trailer park."

Oh, yes, one more thing. The school board has no plans to build another high school in that area. A new high school is scheduled to open in 1990, but it's on the east side of the county. Transfer the students to other schools? Forget that. Every other high school in Orange County is either filled or overcrowded too. More than 3,300 students attend Winter Park High School though it was built for only 2,269.

There are plans for another elementary school in that west Orange area. But with the commission allowing so many more families in that area, that school too might open to 10:30 lunches or 9 a.m. brunches.

□ □ □

As you can see, unmanaged growth doesn't happen haphazardly. That is Florida's Shame. The county commissioners knew that Dr. Phillips High was overcrowded. *Everybody* knows that. They knew Palm Lake was jammed as well. Yet they overturned their own rules to approve more houses on each acre anyway. Approved, approved, approved. Sounds like some entertainment from the Theater of the Absurd. Sadly, it's all too real. Managed growth? What a joke.

It's clear who suffers from all this—the students. Who benefits? The same old gang—landowners and developers, their architects, engineers and attorneys. Land values skyrocket and fees come rolling in every time the county commission allows urban development of rural land. Worst of all, the ones who make the killing don't have to live there when they're through. Let the poor suckers who buy the houses worry about schools and roads and all that nonsense.

Don't look to the school board for any help. It's the co-conspirator in this mess. School officials didn't even protest the commission's decision to see how many people it could fit in Dr. Phillips High at one time. Not a peep out of them.

They say they didn't know it was coming up. Huh? Everyone else did. Two quarter-page newspaper ads announced the proposed change. What's more, the commission only considers such changes twice a year. Can't school officials keep track of two hearings a year if it means trying to prevent their schools from being unnecessarily crowded?

One more bit of high nonsense from the school board: Its staff now has asked the county commission if it can start building schools in the rural areas even though the county's plan for growth prohibits that—and for good reason. Nothing short of a four-lane highway can encourage high-density growth in rural areas more than a school. To their credit, county planners will ask the county commission to deny this ludicrous request.

How do you turn this dreary record around?

• **The county commission can start treating schools as it does roads, sewers, police or fire—services that are considered before a development is approved or higher densities allowed.**

There's no reason why the commission can't consider a bulging school as a reason to deny a developer's request. Adequate schools are at least as important as adequate roads and sewer systems. Shouldn't the prospect of students lunching during the breakfast hour or taking world studies in the locker room be every bit as daunting as a traffic jam or a drain backup?

• **The school board can start raising a fuss when county commissioners put the needs of developers ahead of the needs of students.**

Granted, the school board has no power to tell the county commission what to do. But it can raise a public stink when mismanaged growth overcrowds the schools. That could be every bit as powerful as an official veto. All that's needed is a little gumption. Surely, the stores haven't sold out of that.

The grub for growth. It does more than hold drivers hostage on I-4. Now it's strangling our schools.

THE GREAT ESCAPE

WEDNESDAY, NOVEMBER 4, 1987

BY JANE HEALY

CASE NO. 1: Vista Lakes, a megadevelopment of homes and industry just northeast of Orlando International Airport, the 30th-busiest airport in the world. If everything goes as scheduled, Vista Lakes will be built under the flight path of the airport's third runway. In half of this development, jets will make so much noise it will sound as if the garbage disposal is at full tilt in the kitchen while the vacuum is running in the next room. No, homes won't be built in this half but the homeowners won't be far away—say, somewhere near the decibel level of a garbage disposal with a few coffee beans in it.

What have regional planners had to say about Vista Lakes? They are the ones who are supposed to look at things such as airport noise when a megadevelopment is being approved. The answer: absolutely nothing.

CASE NO. 2: Lake Nona, a megadevelopment just southeast of Orlando International Airport. In two years it will sit at the end of the airport's third runway. And what have regional planners had to say about the noise at Lake Nona? This time, they've had plenty to say. They've argued that the Orange County Commission has no business approving Lake Nona unless homeowners there agree never to sue the airport.

□ □ □

How did two huge developments so close to the airport get treated so differently? Because regional planners never got to consider Vista Lakes. It escaped their review by building just under the limit for such scrutiny. So forget any requirement that Vista Lakes homeowners give up their right to sue on this issue.

Vista Lakes is a lawsuit-in-the-making, with the future of the airport at stake. Allow homeowners to move that near the airport and just see if the airport ever gets to build that fourth runway it needs. Worse, it wouldn't be long before Vista Lakes homeowners were piling into a commission meeting, demanding that the planes be routed away from them and back over to Conway northwest of the airport.

How do messes like this get made? Easily—too easily.

Yes, there is a law meant to assure that megadevelopments don't dump their problems on someone else. Regional planners are supposed to review potential noise problems and also check to see if the developments will jam roads or pollute lakes in neighboring counties. But the law has a hole: Build ever so slightly under the threshold and you can laugh all the way to North Carolina retirement.

Vista Lakes, being developed by pizza king Jeno Paulucci, is a case in point. The formula by which planners decide whether a development of homes and industry qualifies for scrutiny is too complex to discuss here, but suffice it to say that, if a development adds up to 104 percent or higher on the scale, the regional planners move in. And where did Vista Lakes come out? 103.9 percent.

Indeed, getting under the limit has become something of an art among developers. Since February alone, four other Orange County megaprojects—Eastmore Commons, Cannongate, Cypress Springs and Sherwood Highlands—have come in just under the threshold.

Mind you, topping the threshold doesn't mean a development automatically gets the scrutiny; it is just automatically considered for it. But apparently even that is too great a risk for some developers. After all, if they can avoid regional planners, they have to contend only with county review. That's like skipping boot camp and going straight to happy hour at the officers' club. Best of all for the developers, taxpayers get to pick up the tab for all the problems left behind.

□ □ □

The cure? The Legislature thought it had found one two years ago: It said developers could start building even before the review was done. Even that wasn't lenient enough for developers. Face it, no matter what the Legislature does, the developers will find a way around it. They always do.

The bottom line, then? The same old one: The decision rests in Orange County, the same place where the future is being decided by fast talk. You've got a development scheme? Walk right on in. What's that—you're palsy-walsy with some commissioners? Here, let us get the door. The crucial question now: What can be done?

• **One cure is for three county commissioners to stand up and** say "no more" to megadevelopments that create regional problems.

That can start this month when Vista Lakes comes up for approval. There's absolutely no reason why the commission should rezone an agricultural area to allow 1,300 homes and apartments near a noisy international airport. But depending on the Orange County Commission to say no to developers is like depending on 747s to fly quietly over Vista Lakes.

WHO'S PALSY-WALSY?

THURSDAY, NOVEMBER 5, 1987

BY JANE HEALY

Sept. 21, 1987: A developer approaches the Orange County Commission. His request: He would like to build more than one home per acre on 55 acres in rural southwest Orange County.

Situation: The county's plan for growth says that no more than one home per acre should be allowed on this rural land. It has no sewer service, is near the sensitive Butler Chain of Lakes and is served by a 20-foot-wide road on one side. Oh, yes, schools in that area are jammed.

Decision: The commission turns down the request on a 3 to 2 vote. But commission Chairman Lou Treadway suddenly announces that he will change his vote if the developer can show that the land will drain properly and that he can get sewer service.

Sept. 22, 1987: The developer resubmits his request. Later he says that he will have no problem getting sewers for his property and has tests showing the land will drain adequately.

Result: The decision is not until the spring, but Mr. Treadway made himself quite clear that he will give the developer just what he wants. Forget the schools, roads and lakes.

Name of developer: Former Orange County Commissioner Lee Chira.

June 16, 1986: An attorney wants the Orange County Commission to let his clients develop 2,900 acres in rural east Orange County for an industrial park.

Situation: The county's plan for growth says that area should stay rural. It is not served by sewer and water lines, has inadequate roads and has no other urban services such as schools and fire stations.

Decision: Approved. Why expect anything else? This is the Gang That Can't Say No, to its friends.

Name of attorney: Former Orange County Attorney Charles Gray.

□ □ □

March 23, 1987: A developer's planning consultant asks commissioners to declare nearly 4,000 acres south of Orlando International Airport urban so that there can be a megadevelopment of homes, stores, offices and industries called Lake Nona.

Situation: The county's plan for growth says that area should stay rural. It has no sewer service, inadequate roads and no schools.

Decision: The same sad song—approved.

Name of consultant: Former Orange County Planning Director Jim Sellen.

Are these isolated examples of how things work in Orange County? In one sense, yes. These are some of the worst decisions the county has made when it comes to managing growth. Remember, the county's original plan for growth in 1980 said there was enough vacant land in the urban area to accommodate development for 20 years. Supposedly, there would be no need to put urban development on rural land.

But, no, this isn't the only time Lee Chira, Charles Gray and Jim Sellen have got exactly what they wanted from the commission. The county's rules be damned.

In late 1985, for instance, the county let Mr. Chira and 11 other developers pay county employees overtime to inspect their developments to see if they should be granted building permits. The result: The developers slid under the Jan. 1 deadline for paying so-called road impact fees.

Getting this speeded-up inspection saved Mr. Chira $533,000 in fees. In effect, the county inspectors worked overtime so that county taxpayers would get stuck with more than a half million dollars in road costs. Makes you wonder who's working for whom, doesn't it?

□ □ □

As for Mr. Gray, he now represents some landowners who want a southern leg of the beltway so they can complete their huge projects in south Orange County.

That's right, a southern leg, when other sections of the beltway are desperately needed to handle existing growth. This road is hardly a priority for the rest of the community. Worse, you can just bet what will come roaring down that roadway at 70 miles an hour—the usual fruits of unplanned sprawl: plenty of houses to live in, and plenty of profits for their builders. To heck with schools, parks, secondary roads and adequate police and fire services.

Sounds like a terrible idea, yet last month the county commissioners approved $400,000 to make a preliminary map of that southern belt-way leg. Guess which leg of the beltway will get built soon? Never mind the plans. Just keep your eye on Charlie Gray.

□ □ □

Mr. Sellen has been fortunate as well. He wrote the commission's plan for growth in the late '70s. Is it any wonder that he's so adept at getting around it now? In addition to representing Lake Nona developers, in September he represented a landowner who got the commission to declare urban 135 rural acres near Apopka-Vineland Road east of Windermere.

Want to walk around the growth rules in Orange County? Easy, just be the right person. And, no, it doesn't *have* to be one of those cited above. The commission added 1,200 acres to the urban area in west Orange County last spring after a request from Hugh Lokey's engineering firm. Mr. Lokey, of course, is the former county engineer.

□ □ □

Is there any way to stop commission members from bowing and scraping to their cronies? Probably not. Commissioners are politicians who just can't seem to resist playing politics. You know the rules: Scratch my back; I'll scratch yours. But, if they wanted, commissioners could reduce this assault:

• **They could approve a law that says people who work for the county commission cannot do business with the commission during the two years after they quit.**

Such a law would at least reduce the likelihood of people working for the county with the idea of walking on to some fat-cat developer's payroll a few years later. Broward County has a similar law. So do the state and federal governments. The idea even has been broached as part of Orange County's new charter, which will go to the voters next year. If the commission refuses to approve such a law itself the charter is a good place for it.

Let's put something in the path of the Gang That Can't Say No.

GANG THAT CAN'T SAY NO

FRIDAY, NOVEMBER 6, 1987

B Y   J A N E   H E A L Y

Want a glimpse of a new city? Just go south of Orlando International Airport in a few months, and you might see the makings of one. This city will be called Lake Nona, and about 30,000 people will live there. That's about the same population as Altamonte Springs.

Not only will Lake Nona have 10,000 homes and apartments and millions of square feet of industry, it will have almost as many stores, restaurants and other commercial development as Altamonte Mall.

Now for the punch line: Just eight months ago the Orange County growth plan said this area would stay rural. You know, cows and pastures.

What has happened with Lake Nona tells the story of a system that has failed.

□ □ □

Let's go back for a minute to why this land south of the airport should have stayed rural. Not only does that area lack adequate roads, schools and parks, it will sit at the end of a runway of the 30th-busiest airport in the world.

Oh, Lake Nona developers say they will build roads for the 250,000 cars that will go in or out of this project each day. But what about the other roads needed for the growth Lake Nona surely will spur in the 2 miles between it and Osceola County?

And, yes, the developers will donate land for schools and parks. But donating land for a park or a school doesn't build a school or develop a park. That is something the county commission and school board would have to do even though they have no such plans and no such money.

Yet last March county commissioners agreed to add Lake Nona's 3,790 acres to the urban area, which means it can be developed at much greater densities. That's on top of the 1,200 Lake Nona acres that commissioners turned urban overnight four years ago. Go right ahead, they said, don't let us get in your way of making a quick buck.

Commissioners were in such a rush to please Lake Nona's developers they turned this land urban even before the regional planning council —which reviews large developments for their effects on surrounding areas—had given Lake Nona the nod.

So guess what? When the project came before the planning council in July, it said it doesn't make sense to allow homes so near the airport.

Lake Nona's developers don't agree with this, of course, and are arguing—you guessed it—that they should have a right to build because the commission already has declared their land urban. Can you believe that? Once again, commissioners have found themselves in a bind because they couldn't say no. Their own lousy decision in March is being thrown back at them. What a mess. It's Larry, Curly and Moe at the helm.

There is one hope left, though it's ever so slight. The Lake Nona project comes before commissioners one more time on Nov. 17. They can turn down Lake Nona. The airport noise alone argues against approving this development.

Maybe it's too much to expect the commission to say no. Most of the commission laughs at planning. Commissioner Vera Carter has been the lone voice to manage growth for the past seven years, and at times even she gives in. Linda Chapin, who joined the commission a year ago, also has said no a couple of times. Maybe she, too, will develop a strong voice to manage growth.

But Lou Treadway, Tom Dorman and Hal Marston—the commission majority—are just about as serious about managing growth as they are about turning down campaign contributions from the development industry. Mr. Dorman voted against International Corporate Park but has shown little other interest in saying no.

Make no mistake about it: We're not opposed to growth. Orange County is going to grow, and it should. But we're for the right kind of growth—growth that comes with the necessary services. If growth occurs only to strangle our schools and jam our roads, then all of Orange County loses. Not only do residents suffer but so do businesses. So what can be done?

• **A more dramatic approach is needed, one that puts another step between the commission and developers.**

There is a way to do that. The technical name is an Areawide

Development of Regional Impact. That's a mouthful, but it would force commissioners—rather than the developers—to decide ahead of time how an area will develop and how that growth will be paid for.

The rural areas around the proposed beltway desperately need such a plan. So does the area west of International Corporate Park in southeast Orange County and the area east of Windermere. And on and on. All these areas are ripe for growth but, as expected, the commission is doing nothing to plan for it. After all, if there were ironclad plans for these areas, how could commissioners please developers who want to change the plan?

• **The area around the airport also cries for such an approach, but the commission would first have to have the courage to say no to Lake Nona.**

It's still not too late. Here's how such a plan would work: The commission first would study this area to see how it should develop—about how many homes, offices, industrial parks and stores it could stand. Presumably the commission would decide, too, that it's unwise for people to invest their life savings in homes right near the airport runways.

The plan also would detail how much developers have to pay for roads, schools, sewers and parks before they could build. The result: At last developers would pay the real cost of growth rather than stick the rest of us with their bills.

If commissioners later changed their minds about the details of the plan, then they would have to run those changes past regional planners, who would make sure services still would go hand in hand with the growth. No more changing the plan at the commission meeting because three commissioners are pals with a developer.

This is not some pie-in-the-sky concoction that can't work in the real world. Lake County is taking this approach for a 16-square mile undeveloped area at Florida's Turnpike and U.S. Highway 27. Altamonte Springs has done this for its downtown.

Would Orange County commissioners take such an approach and finally start planning? If they want to manage growth, they will. If they want to continue to play palsy-walsy with the developers at everyone else's expense, they will not. A betting person would put odds on a non-stop game of palsy-walsy. That is Florida's Shame.

CHILD OF THE TELEVISION AGE

1988 WINNER IN THE CRITICISM CATEGORY

"For distinguished criticism . . ."

The Washington Post
Tom Shales

If the quality of TV programming has improved at all, Tom Shales of *The Washington Post* probably deserves some credit. Programmers know that whenever millions of viewers tune in to any television show, one pair of very alert and critical eyes is likely among them.

Tom Shales, the TV critic of *The Washington Post,* has made a powerful impact on the industry he covers as well as on American journalism. When Electronic Media conducted a survey of industry executives last September, it found Shales "so dominant in his field" that he was chosen both favorite and least favorite TV critic by those polled, "many of whom insisted that Mr. Shales be tallied in both categories."

Shales takes television seriously and understands how it operates, how it affects viewers, and how it is capable of wrenching the heart or offending the sensibilities. He believes in its promise, is alarmed by its shortcomings and writes about both with unfailing verve and intelligence.

Washington Post readers rely upon Tom Shales. A strongly favorable Shales preview almost always adds several points to local ratings.

But Shales' characteristically confident views, now syndicated in 160 newspapers, reach far beyond the Beltway.

Earlier this year, for example, Shales questioned the suitability of a proposed CBS series based on the "Garbage Pail Kids," writing, "That a major network has decided to produce a cartoon series derived from drawings of mangled and deformed children dramatizes the violent and grotesque lengths to which children's television can now go." The network pulled the show from its Saturday morning lineup only days before it was scheduled to premiere.

Many of the stories submitted here show Shales's range and versatility in his work as a previewer and reviewer of programming. Others, including his coverage of the Reagan-Gorbachev summit, demonstrate his work as an analyst of on- and off-camera coverage, as well as an astute observer of the life many Americans know only through the tube.

Tom Shales is a child of the television age. He is a relentless viewer, and knows that, as a critic, he must assume the role of early warning system.

But Shales never forgets the wider impact of the medium, the way it shapes and reflects more subtle social changes. "What has to be reinvented is not only television, but the way we watch it," he observed of the cosmetic overhaul that television underwent during the 1980s.

A profile in *Channels* magazine last February concluded: "Tom Shales is too good to be ignored and, in the world of daily television, he's all alone at the top." And, because Shales is a writer whose judgment is so widely respected, he has had the kind of influence few critics in any field achieves: he has made the medium better.

—Leonard Downie Jr., Managing Editor
The Washington Post

ON THE AIR
OUT OF THE GARBAGE PAIL

AND ONTO YOUR SCREEN, COURTESY OF CBS

MONDAY, JUNE 15, 1987

BY TOM SHALES

Bustin' Dustin, his limbs tied in knots, lies face down in a battered heap, blood running from his nose. Basket Casey dribbles his own severed head across the gymnasium floor. Screaming Mimi is being chased and stung by a swarm of bees, Travellin' Travis has been crushed under the wheels of a car, and Well Done Sheldon, shot full of arrows, is being burned at the stake.

These are some of the "Garbage Pail Kids" pictured on a popular strain of bubble gum trading cards that have sold in the millions to American children since they first appeared in 1985. Now CBS has announced that it will introduce a new, animated version of "Garbage Pail Kids" in its Saturday morning kiddy cartoon lineup starting this fall. The series—produced, like many TV cartoon shows, in Taiwan —will air immediately following "Pee-wee's Playhouse," when very young children are the target audience.

While CBS insists that the TV series will not feature the mutilations, torture and disfigurement that have made the cards a strange, sick-humor sensation among American youngsters, the network does promise in publicity that the series will be "unorthodox, wild and wacky" and offer "short comedy blackouts straight from the offbeat humor of the cards"—such gags as "Fried Franklin's discovery of electricity."

Children may find this good news. Parents may not. That a major network has decided to produce a cartoon series derived from drawings of mangled and deformed children dramatizes the violent and grotesque lengths to which children's television can now go. The Federal

Communications Commission holds networks and stations to virtually no standards with regard to children's programming.

And so, "Garbage Pail Kids" goes on the air in September.

"This is particularly insensitive of CBS," charges Thomas Radecki, research director of the National Coalition on Television Violence (NCTV). "I think it's a real mistake. The cards are extremely sadistic. They take the most intensive, sadistic fantasies from war and horror movies and turn them into entertainment for young children."

Peggy Charren, president of Action for Children's Television (ACT), says the cards ridicule children who are physically impaired. "The idea that you take handicapping conditions and make them funny, and have to go to that kind of humor on children's television, I find outrageous," Charren says.

"Nothing about the content that's targeted to children surprises me any more," adds Charren, but she chides the networks for "looking at the creepiest toys children play with and turning those into programs." She says the humor of "Garbage Pail Kids" might be all right on "Saturday Night Live" but that "it is not appropriate for Saturday morning."

At CBS, Judy Price, vice president for children's programming, concedes that plans for the "Garbage Pail Kids" TV show have elicited angry mail from parents and concern from worried CBS affiliates. But she insists the program will not deal in the kind of gross-out humor common on the cards, which are manufactured by Topps Chewing Gum Inc.

"We don't go to some of the extremes of the cards," Price says. "There are some of those cards that make my stomach turn. On the cards you see acne, mucus, throw-up, children hurt. You're not going to see that on our show."

"I'm sure they could not possibly make the cartoon the way the cards are," says Radecki. "The cards have things like a little boy chopping off people's heads, a little girl trapped inside a blender, a baby with a huge safety pin through its chest and abdomen. These images are really more brutal than the stuff you see in the worst of the horror movies."

Price says five major characters will star each week. None sounds as grisly or gory as the worst characters on the cards. But, as described by Price, they don't sound particularly innocuous, either. Of heroine Terry Cloth, Price says, "Her face is on her hand," and as for Eliot Mess, "He's a little messed up. Let's just say his body parts are not in the right order."

Children will not be chopped up, decapitated, squished, stretched or otherwise mangled, as they are on the cards, Price promises. "Of course not. We're not going to do anything that is violent. That would be outrageous and gross and irresponsible."

But Radecki thinks the show sounds outrageous and gross and irresponsible anyway. "I can't imagine it being nonviolent," he says. "The whole purpose of the cards is to assault the viewer. By their very conception, they're violent.

"I'm sure CBS will have to tone it down for Saturday morning television, but in a very powerful way, it's giving major social sanction to the cards and their extreme and brutal sadism for young children," Radecki says. "It gives out the message that the cards are appropriate for children, and that leads to even further desensitization to violence."

Price claims the program will remain "within wholesome entertainment boundaries" and says that while "it delivers on certain expectations of youngsters" who've seen and bought the cards, it is nevertheless "not in poor taste."

Does the program break taboos in children's TV? "It does in some ways, yes," Price says. "But not bad-taste taboos. Things that are on the edge of slight irreverence. It's not antisocial, but neither have we turned the characters into Care Bears. If we do, then we are not going to have an audience."

Price dismisses the argument that her supposedly nonviolent program nevertheless promotes, and will help sell, the clearly violent cards. "I don't find that an issue I'm concerned about," she says, "because they've already sold a billion copies. This is very much a part of our popular culture."

Topps had to be talked into licensing the characters for a TV show, Price says. CBS, unlike the other two networks, does not enter into coproduction deals with toy and novelty manufacturers to base TV shows on their products as a way of promoting them; CBS is paying Topps a license fee (undisclosed) for the TV rights to the characters.

"In fact, it was very difficult to convince Topps to do the show," Price says. "I had to chase them and chase them."

"I don't think that's quite accurate," says Topps spokesman Norman Liss from the company's Brooklyn headquarters. "We're delighted that they're doing it. It's just one of our licensing things." A movie is also in the works, but CBS is not involved in that.

Liss won't confirm Price's claim that a billion cards have been sold but says, in answer to criticism of the cards from parents' and antiviolence groups, "Millions and millions of people have been buying this product. Certainly those people were expressing their opinion and their approval. If we thought anything was too gross, we wouldn't put it out."

And so the marketplace speaks again, this time in favor of bubble gum cards (five to a pack, plus gum, for 25 cents) that feature such cartoon characters as Rutherford B. Hay, a pudgy child scarecrow whose left eye has been plucked out by a bird, and Unzipped Zack, a little boy who unzips his face to reveal a demonic skull underneath.

These characters may not appear on the CBS show, but the sensibility behind them is clearly what CBS has bought for its young audience —or rather, for the advertisers (mostly of sugary cereals, fast food and candy) who want to reach them.

Radecki says children's television has become increasingly violent again, after a few years of seeming reform, and both he and Charren blame, in part, former FCC chairman Mark Fowler and his laissez-faire attitude toward children's programming. During Fowler's reign, TV cartoon shows built around, and promoting, current toys, including violent ones, proliferated. Charren calls these shows "program-length commercials" that are disguised as entertainment but relentlessly pitch products to kids.

The District Court of Appeals is expected to rule soon on a suit ACT filed against the FCC for its failure to protect young viewers from such sustained commercial assaults. Radecki is pushing for legislation that would, among other things, ban commercials for violent war toys and require networks and stations to air antiviolence public service announcements aimed at kids.

Radecki says that while one may laugh off a phenomenon like "Garbage Pail Kids," it contributes to increased desensitization to violence in American society and thus to an even more violent culture. "It's a gradual process," he says. "We get desensitized to one step and then take the next step before we realize it. You find increasing acceptance of brutality and sadism as socially appropriate forms of entertainment.

"We all need to take this issue more seriously," Radecki says.

What CBS takes seriously is the proven child-luring power, and revenue-earning potential, of the cards. CBS finished the 1986–87 TV season in second place in the Saturday morning ratings, behind NBC, and would love to move up. Will "Garbage Pail Kids" help bring that about? "I think," says Price gleefully, "we have a very strong chance of having a hit."

'AMERIKA' THE VIEWABLE

ABC'S CONTROVERSIAL MINI-SERIES: A DARING, GRIM VOYAGE

SUNDAY, FEBRUARY 15, 1987

BY TOM SHALES

"Amerika" has its little problems. Its script is uneven, its direction is arch, it succumbs too frequently to stupefying lulls, and its leading man gives a performance so wooden you could make a coffee table out of it.

Not to mention that it has been condemned in advance for alleged gross insensitivity by, it would seem, much of the Western world. Ted Turner compared it to Nazi propaganda. Carl Sagan has called it a "laughable embarrassment." Citizens for This and the Committee for That have rushed to trounce it for supposed Cold Warmongering.

After all that, is "Amerika" worth watching? Yes. It is even worth enduring, and indeed seems at times to constitute a virtual viewer endurance test.

The seven-part, nearly 15-hour ABC mini-series, premiering tonight at 9 on Channel 7 (and concluding a week from tonight at the same time), was written, produced and directed by one man, Donald Wrye, which alone makes it distinctive among long-form television programs—even most short-form ones. But the real novelty here, of course, is the premise. "Amerika" is set in a subdivided and subjugated United States of 1997 that has spent 10 dreary years under Soviet occupation and control.

No one in the movie seems to remember precisely how the Soviets accomplished the dastardly feat of takeover back in that naive year of 1987. There is talk among the populace of the Soviets' having nuked Seattle, but mostly as a demonstration of power, not as the spearhead of an invasive assault. That the mini-series imagines a World War III fought without the use of nuclear weapons has ticked off some of the peace groups making war on it.

All political balderdash aside, "Amerika" deserves credit for its daring grimness, practically unheard of along the prime-time midway; for tackling tough subjects like national morality and human rights in sometimes subtle and affecting ways; for an intense and thoughtful sobriety that is unyieldingly consistent; and for showcasing a few fine, strong, moving performances.

These include Christine Lahti as Alethea, an embittered, acerbic schoolteacher; Cindy Pickett as Amanda, the conscience-stricken wife of a Vietnam vet co-opted into serving as a Soviet factotum; and the handily compelling Richard Bradford as Ward Milford, brother of the movie's hero and a worried, assertive pragmatist.

Such potent contributors help offset the fact that the central character, resistance leader Devin Milford, is played in a dazed, somnambulatory blur by non-actor Kris Kristofferson. There's never been a soggier firebrand than this supposedly galvanizing one-time presidential candidate and former Democratic senator from Massachusetts.

Wrye hasn't given Kristofferson much help. In Part 1, Kris has an entire paragraph of dialogue. The suspense derives from waiting for him actually to speak a sentence. But Kristofferson is a body-language illiterate, too. Looking into those blank, squinty little eyes, one is reminded of lyrics from the rock opera "Tommy": "What is happening, in his head? . . . Ooo-ooh, I wish I knew!"

In Part 2, Sam Neill as Col. Andrei Denisov, a top Soviet honcho, watches old videotape of Milford and declares, "If I could understand this man, I could understand America." That's the biggest insult to America that "Amerika" could deliver. The episode ends with a Soviet-controlled Lincoln Day celebration at which Kristofferson thrills and mobilizes a crowd just by staring at them.

"Amerika" takes place mostly in Milford County, Nebraska, which is being assimilated into a five-state Soviet Socialist Republic called "Heartland," and in Chicago, Ill., now capital of the "Central Administrative Area." In tonight's premiere, Devin Milford is released from "an American gulag" in southwest Texas, after six years of imprisonment and brain laundry, and makes his way, oh so very slowly, back to his namesake home town of Milford, where as an internal exile he is required to remain, but doesn't.

Throughout the mini-series (the first 10 hours of which were available for preview), the action switches back and forth between Chicago and Milford County, with the occasional scene in Washington, where a puppet government set up by the invaders goes through parliamentary motions and a satrap identified as "the last president of the United States" exists only as an impotent transitional symbol. In Part 6, the Soviets will blow up the U.S. Capitol as a way of reminding the populace who's boss.

In poor old Milford, now desolate and crawling with desperate refugees, the Soviets tighten their grip as the mini-series goes on. In a harrowing, 13-minute sequence near the end of Part 3, tanks and helicopters level an exiles' shantytown in the surrounding countryside, crushing women and children in the debris. During one scene from tonight's slow-to-start premiere, breakfast patrons of Herb and Betty's diner are complaining they must settle for soybean cakes and molasses instead of Aunt Jemima pancakes and syrup; by Part 4, Betty herself is being hauled away in a Soviet truck.

Whereabouts of Herb unknown.

Among the Milfordites are Robert Urich as Amanda's husband, the earnestly compromising Peter Bradford, who has been serving as "county administrator" in Milford when the story begins and who is later entreated by the Soviets to become the first "governor general" of the new Heartland region. Urich is sullen much of the time, and his jowls sag mightily and poutily, but his performance is acceptable in a TV-movie way.

The two families whose lives interact in Milford are the Milfords and the Bradfords (to confuse things, the most dynamic of the Milfords is played by a Bradford: Richard). Pickett is strikingly good as Mrs. Bradford and has a real Dorothea Lange populism about her. But it is Lahti, as Devin Milford's sister, who repeatedly awakens scenes from the dead and projects a spirited, earthy insouciance that makes her character vivid and believable.

Unfortunately, in Part 3 she must recite a long, painful monologue about having been raped by occupying soldiers that doesn't seem credible or relevant. Worse, Lahti disappears entirely through all of Parts 4 and 5, returning in Part 6, a victim of Wrye's blundering miscalculation.

Meanwhile, in Chicago, Mariel Hemingway plays Kimberly, a simpering dimwit of an actress who stars in underground theatricals—including, as a Wrye touch, "The Fantasticks," a scene from which opens the mini-series, the point being perhaps that yesterday's innocuous bonbon can be tomorrow's forbidden fruit (or that literally nothing can close "The Fantasticks"?). Kimberly also serves as obedient mistress to Col. Denisov, and it takes her the longest, longest time to see a certain duplicity there.

Based on the way Wrye depicts women, it's feminists, not peaceniks, who should be angriest with him. Most of the women in "Amerika" are helpless drones to sexual desire; they sort of like being occupied. The characters played by Lahti and Hemingway are both sleeping with the enemy, and the wily and lively Wendy Hughes, who plays Devin Milford's traitorous ex-wife Marion, worked her way up through the ranks of the puppet regime in the beds and bathtubs of a particularly sinister Soviet general. Hughes plays Marion just evilly enough to stir memories of the only other mini-series about America under foreign occupation, NBC's "V," in which the invaders were lizards from outer space.

Sexual encounters seem invariably to be initiated by women. The Bradfords' teen-age daughter keeps coaxing her rebel boyfriend mattress-side. Brainless Kimberly goes horizontal at nearly every glimpse of her leaden loverboy. Lahti's Alethea grovels in kinky masochistic subservience to a sadistic East German. You could boil "Amerika" down to the bedroom scenes, put them on an adults-only videotape, and peddle it as "These Women Want It," "Hotski to Trotski" or "Sex Slaves of the Kremlin."

Impressionable viewers may want to investigate the potentials of soybeans as a female aphrodisiac.

Wrye is entitled to harbor regressive male fantasies but not to populate a mini-series with them. One could draw the conclusion from what's seen on the screen that whatever Russian men have, American men don't, and American women crave. Maybe the Soviets gained control just by seducing their way in—*Invasion of the Commie Hunks!*

Now as for the political discussions, the whither democracy stuff, it is there in abundance, and some of it is intelligently provocative. "You lost your country before we ever got here," Neill tells Urich. "You had political freedom, but you lost your passion," he says later. Americans were "self-absorbed and dispirited" when the Soviets moved in, it is declared—also, "weak and divided."

Wrye's most quixotic pontificating is contained in the speeches made by Devin Milford when, we are told, he ran for president in 1988 (he didn't win because his wicked wife betrayed him). Milford announced his candidacy at the Vietnam Veterans Memorial, saying, "Many of us lost our faith in the vision of the country" because of Vietnam and lecturing, "We don't need troops to tell us we've lost our vision . . . Americans have allowed themselves to become immobilized by their own selfish concerns."

These selfish concerns, Milford says, include "minority" issues and those that pit "women against men." At points like this, Wrye's thinking gets woefully muddy. He wants people to participate in democracy but, it would seem, not to speak out for their own interests.

On the other hand, elements of this convoluted litany are reflected in the real-life uproar over the approach of "Amerika"—the notions that we are squishy-soft and constantly bickering among ourselves, for instance. One frequently voiced criticism of "Amerika," by TV reviewers and protesting groups alike, is that it's boring. It's not enough fun. Who wants a dour old civics lesson? Soviet conquest of the United States oughta be entertaining.

If we are squishy-soft, it's television that has helped make us so, endorsing at every juncture the idea that we are entitled to 'round-the-clock frivolity and sport. NBC is entreating viewers to watch the usual witless inanity tonight—in this case a movie called "The Facts of Life Down Under"—with the implied promise that, unlike that killjoy "Amerika," it makes no demands whatever on the mind.

Bickering special-interest groups, meanwhile, have veritably tumbled out of the woodwork in the rush to condemn "Amerika," quibbling and haggling over its ostensible threats and dangers before any of their members had glimpsed a single frame. It's almost as if they were striving to validate the movie's contention that we have become a nation of self-absorbed crybabies. Or whinebabies anyway.

If we are a pack of bickering brats, "Amerika" itself may not make the point as well as pre-reaction to "Amerika" has. As for the complaint that "Amerika" is beastly to the Russians, that's a phony. Wrye seems to have gone overboard to de-nationalize his villains. They aren't Russian stereotypes. Wrye wanted them to work as generic symbols of oppression, and they do. They may remind a viewer of a superintendent, instructor or editor, for example—one or more of the petty bureaucrats encountered every day.

Among the most telling details in Wrye's detailed canvas are the little portraits of those who are not that uncomfortable under totalitarian rule, who like the sense of order, who even thrive under the rigid new codes. You can walk down a street and pick such people out of a crowd, or see them in footage on the evening news, urging that books be banned from classrooms or that some other freedom be curtailed.

The Russians may be offended by the portrayals even though they're low-profile Russianness. Well isn't that a pity? Isn't that a crime? The Soviets don't look good in "Amerika," no, but they don't look so hot in Afghanistan, either. KGB agents didn't look cute roughing up Russian Jews and snipping the cable of an ABC crew in news tape aired Thursday night on U.S. TV, either. All part of the new "openness," of course.

It's been widely alleged that "Amerika" is intended partly as an apology for "The Day After," ABC's 1983 shocker about an imagined nuclear attack. The program irritated conservatives nearly to the degree that "Amerika" has inflamed liberals. If anything, "Amerika" seems more an apology for last summer's egregious "Liberty Weekend" pageant, also seen on ABC. Viewers beheld this horrendous Las Vegas glitz orgy and imagined that it had some incomprehensible relationship to democratic values and love of country.

Watching 200 Elvis impersonators or a fireworks display is about as serious as many people want to get about patriotism. Wrye asks more—more of the citizenry than is usually asked, and more of viewers than television usually asks. Part of what's required is patience at waiting through the long empty stretches, but another part is a willingness to confront material that at its best is challengingly complex and densely textured and relatively free of snap answers.

Often deficient as drama, not uniformly sophisticated in its political noodling, unbearably slack at times, "Amerika" is nevertheless commendable for its seriousness. ABC's and Wrye's motives have been trashed by agitated detractors, but if anything, "Amerika" is a good deal less exploitive than the typical TV, pander, and clearly has higher aspirations.

It does make you think about, (and gives you plenty of quiet time to reflect upon) pertinent fundamentals, matters of citizenship and conscience, in ways that few entertainments have tried to do. So bring a snack. Bring a pillow. Bring another TV set if necessary. But try to drop by. "Amerika" needs you. And in some curious, elusive way, America may even need "Amerika."

TELEVISION IN THE '80S: EMPTY AS EVER, BUT SPECTACULARLY STYLISH

SUNDAY, APRIL 12, 1987

BY TOM SHALES

Television looks better than ever. Honest! Program content may not have improved an iota, but form is definitely thriving. A supposedly visual medium is becoming dynamically visual at last. If there still is little worth watching, there now is more worth seeing.

It used to be that scant care was lavished on how something looked on TV, unless it was a plate of fluffy mashed potatoes in a commercial or an anchorperson's equally fluffy hair. Television programs tended to arrive on the screen brandishing the same styleless style, factory-made anonymousness marked by flat lighting, humdrum art direction and lackadaisical composition.

Then something happened. A few somethings happened. One was "Miami Vice," perhaps the first prime-time entertainment show in history to be pitched to viewers largely on the way it looked. Another was MTV, the cable network, which displays its high-fashion music videos in a showcase full of witty, gleaming animated graphics.

Suddenly, television was pretty. And getting prettier. An old law of TV maintains that only the worst trends proliferate, but here, something encouraging seems to be growing increasingly popular. The result: Video Nouveau, television of the '80s, arguably empty but wrapped in a coat of beguiling deluxe gloss.

"Miami Vice" may have spearheaded the trend in prime time, but now other producers have grabbed the baton and are running with it. The latest and most obvious example is ABC's inventive "Max Headroom," a wizardly mishmash set "20 minutes into the future" and lavished with the kind of production details that TV producers usually consider frivolous, or simply beyond reach.

"Max" has visual density. There may not be a lot more to it than what meets the eye (and the second episode was a drastic letdown from the first), but what meets the eye has detail and complexity beyond

357

that of most mortal television. You feel there's almost too much on the screen to take in, a rare sensation when it comes to TV watching. But viewers are becoming increasingly comfortable with that because of all the theatrical movies they consume on pay-cable and their VCRs.

As a practical matter, TV producers cannot command for their shows the kind of care and time expended on the production of a top-flight movie. But ways can be found to enhance the visual texture of a TV series and give it a distinctive consistency. At that, the producers and craftspeople behind the grinning and stammering Max have succeeded to a happily spectacular degree.

One young viewer told me after a recent encounter with Max, scheduled to be Newsweek's cover boy tomorrow, that the show's visual content was so heavy it gave him a headache. What a compliment to the producers! Way to go, Maxie baby!

Several years ago an ABC program executive, explaining why a hilarious satire called "Police Squad!" was canceled, decreed that the show was so fast and clever, viewers were required to pay too much attention to it. This dunce, since departed, was offering a tacit admission that most TV shows are designed not to be watched so much as glanced at. You don't partake of TV; you just have it "on" like the light in an aquarium.

That executive got the heave-ho, but his philosophy hung around. Now television may be developing a bit more self-respect. You do have to pay attention to "Max Headroom" or you really might miss something—if not something germane, at least something diverting, and very likely something enigmatically picturesque. What has to be reinvented is not only television but the way we watch it.

Other shows could be lumped into the Video Nouveau genre. NBC's colossal-to-stupendous flop "Amazing Stories" may be a bust as mind-expanding fantasy, but the show has a very rich look, perhaps the richest on TV now that the revived "Twilight Zone" is kaput. NBC's "L.A. Law" is a high-content and high-impact weekly drama, but it has a shimmering visual luster that is highly tactile. The program is shot on film but, as is increasingly the custom, edited electronically, on video-tape. The same network's dour "Crime Story" is covered in supple velour.

ABC's "Moonlighting" has included visual satire of old movie styles, but what predominates are the fuzzy-wuzzy lenses used on glamoroso close-ups of Cybill Shepherd. One episode, however, was filmed in black and white as a *film noir* homage (TV has yet to see a true *tape noir* production). It says something about the growing sophistication of the audience as well as of the producers that such knowing asides can be brought off in prime time.

Only one nonfiction television program could be shoehorned into the Video Nouveau category and that one is, of course, "West 57th." This forward-looking magazine-format production from CBS News is the bouncing brainchild of Madison Avenue-bred maverick Andrew Lack, executive producer. Lack went into this assignment determined to summon forth a TV magazine for the TV generation, not the print generation, and when "West 57th" returned recently for its third run on the network, its visual credentials were intact.

At first derided within the News division for its youth-baiting hyperglitzics, "West 57th" brandished such an emphatic, nearly nihilistic, kind of newness that initial critical reaction to the program was largely, and sometimes vehemently, negative.

People were suspicious of a news production that looked this good. Of course they hadn't been paying attention. In recent years the physical appearance of "The CBS Evening News With Dan Rather" had been upgraded dramatically; the editing pace within stories had been accelerated (sometimes excessively) and the art of electronic photography, on tape rather than the increasingly anachronistic film, was being perfected before our very eyes, and the CBS eye as well.

CBS has always enjoyed an enormous advantage over the other networks in terms of design. Cofounder and former chairman William S. Paley made good taste, at least in graphics and artwork, the eleventh commandment. The impeccable CBS art department has unfortunately been among the divisions devastated by budget cutbacks and layoffs dealt by new CBS chief executive Laurence A. Tisch, the domed avenger. But so far, no decline is evident in the CBS look on the air.

Compare this year's CBS Super Bowl with last year's NBC Super Bowl; the CBS trappings were incalculably more handsome. A tiny detail like the animated graphics and music that open the brief, nightly "We the People" segments on CBS (the "Bicentennial Minute" concept updated for the bicentennial of the U.S. Constitution) reaffirms that CBS still has the best eye in the business. How long this image of excellence will prevail is questionable; the gap between CBS style and CBS substance, as far as prime-time entertainment programming goes, has grown embarrassingly wide. Yawning even. Yeah, yawning.

Soon, one fears, CBS may be like Madame Tussaud's. It will have the best-dressed stiffs in town.

MTV's rock graphics are currently the flashiest on television—even its promos bubble with kinetic esprit (not to mention panache)—and the music-video network's influence is spilling out into the cable spectrum, inspiring such money-losing propositions as the Lifetime Channel to upgrade at least the look of what is offered to viewers. MTV's graphics and animated logos are the state of the art in television and have inspired healthy imitation.

One winces on behalf of MTV when its gorgeous visual hum must be interrupted for something as tacky as a Civil War chess set commercial or one of those 532-greatest-hits record blurbs. And yet the style consciousness of MTV is so high that, in context, even these blemishes take on a mild pop-art allure, as if they were parodies of importuning ugliness instead of the real thing.

Once it was axiomatic that if one went looking for innovation in network television, prime time was always the last place to find it. As the networks have been forced into competition with cable and with the home programming facilitated by VCRs, that has become less the case. NBC Entertainment President Brandon Tartikoff may put style and appearance low on his list of program priorities, but at least they're there somewhere, and other networks have had to follow suit, if slowly.

In the fringes of network time, meanwhile, is where the most provocative experimentation goes on. "Late Night With David Letterman" may be chiefly notable for its host and guiding spirit, one of the most ingratiating natural wits of our time (you know, that goofy-looking guy with the rigatoni hair), but the program has a delightful visual verve as well. The general funkiness of the studio setting comes across as charming, and the photographic "bumpers" that precede and follow commercials ("Late Night" delivery service, "Late Night" delicatessen) are attention-getting award-winners.

The Letterman show is infused with a sensibility carried over into all details. It's handmade, not machine-made, TV. The same is true of the most visually stylish program currently on any network, "Pee-wee's Playhouse," a new classic of kid-vid and hip-vid that CBS airs on Saturday mornings. Ostensibly children's fare, "Pee-wee" obviously attracts a sizable adult audience (sizable adults, and normal ones). Not for nothing does CBS run promos for Dan Rather's newscast right there in the middle of Pee-wee's funcast.

From the opening sight of an animated beaver chewing on a sign, through the artificial woods through which one must traipse to get to Pee-wee's place, "Playhouse" is a trip to the circus every week, and sometimes you may feel as if you're seeing it all from inside the calliope. A mesmerizing amalgamation of theatrical, cinematic and electronic effects, "Pee-wee's Playhouse" is an incomparable romp ripe to be heaped with art-director honors.

The design concept of the playhouse—the magic screen, beatnik puppets, genie-in-a-box, and the living popsicles and ice cubes that skate and cavort inside the fridge—expands and glorifies Pee-wee's conceit, that of being a kid reluctantly imprisoned in an adult's body. The artwork lends just enough concrete detail to the program's alternately zany and warm evocations of childhood.

Ironically, "Pee-wee's Playhouse" uses television to celebrate the pre-television fantasy life of children, as well as spoofing the long tradition of pandering kiddie-show entertainments.

"Pee-wee's Playhouse" and "Max Headroom" are probably the two most design-intensive programs on commercial TV right now. "Miami Vice" hews to its style—even if producer Michael Mann's famous "no earth tones" edict has since been retired—but the program seems terribly passé somehow. That may be a problem for style-conscious TV shows. The very styles they set can change. They're picked up by others, like those ever-alert scavengers on Madison Avenue, and grow tired.

"Max's" ambiance and décor clearly owe a lot to "Blade Runner" and the "Road Warrior" movies, although it should be pointed out that one of the first pop entertainments to depict the future as looking rather junky was "Star Wars," with its seedy cantina bar and rattletrap Millennium Falcon. The old image of the future as being sleek, shiny and germless has been supplanted in pop fantasies by a more cynical one.

Peter Wagg, executive producer of "Max Headroom" both here and in its earlier incarnation on England's Channel 4, says a "tremendous amount" of effort is exerted to give "Max" the right look. "We want to maintain a depth of production value that keeps people coming back week after week," says Wagg from Lorimar Productions in Hollywood, where "Max" is made.

Attention to detail has not often been a preoccupation of TV producers. Just getting the darn thing finished on time took precedence. Wagg says a new "nontelevision attitude" is surfacing in television that involves making mere TV shows look as good, or almost as good, as movies. The look does not come cheap. "Max" reportedly comes in at around $1.4 million an hour.

"I tell everybody, 'Every idea you've ever had, and people have told you you can't do, bring over here,' " says Wagg. "This is a very challenging show for everyone concerned—including, hopefully, those watching." No one anticipated "the sheer magnitude" of producing "Max" for weekly network TV, Wagg says, so "casualties are falling all over the battlefield at the moment" because "people are literally burned out" from the extra work it takes to push "Max" to the max.

In fact, the network asked Wagg for three more shows in addition to the original six it ordered for this season, and Wagg had to decline. Should ABC pick up "Max" for the fall, some scaling down seems inevitable, but the wily Wagg is determined to sustain as much of the production sheen as he can.

If "Max Headroom" succeeds, it will be good for television, just as the success of MTV and "Miami Vice" and, yes, "Pee-wee's Playhouse" have been good for television. As production design and art direction are upgraded, so the more substantive aspects of programmaking are likely to improve. An audience that starts taking visual excellence for granted is less likely to settle for the crummy and the shoddy however it manifests itself on the tube.

Not often when covering TV does one get to report on a change for the better. Video Nouveau may be one, and a change with wide-ranging potential. Seen any good television lately? It's increasingly likely that you have. One of the great things about TV is its infinite capacity for rejuvenation. Who knows but that its second childhood might even surpass its first.

ON THE AIR
THE DIVERTING DEMOCRATS

ON PBS, TELLING GLIMPSES OF SEVEN '88 CONTENDERS

FRIDAY, JULY 3, 1987

BY TOM SHALES

What a chore to tear oneself away from "Aliens" on HBO for "Democrats" on PBS. But it turns out the Democrats were a good show, too, if not precisely a hair-raising thriller.

William F. Buckley Jr. invited the seven most likely Democratic presidential contenders to join him in Houston Wednesday night for a "Firing Line Special." Buckley, the gourmet conservative, announced that the program would be "unsparingly partisan but scrupulously fair" and had asked "Mr. Democrat," former party chairman Robert Strauss, to cohost.

The structure was looser and more productive than the rigid League of Women Voters debates that precede elections.

Surely only our hardiest pundits are already in a 1988 election mood. But the program offered enlightening glimpses of the Democratic hopefuls, enough to afford a preliminary fix not so much on what kind of president each would make as on what kind of campaigner each will make. And how great a communicator. Everyone knows how important that is.

The bright new star to emerge was Sen. Paul Simon of Illinois, who is also the most unassuming of the bunch. He seemed level headed, forthright and peppery—as effortlessly folksy as Orville Redenbacher and, best of all, bracingly Trumanesque. Ronald Reagan never tired of comparing himself to FDR; maybe Simon could succeed Reagan as Truman succeeded Roosevelt. Maybe the country will want to go from head in the clouds to feet on the ground.

True, Simon looks a bit like Oscar Levant. He has oddly floppy earlobes. But these flaws are more like endearing badges of honor; Simon's neither simple nor synthetic. "If you want a slick, packaged product, I'm not your candidate," he said, stating the obvious and vowing to continue wearing those quaint bow ties no matter what.

Simon, who has such a rich baritone that he could be the announcer for the Metropolitan Opera broadcasts, is the most engaging new eccentric to hit television since Alf. Not Alf Landon; Alf the extraterrestrial.

Bruce Babbitt, the former Arizona governor, has a touch of Jimmy Stewart about him, but he also has a touch of Jimmy Carter—the lines in his face bring back Carter memories one doesn't want brought back—and parading around in flannel shirts (each candidate was allowed to bring a 90-second taped autobiography) doesn't help.

Jesse Jackson, who has sought the office before, obviously has a tremendous oratorical advantage over other contenders. He was the only candidate on the Buckley show to rise for his final summation. Jackson was so eager to prove a grasp of foreign affairs that he may have slighted domestic matters. He definitely had the most fashionable lapels.

After Jackson prescribed medicine for America's horrendous trade imbalance, Buckley grinned and said, "I happen to agree, but I don't want to embarrass you." Ah, Bill, ever the sly boots. And sometimes the Cheshire rat.

Richard A. Gephardt, representative from Missouri, appeared rather wimpish and ineffectual. He casts a fuzzy shadow. When Buckley, as the first question of the night, asked each candidate to say which presidential portraits he'd post in the Oval Office, Gephardt was a poor sport and wouldn't play along, saying "the real issue" was blah blah blah and declaring he'd put the Constitution on the wall. A copy, presumably.

Couldn't he have just answered the darn question? At least Gephardt did have the guts to say, on the subject of a balanced budget, "What Ronald Reagan needs is guts."

Michael S. Dukakis, the Massachusetts governor, has a pleasing, cushioned television manner, very relaxed and conversational and, alas, not very exciting. Television calls for a politician to be easygoing and electrifying at the same time. It calls for that mainly because Ronald Reagan, in his prime, anyway, was able to do it.

Albert Gore, senator from Tennessee, reinforced his image as a plain, dull square. He looks like Clark Kent—but a Clark Kent who would never dream of undressing in a phone booth. Nor perhaps anywhere else. Having a wife who sniffs out naughty rock lyrics hardly mitigates the impression. Gore opens his mouth and one feels a snooze coming on. But he was good sparring with, and getting the best of, Buckley during a tiff over "Star Wars" experts and projected costs.

Finally there is Joseph R. Biden Jr., senator from Delaware, and famous George Shultz tongue-lasher. Biden seems bright, tough and bold. Also very, very scary. One might even say terrifying. He has Rod Serling's upper lip, which is no shortcoming, but suggests maybe he should only be president of the Twilight Zone.

Like Gephardt, Biden refused to play along with Buckley's harmless, colorful opening question. The candidate appears to be overadvised and suffering from excessive consultitis. Worse, he comes across on TV as someone whose fuse is always lit. Unless we ditch television for the remainder of the campaign, Biden will never be president.

Except for some sluggish camera work, the program ran smoothly, but someone should have handed Buckley a cough drop, because he began the program loudly clearing his throat and kept that up through all two hours. Apparently he was ill. But a viewer might have interpreted all the noisy throat clearing as an intrusive rhetorical trick. Maybe Bill has been spending too much time out on the bounding main aboard his yacht.

He gingerly avoided asking the candidates for their reaction to Reagan's announcement of Judge Robert H. Bork to fill a Supreme Court vacancy. By repeatedly anticipating "Reagan-bashing" and the "torturing and dismembering of Ronald Reagan," Buckley tried to make the Democrats look as though they were being mean to the old boy, but there was no meanness at all.

Perhaps, actually, it's time for some.

Buckley's adversarial posture was probably helpful. It kept the candidates on the alert and helped prevent doldrums. Nearly everyone may be dreading the long campaign year ahead, but this "Firing Line Special," produced and directed by Warren Steibel, got it off to a promising start. It said to the viewing electorate, "Maybe this won't be as bad as you think."

It also indicated that maybe it's the *other* Paul Simon who will soon be known as "the other Paul Simon."

TWO PEARLS IN PRIME TIME

'HOOPERMAN' & 'SLAP' ARE CUTS ABOVE THE REST

WEDNESDAY, SEPTEMBER 23, 1987

BY TOM SHALES

"Hooperman" and "The 'Slap' Maxwell Story," two weirdly wonderful ABC comedies premiering tonight, are so good you may not only want to watch them, you may want to buy each of them a drink. At the very least, a toast should be raised: to the good health of shows like this.

John Ritter stars as an unorthodox San Francisco cop, Harry Hooperman, in "Hooperman," at 9 on Channel 7, and Dabney Coleman plays downright uncouth sportswriter Slap Maxwell in his "Story," at 9:30 on Channel 7.

Together these shows make a great hour of misfit comedy that also serves as a barricade against that proverbial rising tide of mediocrity we're always hearing so much about.

"Hooperman" was created, and the premiere written, by Steven Bochco and Terry Louise Fisher of "L.A. Law," and produced and directed by Gregory Hoblit. They all won Emmys the other night, for what that's worth. "Hooperman" is worth a lot. It's about a caring guy who is not a cliché and who is willing to admit, every now and then, that life has gotten him down.

Life *can* get you down. The only people life never gets down, usually, are characters in situation comedies.

"You know your trouble, Hooperman?" growls a porky, Borky cop named Pritzger in the precinct house. "You're a liberal, snot-nosed, civil service lifer."

"That was just a lucky guess, Pritzger," Hooperman responds. In

367

the role, John Ritter banishes memories of the tumbling goof he played for years on "Three's Company"—now he's more crestfallen than pratfallen—and creates an instantly likable rumpled hero.

To call "Hooperman" a sitcom demeans it. Some out in Hollywood are floating the term "dramedy" to describe the relatively new breed of show that "Hooperman" personifies—comic in outlook yet 99 percent gag-free. Bochco and Fisher fall back now and then on their old trick of alternating pathos with farce, but "Hooperman" somehow stays grounded in a solid reality of its own.

Ritter is an unexpendable reason why.

In the first episode, Harry starts out on a typical day, waking in his plebe-chic San Francisco apartment house, exchanging morning chatter with his friend the landlady and trying to avoid her mean-spirited little dog. Later in the day, Harry learns that the landlady has been killed in a stupid, bungled robbery. Then he learns how close they really were; she has left him her apartment building.

Thus has the premise been set up with inventive finesse. When Harry is not beleaguered as a cop, he will be besieged as a landlord. Ritter pinpoints the sense of decency and the seasoned resignation that will help see Harry through.

The producers and writers did make a few mistakes. Bochco cast his wife, Barbara Bosson, as the standard-issue nasty nemesis police captain (the fact that it's a woman instead of a man hardly shatters the cliché), and Bosson is annoying.

A running gag about a gorgeous woman cop (Sydney Walsh) who tirelessly pursues a firmly resistant gay cop (Joseph Gian), while having a certain bittersweet charm, seems anachronistic and naive considering the AIDS scare and the fact that the show is set in San Francisco.

But so many things have been done right. And righter than Ritter you couldn't get; he captures and ennobles Harry's battle-scarred optimism and makes him a true citizen of the '80s. He's especially adept at coaxing a potential leaper off a ledge with a dramatic demonstration that owes a little something to "Late Night With David Letterman" (as do we all).

Also adding considerably more than two cents' worth at the precinct are Felton Perry as Clarence McNeil and Clarence Felder as the supremely cynical Pritzger and, arriving on a wildly hopeful note at the apartment house, Deborah Mullowney as a living salvation named Susan Smith.

"Hooperman's" finest moment occurs near the fade-out. Harry succumbs to grief over the loss of a loved one, and that is something one rarely sees on prime-time television. Usually when characters die they disappear like blips from a video game. Harry quietly remembers.

At that moment, "Hooperman" goes from simply wow to oh-my-God.

If Harry Hooperman is rumpled, what is Slap Maxwell? Crumpled, actually, and just about at the end of his rope, except you get the feeling he was born there, too. With his portrayal of Slap, Dabney Coleman does more than add to his list of memorable characterizations. He achieves a metamorphosis of virtually scientific elegance.

Seldom in the history of popular entertainment has a broken-down old schlub had such towering stature. Slap Maxwell is a small-town sports columnist who's eyeball to eyeball with 50. And 50 is not blinking. Slap doesn't get respect, doesn't get understanding, can't even quite worm his way into qualifying for pity, yet the man has a heroism about him that borders on the mythic.

The Slapper, as he sometimes calls himself, is the creation of writer-producer Jay Tarses, and like Tarses's recent NBC experiment, "The Days and Nights of Molly Dodd," the Maxwell saga is less a situation comedy than an unfolding, serialized novel. Tarses and Coleman teamed earlier on "Buffalo Bill," a show that never quite got its rhythms right.

It was easy to admire "Molly Dodd" and "Buffalo Bill," but hard to like them. That comes easier with " 'Slap' Maxwell," because although Tarses and Coleman have pushed their hero to the outermost limits of irredeemability, you can still see a spark there of something that merits attention and even, dare we say, devotion.

" 'Slap's' " story is structured unlike any other comedy on the air. Scenes are long, speeches ramble on, sets are alarmingly drab and dreary. No one has even installed computer terminals at Slap's ragtag newspaper, The Ledger, from which he is noisily fired in Episode 1, but by which he is reluctantly rehired, thank heaven, in Episode 3.

One beneficial effect of "Moonlighting" is that it has made banter marketable on television again, and " 'Slap' Maxwell" is banter-intensive. Some of it is priceless. Slap has a relationship, of sorts, with

Judy, the staff secretary, played as the Annie Oakley of zinger-flingers by Megan Gallagher. In an early scene, Slap fumbles another pass and gets what would seem the latest in a long line of rejections.

Judy: "You're ugly, and you smoke cigars."

Slap: "I'd quit cigars."

Judy: "Then you're halfway there."

Every scene is a potentially ego-crushing encounter for Slap, but the ego is the one part of him that hangs in there, and you honestly do root for it. Retiring to a bar and the solace grumblingly proffered by the bartender, Dutchman (Bill Cobbs, clearly one who has heard it all), Slap philosophizes about getting sacked.

Slap: "You know, actually, this might be the best thing that could happen to me. New lease on life. It's a big world out there. Sky's the limit. There's a bus called Destiny waiting for me, and I'm going to ride it down the highway to tomorrow."

Dutchman: "Six clichés in 10 seconds!"

Slap: "Was it six?"

Dutchman: "Takes your breath away."

Some of the best, choicest exchanges, though, are between Slap and his editor, Nelson Kruger (Brian Smiar), from whom malaprops drip like water off a duck's hat. In the third episode, Slap, his sports column having been taken from him, has written a feature story on hats, and Kruger eats it up.

Kruger: "I like it. It speaks of bygone days when life was simpler, before the world got all jammed up. You know what era it calls to mind?"

Slap: "The era of hats?"

Kruger: "Yeah. Snap-brims and derbies and skimmers; you remember them?"

Slap: "I do. Let's name all the different hats."

For the first couple of shows, Slap goes around telling everyone Kruger has a glass eye. Then he changes it to a peg leg. One of the salubrious side effects of " 'Slap' Maxwell" is that it dramatically reasserts the moral superiority writers, however lowly, have always enjoyed over editors, however lofty. " 'Slap' Maxwell" is a show about the joy of writing in more ways than one.

At every turn, Tarses steers away from the comfy sitcom staples.

For instance, an extremely cute little Japanese girl, Slap's neighbor, shows up looking for her lost dog in Episode 2. Slap slams the door in her face.

Susan Anspach will be appearing, to great advantage, starting next week, as Slap's wife, who moved out on him 15 years ago but whom he still expects back. He comes muling around about his midlife crisis and does a whither-I-goest soliloquy at the window. "Your life is always in a crisis," she reminds him. "It's mother's milk to you. You thrive on it."

As Slap thrives on crisis, so there will be a certain kind of viewer who will thrive on "Slap." Even those who find it a bit mannered (each episode opens with someone punching Slap—a nun does the honors in No. 2), surely will see the crazed power and the shaggy glory in Coleman's performance.

It's the stuff that dreams are made of, in the sense that so is a banana split before bed. I meant it about raising a toast: To Harry! To Slap! And even . . . to television! Takes your breath away.

ON THE AIR
THE PAGEANT ON A DAY OF GRACE

WEDNESDAY, DECEMBER 9, 1987

B Y   T O M   S H A L E S

Admit it, it was thrilling. Ronald Reagan, Mikhail Gorbachev, the signing of the treaty, the ceremonial panoply, the quotations from Ralph Waldo Emerson, and that little saunter the two world leaders took down a red-carpeted hallway between the East Room and the State Dining Room of the White House.

"Nice moment here," understated Dan Rather on CBS as a camera followed the two ambling men. Gorbachev stopped to shake hands with an unseen person behind a pillar. The Marine Band played a sprightly air.

NBC had the same shot, but ABC unwisely went to a map of the White House, missing one of the small informal details that helped make yesterday's signing of the INF treaty enormously moving to watch on TV.

When the two men got to the State Dining Room and were outfitted with earpieces for the simultaneous translations, Ronald Reagan approached the podium and said, "Well thank you, and thank you all very much. And, I think that maybe I got out the wrong set of notes here. Still," he continued, unfazed, as he brought out the right set, "I do say thank you very much."

In making his bid for greatness, The Gipper sacrificed not a scintilla of his incomparable charm.

Earlier, during presigning remarks in the East Room, Reagan had revived yet again his favorite Russian maxim, "Trust, but verify." Gorbachev began to chuckle. "You repeat that at every meeting," he chided. "I like it," Reagan said cheerfully. Then he continued with his talk.

Network reporters were still combing the earth to ferret out every conceivable objection or complication to the treaty, and estimating its chances for ratification (on CBS, Jeane Kirkpatrick predicted there'd be no problem getting it approved), but no amount of carp nor cavil could sour the overwhelming sense of accomplishment and fellowship. This was Christmas, Hanukah, the Fourth of July and your most fondly remembered birthday party all rolled into one.

On NBC, correspondent John Hart said from Moscow that for an American to wander the streets of that capital and speak of the historic agreement being signed in Washington was to "risk getting a bear hug" from a Soviet citizen. The world has relatively few opportunities for such salubrious celebration. Who could be blamed for not wanting to hear any discouraging words?

Not that television anchors and reporters should have showered the occasion with gush, and few if any did. They instead seemed a bit in the way; the event was too big for them, and they didn't know quite what to do with it.

They are not allowed to just sit back and say how wonderful it all is. But they must have been tempted. "Nice moment there" was about as close as it got.

Reagan's short speech in the State Dining Room was one of the most gracious and deftly delivered of his presidency, which is certainly saying something. How odd that both the American and Soviet leaders quoted Emerson. Perhaps we're in for a big transcendentalist revival. Worse things could happen. And better things, too.

Quoting an unnamed Russian soldier present at the end of World War II, Reagan said the treaty helped ensure "a time to live." He said America was more than free markets and materialism: "The true America . . . is a land of faith and family." In the context of the occasion, these did not sound like platitudes.

Reagan concluded his speech and NBC's Tom Brokaw couldn't think of anything to say but, "President Reagan—getting in a pitch for human rights," as if this were a sports event. Later, Brokaw reported that the Americans would be hosting a black-tie dinner at the White House later that night and said, "We'll see whether the Soviet side shows up in formal wear."

Right, Tom, we'll see. There was little danger of Brokaw being carried away by the emotions of the occasion. Too bad.

It was Gorbachev's speech that contained all the pitching. One sympathized with Reagan having to stand there while the Soviet leader praised Lenin. Yech. This was clearly a campaign speech for the folks back home, and the folks back home were watching. Mark Phillips reported on CBS from a square in Moscow over which a giant TV screen loomed, turning the live transmission from the States into a luminous billboard.

Phillips said there had been "spontaneous, and I mean spontaneous, applause."

Pictures from Moscow became a bone of contention between ABC News and NBC News, however, disrupting the overall harmoniousness of the day. ABC charged that during coverage of the morning's activities, NBC punched up ABC's pictures of crowd reaction in Moscow three times. "Once could have been a mistake, but three times smacks of deliberate action," ABC News spokeswoman Elise Adde charged.

Joseph Angotti, executive producer of NBC's coverage, said, "It was not thievery" and called the incident "just such a simple little thing." He said the pictures were coming over "on our bird," meaning on NBC's satellite time, and that the moment he heard there was some dispute about whose pictures they were, he stopped using them.

"I'm still not convinced it wasn't material we had every right to use," Angotti said. "I'm not absolutely convinced we did the wrong thing, but I don't think they'd lie."

It isn't always easy to know whose feed is whose, Angotti said.

Trust, but verify! There you go again.

All three networks have aired special reports on the summit as well as live unfolding coverage. NBC put together an all-star show Monday night, with Brokaw playing host to a rapid succession of correspondents and guest experts—one of them Soviet spokesman Gennadi Gerasimov, who said of Gorbachev, "He's in a businesslike mood." White House correspondent Chris Wallace was on and off in about 30 seconds, zip zip.

From Moscow, Hart held up a Pravda headline: "Great Expectations."

The Cable News Network (CNN) was the only network to cover, live, Gorbachev's get-acquainted session with an invited crowd of celebrities late yesterday afternoon. Yoko Ono, Billy Graham and John Denver were there—one of the few summit events likely to turn up on "Entertainment Tonight."

Seated at an ornate table in an ornate room of the Soviet Embassy, the Soviet leader responded to "Dear Gorby" letters sent to him by young people. Nothing much of substance, but another chance to / stare long and hard at the *glasnost* guy, and attempt to determine if he's on the level.

Last night, from 9:32 to 9:50, ABC was the only network to air, live from the White House, the Reagan and Gorbachev toasts that ended the state dinner. Peter Jennings anchored. CNN, supposedly an all-news network, did not interrupt its scheduled talk show for the toasts. Both the president and Gorbachev looked very tired. They earned their paychecks yesterday.

The elusiveness of Raisa Gorbachev was apparently frustrating network reporters. "She literally whipped through town," correspondent Anne Garrels told Brokaw. Mrs. Gorbachev did a whirlwind ride-by of monuments and historical sites, leaving her limo only for minutes. "She never got up to the top of the Jefferson Memorial," noted Garrels.

Henry Kissinger made the network rounds, as did former assistant defense secretary Richard Perle (an unusually assured and calming presence on the air). Howard Baker showed up, tight-lipped, on "ABC World News Tonight," and George Shultz, in his tux, dropped by "The CBS Evening News." Sen. John Glenn (D-Ohio) was on more than one network, sizing up the treaty's chances once it hits the Hill. This was not a day for sour grapes, or grapes of wrath for that matter, and nobody was very eager to toss any. Caspar Weinberger got into a spat with a Russian on "CBS This Morning," but you know how he is.

Many of the Soviet experts employed by the networks have beards; it's an oddly consistent facial feature. Maybe they become what they behold. CBS correspondent Wyatt Andrews, as it happens, is actually starting to look like the Kremlin, gray and impervious. Dan Rather had to suffer through the pompous verbosity of Soviet scholar Georgi Arbatov on an otherwise pithy CBS special Monday night, but yesterday got a delightful visit from Vitaly Korotich, editor of the allegedly feisty Soviet magazine Ogonyok.

Rather met Korotich when he anchored the "Seven Days in May" special CBS did in the Soviet Union earlier this year. In the CBS booth on the Ellipse yesterday, Korotich interrupted one of his own responses to a Rather question by saying, in English, "but excuse me for long answer."

One thing these Soviets will have to learn if they are going to come over here and be on television is to keep it short. Lord knows we are not known for our vast attention spans. And yet as the events transpired yesterday, one well might have wished it could all have been slowed down and stretched out so that the magnitude of it would sink in better.

Maybe one sports-coverage touch would have helped: instant replays of the signing and the hearty handshake that followed.

To begrudge television its absurdities would be to deny the very nature of the beast. On the outer fringes of summit coverage, Rona Barrett guest-hosted "Larry King Live" on CNN Monday night and complained to Soviet spokesman Vladimir Posner that we Americans see far too few "attractive" Russians and that too many of them run around in those awful "fur hats."

Posner, a seasoned slickster, didn't let this ruffle him. He assured Barrett that the Soviets are a "handsome" people, and that she'd run around in a fur hat too if she was in chilly Moscow. Miss Rona seemed to understand.

Undoubtedly there are those who think there's been too much summit coverage. Surely the networks will report having received phone calls of protest over preempted soap operas. Just as surely, most who watched the ceremonies and caught the little grace notes yesterday have to be encouraged. To top it all off, Coca-Cola prepared a special commercial for the milestone, an international children's chorus singing about peace.

"As the leaders of the world come together," the ad concludes, "we offer this message of hope." Message received. Loud and clear. Who was it?—oh yeah, it was Emerson—who said, "Nothing can bring you peace but yourself." But then, he never got to drink a Coke.

Or watch TV.

ELEVEN

DAVE BARRY'S QUIRKY 'YUK SYSTEM'

1988 WINNER IN THE COMMENTARY CATEGORY

"For distinguished commentary . . ."

The Miami Herald
Dave Barry

Loyal readers of Dave Barry's column in *The Miami Herald* probably shuddered when he announced he might have to "class up his act" to win the attention of the Pulitzer Prize Committee. Luckily for us, he impressed the committee with his irreverence.

There are several million famous quotations, most of them from Mark Twain, about what a mistake it is to try to analyze humor. I agree with these quotations. I have no idea *why* I think something is funny; I just do. And I know that often the very same things that strike me as truly hilarious strike other people—people I respect; my *wife*, in fact—as pure snake poop.

So I'm not comfortable writing analytically about humor writing. I don't want to create the illusion that I use some kind of Logical Yuk System. What I do is, I sit in front of the computer, stare at the screen, write a sentence, read it over, change a word here, add a word there, rework the punch line and rework it again; until finally, mysteriously, there comes that strange and wonderful moment when I look at what I've produced and say: "This stinks." Then I go for coffee.

Anyway, about the pieces in this book:

The one that's most typical of what I do is the column on the Iran-Contra affair. The theory I go on, when I write this kind of column, is that nothing you could ever make up is as funny as what real people actually do, especially if these people work for enormous, rich, powerful, chronically boneheaded institutions such as the United States government. Of course I've embellished it somewhat with vicious cheap-shot descriptive words, but basically, if people laugh at this, they're laughing at the very foreign policy they have paid God knows how many millions of dollars for, not at my fertile imagination. The funniest stuff is usually the truest stuff, if you ask me, and one of the great mysteries of journalism is how we so often take astoundingly comical events such as the presidential election campaigns, and, through enormous expenditures of manpower and money, render them boring.

The piece about New York City was basically a gift. It resulted from a *New York Times Sunday Magazine* cover story announcing that Miami has problems with drugs, crime and ethnic tension, which of course came as a massive surprise to one and all. A lot of Miami's civic leaders, who don't even like to admit we have *humidity,* let alone drugs and crime, got very upset about *The Times* story, but they had no good way to fight back. At the *Herald,* however, we have a very sharp photographer named Chuck Fadely, who thought of a wonderful idea: Let's not defend Miami; let's viciously and irresponsibly attack New York. And so we did, and we ran it as a cover story in *The Herald*'s Sunday magazine, *Tropic.*

The story got an enormous amount of publicity, far more than if we had published, say, a simple home cure for heart disease. We apparently tapped into a rich vein of hostility toward the Big Self-Important Apple. The truth is that I, personally, *like* New York, but I like to think that none of this affection is detectable in the story.

The essay about my mom is a real anomaly for me. When I wrote it, I wasn't really thinking about getting it published; I was trying to deal with my feelings, mostly guilt. But I was glad that *Tropic* ran it, because a lot of people wrote to say that they'd been dealing with the same kinds of problems, and that it helped them to read about someone else's situation.

Before I relinquish this soapbox, I'd like to stick a plug in for Sunday magazines. They're often dismissed by real journalists as dumping grounds for fluff, and a lot of them are in financial trouble, but I think we need them. The stories reprinted here—a semitasteless political satire, a long humor piece and a short, intensely personal essay—might not have been printed at all if it weren't for *Tropic.* It's hard to find a place in newspapers for writing that deviates from traditional news-and-features journalism; we need magazines to give newspapers a chance to be quirky, experimental, strange and funny.

At least *I* think it's funny.

—Dave Barry
The Miami Herald

CAN NEW YORK SAVE ITSELF?

SUNDAY, AUGUST 30, 1987

BY DAVE BARRY

Here at The Miami Herald we ordinarily don't provide extensive coverage of New York City unless a major news development occurs up there, such as Sean Penn coming out of a restaurant. But lately we have become very concerned about the "Big Apple," because of a story about Miami that ran a few weeks ago in the Sunday magazine of The New York Times. Maybe you remember this story: The cover featured an upbeat photograph of suspected Miami drug dealers being hand-cuffed face-down in the barren dirt next to a garbage-strewed sidewalk outside a squalid shack that probably contains roaches the size of Volvo sedans. The headline asked:

CAN MIAMI SAVE ITSELF?

For those readers too stupid to figure out the answer, there also was this helpful hint:

A CITY BESET BY DRUGS AND VIOLENCE

The overall impression created by the cover was: *Sure Miami can save itself! And some day trained sheep will pilot the Concorde!*

The story itself was more balanced, discussing the pluses as well as the minuses of life in South Florida, as follows:

• **MINUSES:** The area is rampant with violent crime and poverty and political extremism and drugs and corruption and ethnic hatred

• **PLUSES:** Voodoo is legal.

I myself thought it was pretty fair. Our local civic leaders reacted to it with their usual level of cool maturity, similar to the way Moe reacts when he is poked in the eyeballs by Larry and Curly. Our leaders held emergency breakfasts and issued official statements pointing out that much of the information in The Times story was Ancient History dating all the way back to the early 1980s, and that we haven't had a riot for, what *months* now, and that the whole drugs-and-violence thing is overrated. Meanwhile, at newsstands all over South Florida, crowds of people were snapping up all available copies of The Sunday Times, frequently at gunpoint.

All of which got us, at The Herald, to thinking. "Gosh," we thought. "Here the world-famous New York Times, with so many other things to worry about, has gone to all this trouble to try to find out whether Miami can save itself. Wouldn't they be thrilled if we did the same thing for them?" And so it was that we decided to send a crack investigative team consisting of me and Chuck, who is a trained photographer, up there for a couple of days to see what the situation was. We took along comfortable walking shoes and plenty of major credit cards, in case it turned out that we needed to rent a helicopter, which it turned out we did. Here is our report:

DAY ONE

We're riding in a cab from La Guardia Airport to our Manhattan hotel, and I want to interview the driver, because this is how we professional journalists take the Pulse of a City, only I can't, because he doesn't speak English. He is not allowed to, under the rules which are posted right on the seat:

NEW YORK TAXI RULES
1. DRIVER SPEAKS NO ENGLISH.
2. DRIVER JUST GOT HERE TWO DAYS AGO FROM SOME-PLACE LIKE SENEGAL.
3. DRIVER HATES YOU.

Which is just as well, because if he talked to me, he might lose his concentration, which would be very bad because the taxi has some kind of problem with the steering, probably dead pedestrians lodged in the mechanism, the result being that there is a delay of eight to 10 seconds between the time the driver turns the wheel and the time the taxi actually changes direction, a handicap that the driver is compensating for by going 175 miles per hour, at which velocity we are able to remain airborne almost to the far rim of some of the smaller potholes. These are of course maintained by the crack New York Department of Potholes (currently on strike), whose commissioner was recently indicted on corruption charges by the Federal Grand Jury to Indict Every Commissioner in New York. This will take some time, because New York has more commissioners than Des Moines, Iowa, has residents, including the Commissioner for Making Sure the Sidewalks Are Always Blocked By Steaming Fetid Mounds of Garbage the Size of Appalachian Foothills, and, of course, the Commissioner for Bicycle Messengers Bearing Down on You at Warp Speed with Mohawk Haircuts and Pupils Smaller Than Purely Theoretical Particles.

After several exhilarating minutes, we arrive in downtown Manhattan, where the driver slows to 125 miles so he can take better aim at wheelchair occupants. This gives us our first brief glimpse of the city we have come to investigate. It looks to us, whizzing past, as though it is beset by serious problems. We are reminded of the findings of the 40-member Mayor's Special Commission on the Future of the City of New York, which this past June, after nearly two years of intensive study of the economic, political and social problems confronting the city, issued a 2,300-page report, which reached the disturbing conclusion that New York is "a nice place to visit" but the commission "wouldn't want to live there."

Of course they probably stayed at a nicer hotel than where we're staying. We're staying at a "medium priced" hotel, meaning that the rooms are more than spacious enough for a family of four to stand up in if they are slightly built and hold their arms over their heads, yet the rate is just $135 per night, plus of course your state tax, your city tax, your occupancy tax, your head tax, your body tax, your soap tax, your ice bucket tax, your in-room dirty movies tax and your piece of paper that says your toilet is sanitized for your protection tax, which bring the rate to $367.90 per night, or a flat $4,000 if you use the telephone. A bellperson carries my luggage—one small gym-style bag containing, primarily, a set of clean underwear—and I tip him $2, which he takes as if I am handing him a jar of warm sputum.

But never mind. We are not here to please the bellperson. We are here to see if New York can save itself. And so Chuck and I set off into the streets of Manhattan, where we immediately detect signs of a healthy economy in the form of people squatting on the sidewalk selling realistic jewelry. This is good, because a number of other businesses, such as Mobil Corp., have recently decided to pull their headquarters out of New York, much to the annoyance of Edward Koch, the feisty, cocky, outspoken, abrasive mayor who really gets on some people's nerves, yet at the same time strikes other people as a jerk. "Why would *anybody* want to move to some dirt-bag place like the Midwest?" Mayor Koch is always asking reporters. "What are they gonna do at *night?* Huh? *Milk the cows?* Are they gonna wear bib overalls and sit around *canning their preserves?* Huh? Are they gonna . . . Hey! Come back here!"

But why *are* the corporations leaving? To answer this question, a polling firm recently took a scientific telephone survey of the heads of New York's 200 largest corporations, and found that none of them were expected to arrive at work for at least two more hours because of massive transit delays caused by a wildcat strike of the 1,200-member Wildcat Strikers Guild. So you can see the corporations' point: It *is* an inconvenience, being located in a city where taxes are ludicrously high, where you pay twice your annual income to rent an apartment that could easily be carried on a commercial airline flight, where you spend two-thirds of your work day trying to get to and from work, but as Mayor Koch philosophically points out, "Are they gonna *slop the hogs?* Are they gonna . . ."

Despite the corporate exodus, the New York economy continues to be robust, with the major industry being people from New Jersey paying $45 each to see *A Chorus Line.* Employment remains high, with most of the new jobs opening up in the fast-growing fields of:

- Person asking everybody for "spare" change.
- Person shrieking at taxis.
- Person holding animated sidewalk conversation with beings from another dimension.
- Person handing out little slips of paper entitling the bearer to one free drink at sophisticated nightclubs with names like The Bazoom Room.

As Chuck and I walk along 42nd Street, we see a person wearing an enormous frankfurter costume, handing out coupons good for discounts at Nathan's Famous hot dog stands. His name is Victor Leise, age 19, of Queens, and he has held the position of giant frankfurter for four months. He says he didn't have any connections or anything; he just put in an application and, boom, the job was his. Sheer luck. He says it's OK work, although people call him "Frank" and sometimes sneak up and whack him on the back. Also there is not a lot of room for advancement. They have no hamburger costume.

"Can New York save itself?" I ask him.

"If there are more cops on the streets, there could be a possibility," he says, through his breathing hole.

Right down the street is the world-famous Times Square. Although this area is best known as the site where many thousands of people gather each New Year's Eve for a joyous and festive night of public urination, it also serves as an important cultural center where patrons may view films such as *Sex Aliens, Wet Adulteress* and, of course, *Sperm Busters* in comfortable refrigerated theaters where everybody sits about 15 feet apart. This is also an excellent place to shop for your leisure product needs, including The Bionic Woman ("An amazingly lifelike companion") and a vast selection of latex objects, some the size of military pontoons. The local residents are very friendly, often coming right up and offering to engage in acts of leisure with you. Reluctantly, however, Chuck and I decide to tear ourselves away, for we have much more to see, plus we do not wish to spend the rest of our lives soaking in vats of penicillin.

As we leave the area, I stop briefly inside an Off-Track Betting parlor on Seventh Avenue to see if I can obtain the Pulse of the City by eavesdropping on native New Yorkers in casual conversation. Off-Track Betting parlors are the kinds of places where you never see signs that say, "Thank You For Not Smoking." The best you could hope for is, "Thank You For Not Spitting Pieces Of Your Cigar On My Neck." By listening carefully and remaining unobtrusive, I am able to overhear the following conversation:

FIRST OFF-TRACK BETTOR: I like this (*very bad word*) horse here.

SECOND OFF-TRACK BETTOR: That (*extremely bad word*) couldn't (*bad word*) out his own (*comical new bad word*).

FIRST OFF-TRACK BETTOR: (*Bad word*).

Listening to these two men share their innermost feelings, I sense concern, yes, but also an undercurrent of hope, hope for a Brighter Tomorrow, if only the people of this great city can learn to work together, to look upon each other with respect and even, yes, love. Or at least stop shoving one another in front of moving subway trains. This happens a fair amount in New York, so Chuck and I are extremely alert as we descend into the complex of subway tunnels under Times Square, climate-controlled year-round at a comfortable 172 degrees Fahrenheit.

Although it was constructed in 1536, the New York subway system boasts an annual maintenance budget of nearly $8, currently stolen, and it does a remarkable job of getting New Yorkers from Point A to an indeterminate location somewhere in the tunnel leading to Point B. It's also very easy for the "out-of-towner" to use, thanks to the logical, easy-to-understand system of naming trains after famous letters and numbers. For directions, all you have to do is peer up through the steaming gloom at the informative signs, which look like this:

A 5 N 7 8 C 6 AA MID-DOWNTOWN 7⅜
EXPRESS LOCAL ONLY LL 67 ♦
DDD 4♠ 1 K ★ AAAA 9 ONLY
EXCEPT CERTAIN DAY BB ® ® 3
MIDWAY THROUGH TOWN 17D
WALK REAL FAST AAAAAAAAA 56
LOCALIZED EXPRESS -6
"YY" ♣ 1,539
AAAAAAAAAAAAAAAAAA

If for some reason you are unsure where to go, all you have to do is stand there looking lost, and within seconds a helpful New Yorker will approach to see if you have any "spare" change.

Within less than an hour, Chuck and I easily locate what could well be the correct platform, where we pass the time by perspiring freely until the train storms in, colorfully decorated, as is the tradition in New York, with the spray-painted initials of all the people it has run over. All aboard!

Here is the correct procedure for getting on a New York subway train at rush hour:

1. As the train stops, you must join the other people on the platform in pushing forward and forming the densest possible knot in front of each door. You want your knot to be so dense that, if the train were filled with water instead of people, not a single drop would escape.

2. The instant the doors open, you want to push forward as hard as possible, in an effort to get onto the train *without letting anybody get off*. This is *very important*. If anybody does get off, it is legal to tackle him and drag him back on. I once watched three German tourists—this is a true anecdote—attempt to get off the northbound No. 5 Lexington Avenue IRT train at Grand Central Station during rush hour. "Getting off please!" they said, politely, from somewhere inside a car containing approximately the population of Brazil, as if they expected people to actually *let them through*. Instead, of course, the incoming passengers propelled the Germans, like gnats in a hurricane, *away* from the door, deeper and deeper into the crowd, which quickly compressed them into dense little wads of Teutonic tissue. I never did see where they actually got off. Probably they stumbled to daylight somewhere in the South Bronx, where they were sold for parts.

Actually, though, there is reason to believe the subways are safer now. After years of being fearful and intimidated, many New Yorkers cheered in 1985 when Bernhard Goetz, in a highly controversial incident that touched off an emotion-charged nationwide debate, shot and killed the New York subway commissioner. This resulted in extensive legal proceedings, culminating recently when, after a dramatic and highly publicized trial, a jury voted not only to acquit Goetz, but also to dig up the commissioner and shoot him again.

Chuck and I emerge from the subway in Lower Manhattan. This area has been hard hit by the massive wave of immigration that has threatened to rend the very fabric of society, as the city struggles desperately to cope with the social upheaval caused by the huge and unprecedented influx of a group that has, for better or for worse, permanently altered the nature of New York: young urban professionals. They began arriving by the thousands in the 1970s, packed two and sometimes three per BMW sedan, severely straining the city's already-overcrowded gourmet-ice cream facilities. Soon they were taking over entire neighborhoods, where longtime residents watched in despair as useful businesses such as bars were replaced by precious little restaurants with names like The Whittling Fig.

And still the urban professionals continue to come, drawn by a dream, a dream that is best expressed by the words of the song *New York, New York* which goes:

Dum dum da de dum
Dum dum da de dum
Dum dum da de dum
Dum dum da de dum dum.

It is a powerfully seductive message, especially if you hear it at a wedding reception held in a Scranton, Pa., Moose Lodge facility and you have been drinking. And so you come to the Big Apple, and you take a peon-level position in some huge impersonal corporation, an incredibly awful, hateful job, and you spend $1,250 a month to rent an apartment so tiny that you have to shower in the kitchen, and the only furniture you have room for—not that you can afford furniture anyway—is your collection of back issues of *Metropolitan Home* magazine, but you stick it out, because this is the Big Leagues (*If I can make it there, I'll make it anywhere*), and you know that if you show them what you can do, if you really *go for it* then, by gosh, one day you're gonna wake up, in The City That Never Sleeps, to find that the corporation has moved its headquarters to Plano, Texas.

Now Chuck and I are in Chinatown. We pass an outdoor market where there is an attractive display consisting of a tub containing I would estimate 275,000 dead baby eels. One of the great things about New York is that, if you ever need dead baby eels, you can get them. Also there is opera here. But tonight I think I'll just try to get some sleep.

At 3:14 a.m. I am awakened by a loud crashing sound, caused by workers from the city's crack Department of Making Loud Crashing Sounds During the Night, who are just outside my window, breaking in a new taxicab by dropping it repeatedly from a 75-foot crane. Lying in bed listening to them, I can hardly wait for . . .

DAY TWO

Chuck and I decide that since we pretty much covered the economic, social, political, historical and cultural aspects of New York on Day One, we'll devote Day Two to sightseeing. We decide to start with the best-known sight of all, the one that, more than any other, exemplifies what the Big Apple is all about: the Islip Garbage Barge. This is a barge of world-renowned garbage that originated on Long Island, a place where many New Yorkers go to sleep on those occasions when the Long Island Railroad is operating.

The Islip Garbage Barge is very famous. Nobody really remembers *why* it's famous; it just *is,* like Dick Cavett. It has traveled to South America. It has been on many television shows, including—I am not making this up—*Phil Donahue.* When we were in New York, the barge—I am still not making this up—was on trial. It has since been convicted and sentenced to be burned. But I am not worried. It will get out on appeal. It is the Claus Von Bulow of garbage barges.

Chuck and I find out from the Director of Public Affairs at the New York Department of Sanitation, who is named Vito, that the barge is anchored off the coast of Brooklyn, so we grab a cab, which is driven by a man who of course speaks very little English and, as far as we can tell, has never heard of Brooklyn. By means of hand signals we direct him to a place near where the barge is anchored. It is some kind of garbage-collection point.

There are mounds of garbage everywhere, and if you really concentrate, you can actually see them giving off smell rays, such as you see in comic strips. Clearly no taxi has ever been here before, and none will ever come again, so we ask the driver to wait. "YOU WAIT HERE," I say, speaking in capital letters so he will understand me. He looks at me suspiciously. "WE JUST WANT TO SEE A GARBAGE BARGE," I explain.

We can see the barge way out on the water, but Chuck decides that, to get a good picture of it, we need a boat. A sanitation engineer tells us we might be able to rent one in a place called Sheepshead Bay, so we direct the driver there ("WE NEED TO RENT A BOAT"), but when we get there we realize it's too far away, so we naturally decide to rent a helicopter, which we find out is available only in New Jersey. ("NOW WE NEED TO GO TO NEW JERSEY. TO RENT A HELI-

COPTER.") Thus we end up at the airport in Linden, N.J., where we leave the taxi driver with enough fare money to retire for life, if he ever finds his way home.

Chuck puts the helicopter on his American Express card. Our pilot, Norman Knodt, assures me that nothing bad has ever happened to him in a helicopter excepting getting it shot up nine times, but that was in Vietnam, and he foresees no problems with the garbage-barge mission. Soon we are over the harbor, circling the barge, which turns out to be, like so many celebrities when you see them up close, not as tall as you expected. As I gaze down at it, with the soaring spires of downtown Manhattan in the background gleaming in the brilliant sky, a thought crosses my mind: I had better write at *least* 10 inches about this, to justify our expense reports.

Later that day, I stop outside Grand Central Station, where a woman is sitting in a chair on the sidewalk next to a sign that says:

Tarot Cards
Palm Reading

I ask her how much it costs for a Tarot card reading, and she says $10, which I give her. She has me select nine cards, which she arranges in a circle. "Now ask me a question," she says.

"Can New York save itself?" I ask.

She looks at me.

"That's your question?" she asks.

"Yes," I say.

"OK," she says. She looks at the cards. "Yes, New York can save itself for the future."

She looks at me. I don't say anything. She looks back at the cards.

"New York is the Big Apple," she announces. "It is big and exciting, with very many things to see and do."

After the reading I stop at a newsstand and pick up a copy of Manhattan Living magazine, featuring a guide to condominiums. I note that there are a number of one-bedrooms priced as low as $250,000.

Manhattan Living also has articles. "It is only recently," one begins, "that the word 'fashionable' has been used in conjunction with the bathroom."

DAY THREE

Just to be on the safe side, Chuck and I decide to devote Day Three to getting back to the airport. Because of a slip-up at the Department of Taxi Licensing, our driver speaks a fair amount of English. And it's a darned good thing he does, because he is kind enough to share his philosophy of life with us, in between shouting helpful instructions to other drivers. It is a philosophy of optimism and hope, not just for himself, but also for New York City, and for the world:

"The thing is, you got to look on the lighter side, because HEY WHAT THE HELL IS HE DOING! WHAT THE HELL ARE YOU DOING YOU (*very bad word*)! Because for me, the thing is, respect. If a person shows me respect, then HAH! YOU WANT TO SQUEEZE IN FRONT NOW?? YOU S.O.B.!! I SQUEEZE YOU LIKE A LEMON!! So I am happy here, but you Americans, you know, you are very, you know WHERE IS HE GOING?? You have to look behind the scenery. This damn CIA, something sticky is going on WHERE THE HELL IS THIS STUPID S.O.B. THINK HE IS GOING??? behind the scenery there, you don't think this guy, what his name, Casey, you don't LOOK AT THIS S.O.B. you don't wonder why he *really* die? You got to look behind the scenery. I don't trust *nobody*. I don't trust my own *self*. WILL YOU LOOK AT . . ."

By the time we reach La Guardia, Chuck and I have a much deeper understanding of life in general, and it is with a sense of real gratitude that we leap out of the cab and cling to the pavement. Soon we are winging our way southward, watching the Manhattan skyline disappear, reflecting upon our many experiences and pondering the question that brought us here:

Can New York save itself? Can this ultra-metropolis—crude yet sophisticated, overburdened yet wealthy, loud yet obnoxious—can this city face up to the multitude of problems besetting it and, drawing upon its vast reserves of spunk and spirit, as it has done so many times before, emerge triumphant?

And, who cares?

JUST-A-MOMENT

LOST IN AMERICA

SUNDAY, NOVEMBER 29, 1987

BY DAVE BARRY

My mother and I are driving through Hartford, Conn., on the way to a town called Essex. Neither of us has ever been to Essex, but we're both desperately hoping that my mother will want to live there.

She has been rootless for several months now, moving from son to son around the country, ever since she sold the house she had lived in for 40 years, the house she raised us in, the house my father built. The house where he died, April 4, 1984. She would note the date each year on the calender in the kitchen.

"Dave died, 1984," the note would say. "Come back, Dave."

The note for July 5, their anniversary, said: "Married Dave, 1942. Best thing that ever happened to me."

The house was too big for my mother to handle alone, and we all advised her to sell it. Finally she did, and she shipped all her furniture to Sunnyvale, Calif., where my brother Phil lived. Her plan was to stay with him until she found a place of her own out there.

Only she hated Sunnyvale. At first this seemed almost funny, even to her. "All my worldly goods," she would say, marveling at it, "are in a warehouse in Sunnyvale, Calif., which I hate." She always had a wonderful sense of absurdity.

After a while it didn't seem so funny. My mother left Sunnyvale to live for a while with my brother Sam, in San Francisco, and then with me, in Florida; but she didn't want to stay with us. What she wanted was a home.

What she really wanted was her old house back.

With my father in it.

Of course she knew she couldn't have that, but when she tried to think of what else she wanted, her mind would just lock up. She started to spend a lot of time watching soap operas.

"You have to get on with your life," I would tell her, in this new, parental voice I was developing when I talked to her. Dutifully, she would turn off the TV and get out a map of the United States, which I bought her to help her think.

"Maybe Boulder would be nice," she would say, looking at Colorado. "I was born near Boulder."

"Mom," I would say in my new voice. "We've talked about Boulder 50 times, and you always end up saying you don't really want to live there."

Chastened, she would look back at her map, but I could tell she wasn't really seeing it.

"You have to be *realistic,*" I would say. The voice of wisdom.

When she and I had driven each other just about crazy, she went back out to California, and repeated the process with both of my brothers. Then one night she called to ask, very apologetically, if I would go with her to look at Essex, Conn., which she had heard was nice. It was a bad time for me, but of course I said yes, because your mom is your mom. I met her in Hartford and rented a car.

I'm driving; my mother is looking out the window.

"I came through Hartford last year with Frank and Mil, on the way to Maine," she says. Frank was my father's brother; he has just died. My mother loved to see him. He reminded her of my father.

"We were singing," my mother says. She starts to sing.
I'm forever blowing bubbles
Pretty bubbles in the air.

I can tell she wants me to sing, too. I know the words; we sang this song when I was little.
First they fly so high, nearly reach the sky
Then like my dreams, they fade and die.

But I don't sing. I am all business.

"I miss Frank," says my mother.

Essex turns out to be a beautiful little town, and we look at two nice, affordable apartments. But I can tell right away that my mother doesn't want to be there. She doesn't want to say so, after asking me to fly up from Miami, but we both know.

The next morning, in the motel coffee shop, we have a very tense breakfast.

"Look, Mom," I say, "you have to make some kind of decision."
Sounding very reasonable.

She looks down at her map. She starts talking about Boulder again.
This sets me off. I lecture her, tell her she's being childish. She's
looking down at her map, gripping it. I drive her back to Hartford,
neither of us saying much. I put her on a plane; she's going to Mil-
waukee, to visit my dad's sister, then back to my brother in Sunnyvale, Calif. Which she hates.

The truth is, I'm relieved that she's leaving.

"You can't help her," I tell myself, "until she decides what she
wants." It is a sound position.

About a week later, my wife and I get a card from my mother.

"This is to say happy birthday this very special year," it says. "And
to thank you for everything."

Our birthdays are weeks away.

About two days later, my brother Phil calls, crying, from a hospital. My mother has taken a massive overdose of Valium and alcohol.
The doctors want permission to turn off the machines. They say there's
no hope.

We talk about it, but there really isn't much to say. We give the
permission.

It's the only logical choice.

The last thing I saw my mother do, just before she went down the
tunnel to her plane, was turn and give me a big smile. It wasn't a
smile of happiness; it was the same smile I give my son when he gets
upset listening to the news, and I tell him don't worry, we're never
going to have a nuclear war.

I can still see that smile any time I want. Close my eyes, and there
it is. A mom, trying to reassure her boy that everything's going to be
OK.

A BOLDFACED LIE

SUNDAY, JULY 12, 1987

BY DAVE BARRY

Unless you are unemployed, sick, or a journalist, you probably have not had time to keep up with the hearings that have been held, over the course of the past year or two, by the Congressional Committee To Drone On About The Iran-Contra Scandal Until Everybody Involved Is Dead. So today, as a public service, we're going to provide the following convenient summary of the entire affair, putting the names of **KEY ELEMENTS** in easy-to-read **BOLDFACE**. There will be a quiz.

It all started when some **EXTREMIST MANIAC LUNATICS** took some **AMERICAN HOSTAGES**, which upset **RONALD REAGAN**, who to the best of his recollection was **PRESIDENT OF THE UNITED STATES** at the time, so he naturally sold **WEAPONS** to the **EXTREMIST MANIAC LUNATICS** in exchange for **MONEY**, which was funneled, with the help of various **COURAGEOUS PATRIOTS** who received nothing for their efforts except **A SENSE OF SATISFACTION AND EIGHT MILLION DOLLARS**, to the crack **FOREIGN-POLICY ADVENTURE SQUAD** headed by **LT. COL. OLIVER NORTH** (Secret Code Name "**MANHOOD TESTICLE**"), who, with his loyal staff, **FAWN HALL**, who has been offered $500,000 by **PENTHOUSE MAGAZINE** to pose **NAKED**, occupied an office in the **WHITE HOUSE**, but was in no way whatsoever connected with **ANYBODY HIGHER UP**, because of course it is a **COMMON PRACTICE** for **TOTALLY RANDOM UNOFFICIAL PEOPLE** such as **INSURANCE AGENTS** and **ACCORDION TEACHERS** to have **WHITE HOUSE OFFICES**, and thus it was that **COL. NORTH**, acting completely on his **OWN**, decided to divert the **MONEY** to the **CONTRAS**, who are at war with **IRAQ**, no, wait, sorry, it is **IRAN** that is at war with **IRAQ**, which is the country that shot one of our ships, which naturally caused **PRESIDENT REAGAN** (Code Name "**GRINNING VEGETABLE**"), to speak out angrily against—this is the truth—**IRAN**, which as some of you may recall is the very same country he sold the **WEAPONS** to, but we are drifting away from our **CENTRAL POINT**, which is that **COL. NORTH** was merely trying to insure that the **CONTRAS** received an adequate supply of **MONEY** in order to carry out the **REAGAN ADMINISTRA-TION'S SECRET PLAN** (Don't tell **ANYBODY!**) to overthrow the government of **NICARAGUA**, a role in which the **CONTRAS** have proved to be as effective, militarily, as a **BUCKET OF DEAD SHRIMP.**

Now that you're up to date on this important scandal, you might want to take some time off from work and watch a few episodes of The Iran-Contra Hearings TV Show. The best time to tune in is when a Reagan administration official is testifying, and the committee tries to trick him into making a coherent statement:

CONGRESSPERSON: Please state your name and title, and reveal what the U.S. foreign policy is.

WITNESS: My name is Elliott Abrams; my title is Assistant Administrative Associate Sub-secretary of State for Reminding Everybody of a Small Hairless Nocturnai Rodent; and the U.S. foreign policy is . . .

(The entire committee leans forward in breathless anticipation . . .)

WITNESS: . . . a SECRET!

AUDIENCE: *(Loud applause)*

CONGRESSPERSON: Ha ha! You really had us going there! Don Pardo, tell our witness what exciting gifts he'll receive for testifying here today!

DON PARDO: Bob, he'll receive . . .

The danger, of course, is that one day a witness will slip up and reveal the foreign policy, which is why the Reagan administration, as a Security Measure, is now changing it on a daily basis. It is also kept in a locked box, for which there is only one key. Which the president, as an added precaution, has misplaced.

QUIZ: TEST YOUR
SCANDAL KNOWLEDGE

1. Would you pose naked for $500,000? Me too.

PITHY INTO THE WIND

B Y   D A V E   B A R R Y

The burgeoning Iran-Contra scandal is truly an issue about which we, as a nation, need to concern ourselves, because (Secret Note To Readers: Not really! The hell with the Iran-Contra affair! Let it burgeon! I'm just trying to win a journalism prize, here. Don't tell anybody! I'll explain later. Shhhh.)

When we look at the Iran-Contra scandal, and for that matter the mounting national health-care crisis, we can see that these are, in total, two issues, each requiring a number of paragraphs in which we will comment, in hopes that

(. . . we can win a journalism prize. Ideally a Pulitzer. That's the object, in journalism. At certain times each year, we journalists do almost nothing except apply for the Pulitzers and several dozen other major prizes. During these times you could walk right into most newsrooms and commit a multiple ax murder naked, and it wouldn't get reported in the paper, because the reporters and editors would all be too busy filling out prize applications. "Hey!" they'd yell at you. "Watch it! You're getting blood on my application!")

we can possibly, through carefully analyzing these important issues —the Iran-Contra scandal, the mounting national health-care crisis, and (while we are at it), the federal budget deficit—through analyzing these issues and mulling them over and fretting about them and chewing on them until we have reduced them to soft, spit-covered gobs of information that you, the readers, can

(. . . pretty much ignore. It's OK! Don't be ashamed! We here in journalism are fully aware that most of you skip right over stories that look like they might involve major issues, which you can identify because they always have incomprehensible headlines like "House Parley Panel Links NATO Tax Hike To Hondurans In Syrian Arms Deal." Sometimes we'll do a whole *series* with more total words than the Brothers Karamazov and headlines like: "The World Mulch Crisis: A Time To Act." You readers don't bother to wade through these stories, and you feel vaguely guilty about this. Which is stupid. You're not *supposed* to read them. We *journalists* don't read them. We use modern computers to generate them solely for the purpose of entering them for journalism prizes. We're thinking about putting the following helpful advisory over them: "CAUTION! JOURNALISM PRIZE ENTRY! DO NOT READ!")

gain, through a better understanding of these very important issues —the Iran-Contra scandal; the health-care crisis (which as you may be aware is both national AND mounting); the federal budget deficit; and yes, let's come right out and say it, the Strategic Defense Initiative —you readers can gain a better understanding of them, and thus we might come to an enhanced awareness of what they may or may not mean in terms of

(. . . whether or not I can win a Pulitzer Prize. That's the one I'm gunning for. You get $1,000 cash, plus all the job offers the mailperson can carry. Unfortunately, the only category I'd be eligible for is called "Distinguished Social Commentary," which is a real problem, because of the kinds of issues I generally write about. "This isn't Distinguished Social Commentary!" the Pulitzer judges would say. "This is about goat boogers!" So today I'm trying to class up my act a little by writing about prize-winning issues. OK? Sorry.)

how we, as a nation, can, through a deeper realization of the significance of these four vital issues—health care in Iran, the strategic federal deficit, mounting the Contras, and one other one which slips my mind at the moment, although I think it's the one that's burgeoning—how we can, as a nation, through Distinguished Social Commentary such as this, gain the kind of perspective and foresight required to understand

(. . . a guy like noted conservative columnist George Will. You see him, on all those TV shows where he is always commenting on world events in that snotty smartass way of his, with his lips pursed together like he just accidentally licked the plumbing in a bus-station restroom, and you quite naturally say to yourself, as millions have before you: "Why doesn't somebody just take this little *dweeb* and stick his bow tie up his nose? Huh?" And the answer is: Because a long time ago, for reasons nobody remembers anymore, *George Will won a Pulitzer Prize.* And now he gets to be famous and rich and respected *for ever and ever.* That's all I want! Is that so much to ask?!)

what we, and I am talking about we as a nation, need to have in order to deeply understand all the issues listed somewhere earlier in this column. And although I am only one person, one lone Distinguished Social Commentator crying in the wilderness, without so much as a bow tie, I am nevertheless committed to doing whatever I can to deepen and widen and broaden and lengthen the national understanding of these issues in any way that I can, and that includes sharing the $1,000 with the judges.

TWELVE

AIDS IN THE HEARTLAND

1988 WINNER IN THE FEATURE WRITING CATEGORY

"For a distinguished example of feature writing giving prime consideration to high literary quality and originality . . ."

St. Paul Pioneer Press Dispatch
Jacqui Banaszynski

"So often, the AIDS epidemic is written about in terms of numerical milestones: the 200th case, the 100th death. As the numbers grow, the victims become cases rather than people, distanced from names and faces, and the rest of us grow immune to the horror." * Jacqui Banaszynski skillfully cut through the statistics.

It was an unseasonably hot evening in May 1987, when I rode the elevator up to a Spartan apartment in downtown Minneapolis and asked a man if I could watch him die.

I had met Dick Hanson and his partner, Bert Henningson Jr., three months earlier at their farm near Glenwood, in west-central Minnesota. Hanson was on a temporary rebound from his second bout of near-fatal pneumocystis pneumonia—the most common killer of AIDS patients. Henningson was experiencing mild fatigue, chills and diarrhea—the early warning signals of acquired immune deficiency syndrome.

Photographer Jean Pieri and I visited the farm several times that spring, chatting at the kitchen table while Henningson baked bread or listening to Hanson's rambling stories of political battles. We were struggling to find a focus, searching for a story that would go a step beyond the informational coverage of AIDS, a story that would not only humanize the AIDS crisis but enlighten and, perhaps, nudge society toward a more compassionate understanding of this stigmatized killer.

The notion of following an AIDS patient from diagnosis through death was hardly a novel one. I had read that story in several large newspapers—primarily from the east and west coasts—and it had been on our list of AIDS-related stories since late 1985.

It took us almost a year of false starts before we found Dick Hanson. Most AIDS sufferers were unwilling to go public with their homosexuality or their illness—fearing loss of jobs and home, rejection by

---

* From the nomination letter written by Deborah Howell, Editor of the *St. Paul Pioneer Press Dispatch*.

family and friends and, in the case of a divorced mother, loss of parental visitation rights.

Hanson's situation was different. He had been out of the closet since 1980, when he stood on the floor of a state political convention and announced he was a homosexual, hoping the revelation would sway support for a gay rights resolution. He had been in a committed relationship with Henningson since 1982, and their partnership was acknowledged by their families and friends. He and Henningson had been photographed together standing in their farm field for a 1983 *Newsweek* cover story titled "Gays in America."

That made Hanson accessible. The sensitive issues of secrecy that so often accompany AIDS stories were irrelevant. As lifelong political activists—some would say radical rabble-rousers—Hanson and Henningson also understood the power of the mass media, and were interested in using the voice of an establishment newspaper to carry their message about AIDS to a mainstream audience.

We initially thought Hanson's story was the grist of a good, straightforward profile—one that needed to be done quickly because he was so well-known in political circles, his illness was beginning to make news, and we didn't want the competing newspaper in Minneapolis to discover him first.

But as I conducted interviews for that profile, my notebook slowly began to fill with sprinklings of journalistic gold. Rather than putting the story together, Jean and I kept returning to the farm on weekends, or to the Minneapolis clinic the men visited each week, or to their subsidized and sterile downtown apartment, where they lived during the week so Henningson could work and Hanson could receive medical treatment.

During those visits, Hanson and Henningson grew to know us as people as well as journalists, and began to talk on a more personal level. One night over dinner at a local steakhouse, while my notebook was closed, Hanson and Henningson talked freely about themselves, their relationship, their families, their lost hopes and their fears.

That evening, I knew I had a story that was more real, more special, than I had dared to hope. It was, above all, a love story. It was a rare glimpse into a homosexual relationship—the kind of relationship that mystifies most and disgusts many but that has become an undeniable part of our culture. It also was the first time AIDS was going to be confronted openly in small-town Minnesota.

Soon after that, I asked Hanson if we could witness his death, if we could try to tell the whole story of AIDS—life and death, love and hate, family support and family strife, politics, money, morality, religion, law, medicine and sex.

We talked for a long time that night about what it would mean—for him and Henningson, for me and for our readers. We talked about the potential invasion of his privacy, about the inevitable anger of his relatives, about the scorn the story would generate, about the logistics of a reporter and photographer having access to the most personal aspects of his life, about negotiating the rough waters of mutual trust. Hanson barely hesitated before he said yes.

We called our story "AIDS in the Heartland." It was written as it happened, with no set timetable. The challenge was to remain flexible enough to respond to events and, at the same time, build a literary structure that would sustain us indefinitely, through as many as four or five segments. We also had to help the readers through each piece —reminding them of what had happened before without repeating ourselves. The solution was to package the stories in our Sunday "Focus" section, clearing everything from that section except the editorial pages.

I began each piece with an italic scene-setter that told the reader where the story had been and where it was going and also creating a mood. It proved a good technique—one that still worked eight months later when I wrote an epilogue section about Henningson.

The reporting challenges were considerable. We were asking Hanson and Henningson to hand us their lives—and their deaths. That required the utmost honesty about our roles as journalists—roles that became difficult to define as Jean and I grew to care deeply about these men. I waded into the center of a deeply divided family and managed —again through honesty and patience—to gain interviews with each family member despite their hostility toward the press for publicizing their secret. I had an obligation to report intensely personal and painful events honestly—and yet to do so with respect for the subjects.

The greatest challenge was to recognize my emotional involvement in the story—to use that emotion to breathe passion into my writing but to detach myself enough to remain focused on the truth. For that delicate balance I relied on the soul and artistry of Jean Pieri, the compassionate guidance of assistant metro editor Jack Rhodes, the unerring faith of assistant to the managing editor Steven Smith and the disciplined editing of executive editor Deborah Howell. Others in the newsroom inspired me with their questions and concern.

As Hanson's health deteriorated rapidly, we published under considerable deadline pressure. Jean and I devoted hundreds of hours to the story over the course of a year. I worked on it full-time—weekends and evenings included—from mid-May to mid-August.

The first chapter introduced Hanson and Henningson, took readers to their farm and the clinic, described their struggle to maintain dignity and hope, and teased about the issues shaping their lives—the family stress, their sexual history, their mutual commitment, Henningson's failing health. The second chapter carried voices of Hanson's neighbors and relatives, and was a powerful statement about the societal pain surrounding AIDS.

The final chapter caught us by surprise, prompted by Hanson's death at sunrise on July 25, 1987. It chronicled his last hours, took readers to a cathartic memorial service at his country church and ended with Henningson grieving for Hanson—and for himself as his own fight with AIDS began in earnest.

Many readers were not happy with the detail or depth of the series. Some accused the paper of glorifying homosexuality, trading on death, exploiting a family's private pain.

We took those concerns seriously, and made several difficult ethical decisions: A photograph of the two men kissing would not be published, but we would be explicit in writing about Hanson's active sexual history; some especially raw exchanges between relatives were not repeated because they exposed too much privacy without enhancing the story; statements about Henningson's medical status remained vague until he gained a farm loan.

But we continued to publish. Managing editor Mark Nadler explained to readers that our intention was not to present a "ghoulish death watch." Rather, it was an attempt to debunk some of the stereotypes of AIDS and to lift the shroud of ignorance from the disease.

"That kind of ignorance is dangerous for all of us," Nadler wrote. "Moreover, ignorance breeds fear, and a search for culprits rather than cures. Dick Hanson is no culprit. Whatever you may think of his politics or sexual orientation, it is impossible to read his story and think of him as anything other than a decent, sensitive man determined to make some sense of the tragedy that has befallen him and thousands of others. His is the great tragedy of our times, and his is a story worth telling."

By the time of Hanson's death, many readers began to change their minds—about the story, and about their fellow human beings who happened to be suffering from AIDS. A nurse from rural Wisconsin said she had not been able to treat AIDS patients before reading the series. Mothers wrote of coming to terms with their sons' homosexuality. And a federal judge wrote this: "Your series humanized and focused a terror that is swiftly becoming pervasive. Your work was sympathetic but objective and in a most skillful fashion helped teach the community to care."

—Jacqui Banaszynski
St. Paul Pioneer Press Dispatch

AIDS IN THE HEARTLAND

ILL ACTIVIST STRUGGLES TO CARRY ON

SUNDAY, JUNE 21, 1987

BY JACQUI BANASZYNSKI

Death is no stranger to the heartland. It is as natural as the seasons, as inevitable as farm machinery breaking down and farmers' bodies giving out after too many years of too much work.

But when death comes in the guise of AIDS, it is a disturbingly unfamiliar visitor, one better known in the gay districts and drug houses of the big cities, one that shows no respect for the usual order of life in the country.

The visitor has come to rural Glenwood, Minn.

Dick Hanson, a well-known liberal political activist who homesteads his family's century-old farm south of Glenwood, was diagnosed last summer with acquired immune deficiency syndrome. His partner of five years, Bert Henningson, carries the AIDS virus.

In the year that Hanson has been living—and dying—with AIDS, he has hosted some cruel companions: blinding headaches and failing vision, relentless nausea and deep fatigue, falling blood counts and worrisome coughs and sleepless, sweat-soaked nights.

He has watched as his strong body, toughened by 37 years on the farm, shrinks and stoops like that of an old man. He has weathered the family shame and community fear, the prejudice and whispered condemnations. He has read the reality in his partner's eyes, heard the death sentence from the doctors and seen the hopelessness confirmed by the statistics.

But the statistics tell only half the story—the half about dying.

Statistics fail to tell much about the people they represent. About people like Hanson—a farmer who has nourished life in the fields, a peace activist who has marched for a safer planet, an idealist and gay activist who has campaigned for social justice, and now an AIDS patient who refuses to abandon his own future, however long it lasts.

The statistics say nothing of the joys of a carefully tended vegetable garden and new kittens under the shed, of tender teasing and magic hugs. Of flowers that bloom brighter and birds that sing sweeter and simple pleasures grown profound against the backdrop of a terminal illness. Of the powerful bond between two people who pledged for better or worse and meant it.

"Who is to judge the value of life, whether it's one day or one week or one year?" Hanson said. "I find the quality of life a lot more important than the length of life."

Much has been written about the death that comes with AIDS, but little has been said about the living. Hanson and Henningson want to change that. They have opened their homes and their hearts to tell the whole story—beginning to end.

This is the first chapter.

The tiny snapshot is fuzzy and stained with ink. Two men in white T-shirts and corduroys stand at the edge of a barnyard, their muscled arms around each other's shoulders, a puzzled bull watching them from a field. The picture is overexposed, but the effect is pleasing, as if that summer day in 1982 was washed with a bit too much sun.

A summer later, the same men—one bearded and one not, one tall and one short—pose on the farmhouse porch in a mock American Gothic. Their pitchforks are mean looking and caked with manure. But their attempted severity fails; dimples betray their humor.

They are pictured together often through the years, draped with ribbons and buttons at political rallies, playing with their golden retriever, Nels, and, most frequently, working in their lavish vegetable garden.

The pictures drop off abruptly after 1985. One of the few shows the taller man, picking petunias from his mother's grave. He is startlingly thin by now; as a friend said, "like Gandhi after a long fast." His sun-bleached hair has turned dark, his bronze skin pallid. His body seems slack, as if it's caving in on itself.

The stark evidence of Dick Hanson's deterioration mars the otherwise rich memories captured in the photo album. But Hanson said only this:

"When you lose your body, you become so much closer to your spirit. It gives you more emphasis of what the spirit is, that we are more important than withering skin and bone."

□ □ □

Hanson sat with his partner, Bert Henningson, in the small room at Minneapolis' Red Door Clinic on April 8, 1986, waiting for the results of Hanson's AIDS screening test.

He wouldn't think about how tired he had been lately. He had spent his life hefting hay bales with ease, but now was having trouble hauling potato sacks at the Glenwood factory where he worked part time. He had lost 10 pounds, had chronic diarrhea and slept all afternoon. The dishes stayed dirty in the sink, the dinner uncooked, until Henningson got home from teaching at the University of Minnesota-Morris.

It must be the stress. His parents had been forced off the farm and now he and his brothers faced foreclosure. Two favorite uncles were ill. He and Henningson were bickering a lot, about the housework and farm chores and Hanson's dark mood.

He had put off having the AIDS test for months, and Henningson hadn't pushed too hard. Neither was eager to know.

Now, as the nurse entered the room with his test results, Hanson convinced himself the news would be good. It had been four years since he had indulged in casual weekend sex at the gay bathhouse in Minneapolis, since he and Henningson committed to each other. Sex outside their relationship had been limited and "safe," with no exchange of semen or blood. He had taken care of himself, eating home-grown food and working outdoors, and his farmer's body always had responded with energy and strength. Until now.

"I put my positive thinking mind on and thought I'd be negative," Hanson said. "Until I saw that red circle."

The reality hit him like a physical punch. As he slumped forward in shock, Henningson—typically pragmatic—asked the nurse to prepare another needle. He, too, must be tested.

Then Henningson gathered Hanson in his arms and said, "I will never leave you, Dick."

□ □ □

Hanson is one of 210 Minnesotans and 36,000 Americans who have been diagnosed with AIDS since the disease was identified in 1981. More than half of those patients already have died, and doctors say it is only a matter of time for the rest. The statistics show that 80 to 90 percent of AIDS sufferers die within two years of diagnosis; the average time of survival is 14 months after the first bout of pneumocystis—a form of pneumonia that brought Hanson to the brink of death last August and again in December.

"For a long time, I was just one of those statistics," Hanson said. "I was a very depressing person to be around. I wanted to get away from me."

He lost 20 more pounds in the two weeks after receiving his test results. One of his uncles died and, on the morning of the funeral, Hanson's mother died unexpectedly. Genevieve Hanson was 75 years old, a gentle but sturdy woman who was especially close to Dick, the third of her six children. He handled the arrangements, picking gospel hymns for the service and naming eight of her women friends as honorary pallbearers—a first in the history of their tiny country church.

But Hanson never made it to his mother's funeral. The day she was buried, he collapsed of exhaustion and fever. That night, Henningson drove him to Glenwood for the first of three hospitalizations—42 days worth—in 1986.

"Dick was real morbid last summer," Henningson said. "He led people to believe it was curtains, and was being very vague and dramatic. We all said to be hopeful, but it was as if something had gripped his psyche and was pulling him steadily downward week after week."

Hanson had given up, but Henningson refused to. He worked frantically to rekindle that spark of hope—and life. He read Hanson news articles about promising new AIDS drugs and stories of terminal cancer patients defying the odds. He brought home tapes about the power of positive thinking and fed Hanson healthy food. He talked to him steadily of politics and all the work that remained to be done.

He forced himself, and sometimes Hanson, to work in the garden, making it bigger than ever. They planted 58 varieties of vegetables in an organic, high-yield plot and christened it the Hope Garden.

But Hanson returned to the hospital in August, dangerously ill with the dreaded pneumonia. His weight had dropped to 112 from his usual 160. He looked and walked like an old-man version of himself.

"I had an out-of-body type experience there, and even thought I had died for a time," he said. "It was completely quiet and very calm and I thought, 'This is really nice.' I expected some contact with the next world. Then I had this conversation with God that it wasn't my time yet, and he sent me back."

Hanson was home in time to harvest the garden, and to freeze and can its bounty. He had regained some of his former spunk, and was taking an interest again in the world around him.

"I'd be sitting next to him on the couch, holding his hand, and once in a while he'd get that little smile on his face and nod like there was something to hold on to," Henningson said. "And a small beam of life would emerge."

A month later, Hanson's spirits received another boost when he was honored at a massive fund-raising dinner. Its sponsors included DFL [Democratic-Farmer Labor party] notables—among them Gov. Rudy Perpich, Lt. Gov. Marlene Johnson, St. Paul Mayor George Latimer, Minneapolis Mayor Don Fraser and Congressmen Bruce Vento and Martin Sabo—and radical political activists Hanson had worked with over the years, farmers who had stood with him to fight farm foreclosures and the West Central power line, women who remembered his support during the early years of the women's movement, members of the gay and lesbian community and other AIDS sufferers.

What started as a farewell party, a eulogy of sorts, turned into a celebration of Hanson's life. Folk singer Larry Long played songs on an Indian medicine man's healing flute. Friends gathered in a faith circle to will their strength to Hanson. Dozens of people lined up to embrace Hanson and Henningson. For most, it was the first time they had touched an AIDS patient.

"People are coming through on this thing and people are decent," Hanson said. "We find people in all walks of life who are with us on this struggle . . . It's that kind of thing that makes it all worth it."

So when the pneumonia came back in December, this time with more force, Hanson was ready to fight.

"The doctor didn't give him any odds," Henningson said. Hanson was put on a respirator, funeral arrangements were discussed, estranged relatives were called to his bedside.

"He wrote me a note," Henningson said. " 'When can I get out of here?' He and I had never lied to each other, and I wasn't about to start. I said, 'You might be getting out of here in two or three days, but it might be God you're going to see. But there is a slim chance, so if you'll just fight . . .' "

People from Hanson's AIDS support group stayed at the hospital round the clock, in shifts, talking to him and holding his hand as he drifted in and out of a coma. Friends brought Christmas to the stark hospital room: cards papered the walls and a giant photograph of Hanson's Christmas tree, the one left back at the farmhouse, was hung.

The rest was up to Hanson.

"I put myself in God's healing cocoon of love and had my miracle," he said. "I call it my Christmas miracle."

He was released from intensive care on Christmas Eve day and since has devoted his life to carrying a seldom-heard message of hope to other AIDS patients, to give them—and himself—a reason to live as science races to find a cure.

"I'd like to think that God has a special purpose for my life," he said. His smile under the thinning beard is sheepish; faith is personal, and easily misunderstood.

"I don't want to come across like Oral Roberts, but . . . I believe that God can grant miracles. He has in the past and does now and will in the future. And maybe I can be one of those miracles, the one who proves the experts wrong."

□ □ □

Hanson has spent his life on the front line of underdog causes—always liberal, often revolutionary and sometimes unpopular.

"Somewhere along the line Dick was exposed to social issues and taught that we can make a difference," said Mary Stackpool, a neighbor and fellow political activist. "That's what Dick has been all about —showing that one person can make a difference."

Hanson put it in terms less grand: "You kind of have to be an eternal optimist to be a farmer. There's something that grows more each year than what you put into the farm. . . . I've always been involved in trying to change things for the better."

He was born into the national prosperity of 1950 and grew up through the social turmoil of the 1960s. A fifth-grade teacher sparked his enthusiasm in John F. Kennedy's presidential campaign. He was 13 when his father joined the radical National Farmers Organization, took the family to picket at the Land O'Lakes plant in nearby Alexandria and participated in a notorious milk-dumping action.

He later led rural campaigns for Eugene McCarthy, George McGovern, Mark Dayton, [a Minnesota businessman who ran for the U.S. Senate], and his current hero, Jesse Jackson. He led protests against the Vietnam War, and was a conscientious objector. He organized rival factions to try to stop construction of the high-voltage power line that snakes through western Minnesota.

He was an early member of the farm activist group Groundswell, fighting to stop a neighbor's foreclosure one day, his own family's the next. The 473-acre Hanson farm has been whittled to 40 by bankruptcy; Hanson and Henningson are struggling to salvage the farmhouse and some surrounding wetlands.

He has been arrested five times, staged a fast to draw attention to the power line protest and stood at the podium of the 1980 DFL district convention to announce—for the first time publicly—that he was gay. That same year, he was elected one of the first openly gay members of the Democratic National Committee and, in 1984, made an unsuccessful bid for the party's nomination for Congress from the Second District. In 1983, he and Henningson were photographed in their fields for a 1983 Newsweek magazine story about gays responding to the AIDS crisis; neither knew at the time they carried the virus.

"He just throws himself into a cause and will spare nothing," Stackpool said. "He will expose himself totally to bring out the desired good."

Now the cause is AIDS. The struggle is more personal, the threat more direct. But for Hanson, it has become yet another opportunity to make a difference.

"He's handling this just as he would anything else—with strength and lots of courage and hope," said Amy Lee, another longtime friend and fellow activist. "And with that pioneering spirit. If there's anything he can do, any way he can help other victims, any time he can speak—he'll go for it."

Hanson has become one of the state's most visible AIDS patients. He and Henningson are frequently interviewed for news stories, were the subject of a recent four-part series on KCMT-TV in Alexandria and speak at AIDS education seminars in churches and schools throughout the state. Last month, Hanson addressed the state Senate's special informational meeting on AIDS.

"I want to take the mask off the statistics and say we are human beings and we have feelings," he said. "I want to say there is life after AIDS."

Rather than retreat to the anonymity of the big city, as many AIDS sufferers do, Hanson has maintained a high political profile in Pope County. He is chairman of the DFL Party in Senate District 15. He and Henningson continue to do business with area merchants and worship weekly at the country church of Hanson's childhood, Barsness Lutheran.

"I've always been a very public person and I've had no regrets," Hanson said. "One thing my dad always emphasized was the principle that honesty was the most important thing in life."

Hanson and Henningson use their story to personalize the AIDS epidemic and to debunk some of the stereotypes and myths about AIDS and its victims. They are farmers who have milked cows, slopped hogs and baled hay like everyone else. Their politics and sexual orientation may disturb some. But their voices and values are more familiar, and perhaps better understood, than those of some of their urban counterparts.

"It makes people aware that it can happen here," said Sharon Larson, director of nursing at Glacial Ridge Hospital in Glenwood.

That honesty has carried a price. A conservative Baptist minister from Glenwood criticized their lifestyle at a community forum and again in a column in the Pope County Tribune. Some of Hanson's relatives were upset by the Alexandria television show and demanded he keep his troubling news to himself. There have been rumblings in his church from people concerned about taking communion with him, and a minor disturbance erupted in a Glenwood school when his niece was teased about him.

But his connections also carry clout.

"It brings it a little closer home to the guys in the Capitol who control the purse strings," a fellow AIDS patient said.

When they speak, Hanson and Henningson touch on a variety of topics: the need for national health insurance to guarantee equitable care, the cruelty of policies that force AIDS patients into poverty before they are eligible for medical assistance, the need for flex-time jobs so AIDS sufferers can continue to be productive, the imperative of safe sex.

They also stress the personal aspects of the disease: the need for patients to be touched rather than shunned, the importance of support from family and friends and, most dear to Hanson, the healing powers of hope.

"I know there are some who die because they give up," he said. "They have no hope, no reason to fight. Everything they're faced with is so desperate and dismal. . . . I believe the biggest obstacle for us who have AIDS or AIDS-related complex is fighting the fear and anxiety we have over the whole thing. Every positive thing, every bit of hope is something to hold on to."

□ □ □

Next month, Hanson and Henningson will celebrate five years together, perhaps with a gathering of friends and an exchange of rings. They exchanged vows privately that first summer while sitting in their car under the prairie night.

"We asked the blessing of the spirit above," Hanson said. "It was a pretty final thing."

At first blush, they seem an unlikely couple.

"Bert the scholar and Dick the activist . . . In some ways they're just worlds apart," Stackpool said. "But politics brought them together, and now they take delight in those differences and in their special traits. They've figured out things many married couples never come close to figuring out."

Henningson is bookish and intense, a Ph.D. in international trade, a professor and essayist. He is a doer and organizer. He charts the monthly household budget on his Apple computer, itemizing everything from mortgage payments to medicine to cat food. He sets a hearty dinner table, which is cleared and washed as soon as the last bit of food is gone. He buries himself in his work during the week, becomes reclusive when he retreats to the farm on weekends and has worked hard over the years to control an explosive temper.

Hanson is more social, an easygoing, non-stop talker with a starburst of interests. He spent 12 years detouring through social activism before finally earning a bachelor's degree in political science at the university's Morris campus. He has a political junkie's memory for names, dates and events, thrills in company and is quick to offer refreshments, having inherited his mother's belief in friendship through food.

But they also have much in common.

Henningson, 40, grew up on a farm near Graceville, in neighboring Big Stone County. His life paralleled Hanson's in many respects: the radical farm movement, anti-war protests, involvement in liberal political campaigns.

Both suppressed their homosexuality until they were almost 30. Hanson kept so active with politics and the farm that he didn't have time for a social life. After acknowledging his homosexuality, his sexual life involved weekend excursions to the Twin Cities for anonymous encounters at the gay bathhouse.

"I had to taste all the fruit in the orchard," he said. "I had some real special relationships, but if they suggested it just be us I felt trapped, like they were closing in on me."

Henningson threw himself into graduate school, tried marriage and took on a demanding career in Washington, D.C., as an aide to former U.S. Rep. Richard Nolan. He divorced and returned to Minnesota, where he enrolled in a human sexuality program at the University of Minnesota. He had three homosexual involvements before meeting Hanson at a political convention.

"There were some major forces working in the universe that were compelling us together," Henningson said. "I don't know that we even had much to say about it. I've always believed in serendipity, but I also feel you have to give serendipity a little help. So I didn't sit back and wait for Dick to call—I called him."

Any doubts Hanson had about their relationship were squelched by his mother. She visited the farmhouse one Sunday morning with freshly baked caramel rolls, which she served Hanson and Henningson in bed. Henningson was accepted as part of the family, moved to the farm and eventually assumed financial responsibility for the family's farm operations.

"It was so good to work together, to sweat together, to farrow those sows and help the sows have those little piglets," Henningson said. "We literally worked dawn to dusk."

That hard but somewhat idyllic life has been altered drastically by AIDS. Hanson does what he can, when he can, perhaps baking cookies or doing the laundry. But the burden of earning an income, running the house and caring for Hanson has fallen heavily on Henningson's shoulders.

Hanson's medical bills—totalling more than $50,000 so far—are covered by welfare. Henningson's temporary job at the state Department of Agriculture, where he writes farm policy proposals, pays their personal bills, helps pay their apartment rent in the Twin Cities so Hanson can be near medical care during the week and allows them to keep the farmhouse.

"Dick's optimism is fine," Henningson said. "But you have to help optimism along now and then with a little spade work. I ended up doing all of the work with no help. What could have happened is that I could have grown resentful and blamed the victim.

"But I tried to put myself in his shoes—having pneumonia twice —and with all my anger and short temper, could I live with that? Could I even get through that? I'd probably have the strength to go to a field and dig a hole and when the time came crawl in and bury myself. But I don't know if I'd have the strength to do what he did."

So, their commitment to each other remains absolute, perhaps strengthened by facing a crisis together.

"When you know that somebody's going to stand by you, and when they prove that they will, when they go through what Bert's gone through this past year in putting up with me . . . you just know it's very, very special what you have," Hanson said.

□ □ □

Each week, Hanson checks in at the AIDS clinic at Hennepin County Medical Center. He and Henningson make the three-hour drive to Minneapolis every Monday and spend their week in the Twin Cities. Henningson has work through June at the Agriculture Department. Hanson's full-time job is AIDS.

He has his blood tested to determine his white blood cell count—his body's natural defense system. It often is below 1,000; a healthy person's count would be closer to 5,000.

He has a physical exam, chats with two or three doctors, gives encouragement to fellow patients and collects hugs from the nursing staff. He is a favorite with the social workers, who tease him about his lack of interest in the women who flock to his examination room each week for a visit.

He does weekly inhalation therapy, breathing an antibiotic into his lungs to ward off the dreaded pneumonia. Then he buses to St. Paul for a long, healing massage from one of several local massage therapists who donate time to AIDS patients.

Thursday mornings find him at the University of Minnesota Hospital and Clinic for eye treatments. Doctors inject medicine directly into his eyeball to thwart a virus that is attacking his vision. Sometimes the needle punctures a blood vessel, leaving Hanson with bright red patches in his eyes.

On Thursday nights, he and Henningson attend an AIDS support group meeting, where as many as 30 patients, relatives and friends gather to share comfort and information.

For eight months, Hanson has taken AZT, or azidothymidine, an experimental drug believed to prolong life for AIDS sufferers. He takes other drugs to counter the nausea caused by AZT's high toxicity, and he is watched closely for bone marrow suppression. He uses various underground treatments, all with his doctor's knowledge. He rubs solvent on his skin to try to stimulate a response from his immune system, and spreads a home-brewed cholesterol agent on his toast, hoping it will help render the virus inert.

He watches his diet to prevent diarrhea and takes various prescription drugs for depression and anxiety.

His spare time, what there is of it, is devoured by long waits for the bus or slow walks to his various appointments. He naps often to keep his energy level up and spends evenings watching the Twins on TV. Reading has become painful for him, straining his eyes and making him dizzy.

"It comes back and back and back many times," he said. "Is this my total life? Has the illness become such an all-encompassing thing that my life will never be judged by anything but this brand of AIDS?"

Weekends are spent on the farm, where Hanson often can be found kneeling in his flower beds. The impatiens, moss roses and sweet Williams are planted especially thick this summer; Hanson was eager to see their cheerful pinks and reds cover the crumbling stone foundation of the old farmhouse. He insists on having fresh flowers in the house every day, even dandelions and thistles. Once, after pranksters broke the peony bushes in the church cemetery, Hanson gathered up the broken blossoms and took them home, placing them around the house in shallow bowls of water.

Or he can be found singing in the empty silo, practicing hymns for Sunday's church service. His voice is sweet and natural, with a good range. It is inherited, he says, from his mother, who sang to him when he was in the womb and tuned in opera on the radio in the farm kitchen when he was a youngster. He has sung for his brothers' weddings but is better, he says, at funerals.

On hot summer nights, he and Henningson sleep in twin beds in a screened porch upstairs. The room is kept cool by towering shade trees and constant breezes blowing off the marsh that winds in front of the house. From there, the men note the comings and goings of their neighbors: egrets and blue herons, Canada geese that feed on what Henningson calls Green Scum Pond, a doe and her buff-colored fawn. There is an owl in the nearby woods, a peregrine falcon nesting in the farmhouse eaves and an unseen loon that sings to them at dusk.

If the weekend is slow, the weather is mild and his energy is high, Hanson can be found in a dinghy somewhere on Lake Minnewaska, the sparkling centerpiece of Pope County. He's a skilled fisherman, and remembers weekends when he would haul home a catch of 200 pan fish for one of his mother's famous fries.

"I find that going out in the garden is a good way to get away from things, or going fishing, or just visiting with people and talking," he said. "I don't want my whole life to be branded by AIDS."

□ □ □

Hanson awakes in the Minneapolis apartment on a recent morning to the sound of his mother's voice.

"It wasn't part of any dream," he said. "Just her voice, crystal clear, calling."

He has been running a fever for several days, and suffering headaches. His white blood cell count has dropped precipitously. His chatter, usually cheerful, is tinged with fear.

"I got pretty emotional about it," he said. "But Bert held me and said, 'Don't be afraid. Don't fight it.' And I remember a year ago when I was so sick, and she was reaching to me, and I was so scared I was almost pushing her away. And Bert said not to fight it, to let her comfort me even if she's reaching to me on a level we don't understand . . .

"There are days I think I'm just going to get out of this, put this whole thing behind me and get a job and go on with my life again.

Then I have a rough day like this and I have to look at things much more realistically."

Hanson seldom talks of death. When his health is stable, there seems little point. He has beaten the odds before and will, he says, again.

"Intermittently, there has been some denial," said his physician, Dr. Margaret Simpson, director of the sexually transmitted disease clinic at Hennepin County Medical Center. "That's not too surprising. When you're feeling good, it's easy to think this isn't true.

"But he's deteriorating again, and it's worrisome. I don't make predictions, but I think now in terms of weeks and months rather than months and years."

Hanson senses that urgency. But he remains a fighter. His attitude, he says, is not one of delusion but of defiance.

"I think I'll know when the time is right and it's coming," he said. "Should it be, I'm ready to meet my maker. But I'm not ready to give up and say there's nothing that will turn around so I can live."

A week later, Hanson is in the hospital. The headaches are worse, and doctors do a painful spinal tap to determine if the AIDS virus has entered his brain. His white blood cell count is dangerously low, but a transfusion is too risky.

It is the first hospitalization in six months, and only an overnight stay for tests, but it evokes painful memories of the past and fears for the future.

Henningson telephones Hanson's sister.

"I told Mary it may be only three or four months and we have to respond to him accordingly," he said. "Not treat him as someone who's going to die, but accord him the time and attention you want. We can't just say, 'See you next week.' It's not a matter of dealing with certitude anymore, but a great deal of uncertainty about where it's going to lead."

Hanson is quiet this evening and seems distracted. The Twins game plays silently on the hospital room TV, but relief pitcher Jeff Reardon is losing and Hanson pays only passing interest. He gets up once during the evening to vomit and occasionally presses his hand to his temple. But he never mentions the nausea, the throbbing headache or the pain from the spinal tap.

Henningson sits next to him on the bed and thumbs through their photo album, recalling lighter times.

Suddenly, Hanson waves his hand vaguely, at the room, at his life. "I'll miss all this," he confided. "I'll just miss all these wonderful people."

Then he and Henningson discuss—gently—the logistics of his death. Should he be placed in a nursing home if he becomes invalid? Should life-sustaining measures be used if he falls into a coma again? Should he donate his body to research?

The morbid conversation is held in matter-of-fact tones and seems to soothe Hanson. It is Henningson's way of pulling out the emotions, the soft rage and futility that Hanson otherwise would keep tucked inside.

"Talking about things like that helps you understand your mortality, that it may not be much longer," Henningson said. "And that helps relieve your fears. Dick's fears are not so much for himself as for me. Will I live out here all by myself? Will I find someone else? I say don't worry about that, it's out of your control."

But Henningson, too, is shaken. He sits at the window next to Hanson's hospital bed, and holds his hand. Finally, he abandons the diversionary talk and cries. He is worried about losing the farm, about the political hassles involved in getting housing assistance, about getting a job after his contract with the state expires, about not having enough time left with Hanson.

And he can't help but worry about the AIDS virus in his body and his own health prospects. Although he guards his health carefully and is optimistic about medical progress on the AIDS front, he fears that the stress of caring for Hanson is taking its toll. He watches Hanson, and wonders if he is watching his own future.

Then he comforts himself with a wish.

"I want to be cremated and have my ashes thrown in Big Stone Lake. And from there I would flow to the Minnesota River, down to the Mississippi River, all the way to the Gulf. And I'll hit the Gulf Stream and travel the world.

"And I told Dick if he'd like to be cremated, they could put him in Lake Minnewaska, and he would flow to the Chippewa River and then into the Minnesota and the Mississippi and to the Gulf and around the world. And at some point we would merge and we'd be together forever."

He stops, perhaps embarrassed.

"You can't control what happens to people after they're dead," he said. "But even if it doesn't happen, it's a lovely, consoling thought."

CHAPTER II

BY JACQUI BANASZYNSKI

Dick Hanson used to talk about being the first to survive AIDS; now he talks about surviving another week.

After a yearlong battle with acquired immune deficiency syndrome, the Glenwood, Minn., farmer's health is deteriorating rapidly.

"We talk about holding on," said Bert Henningson, Hanson's partner of five years, who also carries the AIDS virus. "But we have to recognize what may be reality and prepare ourselves for it."

The funeral arrangements are checked and rechecked. Visits from family and friends take on more urgency. Precious moments alone, just Hanson and Henningson, are guarded and savored. Where once Hanson threw himself into radical political activism, he now hoards his dwindling strength.

Hanson has taken his battle with AIDS to the public, exposing his own dreams and despairs so that others will feel less alone. He wants others to learn from his loss. But the spotlight on Hanson is harsh, and sometimes catches unwilling players in its glare—relatives who would rather bear their grief in private, others who are angered and embarrassed by their connection with him and some who want no part of him at all.

"This whole illness is a test of humanity, of how we treat our fellow human beings," Hanson said. "If we do the leper thing, and put people away, that's one judgment. But if we do everything we can to give comfort and hope and try to find a cure, that's another judgment."

Chapter Two of Hanson's story is about that test of humanity.

Growing up, the men were like twins. Dick Hanson is barely a year younger than his brother Grant. They shared farm chores; Dick was a patient milker and had a gentle way with the animals, while Grant was a tinkerer who kept the machinery tuned and responsive.

They double-dated in high school, although the socializing never seemed to hold much interest for Dick. They even looked alike, with the same sandy hair that turned lighter in the sun.

"He looks different now, of course," Grant Hanson said.

At 38, Grant Hanson is sturdy from years of physical labor. His hair and beard are bleached from the summer, and his face carries a warm, healthy tan.

But Dick Hanson, 37, is wasting away from AIDS. His frail body is a sallow white, his skin seems translucent, his hair and beard have thinned and turned dark. He bears little resemblance to the ruddy, full-faced man who stands side-by-side with Grant and other relatives in family photographs.

And appearance isn't all that has changed because of AIDS.

Although Grant Hanson remains close to his brother and checks regularly on his condition, AIDS has created an unwelcome barrier between them.

"There's a paranoia about AIDS," Grant Hanson said. "Some people are certain the AIDS virus will live on a doorknob for days on end or you'll catch AIDS from mosquitoes. My wife is very fearful of the disease."

As a result of that fear, Grant Hanson's five children, ages 2 to 12, haven't been allowed to spend time with their Uncle Dick since he became seriously ill last fall. The family has visited the farm only once in recent months; the children stayed in the car while Dick Hanson chatted with them through an open window.

Dick Hanson seldom speaks of such rifts. He prefers to focus on the many kindnesses shown him by family and friends, and to dismiss any unpleasantries, blaming them on misinformation rather than maliciousness.

But he mentioned it recently at an AIDS education seminar in nearby Starbuck, when someone in the audience quoted a Christian radio doctor who said AIDS could be spread by casual contact.

"Because of things like that, I have five nieces and nephews who I can't see, who used to love to come out to the farm and enjoy being with Bert and me and doing things with us," Hanson said. "For a year now they haven't been allowed to do that. And it's one of the things I have missed most in the last year—getting to know these young people—and it has hurt me deeply. I can only hope it will change."

☐ ☐ ☐

Hanson has become one of Minnesota's most visible AIDS patients, trying to educate others about the disease. That visibility has carried a price.

Some of his relatives have been hassled by gossip, letter-writers have accused him of flaunting his homosexuality, and a few family members are furious with him for holding the Hanson name up to public scrutiny.

But, on the whole, Glenwood and Minnesota are passing Hanson's test of humanity.

"You have to deal with so many different aspects of life when you're dealing with this, you're bound to run into some resistance or ignorance," Hanson said. "There are simple-minded people, and I don't bother to waste my time with them. But by and large, people are caring and giving and compassionate if given a chance."

Hanson says he expected no less, although he and Henningson knew they risked rejection by making their situation public. They have been featured in news stories and have spoken at AIDS education forums across the state and at the Minnesota Legislature.

"Our friends told us we were crazy, that we'd be lynched and branded by the hysterics," Hanson said. "But we had to balance that off with what we see as our part of it, what I like to think is the truth."

The slurs that come to him third-hand are more than offset by the favors he receives directly.

He and Henningson recently received a $50 check from strangers —two closeted gay men from Minneapolis who heard about them and wanted to help. Other strangers have sent smaller amounts—$5 or $10—or invaluable words of encouragement. A friend from the Glenwood area called Henningson last week to offer her savings if they needed it.

Neighbors sometimes mow the lawn, and others stop by to leave food in the freezer. Pearl Brosvick, Hanson's neighbor and godmother, brings rhubarb pie on the weekends and homemade doughnuts like those Hanson's mother made.

Brosvick, a childless 73-year-old widow, also sent Hanson a note last winter thanking him for escorting her to communion at Chippewa Falls Lutheran Church. Area residents had just received the news that Hanson had AIDS.

"I don't know that much about AIDS," she said. "And I don't really approve of homosexuality. I don't know if they're born this way and they can't function any other way.

"But we all do things we shouldn't and we can't judge each other."

Several local ministers have risked the wrath of their congregations by supporting Hanson. The Rev. Wayne Mensing of Immanuel and Indherred Lutheran churches in Starbuck urged people at an AIDS seminar to "take a stand and see these people as children of God and be with them in community." And the Rev. Marlin Johnson of Trinity Lutheran Church in Cyrus thanked Hanson and Henningson for sharing their story.

"Whether you agree or disagree or approve or disapprove is irrelevant," Johnson said. "This is such a big problem, you can't go running away off into the boondocks as if it didn't exist. If God can work good out of evil, then we are being blessed by these two fellows because they are so willing to be vocal about it."

Hanson cherishes such comments, little signs that people are listening and learning.

"I am so proud of this rural community," he said. "I think in the big cities it's very easy to get lost in the shuffle and impersonal aspect of the thing. But in the rural area, if you've given to the community all your life as I have, there's a level of decency. If a farmer gets sick or his barn burns down, the neighbors get together and bring food. There's a time to come together, even if you don't like the person, no matter what the differences.

"Not a lot of people understand or agree with my lifestyle, but they understand that sense of coming together and that sense of community. That, for me, makes life worth living."

□ □ □

Allen Hanson, 69, drives out to the farmhouse on a recent night to visit his son. They talk of the usual things—the family, the failing farm economy, their mutual dream of someday seeing Jesse Jackson in the White House.

But as he prepares to leave, Allen Hanson tells a strange story, about an age gone by when his own father was dying of inoperable cancer, and about a faith healer who came to town and called upon God, and how doctors later saved his father. And about a time when Allen Hanson himself was sick, stricken with gallstones, and the faith healer again called upon God, and the stones passed and he finally was freed of pain.

Allen Hanson stops his story and looks at his son, lying still as death on the couch.

"I just know if I could find someone like that," he said, "they could help the doctors and take away this illness of yours."

Dick Hanson stands up then, mustering a strength he hasn't felt for days, and clasps his father's hand in both of his. They stay that way for a long, awkward moment—two proud Norwegian farmers who seldom shared a handshake in all the years they shared a life.

Before letting go of his hand, Dick Hanson tells his father how good it is to see him, and how much he appreciates his concern.

□ □ □

It was the first time Allen Hanson had spoken with his son, even obliquely, about AIDS.

"We never discussed it," the elder Hanson said. "I can't explain why. . . . I don't believe in this crying and everything. You got to take the good with the bad in life."

He sits this evening in the living room of a modest rambler near downtown Glenwood, where he moved after losing much of the family's century-old farm to foreclosure and selling the rest to his sons in an attempt to salvage the homestead.

He lives there with two of his five sons, Leland and Tom, and with Leland's wife and teen-age daughter. Allen Hanson's only daughter, Mary Hanson-Jenniges, has walked over from her nearby apartment, and son Grant stops by on his bicycle. Allen Hanson's oldest son, John, lives with his family in Brooten, some 25 miles away.

It is an uncomfortable evening for Allen Hanson. He seems pleased by the company, but troubled by the conversation. He says he is confused about the strange and frightening disease that has attacked Dick, his third child, and that has fractured his family.

Allen Hanson says he never thought much about his son being gay, that it didn't really matter. Nor does he mind that Dick Hanson has taken his homosexuality and his fight with AIDS public. None of the townsfolk have said anything to him about it and, if they do, he's used to controversy.

As one of the first farmers in the area to try contour plowing, he was ridiculed by traditionalists who "probably thought I'd been drinking." As an early leader of the radical National Farmers Organization, he alienated neighbors who belonged to the conservative Farm Bureau.

But this issue is different, beyond Allen Hanson's understanding or control. "I'm sitting here thinking of what the heck I done wrong," he said. "The last year I lost everything I got . . . the farm, my wife, everything."

He doesn't mention Dick directly in the litany of loss. But he spreads the family photo albums on his lap, pointing out the prouder times, the times that made more sense. Rather than talk about the son who is gay and dying of AIDS, he talks about the son who was, like him, a promising farmer and avid fisherman.

"Those pictures in there, years ago, he was built real good," he said. "He was strong. He could handle those bales like a good, healthy person, and he had good arms on him.

"And I can't help but think of the fun Dickie and I had fishing on this lake. We caught some fish there, I tell you . . . Dickie and I haven't fished together for a couple years now."

He talks of the time Jesse Jackson visited Glenwood and drank some of his wife's good coffee, and the time he rode with the WCCO-TV helicopter to cover a story in the area. He brings out his daughter's wedding picture and many of the awards he won as a young farmer—anything to keep the conversation on safe, pleasant terrain.

But the anguish that has torn his family apart is not to be mended by nostalgia. Allen Hanson's memories are lost beneath the squabbling voices of his children—voices of grief, anger and resentment.

"You can't understand what this is doing to us as a family," Tom Hanson said. "It split us, big time."

The children—Dick Hanson's four brothers and one sister—share their stories reluctantly.

Each has been touched by AIDS in varying degrees and ways, depending on their ties to their brother. Their positions polarized after Hanson's story was aired on Alexandria television in April and, more recently, was covered by Twin Cities newspapers and TV stations. Between Hanson's avid crusade for AIDS education and the fishbowl existence of small-town living, they are robbed of the luxury of private emotions.

So they talk, some out of compassion for other families visited by AIDS, some out of a simple desire to support their brother, some out of a need to distance themselves from him, some out of anger at him for bringing his suffering—and its accompanying stigma—home.

Dick Hanson is painfully aware of the family's turmoil, but if he has criticisms or conflicts, he keeps them to himself.

"But I can't shelter people from reality," he said. "Even the people you love the most, sometimes you have to hurt them. I have to do what I think is right."

Tom Hanson, 28, is the youngest of Dick Hanson's brothers, a big, brusque man who family members say is prone to outbursts of rage. He lives in his father's house in town, having sold his dairy herd as part of a government buy-out. He still grows crops on 190 acres of the family's farmstead.

"Dickie helped me get the farm, the one thing I've always wanted," he said. "It's just like a twist in my stomach. It hurts because he helped me so much. But just because somebody does something good . . . Every day something happens and I get madder and madder and madder."

Tom Hanson is angry at Dick Hanson for making news of such a shameful disease, at his sister, Mary, for siding with Dick, at his brother Grant because "he's not man enough" to say that homosexuality is wrong, at a local minister for refusing to denounce homosexuality from the pulpit, at the media for exploiting his family.

"I feel Dickie is helping the public by talking about this," he said. "But he could have done it without bringing his name into it or his picture or the town. This is not fair what he's doing to the family.

. . . It's not easy being single trying to go through this, having girls come up and say, 'His brother's gay and he has AIDS. Is he gay, too?'

"At least I'm polite enough to call them 'gays.' And I still respected Dickie as my brother for years after I found out he was that way. I've always been nice to Dickie. When he came out of the hospital, he said he'd like to go ice fishing. So I moved the icehouse closer to shore and drilled some holes for him and I tried to be nice. And in return, the favor I get back is he comes on TV without consulting all the family, with no consideration what it'd be like in a small town. He never stopped to think of the innocent people who would be suffering for his glory."

He is cut short by his sister. The two haven't spoken for weeks, their relationship strained by her steadfast loyalty to Dick.

"Can I ask you one question?" Mary Hanson-Jenniges is near tears, her voice low and controlled. "Have you thought about what life will be like without Dick? What will you complain about when he's gone?"

She is 32, has a degree in psychology from St. Cloud State University and works as a social service director at a Glenwood nursing home. She lived at Dick Hanson's farm for a time before she was married, and later she and her husband were frequent visitors with their lively daughter, now 2.

The baby no longer goes to the farm for fear she'll pass some childhood illness on to her uncle. Hanson-Jenniges often cooks for her brother, making meals from their mother's recipes—glorified rice and custard and other bland foods that Hanson can digest.

"As a result of my supporting Dick I've been shunned by some of the family," she said. "I probably would have felt more comfortable if he had not been public, because I'm more a private person. I can't say I don't worry about what people think, because I do. But I'm proud that Dick is my brother and has the courage to stand up and do what he does.

"In the family, I was the first to know. I went through a mourning period when he told me. I cried and cried and cried. I figured that was the worst thing that could ever happen to me. Then three weeks later my mom died.

"And for a while, there were probably a couple of months where I hadn't adjusted to Mom's death, I almost felt angry at Dick for having AIDS. I just lost Mom and now the next most important person in the world may leave me, too. I think Grant is hurting inside just like I am right now. You start grieving before somebody's gone."

Grant Hanson is a quiet man who observes the rest of the family's emotion without comment, refusing to be drawn into the fray. "At this point in time, everybody's got their mind pretty well set," he said. "Being mad doesn't change anything."

Grant, a mechanic and a veteran of the U.S. Navy Seabees, is routinely tested for AIDS twice a year when he gives blood and reads everything he can about the disease. AIDS is his concern, he says, not people's sexual preferences.

"If there's truly a body chemistry so that there's a sexual desire in Dick for another man equal to mine for a woman, then I can understand that," he said.

Grant Hanson is careful not to say too much; he wants to protect his own family's privacy as much as possible. But he acknowledges that his affection for Dick Hanson is at odds with his wife's fear of AIDS, and their five children are caught in the middle.

"My desire would be that between what they hear at home and what they hear from the hygiene types at school, they'll make wise choices," he said. "It reaches a point where you let go of them on the bicycle, and it reaches a point where you can't control everything they do. You just hope they'll carry on what you've tried to teach them.

"And you pray for the people with AIDS. They say there is no cure, that the likelihood of a cure in this century is next to nil, so you just pray for time."

Leland Hanson, the fourth son, is 35 and unemployed. His wife works as a medical secretary and they are active in a Lutheran church in Sunberg. He says he is a recovering alcoholic; if he can overcome his desire for alcohol, he believes his brother can overcome his desire for homosexual relations.

"You look at where the gays were marching in the streets, and right in the Bible it says you'll die and your blood will be upon you," he said. "And AIDS is now in the blood. God will take that for just so long. He's still in control and now they're dying and there's not a damn thing we can do about it.

"If I was given a 95 percent chance of dying, and I'm dying from a sin that I committed, and God gave me another chance to live, I'd be hollering at the top of my lungs that this is wrong. But that's not what he did. God didn't give him a second chance so he could splatter his name across the paper.

"I went down to my church and the first two people I met said, 'Is Dick Hanson your brother?' And I walked away. Enough is enough."

John Hanson, 43, is the oldest and, he says "the mediator between the whole bunch." Because he lives in another town, he is less entangled in family politics. He is a part-time farmer who buys hay and straw from area farmers and hauls it to dairy operations and to the race track in Shakopee. He sees Dick Hanson every few weeks when he brings his two teen-age sons to the farm to do chores.

"I feel sorry for him. He seems to be a fairly good person. He's always been real nice to my family.

"But I wish they just wouldn't have so much publicity. We got kids in school and there's always some who pick on them, and this is an excuse. Down in the Cities, there's this gay business going on and they don't think too much of it. But up here in the small communities, it becomes a big deal.

"There are a few who ask, 'Are you related to that guy up in Glenwood?' My sons tell them we're not related."

□ □ □

There is talk. In a town like Glenwood, population 2,500, there is bound to be.

Much of the talk is rumor, and unfounded, based on fears about AIDS and how it is spread.

Like the time Mary Hanson-Jenniges was chatting with a nursing home official from a neighboring county. He mentioned there was an AIDS patient in Pope County who died last winter. He was speaking of Dick Hanson.

Or the time Hanson-Jenniges was asked by a colleague if, because of her brother, she had been tested for AIDS. Flabbergasted, she didn't answer. But when a second person asked her the same question, she was ready.

"No, I haven't," she said. "I don't have sex with my brother or share needles with him."

But it is mostly just talk.

"Dick's problem hasn't been a big community issue," said John Stone, owner and editor of the local weekly newspaper, the Pope County Tribune. There has been no coverage of Hanson's illness or his public speeches in the Tribune.

"Dick has not been a real active member of this community for many, many years, and a lot of people have no idea who he is," Stone said. "I'm not sure people understand a person like him, who puts issues ahead of his own personal life. He's a crusader of sorts."

"The community interest is zip," agreed Gary Wenschlag, principal of Glenwood High School. "Most people feel he's just one of those weird people and they're not going to deal with it. It's like any other issue . . . a few get right in the middle of it and the rest stay home and mow their lawns and go on about their lives."

Wenschlag spoke to a group of junior high school students about AIDS in April after Hanson's niece, a seventh-grader, left school for half a day when she was teased about him.

"Kids were teasing her that she had AIDS and that her uncle was a sexual pervert and things like that," he said. "The focus was more on the sexuality of it than on AIDS.

"So I told them to think of it from their perspective—maybe you have an uncle, or brother or someone who isn't exactly the person you might want them to be. And I tried to clarify the issue. She has an uncle who's gay; that's a fact. And he has AIDS; that's a fact. And when you go into the ninth grade, he'll be dead. That sounds pretty brutal, but that's the way it is and we need to confront that."

Hanson's presence has forced other townspeople to confront AIDS, too. He has been admitted without question at Glenwood's Glacial Ridge Hospital, although the medical staff wore gowns, gloves and masks when treating him—something that seldom occurs in Twin Cities hospitals except when doctors or nurses are drawing blood.

"People may have been a little skittish at first, but no one refused to treat him," said Sharon Larson, the hospital's director of nursing.

Hanson's family dentist cleared his calendar of patients to accommodate Hanson's need for dental work one day last year—and to avoid any panic among other clients. He continues to check on Hanson's health, and has offered to work Saturdays, if necessary, to treat Hanson. But he asked that his name not be published because he fears he will lose business if townspeople know he is treating an AIDS patient.

Local health officials capitalized on the curiosity surrounding Hanson by organizing AIDS education seminars in Glenwood and neighboring Starbuck that drew, combined, about 250 people. Hanson and Henningson were invited to tell their stories.

At the Glenwood seminar, a Baptist minister raised biblical objections to homosexuality, but was quieted by a Catholic priest who turned the conversation back to the topic—AIDS.

Some members of Barsness Lutheran Church, the tiny country church Hanson has attended since birth, were concerned about sharing communion wine with him. With Hanson's consent, the Rev. Carl Listug provided Hanson with a disposable plastic cup. Since then, Hanson has been welcomed warmly at the church, and has been asked to sing a solo when he is feeling well enough.

"Here is someone who was baptized in the church and grew up in the church and was confirmed in the church," Listug said. "We're not going to turn our backs on him now and have nothing to do with him because he's a homosexual and has AIDS. There's a history there."

□ □ □

Pastor Listug has been the minister of Barsness Lutheran Church for 18 years and has come to know the Hanson family well—burying, baptizing and marrying many of them. His parsonage is just down the gravel road from Dick Hanson's farm. Hanson used to teach Sunday school at the church, and Listug was a kind listener when Hanson struggled with his decision to be a conscientious objector to the Vietnam War.

So when Hanson was first hospitalized with AIDS last year, Listug paid a requisite visit.

"When I left the hospital, I realized I hadn't shaken his hand," he said. Listug's reluctance to touch Hanson forced him to face his own fears about AIDS.

"And I worked through that, and the way I came out of it was I'm not going to let that fear prevent me from ministering to Dick."

The next time Listug was called to Hanson's bedside, he made a point of taking the dying man's hand.

Since then, the minister has attended church-sponsored seminars about AIDS and homosexuality, trying to learn as much as he can so he can guide his congregation in their response to AIDS and its victims. He has preached about AIDS from the pulpit, encouraging compassion and acceptance.

"To me, this is a ministry issue and it doesn't mean that I approve of his whole lifestyle," Listug said. "The focus is on ministering to Dick, who has AIDS."

For those in the congregation who might be discomfitted by Hanson's homosexuality and by the publicity he is receiving, the pastor offers some biblical wisdom, specifically, from the Book of Matthew.

"Matthew 7 said 'Judge not that you will not be judged,' " he said. "And in Matthew 9 and 10, Jesus was eating with sinners. He takes the risk of reaching out to people, even though the Pharisees are worried about their image.

"So if someone demanded that Dick not receive communion or not be allowed in church, I would say, 'Do you want me to abandon him? We're all sinners; the rest of us need grace, too.' "

Listug's approach is at odds with the Rev. Merrill Olson, pastor of the First Baptist Church in Glenwood.

"According to the Bible, homosexuality is wrong, an abomination unto the Lord," Olson said. "So a person who is homosexual and has AIDS has to realize the spiritual consequences of it, meaning they have to repent of it.

"So many churches and pastors override that whole issue. They say, 'We'll love them no matter what they've done.' But if we say we love them and accept them in spite of what they're doing, that's totally wrong."

Olson says Hanson would be welcome to worship in his church, but would not be allowed to receive communion until he repented of the sin of homosexuality.

Olson has purchased space in the Pope County Tribune to make his point, and spoke out against Hanson's homosexuality at the AIDS seminar in Glenwood. He objects to the promotion of condoms and safe sex in the war against AIDS, saying it is "treating the sin" rather than stopping it.

"As long as behavior doesn't change, we'll have AIDS and premarital sex and homosexuality and all kinds of debauchery and every immoral thing you can think of," Olson said.

Listug is aware of Olson's comments, and those of his other critics, and of the moral dilemma posed by AIDS.

But he again turns to Matthew, this time paraphrased on his favorite poster. It shows a starving child in dirty, tattered clothing, and carries the caption: "I was hungry and you debated the morality of my appearance."

"We can get into an academic thing of debating the morality of the issue instead of seeing the human being before us," Listug said.

□ □ □

The lush vegetable garden is overgrown and untended. Weeds poke through the thick straw mulch. The spinach and lettuce long ago flowered and turned bitter, before Henningson had a chance to harvest them. The other crops are ripening quickly under the humid summer sun—fat cabbages, gleaming white cauliflower and crisp broccoli, juicy peas and sweet strawberries. The raspberries are almost done for the season, and the tomatoes will redden soon.

"I found with the garden I don't have time to process it this year," Henningson said. "So I'm giving it away, all of it. Alice and John were here last Sunday and filled up their buckets with raspberries and I gave some cauliflower and broccoli to Mary."

He sits on the crumbled concrete stoop of the old farmhouse, looking at the garden that has been his pride and joy for the five years he has lived here with Hanson. Last summer, after Hanson fell ill, they named it the Hope Garden and look to it as a symbol of Hanson's stubborn will to survive.

"I find I just love to look at it," Henningson said. "I'll have to tell Dick there's a scarlet gladiola on the way. He got those for his birthday. Two people gave him bags of gladiola bulbs and two people gave him begonias."

Hanson is asleep inside, on the couch in the front room. It is cool there, and blessedly quiet after noise and smells of the Twin Cities, where Henningson works during the week while Hanson undergoes medical treatment.

It is Hanson's first visit to the farm in almost a month. He was hospitalized at Hennepin County Medical Center three times in June, for 13 days.

The garden has become a luxury for him, as have visits from friends and his beloved Minnesota Twins games. Watching the TV makes him dizzy. And he's been so exhausted he chose not to attend an annual Fourth of July party at the nearby lake home of Alice Tripp, a longtime friend and fellow political activist.

Dozens of friends would be there—compatriots who stood with him to try to block construction of the West Central power line, who campaigned with him for liberal Democratic candidates and who were arrested with him in farm foreclosure protests.

The party would have had special meaning this year: It marked the fifth anniversary of the night Hanson and Henningson exchanged private vows of commitment to each other, asking God to be their witness.

But Hanson and Henningson stayed home. "It would just be too hard to pull away from people and say goodbye," Hanson said. His melancholy is softened some by two red roses, given him that morning by Henningson to celebrate their years together. Hanson places them nearby so they catch his eye whenever he awakes from his frequent naps.

It is little things that tax him now. He suffered severe and unexplained headaches in early June. Doctors tried a host of pain-relieving medicines, but they only caused nausea and a dangerous loss of weight. They finally settled on methadone treatments and the headaches are less painful, but Hanson still cannot digest solid food.

Two weeks ago, an abscessed tooth had to be removed. The Novacain didn't take effect, but oral surgeons cut through the jawbone and pulled the tooth anyway, fearing that Hanson's weakened immune system would not be able to fight the infection by itself. Henningson left the building rather than listen to Hanson's screams. Hanson merely said: "It was the most unpleasant thing I've dealt with in a year-and-a-half with AIDS."

But Dick Hanson remains a fighter, struggling to maintain his weight—which has again dropped below 120—on a diet of Jell-O, Carnation Instant Breakfast and a chocolate-flavored protein drink. He still cherishes the quiet and fresh air of the farm, and watches the news each night with the avid interest of a lifelong political junkie. And he counts his small victories, like making it upstairs by himself to shower, or spending a few minutes on the stoop looking at the garden.

□ □ □

"I'm really thankful I've had the last six months," Hanson said. "The doctors gave up on me six months ago and I was in a very low physical condition. So I'm really thankful for all the things I've been able to do, all the speaking engagements, and talking at the Capitol. Maybe this is the purpose, maybe I was given this extra time in

December so I could inspire the Legislature and the public through the media.

"The last couple of days in the hospital, and then here at home, I seem to have sensed spirits in the room, like people around me. The presence has been so real when I open my eyes up I expect to see them, and possibly I . . . see the vague framework of someone.

"It seems they were there to comfort me and seems real natural with the environment. Mom was one of them, I know. The others I don't recognize. But I never knew my grandmothers. They died before I was born. So there are people in the family tree who would be concerned who I don't know.

"It's been scary in the past when I've felt the spirits. But this time it was a good feeling. Except maybe it means the time is closer for me to leave this world, and that always brings sad tears, to think of missing my friends and Bert and my family. But I guess it's kind of nice to know there is some kind of warning or signal, too, so if there's something I want to say or do before I leave . . . like telling Bert how much I love him.

"Bert and I had a talk last night. He kind of prodded me like he does when he knows I need to talk. We talked about the time left, and he probed my wishes for a service, if it would be soon. He wanted to know if I had any changes in my mind for the plans we had talked about earlier."

He turns to Henningson then, trying to remember. "By the way, what did I say?"

"You left it up to me," Henningson answered.

Hanson shakes his head. "I left it up to you," he said. "Typical me . . . when there are tough choices to make, leave it up to Bert."

Then, Hanson laughs, a surprisingly deep and healthy laugh.

THE FINAL CHAPTER

S U N D A Y ,   A U G U S T   9 ,   1 9 8 7

B Y   J A C Q U I   B A N A S Z Y N S K I

Dick Hanson died Saturday, July 25. It was 5:30 a.m., farmers' time, when the night holds tight to a last few moments of quiet before surrendering to the bustle of the day.

Back home in rural Glenwood, Minn., folks were finishing morning barn chores before heading out to the fields for the early wheat harvest. Members of the Pope County DFL Party were setting up giant barbecue grills in Barsness Park, preparing for the Waterama celebration at Lake Minnewaska.

In the 37 years Hanson lived on his family's farm south of Glenwood, he had seldom missed the harvest or the lakeside celebration. As the longtime chairman of the county DFL, it always had been his job to run the hotdog booth.

But today he was in a hospital bed in downtown Minneapolis. The blinds of the orange-walled room were drawn against the rising sun. He had suffered a seizure the morning before. Doctors said it probably left him unaware of his surroundings, beyond pain and—finally—beyond struggling.

Yet those closest to him swore he could hear them, and knew what was happening, and knew it was time.

"Three times during the course of the night he brought his hands together and his lips would move, and you knew he was praying. I can't help but think he was shutting himself down," said Roy Schmidt, a Minnesota AIDS Project official and longtime friend who stayed with Hanson that last night.

Hanson died holding the hands of the two people most dear to him—his sister, Mary Hanson-Jenniges, and his partner of five years, Bert Henningson.

"Amazing Grace" was playing softly on a tape machine in the corner of the room. It was Hanson's favorite hymn, the one he had sung over his mother's grave barely a year ago.

This is the final chapter of Hanson's story. After having lived a year longer than he was expected to, he grew weary of fighting for his life and was willing —if not eager—for it to end. After his death, he was cremated. Mourners came to his childhood church for a memorial service that was vintage Hanson —traditionally religious but politically radical and, inevitably, controversial.

Henningson is left behind on the farm with a legacy of love—and death. For now he, too, is sick, suffering early symptoms of acquired immune deficiency syndrome. No sooner will he finish grieving for Hanson than he must begin grieving for himself.

□ □ □

Dick Hanson spent the last weekend of his life at the farm where he grew up. It is there he began his goodbyes.

Grant Hanson came to the farmhouse for the first time in months. Of Hanson's four brothers, he was closest to Dick in age, temperament, and affection.

Grant was alone. His wife never had gotten over her overwhelming fear of AIDS and had forbidden Grant any close contact with Dick, worried he would carry the virus home to their five children.

"I think Grant wanted very much to touch me and hug me," Hanson said. "But he said he couldn't lie about it to Joyce and she'd just be so upset if she thought he got too close. So he just sat across the room from me.

"But we had a very deep talk. He said if there was any of the four brothers he could have farmed with, it was me. I guess I've always known that, but it was nice to hear him say that. And it was just something special that he came out and came into the house for the first time."

Allen Hanson made two visits to the farm that weekend to see his son. They never spoke directly of death.

"Dad has been coming out every Friday night on his own and has sat for a long time and has not wanted to leave," Hanson said. "But this last time seemed like a special time for him. He doesn't want to talk about me dying. I guess I haven't found the right words to talk to him about the situation. I was just hoping somehow he could see I was at peace.

"My sister Mary came out with him on Sunday. It was hard for her to see me use the cane and have trouble walking. I guess I stumbled a few times, and when I went outside Bert had to hold my hand. She just had to leave the room and go outside and cry. It was just too hard for her. Bert talked to her and said he has watched me every day, and he said I'm the same person. The inner person of me is still there, and the outer body is something you just have to see past. It's like people growing old together, you just have to accept it.

"So Bert stayed outside with Dad for a while and Mary came back in and sat on the couch and we just had a real deep conversation. I just said, 'Do you know that I'm at peace? I could go the next hour or the next day and be ready.' I think by the time she left she really believed me.

"I just felt like I was saying my goodbyes to each and every one of them. So even though I may never make it back, I felt I had a chance to be with them in a very special way."

Hanson was alienated from his three other brothers in early spring, when an Alexandria television station did a series of stories about him. The brothers were angered and embarrassed by Hanson's decision to tell his story publicly, and accused him of bringing shame on the family.

But Leland Hanson, a conservative Christian who is younger than Hanson by a year, telephoned after hearing his brother had been admitted to the hospital. Hanson's oldest brother, John, had stopped at the farm a few weeks earlier for a short visit, and also called the hospital.

Hanson never heard from Tom, his youngest brother and longtime fishing companion.

□ □ □

Hanson entered the hospital two days later after a vicious bout of vomiting. He predicted it was his last hospitalization, and he seemed almost anxious to die. His characteristic cheerfulness was gone. He still talked occasionally of gaining weight and living several more months, but now the phrases of hope rang hollow, as if they were expected but not meant.

"The time is close," he said to friend Roy Schmidt, who pretended not to hear.

"He's pretty much given up," said his physician, Dr. Margaret Simpson. "Dick has always been an eternal optimist, and somehow he always bounced back before. But in the last two months, there's been a major turnaround. . . . Most people just get tired of feeling this bad. They say, 'I don't want to die, but I don't want to live like this.' "

Yet a core of spunk remained. The sugar-water dripping into his veins perked him up, "giving me the opportunity to just gab away a few more days," he said.

A stream of visitors crowded to his bedside. He had to strain to see them through his blurred vision, or depend on his partner, Bert Henningson, to identify them. He comforted them as they cried, clutching their hands and reminding them each of some special moment or gesture that had enriched his life.

He insisted on sitting up as often as he could during the day, and tried to shake himself out of his morphine doze whenever he had visitors. Henningson teased that Hanson was just testing people "to see how interesting a conversationalist they are."

Hanson brightened most at the talk of politics. He scowled at the news that conservative Cardinal John O'Connor of New York was named to the president's AIDS task force. He smiled in satisfaction when a political crony from Glenwood reported she had been granted a long-sought audience with a state legislator after dropping Hanson's name.

A sympathy call from Gov. Rudy Perpich was cause for quiet pride —and prompt action.

"He praised me for being willing to be public, and for challenging people to be responsive in a public way to what we've done," Hanson said. "And he asked if there was anything he could do to help."

The next day, with Henningson's help, Hanson fired off a two-page letter to Perpich suggesting changes in state law to force nursing homes to accept terminal AIDS patients.

Hanson also remained a keen critic of the news media, constantly analyzing whether they were doing an adequate job to increase the public understanding of AIDS. He pumped Henningson for information about federal funding for AIDS research, laws guaranteeing compassionate treatment of patients or medical advances that might help the next generation of sufferers.

And he kept a healthy hold on his ego. He was fascinated to see himself in a follow-up story on the Alexandria television station, to witness the shocking change in his looks over the last two years.

He died just before People magazine ran a cover story about AIDS in America, and before Newsweek ran its dramatic photo package called "The Face of AIDS," a haunting panoply of 302 men, women and children who have died of AIDS in the past year.

Hanson would have been pleased to know his picture was included.

□ □ □

In the end, Hanson starved to death.

Since he became ill in late 1985, the AIDS virus had waged an insidious attack throughout his body. His skin broke out in herpes' rashes. A related virus ate at his optical nerves, methodically destroying his eyesight. He frequently ran fevers as high as 104 degrees, and more frequently lay huddled under heavy blankets as icy rivulets of sweat soaked through to the mattress. Sometimes he had diarrhea, while other times he would go two or three weeks between bowel movements. His weight plummeted from 160 to 112.

He fought back with blood transfusions, eye injections, inhalation therapy, toxic drugs and homebrewed organic compounds, but his greatest medicines seemed to be faith and a stubborn will to survive. He defied the odds last August, and again in December, when he was expected to die from pneumocystis pneumonia, the most common killer of AIDS patients.

While he regained some of his lost weight and strength from the experimental drug AZT, he also was boosted by the fresh bounty of his garden and by home-baked treats from his country neighbors.

He used the time he had left to crusade, traveling the state, preaching a gospel of hope and acceptance for AIDS sufferers. For several months, he felt so good he vowed to be the first to survive the fatal virus. After a life of championing underdog causes, it would be his greatest triumph.

Then the nausea returned two months ago, leaving him unable to digest solid foods and launching a precipitous weight loss. As his 5-foot-10 frame shrunk and shriveled, his feet and hands and head seemed to grow enormous.

He walked with a cane, when he walked at all, shuffling to negotiate through doorways and around furniture. He fell once when he was alone, landing on his back on the bed board, and was unable to move for almost an hour.

He had grown suddenly old. He trembled with the sheer effort of sitting up and with a constant chill that was impervious to the muggy summer heat. His face at times looked ancient, the forehead protruding atop the fleshless skull, the eyes bulging over pronounced cheekbones.

Yet the same face could look disarmingly young. The worry lines that once creased his forehead were gone and the soft laugh lines were pulled smooth as his skin stretched tautly over his skull.

The heavy gold-framed glasses no longer fit his face, edging each day nearer the tip of his nose, constantly threatening to slip off. His brown eyes were often cloudy and distant, like a child's lost in a world of fantasy.

The uncontrolled vomiting started a week before he died. He had nibbled on a neighbor's moist zucchini bread, declaring it so tasty he abandoned his precautionary avoidance of solid foods. When the retching began that night, nothing would stay down, not even medicine.

Three days later, he was rushed to the hospital, dangerously dehydrated. He weighed 107 pounds, his skin as dry as parchment and cold to the touch.

He refused a feeding tube and requested a do-not-resuscitate order. He tried to decline all medicines, even painkillers, so death would come more quickly. Simpson insisted only on keeping him comfortable, sympathizing with his desire to die.

"She felt it was a terrific period of time I'd had, and that I had done a lot since December," Hanson said two days before he died. "She said I shouldn't feel guilty about not wanting to do every little thing possible to extend my life."

He lived on crushed ice those last four days. His sister, Mary Hanson-Jenniges, or Henningson stayed with him round-the-clock to spoon-feed him, wash his beard and change his soiled hospital gowns.

As he neared the end, he struggled against an increasingly dense fog brought on by the morphine he was given every eight hours.

"It's about all we can give him," Simpson said.

□ □ □

Hanson suffered a seizure on his third day in the hospital, while Henningson was giving him his morning shower.

It was part of the hospital ritual—a shower and shampoo every other day if Hanson was up to it, a bed bath if he was not. It was the only physical intimacy the two men had left.

In the shower, Henningson chattered at Hanson about mundane things. He said he had stayed up late the night before, after leaving the hospital, to watch the magnificent thunderstorms that brought

100-year-rains to the city, thunderstorms that Hanson missed because he was fuzzy with morphine and because hospital policy required that the shades be drawn in case of shattering glass.

And Henningson updated Hanson about the latest political news— another ritual. As Hanson's eyesight failed and his headaches worsened, he relied on Henningson for his daily fix of news from Washington, D.C., or St. Paul or the Metrodome.

Henningson was telling him about the Iran-contra hearings, about Secretary of State George Shultz's startling testimony, when the seizure began.

"I was just saying, 'I'll tell you all about it when we get you back in bed,'" Henningson said later that morning. "And suddenly he started pushing out at me, very rigid and quite strong. I had to get a nurse to help me.

"And now there's no more recognition or response. He may be able to hear us, but there's no way to know. But if he is beyond hearing us, he's in effect been released. Now it's just a matter of the body going along. There will be no more pain, no suffering. Oh, I hope so."

□ □ □

The doctor said Hanson's organs were still strong, his farmer's heart and lungs pumping in defiance of the coma-like trance. He could live as long as two weeks like that, his eyes open but unblinking, his knees drawn up, legs twitching and arms tugging toward his chest, trying to curl up like a baby, his head cocked oddly to one side.

But others sensed it wasn't so.

Henningson ushered out the last of the day's many visitors, and drove to his South Minneapolis apartment for much-needed sleep. He awoke about 3 a.m. and cried and prayed and waited.

Hanson-Jenniges refused to return home to Glenwood that day and didn't bother with sleep that night. She sat at her brother's bedside, wearing the same clothes she had been in for three days, and watched his sunken chest move shallowly up and down. She prayed through the night for his death.

Alice Tripp, Hanson's old friend and political compatriot from Sedan, had driven to Minneapolis with Hanson-Jenniges. Tripp was asleep in the guest room of her daughter's house in suburban Minneapolis when something woke her about 4 a.m. She lay awake until daylight, thinking of the young man who had stood with her on countless picket lines and motivated her to run for governor in 1978, quietly convincing her and dozens of other women in rural Minnesota they could make a difference.

Jane Ireland, a chaplain from Hennepin County Medical Center, also awoke at 4 a.m. She was going to telephone Hanson's hospital room but, for some reason, didn't. Her concentration on him was so intense that later, when the phone did ring, she didn't hear it.

And back in Glenwood, Pearl Brosvick had trouble sleeping. She spent a restless night alone in the large farmhouse, where she had nursed her invalid husband for more than 20 years before he died, and where her godson, Dick Hanson, had whiled away rainy afternoons playing with other farm youngsters—the only children Brosvick ever had.

Sometime during the darkest hours of the morning, Hanson's breathing grew labored. His sister asked the nurse to give him a slow measure of oxygen through the mask—enough to smooth his breathing but not enough to keep him alive. She put some soothing music in the tape machine, just in case Hanson could hear, and called Henningson.

Henningson took his time returning to the hospital. He showered and finished his prayers and savored the quiet time, sensing it was about to end.

He reached Hanson's beside at 5:20 a.m. Ten minutes later, Hanson died.

"I think he waited for me," Henningson said.

□ □ □

Henningson's voice echoed in the vast basement vault of the Minnesota Cremation Society in South Minneapolis. He sat alone with Hanson's shrouded body, waiting for the cremation to begin.

Hanson always had been the stronger singer, his clear voice and natural pitch carrying the melody of folk songs while Henningson followed with a self-conscious harmony.

But this morning there was no one to hear Henningson as he sang Hanson's favorite hymns, "Amazing Grace" and "Swing Low, Sweet Chariot." And "Joe Hill," the ballad of the martyred union organizer.

"I've been singing him 'Joe Hill' for the last several weeks because in the song it says, 'I never died, said he,' " Henningson later told the six people—brought together only by a common friendship with Hanson—who waited for him in the hushed, formal parlor upstairs.

Henningson had been uneasy about the cremation. He faced criticism from some of Hanson's relatives who preferred a traditional burial. Others had wanted the body embalmed for a viewing.

But Henningson was determined to honor Hanson's wishes to be autopsied for study by AIDS researchers and then to be cremated.

"The ancient Greeks and the Indians, they all have the tradition of the funeral pyre where residual spirits are released," Henningson said.

"We had a philosophical difficulty with burial, doing that to the earth, and Dick was an environmentalist who cared for the earth. . . . And I didn't want to put Dick in the earth with the AIDS virus in him. They can drain the blood in embalming, but the virus is still in the tissues. Burning is a purifying thing and it kills the virus."

After months of being a no-nonsense caretaker for Hanson, Henningson suddenly felt shaken and unsure. The despair that gripped him in the wake of Hanson's death took him by surprise. His hands were icy when he entered the vault, and he said his voice trembled as he began to sing.

"Then I felt calmer and I put my head down," he said. "Then my head was pulled up, and I felt my mouth fall open and I felt warmer than I had been in days. And I knew the spirit had come into me and he was free and he was with me.

"They say the spirit stays around awhile so we can learn not to be apart. But I thought, 'I'm going to have to share you.' Then I just laughed out loud, because that's the way it always was, I always had to share my time with Dick. And there are lots of people now who will want part of his spirit."

☐ ☐ ☐

It was already dark when Henningson arrived at the farm the next evening. He was tired, and still had much to do. He had to prepare for Saturday's memorial service—last-minute visits with the minister and the florist, and a thorough cleaning to rid the house of countless medicine bottles, stained sheets, sweat-soaked bed cushions and other vestiges of terminal illness.

But those things would have to wait. Henningson went straight upstairs to the screened porch that overlooks the marshes in front of the farmhouse. He found the old pink candle, set it on the small table by the middle window and lit it, placing Hanson's Bible and the urn of ashes next to it. Henningson lay on one of the metal-frame cots, watched the candle's flame and remembered.

"We rehabbed the porch in the summer of '84 so we could use it," he said later. "The screens had been torn out by kids or whatever, so we screened it up and Dick's mother went to her auctions and got cots and a table for 50 cents or something ridiculous.

"It was dry that summer, not humid. The strawberries were especially good and I found a recipe for an old-fashioned, biscuit-type of shortcake. We would use the porch in the evenings. We'd spend all day with the hogs, then go up there and have our biscuits and strawberries and cream. There were good memories up there.

"That was an election year, and Dick was running for Congress. And often what I'd do, when Dick was out on the campaign trail, I'd light the pink candle and wait for him to come home. It was a nice signal for him to see as he drove in."

On this night, Henningson again lit the candle. But his sentimental vigil was brief, cut short by practicality. He fought sleep a while longer, but felt himself sinking into the thin mattress.

The last few months of caring for Hanson had extracted an ironic price. Stress had activated the AIDS virus, which had lain dormant in Henningson's body for so long but now was attacking his strength with a vengeful speed.

He blew out the candle, took two sleeping pills to ward off anxiety and set his alarm for 3 a.m., when he was scheduled to take his next dose of life-prolonging AZT.

□ □ □

The mourners came a week after the death, driving down the dusty prairie road to tiny Barsness Lutheran Church. As they entered the stuffy lobby of the white-washed sanctuary, they passed a table loaded with the treasures of Hanson's life—a "great bazaar," as Henningson called it.

They saw his degree from the University of Minnesota-Morris. Photos of his biggest fish and proudest garden and of his family at his only sister's wedding. His formal campaign portrait from his run for Congress in 1984. His fishing license and the black rod and reel he used to take hundred of walleyes out of Lake Minnewaska.

His well-thumbed Bible was there, next to a rusty planting trowel and a jar of decorative corn from one of his harvests. His grubby power-line protest T-shirt was neatly folded and covered with shards of green glass and metal—the broken transformers and sawed-off bolts from the transmission towers downed during those protests.

There were a few buttons from his various political alliances, although Hanson had donated most of the collection to a DFL fundraiser. And a tattered red bandana he wore around his arm during farm foreclosure demonstrations—a symbol of his willingness to be arrested.

The display was crowned by a splendid bouquet of gladiolas—flowers that Hanson had grown in the garden next to the farmhouse.

Friends fingered the trinkets and remembered, their laughter torn with tears.

"We have lost a rare friend, a man of courage and vision who raised so many of our hopes," said Anne Kanten, assistant commissioner of the Minnesota Agriculture Department, who gave the eulogy at Hanson's request. "His tenacity frustrated us, and his courage absolutely scared us to death. The greatest tribute we can pay him is to continue the struggle. We have to march and lead and change the systems that need changing. That is the legacy Dick Hanson left us."

But Hanson's legacy, like his life, was burdened by disapproval and controversy. Some relatives and neighbors bristled at his public homosexuality and were disturbed to find reminders of it at the memorial service.

In the middle of the table in the church lobby lay a yellowed copy of Equal Times, a Minneapolis-based gay newspaper that carried a front page story about Hanson's fight with AIDS. Pinned to the paper was a small button, black with a pink triangle—the sign used to identify homosexuals in Nazi Germany and now a universal symbol of pride for gays and lesbians.

Conservative church members took exception to those items, not wanting it to look as if they condoned homosexuality. Others resented the presence of outsiders—a reporter and photographer who were chronicling Hanson's death, and a caravan of mourners from the Minneapolis gay community. And some still feared contact with the AIDS virus.

"People at the church said there was too much gay stuff involved in the service," Henningson said. "But that was a very significant part of Dick's life, that and his struggle in the last year. How can we deny that?"

The greatest resistance came from within the Hanson family, a large family—five siblings, three spouses and numerous nieces and nephews —that shrunk when asked to stand together at his death. A shaky and confused Allen Hanson greeted the mourners at the service, flanked only by his daughter, Mary, and son, Grant. Two of the three pews reserved for the Hanson family remained largely empty.

Leland Hanson came to the church with his wife and teen-age daughter, but left abruptly before the service began. He declined to comment, but family members said he was angered at the presence of a photographer.

Tom Hanson waited until all the mourners were seated, then entered the church through a side door. He sat alone in the choir loft, telling one of his brothers he would not sit in a church filled with homosexuals. He left before the service ended, refusing to greet mourners or to join the modest luncheon afterwards in the church basement.

John Hanson quietly sat in the front of the church with his two grown daughters. But his wife, Kathy, and their teen-age sons did not attend. Kathy Hanson has said she wanted nothing to do with Dick Hanson, and the boys—who have been teased at school—have been advised to deny they were related to him.

Grant Hanson's wife, Joyce, stayed home with her five young children. She called Henningson with condolences before the service but said she couldn't overcome her fear of AIDS.

"I really cared for Dickie," she said. "Maybe I should have gone. Maybe it would be different if it was just me, but I have to think about the kids."

In contrast, Henningson was surrounded by family members. His parents drove over from Ortonville, in neighboring Big Stone County. A few of his uncles were there, and his two brothers and their families.

His sister called from Portland, Ore., to say she would be praying for him during the service.

"This is not a family that will abandon him," Ailys Henningson said of her son.

Behind the two families, the pews of the simple church were packed with about 150 mourners—public officials, anti-establishment radicals, farmers and homosexuals sitting shoulder-to-shoulder in their Sunday best.

"There's one thing we all have in common," said the Rev. Earl Hauge, a farmer and former state legislator, who presided over the service in the absence of Barsness Pastor Carl Listug, who was on vacation. "We have all been irritated by Dick at one time or another.

"There are times when we wanted to be left alone and left in peace, but he was always pushing us to carry on the cause. And he was an irritant to himself. If you had trouble accepting him, remember it took almost 10 years for him to accept himself that he was different, perhaps gay."

State Rep. Glen Anderson, DFL-Bellingham, and state Sen. Gary DeCramer, DFL-Ghent, were there. Gov. Rudy Perpich and his wife, Lola, sent a lush bouquet of pink and white roses for the altar. Other DFL leaders sent condolences from the party's central committee meeting in Grand Rapids. There were representatives from the Minnesota AIDS Project and the Minnesota Health Department.

But the majority of mourners were women, many of them well into the second half of their lives, the same women whom Hanson had found most responsive to his political radicalism and most accepting of his personal lifestyle.

Ten were selected by Hanson before his death to serve as honorary pallbearers. They were his political protégés: Alice Tripp, a sturdy second mother who stood with him to block construction of the United Power Association high-voltage transmission line; elegant Mary Stackpool of Glenwood, who made a bid for the state Senate last year under Hanson's tutelage; Lou Anne Kling, a former DFL county chairwoman from southwestern Minnesota who was involved in the Groundswell farm movement; and lively Nancy Barsness, who, with Hanson's backing, returned to college after her children were grown, graduating with straight A's.

"Dick was well aware of the negative social pressures that discouraged women from seeking active public roles," Henningson said in a formal thank-you speech to the congregation. "He helped escort them along the way before he died, and he asked that these women be his escorts now as he begins his journey to a long and boundless life."

The other women were even older and less well known, but no less precious to Hanson. They were members of the Martha Circle of the Barsness Ladies Aid, a group Hanson's mother belonged to, and a group that, to him, represented respectability and acceptance.

While some paid their respects at the service, others worked downstairs in the church kitchen, preparing a meal of sandwiches and cakes. The get-well card Hanson received from the Martha Circle when he first was diagnosed with AIDS had remained one of his most cherished possessions.

"That card was the first indication that people here would not abandon him, but would show him true Christian love," Henningson said in his speech. "Dick was a strong and courageous man, willing to challenge authority and fight for justice. But he also was a sensitive soul who did not want to lose his friends here. I believe the welcome you extended gave him a great deal of his strength and peace in his fight with AIDS."

□ □ □

The ugly gossip found its way back to Henningson. A fisherman had been overheard at a local coffee shop, complaining that Lake Minnewaska would be contaminated with AIDS if Hanson's ashes were placed there.

For Henningson, it was just the piece of dark news he needed to trigger his anger and pull him out of a growing despondency. He had spent the previous week fighting for his right, as Hanson's partner and legal executor, to handle Hanson's death. Officials questioned his authority to make decisions about treatment, cremation and the disposal of the ashes, insisting on corroboration from a blood relative.

"There seemed to be great poles emerging at the time of his death, denying our relationship together and trying to shove Dick back in the closet again," Henningson said.

The two men met at a political convention in 1982. Hanson probably already was infected with the AIDS virus, although there was no way to know for sure—a test for the virus had not been developed.

Hanson had spent the previous three years exploring his homosexuality, "coming out and crashing out," as he called it, making up for 15 years of self-denial. He worked alone on the farm for weeks at a time, then traveled to Minneapolis or San Francisco or New York on political and sexual junkets.

"I can point to an awful lot of anonymous, unsafe sex," Hanson said a few months before his death. "The likelihood is I got AIDS because of being much more sexually active. But I don't know that it gains anything to know.

"I have given it a lot of thought. You try to go back and remember why you did something or not. There were social factors. It was just easier to have sex when I went to the Cities for the weekend. Being on the farm was not good for developing long-term relationships. And what would my family think if I brought home someone important to me? So I put a big blame, if there is any, on society's pressure that we had to be anonymous and closeted.

"There were a lot of people from Wisconsin, Iowa, the Dakotas doing the same thing. They were farmers, businessmen, teachers, priests. We just had an awful lot in common, living in an environment that wasn't acceptable to us being ourselves. So there was a lot more going on besides sex. Each time I went in it'd be like a therapy session. I saw each individual as someone who was special and I wanted to get to know a little bit. And there were a pretty good number of people I just visited with and got to know and never had sex with.

"I think of all those people. They had all those same emotions, the same need for some warm, loving embracing and healthy contact. It was good for me to discover that I could give something I didn't think was possible, that I wasn't just some freak not attracted by the opposite sex."

Henningson's sexual history was different. His marriage to a childhood friend had failed, and he had come to terms with his homosexuality through the Program in Human Sexuality at the University of Minnesota.

But gay liaisons had seldom worked for him. He had no tolerance for the fast-lane scene in the bars and bathhouses. After three unsuccessful involvements, he retreated into school, work and political activism—a route that led him to Hanson, whom he read about in a biography of power line protesters.

The men shared an uncannily similar background. Both were farm boys who never quite felt they belonged, who knew they were different before they even had a word for their homosexuality. Both became politically involved with the radical National Farmers Organization while still in grade school. Both were Vietnam War protesters, liberal Democrats and farm activists. Both felt rooted to life on the farm.

But they were temperamental opposites. Henningson's biting wit and quick temper was a balance to Hanson's sugary sincerity. Hanson's yen for the public limelight allowed Henningson to work in the background, where he was most comfortable. When Hanson was overcome with insecurity and self-doubt, he looked to Henningson for a gentle nudge of confidence. Hanson was the talker, Henningson the reader and writer.

Henningson was attracted to Hanson's vulnerability, a personal passivity with family and friends that contradicted his public image as a rabble-rouser.

Throughout his life, Henningson had been a caretaker—lending his car to friends against his father's advice, opening a counseling service for Vietnam veterans, working as an orderly in a Twin Cities nursing home.

Later, when Hanson became ill, it was natural for Henningson to assume the role of provider—earning the money that bought the groceries, laundering the soiled clothes and bedsheets, keeping a matter-of-fact attitude in the face of certain death, refusing to let Hanson wallow in depression or self-pity.

He was the one who said no when Hanson wouldn't, who reminded Hanson when to take a nap or wear a jacket. Once, when Hanson was patiently explaining his AIDS crusade to an abusive caller, Henningson simply unplugged the phone.

"I've always thought our relationship was preordained," Henningson said. "Dick probably got the virus in 1980, before we met. If he had to go through this AIDS bout the last year alone, he wouldn't have made it. So I think it was preordained. I would meet him and be there to take care of him.

"But I would lose my life, too, in the process. . . . Giving up one's own life to allow another to die with dignity . . . that's the purpose for my life."

Henningson said it's "likely" he caught the AIDS virus from Hanson. Though the two exchanged private vows of commitment five years ago, they agreed they could have outside affairs, a not-uncommon arrangement among gay couples.

"If it felt right, we have had light safe sex with others," Hanson said. "I encouraged that as part of a trusting relationship. I feel even post-AIDS there are people who need to not be rejected sexually."

Henningson agreed, knowing they had "reserved a part of our lives that wasn't going to be shared by others." He and Hanson discussed the risk of AIDS when they met, but decided their relationship was worth it.

"I'm half-Danish and, like the Scandinavians, there's a fatalism there," Henningson said. "If life dishes you out a lot of bad things, you roll with it because that's the way life is and there's not much you can do about it. Life's too short to lay guilt and all the rest of that. Nobody goes out and asks for AIDS. Nobody would want something like this. It's just something that happens and you have to deal with it."

□ □ □

The diarrhea struck Henningson in early spring. He paid it little mind at first, thinking he had caught a flu bug from Hanson's young niece. He had tested positive for the AIDS virus a year earlier, just after Hanson first fell ill. But with his background of limited sexual encounters, Henningson felt he was at minimal risk.

"My medical history didn't fit the profile and there was no reason to believe I'd go on to develop symptoms," he said. "So emotionally I was buffered."

But as the year wore on, and the strain of caring for Hanson became greater, Henningson couldn't shake the sickness. He had all the tell-tale signs: diarrhea, night sweats, alternating chills and fever. His weight began a steady drop, just as Hanson's had a year earlier.

Henningson is a small man who consciously kept his weight just below 130 pounds, fearing middle-age spread. By late spring, he was down to 120 and was sewing tucks in the waistlines of his pants. By early summer, he had lost 5 more pounds and was buying pants in smaller sizes. By mid-summer, he weighed less than 110 and was wearing suspenders.

He was diagnosed as having ARC—AIDS-related complex—several months ago, but initially declined to discuss his condition publicly. At the time, he was applying for various loans to try to save the farm from foreclosure and, as he said, "They won't lend money to a dying man."

The farmhouse and surrounding 40-acre wetlands belong to Henningson now, signed over to him by Hanson a year ago and purchased for $8,000 under an agreement with the Federal Land Bank. With Hanson's impending death and his own deteriorating health, he realized it was futile to try to keep the cropland.

Instead, he decided to devote his dwindling energy to caring for Hanson, and to joining Hanson's crusade to educate others about AIDS.

"I realized how important it was in the face of this epidemic to get more public understanding about what has to be done," Henningson said. "Maybe not for me, but for the next generation of AIDS patients who will be getting sick in a year or so. It's a social obligation to them."

☐ ☐ ☐

Henningson's regrets are few. He had no lofty career ambitions, content instead to study history and to write philosophy on his home computer. He never questioned his commitment to Hanson, despite its price. From the day they met, Henningson knew he wanted to spend the rest of his life with Hanson.

Now he wants to spend what is left reflecting on what their time together meant.

"It was like growing old together," he said. "The whole process was just speeded up for us. A couple usually has a lifetime to grow old together. We didn't have that time. We had to compensate for things we couldn't do anymore.

"There was no sex the last month. But that's like growing old, too. My parents have a plaque in their kitchen: 'Lovin' don't last, but good cookin' do.' Relationships change. You move past the passion of the first year and mellow out. You have to or you'll burn yourself out.

"We had stopped kissing on the lips. I didn't want to pass anything on to him. But that Tuesday in the hospital, when it looked like it would be terminal and it would go real fast, we just reached for each other. So then every time I'd be gone and come back into the room, I would kiss him.

"I realized what I missed was that close physical sharing we had. I guess I became more of a mother-comforter. I was so busy. I hadn't realized I missed it. So if there's any mourning I do—although I feel his spirit with me—it's a deferred realization of what we had been missing the last few months. As much as the homophobes try, they can't deny what we have is also a physical relationship."

Henningson has been left pale and tired by the last year. A disturbing rash marred his cheek—acne from the stress or, possibly, something more ominous, herpes or Kaposi's sarcoma, a cancer that attacks 40 percent of AIDS patients.

Yet a heaviness has lifted, leaving him with a sense of relief.

"I've seen spouses after a death, and they have a serenity about them," he said. "It's like they've accepted the death and still feel close to the spouse. They feel no compulsion to find anyone else. They still have a complete life in terms of feeling comforted by the closeness of the spirit.

"I've been a hermit all my life. Even as a child I was reclusive. The calling I had to live with Dick has been good. But if I now go back to being alone, it's not foreign to me. I spent most of my life that way."

He has pulled out his favorite books—acid essays by H. L. Mencken and "Mountain Dialogues" by Frank Waters—and has lined up agriculture research projects that will allow him to work at home. He was accepted into an experimental AZT project at the University of Minnesota Hospital and Clinic and will continue to seek treatment in Minneapolis, where an acquaintance is letting him live rent-free.

He will spend as much time as possible at the farm. Hanson's friends have become his, and can be counted on for companionship. Hanson's brother-in-law, Doug Jenniges, has offered to do the heavy labor, mowing the lawn through fall and plowing the driveway if Henningson tries to keep the farmhouse open through the winter.

Thoughts of his own illness, of Hanson's history repeating itself through him, don't greatly trouble him now. He might have a few years, he said. Or he might have a few months.

"I cry almost every day for might-have-beens," he said. "But it's just a momentary passing tear at something that's especially poignant.

It's just a passing emotion, but it becomes part of your psyche in preparing for the future, and then it's not as terrifying.

"Oh, it'd be nice to think about living a lot longer and having all the time. But there's an attraction to going, too. We hear things about what's waiting for us and we have notions about it, and I'm curious to find out what it is. And if that happens sooner rather than later, that's fine.

"Meanwhile, Dick is there for me, not just on the other side, but here, now. That's something I find very comforting. And I know if I end up feeling more and more ill, there'll be someone out there waiting with an outstretched hand. And I have a very good idea who that'll be. So I won't be alone."

□ □ □

Henningson felt oddly light-hearted as he scattered Hanson's ashes into the stony creek. His bleached blue jeans were held up by suspenders, and a straw Panama hat kept the sun out of his eyes as he walked out to the creek where Hanson had played as a child. The waters there tumble rapidly during spring runoff, eventually spilling into the Minnesota River and along to the Mississippi.

"Dick got a lot of fish out of there and ate them, so throwing his ashes back there as fish food is just returning the favor," he said. "It's part of the natural cycle of the earth, ashes to ashes.

"That may sound a bit too flip, but that's how I felt."

That afternoon, he and Mary Hanson-Jenniges planted a memorial petunia next to the geraniums on Hanson's mother's grave. A few days later, a church member was mowing the cemetery lawn and cut too close around the tombstone. The petunia was mowed down.

Henningson was unperturbed. "The roots are strong. It'll grow back."

THIRTEEN

SCANDALS AND SCARES ON WALL STREET

1988 WINNER IN THE EXPLANATORY JOURNALISM CATEGORY

"For a distinguished example of explanatory journalism that illuminates significant and complex issues . . ."

The Wall Street Journal
Daniel Hertzberg
James B. Stewart

Wall Street Journal reporters James B. Stewart and Daniel Hertzberg were at the heart of America's financial hub when stocks took a nose-dive last October. The pair dissected the crash and made sense out of a confusing whirl of events. They also took a keen look at the unraveling values on The Street.

Both "Terrible Tuesday," our account of what happened the day after history's worst stock market collapse, and "A Dream Gone Wrong," the story of an investment banker who turned to insider trading, began as mysteries. Faced with two of the year's biggest financial news stories, we wanted to know why these startling events occurred. Our quest led us deep into the inner workings of Wall Street, and to discoveries that became news in their own right.

Neither of us was an expert on the stock market, or on white-collar crime. But our years of reporting on other topics had given us a broad base of sources and some expertise about Wall Street, the financial markets, investment bankers and the workings of major financial institutions. Dan Hertzberg previously covered banking, insurance and the New York City fiscal crisis. Jim Stewart is a lawyer, and previously covered law and the legal profession. We first worked together when both of us were assigned to the mergers-and-acquisitions beat, a booming area in recent years that gave us a good vantage point on the excesses of Wall Street.

Our first collaborations were in the mergers-and-acquisitions area in early 1985, and we've worked closely since. We're often asked how two reporters work so closely together over a sustained period of time. There's no easy explanation, but we share an enthusiasm for good stories, for investigative work, and for storytelling, and a willingness to work hard. Dan is 42, Jim 36—old by reporting standards—so we're not prone to juvenile outbursts of ego or competition. We're also different personalities, which means some sources naturally gravitate toward Dan, and others toward Jim, multiplying our access to information.

We constantly trade information, develop new leads, challenge each other's assumptions and encourage each other. We've come to know each other very well—our strengths and weaknesses. Other reporters at *The Journal* joke that we finish each other's sentences.

"Terrible Tuesday" began a week after the stock-market crash of Black Monday. The crash had so dominated the news that we asked if we could do some related stories. We got even more than we asked for: *Journal* managing editor Norman Pearlstine and deputy managing editor Paul Steiger asked us to step away from covering the Wall Street insider trading scandal and investigate the still smoldering ruins of the Great Bull Market of the 1980s. Our only mandate was to find out what happened during the crash and why.

Hundreds of reporters were already swarming over Wall Street, and naturally they were focusing on the dramatic events of Black Monday, when the Dow Jones Industrial Average had plunged a record-breaking 508 points. The next day—Tuesday, October 20—the stock market had ended the day up 100 points, and was largely ignored. But we quickly became convinced that the stock market had been much more badly damaged in the crash than stock exchange officials were acknowledging, and that the New York Stock Exchange—and, indeed, the nation's financial system—had come close to a breakdown on Tuesday. This conclusion flew in the face of the reassuring words pouring from Washington and Wall Street, where leaders praised the resiliency of the nation's financial markets.

We attacked the story on two fronts. First, we worked the phones incessantly, calling dozens of figures in the financial community, not only stock market traders, but commercial bankers, investment bankers, futures traders and financial speculators. Second, we began a minute-by-minute reconstruction of Tuesday's trading, amassing data that covered trading in scores of stocks on the New York Stock Exchange and in complex stock-index futures on other exchanges. We had to educate ourselves in the workings of the futures and options markets, and in doing so discovered the crucial ties between them and the stock exchange itself. We began to learn how a small band of savvy speculators, who are far ahead of government regulators, execute complex trades involving stocks and index futures. We realized that little of this had ever been covered by the press.

Slowly, a piece at a time, the chilling story began to emerge. A veteran NYSE specialist, James Maguire, one of the small group who makes the stock market work, told us how he repeatedly begged one of New York's biggest banks for a $30 million emergency loan to finance his swollen inventory of stocks; the bank turned him down flat. Though he wouldn't name the bank, we learned enough to go to other sources, who identified it as Bankers Trust.

The head of a major Wall Street securities firm told us that he angrily called the Federal Reserve Board after banks cut back on their loans to Wall Street. Indeed, we learned that the Federal Reserve, the secretive guardian of the nation's money supply, had played a crucial role in averting a system-wide financial meltdown. Traders knew that the Fed had flooded the financial markets with money at the time of the crash. We learned from bankers and, ultimately, from top Fed officials themselves that E. Gerald Corrigan, president of the Federal Reserve Bank of New York, and other Fed officials had leaned heavily on large banks in New York to meet Wall Street's soaring credit needs.

As we slowly reconstructed the events of Tuesday, we established that trading in stocks, options and futures had all but stopped during a crucial interval Tuesday. Beyond a doubt, the stock market had effectively stopped functioning and came within minutes of closing. NYSE Chairman John Phelan was out of the country, so Dan flew immediately to London and interviewed him at length at the Connaught Hotel. Mr. Phelan revealed that several major Wall Street firms had called the Securities and Exchange Commission and asked officials there to close the stock market.

One source tipped off Jim to the strange behavior of the Major Market Index, a little known stock-market futures contract traded in Chicago. Sustained digging into trading of the MMI, as the index is known, suggested that concerted buying by one or more major firms in a few crucial minutes propelled the index, and perhaps the whole stock market, upward. Some veteran traders believed the MMI had been manipulated to save the stock market from collapse. Nearly everyone agreed that it could have happened—exposing the vulnerability of the stock market to the machinations of a few futures traders.

With growing excitment, we documented a story that flatly contradicted the official view of the stock-market crash. We found not a resilient stock market on a quick rebound, but "Terrible Tuesday."

In writing this complex story, we decided to use a virtual hour-by-hour narrative, allowing us to show the increasing mood of despair and fear among traders, exchange officials and government regulators. We tried, whenever possible, to tell the story through the eyes of participants, like Ronald Shear, a likable MMI options specialist who tried to sleep Monday night, couldn't, and at 4 a.m. went to a 24-hour restaurant. The result, we hoped, was a story that made readers feel they had lived through this terrifying day, but at the same time gave them a sweeping overall view that almost no participants, even top government officials, had at the time.

"Terrible Tuesday" ran in November, exactly one month after the events we described, and nine months after "A Dream Gone Wrong."

In February three prominent arbitragers—speculators in takeover stocks—had been arrested on insider trading charges, two of them in their offices at large, prestigious firms. One was actually handcuffed. We had a page-one story the next day recounting those events and revealing that the unidentified source who had implicated the three men was Martin A. Siegel, a takeover whiz who had moved from Kidder Peabody & Co. to Drexel Burnham Lambert Inc. and who was considered one of the brightest and fastest rising stars on Wall Street. The day our story appeared, Mr. Siegel pleaded guilty to two felonies and admitted to an insider trading scheme with fallen arbitrager Ivan F. Boesky.

We had covered the Boesky scandal and the earlier Dennis Levine insider trading case; the stories grew naturally out of our work in mergers and acquisitions, since it was the takeover boom that spawned the new wave of insider trading crimes. But with Mr. Siegel, the scandal had finally reached the heart of the Wall Street establishment —old-line, blue-chip firms like Kidder and Goldman Sachs & Co. We sensed that by telling Mr. Siegel's story in detail, we would be illuminating a much broader and more complex phenomenon—the erosion of values at even the highest levels of the financial community.

Because of our relationship with many sources, we can't tell the full story of our reporting. But our success in getting the facts depended on relationships with people that had been cultivated over many months, in some cases, years. They trusted us with information that put their careers at risk and exposed others to possible prosecution. Though some of our sources remain unnamed, we relied on them for verifiable facts—facts that, in each case, we were able to confirm.

"A Dream Gone Wrong" was a deadline story, largely reported and written over a single three-day holiday weekend. Dan's four-year-old son joined us at the office, and for diversion we entertained him with his favorite board game involving dinosaurs. We hadn't had much sleep, but the Siegel story was so absorbing and the reporting so exciting that we ran on adrenaline. We lost all sense of the passage of time.

By the time we started writing, we knew we had the rare factual elements of what could be an unusually exciting story. We had a mesmerizing central character in the handsome, bright, ambitious Mr. Siegel. We had high drama and a climax in the events of the previous week. We had startling new information about Mr. Siegel's relationship with Mr. Boesky and his role at Kidder, a leading financial institution.

We wrote the story in a narrative style that tried to capture all of those elements for readers. Certain details spoke volumes—Mr. Boesky's pink Rolls-Royce, the exchange of cash in a back alley, Mr. Boesky's plea to Mr. Siegel: "Don't you love me anymore?" We wanted readers to relive Mr. Siegel's experiences, and by doing so, begin to understand why he had acted as he did.

For both "Terrible Tuesday" and "A Dream Gone Wrong," we had tremendous support from other people at *The Wall Street Journal:* our editors, lawyers, art and graphics people, fellow reporters. Throughout our careers at *The Journal,* we have been held to exacting standards of accuracy and fairness. At the same time we have been encouraged to think big and aim high, both in reporting and writing. Within reason, we've been given whatever time and resources we asked for. There is no greater thrill than to see, after all these elements have coalesced, stories like "Terrible Tuesday" and "A Dream Gone Wrong" on the front page of *The Journal.*

—James B. Stewart and Daniel Hertzberg
The Wall Street Journal

TERRIBLE TUESDAY

HOW THE STOCK MARKET ALMOST DISINTEGRATED A DAY AFTER THE CRASH

CREDIT DRIED UP FOR BROKERS AND ESPECIALLY SPECIALISTS UNTIL FED CAME TO RESCUE

MOST PERILOUS DAY IN 50 YEARS

FRIDAY, NOVEMBER 20, 1987

BY JAMES B. STEWART AND DANIEL HERTZBERG

NEW YORK—A month ago today, the New York Stock Exchange died. But within an hour or two, it was raised from the dead.

The previous day, Oct. 19, when the Dow Jones Industrial Average plunged 508 points in history's largest one-day loss, has been dubbed Black Monday. But it was on Tuesday, Oct. 20, that the stock market —and by extension all the world's financial markets—faced one of their gravest crises.

Full details of what happened that fateful week are only now emerging and are the subject of major inquiries by a presidential commission, congressional committees and others. But minute-by-minute scrutiny of the events of that Tuesday, plus scores of interviews with key stock, commodities and futures market participants, the Federal Reserve, and investment and commercial bankers, reveals that:

—Stock, options and futures trading all but stopped during a crucial interval on Tuesday. Many major stocks, such as International

Business Machines Corp. and Merck & Co., couldn't be traded. Investors large and small couldn't sell their stock; there were no buyers. The industrial average was meaningless because many of its component stocks weren't trading. The Big Board's market makers, or specialists, were overwhelmed by unfilled sell orders, and their capital was devastated.

—Many banks, frightened by the collapse in prices of stocks that were collateral for loans to securities dealers, refused to extend sorely pressed dealers any more credit. They also called in major loans, imperiling some securities firms.

—Some big investment banking firms, facing catastrophic losses if the market panic continued, urged the New York Stock Exchange to close.

—Only the intervention of the Federal Reserve, the concerted announcement of corporate stock-buyback programs, and the mysterious movement—and possible manipulation—of a little-used stock-index futures contract saved the markets from total meltdown.

The story of that Tuesday discloses major weaknesses in the U.S. financial system and raises the specter that such a crisis could strike again. "Tuesday was the most dangerous day we had in 50 years," says Felix Rohatyn, a general partner in Lazard Freres & Co. "I think we came within an hour" of a disintegration of the stock market, he says. "The fact we didn't have a meltdown doesn't mean we didn't have a breakdown. Chernobyl didn't end the world, but it sure made a terrible mess."

□ □ □

Monday, Oct. 19, 11 p.m. This day was the worst in Wall Street's history—and worst of all for the Big Board's specialists. The specialists, more than 50 little-known but powerful firms, are required by Big Board rules to buy and sell assigned stocks during volatile times to keep prices as orderly as possible. They usually profit handsomely by shrewd trading—a franchise that has long been the envy of large, publicly oriented securities firms prevented by Big Board rules from becoming specialists themselves. Specialists are supposed to provide the last bastion of liquidity; in normal times, they are the reason an investor can buy or sell a stock when no other investors are in the market. On this day, at least, they were clearly not up to the task.

As the market plunged on Monday, the specialists bore the brunt of the fall. "From 2 p.m. on, there was total despair," says James Maguire, the chairman of Henderson Brothers Inc., a big specialist firm that makes markets in about 70 stocks: "The entire investment community fled the market. We were left alone on the field." Forced to buy stock himself when there were no other buyers, Mr. Maguire ended the day with $60 million in stock—three times his normal inventory. Like other specialists, he had to pay for this stock five business days later, the following Monday. To do so, he would have to borrow.

Mr. Maguire phoned his bank, Bankers Trust Co., one of New York's biggest and an important lender to Wall Street. He asked for a $30 million loan, even though Henderson is one of Wall Street's best-capitalized specialist firms. He was stunned by the response. "They stated they were in no position to make commitments," Mr. Maguire says.

Mr. Maguire phoned the bank five times between 11 p.m. and 12:30 a.m. It wouldn't budge.

Other specialists report similar experiences. One, A. B. Tompane & Co., similarly turned down by Bankers Trust, was hurriedly forced into the arms of well-capitalized Merrill Lynch & Co. The two firms shook hands on the merger at 3 a.m. By dawn, nevertheless, the worst was yet to come for the markets.

Tuesday, 6:30 a.m. Big Board Chairman John J. Phelan met a neighbor going down in the elevator of his Manhattan apartment building. The neighbor was concerned not about Monday's 508-point plunge but about rumors that the Big Board might close. "He said, 'My God, if things were bad enough to close the market, things were really bad,' " Mr. Phelan recalls.

Tuesday, 8 a.m. Bank credit is the life-line of Wall Street securities firms, and specialists weren't the only ones rushing to arrange more of it Tuesday morning. Large securities firms had swollen stock inventories, accumulated to accommodate major clients who wanted to sell, or in some cases held as part of the firms' holdings of stocks they expected to be involved in takeovers. Demand for credit was further fueled by an explosion of trading in the government-securities market. Trading by big government-securities dealers surged by

$58 billion to a daily average of $173 billion that week. In addition, arbitragers, who had accumulated billions of dollars of takeover stocks, were also getting squeezed by margin calls.

The big firms fared little better. Phone calls started pouring into officials at the Big Board and the Federal Reserve Bank of New York. Angry securities dealers reported that foreign and U.S. regional banks were cutting back credit to the securities industry. Bankers Trust told Wall Street firms that it would stop extending unsecured credit—loans not collateralized by assets.

Executives at one big Wall Street securities firm were shocked when another U.S. bank Tuesday refused to deliver promptly $70 million in West German marks that it had sold to the firm in a foreign-exchange trade. Apparently, the bank feared that it might not be paid promptly—if at all—for the marks. Securities firms "were beginning to have trouble getting extended credit," Big Board Chairman Phelan says. "Japanese banks threatened to stop" lending, adds the head of one of Wall Street's largest securities firms.

Tuesday, 9 a.m. As the credit markets came to life in the U.S., Federal Reserve officials were swinging into action. In the early-morning hours, from a hotel room in Dallas, Chairman Alan Greenspan had decided to issue a one-sentence statement that in effect would reverse the course of policies that he had set into motion upon taking office two months before. He canceled a speech and headed back to his Washington office.

Meanwhile, E. Gerald Corrigan, the beefy president of the Federal Reserve Bank of New York and a protege of Mr. Greenspan's predecessor, Paul Volcker, was in close touch with the stock exchanges—due to open in half an hour—the banks and the bond market. As the head of the Federal Reserve's key operating unit, which daily buys or sells huge amounts of government securities and international currencies, he is the Fed official most closely in touch with Wall Street. He was to become the agency's point man in dealing with the developing crisis.

After learning of the credit squeeze facing Wall Street, Messrs. Greenspan and Corrigan feared that something far worse than a stock-market panic might be in the offing. If credit dried up, securities firms could start to collapse, much as the banks did after the 1929 crash. Fed officials saw a real threat of gridlock developing in the markets: Even the simplest financial transaction might have become impossible.

To avert that risk, Mr. Greenspan agreed to suspend, at least temporarily, the tightening grip the Fed had imposed on credit in order to head off inflation fears that he had seen building up in the economy. Signaling clearly its determination to prevent a market disaster, the Fed issued its extraordinary statement affirming its "readiness to serve as a source of liquidity to support the economic and financial system."

Even that was an understatement. Acting as the ultimate supplier of funds, the Fed flooded the banking system with dollars by buying government securities and thus quickly driving down short-term interest rates. "The Fed opened the floodgates of liquidity," says David Jones, the chief economist of Aubrey G. Lanston & Co., a major government-securities dealer.

Alerted by calls about the developing credit crisis from Mr. Phelan and others, the Fed leaned heavily on the big New York banks to meet Wall Street's soaring demand for credit. Mr. Corrigan and key aides personally telephoned top bankers to get the message across.

"Right from the beginning, Corrigan understood there was a major problem in the system," says Mr. Phelan, who spoke repeatedly to the New York Fed chief. Mr. Phelan sums up the Fed's strategy as he saw it: "The banks would be kept liquid; the banks would make sure everyone else in the system would stay liquid."

The banks were told to keep an eye on the big picture—the global financial system on which all their business ultimately depends. A senior New York banker says the Fed's message was, "We're here. Whatever you need, we'll give you."

Tuesday, 9:30 a.m. The New York Stock Exchange opened. But many important sectors were at a standstill. Two-thirds of the specialists' total $3 billion of buying power had been wiped out on Monday. Some specialists refused to open trading in stocks until they had enough buy orders to enable the shares to trade at higher prices. Many stocks took more than an hour to open. When they did, they were mostly up from Monday's close. The Dow opened about 200 points higher, an extraordinary gain.

But the euphoria was short-lived. Specialists and major firms quickly unloaded some of their huge inventories, and buyers evaporated. Stock-index futures began to plunge on several exchanges. Program traders and portfolio insurers, whose computer-generated trading had accelerated Monday's fall, were largely absent from the market. Program traders switch money between stock-index futures and the underlying stocks, depending on which is cheaper. Portfolio insurance is a method of hedging a stock portfolio, usually by selling futures contracts on stock indexes when the market falls.

Ordinarily, the huge discount of the futures contracts to the cash value of the underlying stocks would encourage selling of the stocks and buying of the futures. That, in turn, theoretically could trigger some buying of stocks at bargain prices. But as the morning continued, everything was being sold—stocks and futures alike.

Tuesday, 11:25 a.m. Of all securities linked to stock-market indexes, the Major Market Index has been the most secure, even in turbulent markets. It is pure blue chip: 17 of the 20 stocks in the index also are in the Dow Jones Industrial Average. Indeed, the MMI was created to mirror that average.

On Monday night, after the market turmoil that day, Ronald Shear, the American Stock Exchange's likable, balding senior specialist for the MMI, couldn't sleep. At 4 a.m., he gave up trying, and he went to the Brasserie, a 24-hour French restaurant in midtown Manhattan. Later, as the markets opened, he could hardly believe what he saw. One after another, major stocks broke down and couldn't be traded. By 11:30 a.m., when IBM stopped trading, the pace of closings was so fast Mr. Shear had trouble keeping track.

Big Board printouts of the morning's trading paint a harrowing picture of a market in disarray. By 11:25, even Du Pont hadn't opened. Merck opened at 9:46, was overwhelmed by sell orders and closed eight minutes later. Sears closed at 11:12; Eastman Kodak at 11:28; Philip Morris at 11:30; 3M a minute later. Dow Chemical shut at 11:43; USX at 12:51. Many other major stocks also weren't trading. Those that were did so only sporadically, in small numbers of shares or on regional exchanges. Over-the-counter market makers stopped answering their phones.

Specialists didn't have any buy orders, and many simply stopped making markets. Many believed that their capital, much of it in stock that looked as though it couldn't be sold, was gone or nearly gone. The specialists had run out of buying power. "The specialist system just let [stocks] go. People just stood aside," says Leslie Quick Jr., the chairman of Quick & Reilly Group Inc., a big discount brokerage firm.

Suddenly, Mr. Shear heard rumors coursing across the Amex floor. One turned out to be true: Tompane, the USX specialist on the Big Board, was about to be taken over by Merrill Lynch. Another later proved to be false: SEC Chairman David Ruder was about to announce the closing of the exchanges.

Sensing a similar imbalance in the options trading, Mr. Shear called a floor supervisor to check the rules for index-options trading on the Amex. The supervisor confirmed that if stocks representing more than 20% of the underlying capitalization of the index aren't trading, then options trading should stop. From what Mr. Shear saw, well over half the stocks in the index had stopped trading.

Mr. Shear got on the loudspeaker and halted trading in the MMI options.

Tuesday, 12:15 p.m. Leo Melamed, the short, dark-haired, kinetic chairman of the Chicago Mercantile Exchange, was on the phone to Mr. Phelan in New York. The Merc trades the Standard & Poor's 500, the principal futures contract used by program traders and portfolio insurers. Mr. Melamed was alarmed by the unprecedented breakdown in trading of the stocks making up the S&P 500. The Chicago Board Options Exchange, which trades options, had already closed because so many stocks weren't trading. "I was told there were no buyers," Mr. Melamed says. Then, he received a jolt: Mr. Phelan told him that Big Board directors were convening to decide whether to close the stock exchange. Mr. Phelan told him that "a decision was close," Mr. Melamed recalls.

Mr. Melamed suddenly envisioned a selling onslaught of the futures that could exhaust every bit of liquidity on the Merc floor. "We were exposed in a very dangerous way. We couldn't bear the brunt of any panic," he says. At 12:15 p.m., the Merc ordered a halt in trading of S&P 500 futures contracts.

A few blocks away at the Chicago Board of Trade, Chairman Karsten Mahlmann, known by his nickname, "Cash," also was on the phone to the Big Board. His exchange was still trading futures contracts on the MMI. But the situation was worsening: The MMI futures, already trading at the deepest discount to the underlying cash value of the index in its history, plunged further on the news that Mr. Shear had halted options trading on the Amex.

Mr. Mahlmann also was told that the Big Board was thinking of closing. But the Board of Trade was a little better off than the Merc. Trading of the relatively little-used MMI futures contracts had almost ground to a nervous standstill; MMI traders didn't seem to face a flood of orders.

Moreover, Mr. Mahlmann calculated that 17 of the MMI's 20 stocks still were trading, albeit sporadically, on some regional stock exchanges. Just the day before, Mr. Mahlmann had received a phone call from Beryl Sprinkel; the chairman of the President's Council of Economic Advisers urged him to keep the Board of Trade open. And there was the fierce long-standing rivalry between the Board of Trade and the New York exchange, a rivalry that has given rise to a generally defiant attitude at the Board of Trade toward any action adopted by the Big Board.

"We felt we had to stay open to do our job, to provide liquidity," Mr. Mahlmann recalls. Then he and his executives made what turned out to be one of the most critical decisions of the day: They kept the Board of Trade open and continued to trade the MMI futures contract.

Tuesday, 12:30 p.m. Mr. Phelan, Big Board President Robert Birnbaum, other top exchange officials and floor directors representing shellshocked specialists had gathered in Mr. Phelan's office to consider an extraordinary step: closing the New York Stock Exchange. The mood was grim. Mr. Phelan recalls that during the morning the market "was off 100 points and looked like it had potential to drop another 200 or 300. It looked like it would go again; it would be faster and heavier than the day before because there would be panic in the system." Exchange officials feared that selling would cascade as investors were hit with margin calls and big mutual funds dumped stock in the face of huge shareholder redemptions.

Behind the scenes, other pressures on Mr. Phelan to close the Big Board were multiplying. Several big securities firms "called the SEC and asked them to tell us to close," says Mr. Phelan (only the U.S.

president and a stock exchange—but not the SEC—can order a closing). Mr. Phelan won't name the firms, but market sources say Salomon Brothers Inc. and Goldman, Sachs & Co., major firms with huge inventories of securities that were being rapidly devalued, were among those pushing to shut the exchange.

A Goldman official says the firm did discuss the possibility of a temporary closing with SEC Chairman Ruder but didn't recommend it. A Salomon spokesman didn't return a phone call.

"There were pressures from all firms that day to cut hours—to close," Mr. Phelan says. Donald Stone, a Big Board director, says there was also a discussion of a plan—broached on Black Monday—for big Wall Street firms to raise a $1 billion fund to keep specialist firms from going broke.

Mr. Phelan denies suggestions by Mr. Melamed and Mr. Mahlmann that he or other officials gave any indication the Big Board was on the brink of closing. He says he had talked during the morning to White House Chief of Staff Howard Baker. "They said if you can do it [stay open], do it," he relates.

Mr. Phelan says he shared White House fears over the impact of a Big Board closing. Shutting the biggest U.S. securities exchange not only would loudly trumpet the gravity of the stock-market crisis, "but the strain on the country . . . would be taken as an extremely bad sign," he adds. And reopening hundreds of stocks at once could later prove impossible. "If we close it, we would never open it," Mr. Phelan says bluntly.

Despite the intensifying pressures to close, the market was still officially open at 12:30.

Tuesday, 12:38 p.m. With the closing of the Big Board seemingly imminent and the market in disarray, with virtually all options and futures trading halted, something happened that some later described as a miracle: In the space of about five or six minutes, the Major Market Index futures contract, the only viable surrogate for the Dow Jones Industrial Average and the only major index still trading, staged the most powerful rally in its history. The MMI rose on the Chicago Board of Trade from a discount of nearly 60 points to a premium of about 12 points. Because each point represents about five in the industrial average, the rally was the equivalent of a lightning-like

360-point rise in the Dow. Some believe that this extraordinary move set the stage for the salvation of the world's markets.

How it happened is a matter of much conjecture on Wall Street. Some attribute it to a mysterious burst of bullish sentiment that suddenly swept the markets. Some knowledgeable traders have a different interpretation: They think that the MMI futures contract was deliberately manipulated by a few major firms as part of a desperate attempt to boost the Dow and save the markets.

According to this theory, the rally in the MMI futures contract was caused by a relatively small amount of concerted buying by one or more major firms at a time when it was so thinly traded that the orders had an enormous and disproportionate upward thrust. By forcing the futures contract to a premium to the underlying cash value of the index, the buyers of the futures could trigger immediate buying of the stocks in the index and selling of the futures by index arbitragers. Because so many of the MMI stocks are in the Dow, this would enable the NYSE to reopen many of these stocks at higher prices, leading to an upturn in this psychologically important index. At the very least, the buyers could flash a powerful bullish signal to the markets.

Mr. Mahlmann says he doesn't know whether this is what happened, but he says it is possible. "The market was extremely thin at that point," he recalls.

Statistics supplied by the Board of Trade lend circumstantial support to the thesis that the index was driven upward by a small number of sophisticated buyers. During the half hour—12:30 to 1 p.m. in the East, 11:30 to noon in Chicago—that encompassed the extraordinary rally, only 808 contracts traded, representing an underlying cash value of the index of about $60 million. The actual cost to someone buying those contracts can't be precisely determined, but it would have been a small fraction of the cash value.

Of the 808 contracts traded, about 70% were purchased at low commission rates. That indicates that the buying came from major Wall Street firms with their own traders on the floor. Only 30% of the buying came from so-called locals—smaller, independent traders who trade for their own and customers' accounts. The Board of Trade's statistician says this is an abnormally low percentage of local buying. Which firms were doing the buying couldn't be determined. Major firms contacted, including Morgan Stanley & Co., Kidder Peabody & Co., PaineWebber Inc., Goldman Sachs and Salomon Brothers, all either denied that they were responsible for the buying or declined comment.

As news of the rally in MMI futures reached the New York Stock Exchange (major firms maintain open lines both to their traders in Chicago and to specialists in New York), the market got another important psychological boost: the announcement of stock buybacks by major corporations. This, too, appears to have been encouraged by major investment banks, many of which spent Tuesday morning frantically calling chief executives of major clients urging them to buy back their stock. First Boston, for example, called about 200 clients.

"It looks like there's almost a get-together on the part of corporate America to prop up the market," Stanley Abel, a consultant specializing in buybacks, observed that day. Among the companies announcing buy-backs were Shearson Lehman Brothers Holdings Inc., Merrill Lynch, Citicorp, Honeywell, ITT, Allegis, four regional Bell companies and USX.

The precise timing of those announcements and any accompanying purchases are difficult to pinpoint, but some occurred during the crucial hour between 12:30 and 1:30. The USX specialist, for example, says trading in USX was halted at 12:43 p.m. because of a sudden influx of buy orders following the company's buyback announcement.

Floor traders at the Chicago Board of Trade say the major securities firms that maintain direct contact with specialists in New York were the first to learn of such buy orders, which in turn led to further buying by those firms of the MMI futures whenever the contract traded at a discount to the underlying cash index. (Indeed, the locals in Chicago have long complained that because the MMI consists of only 20 stocks, it can be manipulated by the major firms with access to Big Board specialists.)

A graph of Tuesday's movement in the MMI futures contract is consistent with such observations. At 12:45, the MMI contract had moved to a sharp premium to the underlying cash value of the index (so many of the stocks weren't trading that the underlying cash value was calculated using recent trades that probably overstated its true value at the time). The graph shows that the contract immediately turned downward, as traders presumably sold the futures and began to buy the underlying stocks, thereby locking in a profit.

One index arbitrager admits using such a strategy. "I did it very, very cautiously," he says. "I was terrified of the market. But it was a very profitable move."

If the goal of those buying the MMI futures beginning at 12:38 was to drive up the Dow, it succeeded brilliantly.

Tuesday, 1 p.m. Like water on parched earth, buy orders began flowing into securities firms and into the stock exchange.

Banks, including the recalcitrant Bankers Trust, had finally pledged their support after receiving reassurances from the Fed, giving specialists and other firms the financial confidence to execute orders. The Fed told the banks that they were free to increase their borrowings at the Fed's discount window. New York's Chemical Bank increased its loans to securities firms for that week by $400 million above normal, a bank official says.

All told, the 10 biggest New York banks nearly doubled their lending to securities firms that week to $12 billion, pumping in an extra $5.5 billion.

A spokesperson for Bankers Trust says, "We were able to accommodate routinely the financing requirements of our major customers in an environment characterized by great uncertainty. The requirements of most others were met after greater than usual consideration."

As the buy orders reappeared, large, capitalization stocks—especially those in the MMI—began coming back to life. Merck reopened at 1:15, albeit 21 points lower, and IBM reopened at 1:26 at 112, unchanged from two hours earlier. By 2 p.m., when USX reopened, up 62½ cents, all the MMI stocks were trading.

Mr. Phelan told his counterparts at the other exchanges in New York and Chicago that the day's threat of closing had passed, that the immediate crisis was over. At the Amex, Mr. Shear got on the loudspeaker to announce that MMI options would resume trading in 15 minutes. Mr. Melamed ordered the resumption of futures trading on the Merc, and the Board of Trade's Mr. Mahlmann breathed a great sigh of relief. "We were immensely pleased that the market came back and that we were the ones who stayed open," he says.

Tuesday, 4 p.m. The stock market ended its tumultuous day with a record—and psychologically crucial—gain of 102.27 points in the

Dow. Volume was also a record 608,120,000 shares, a little higher than on Black Monday. On the Big Board overall, 1,398 stocks declined. Only 537 gained.

The Dow's rise partly reflected the strong performance of the stocks that make up the MMI. Throughout the afternoon, the MMI futures traded several times at a premium to the cash index, apparently triggering buying of the underlying stocks. The performance of the MMI futures diverged significantly from that of the S&P 500, which remained at a deep discount to the index even after it reopened.

Because of the Fed's aggressive move to drive down interest rates by flooding the system with liquidity, the bond market, too, rallied strongly, providing crucial support for the broader financial system. "If the bond market had been going the same direction as the stock market—down—that would have been the straw that broke the camel's back," Mr. Phelan says.

□ □ □

On Wednesday, Americans woke to newspaper headlines proclaiming the largest rise in the Dow's history. A wave of optimism washed over the exchanges. The stock market that day was to have a real rally —186.84 points on the Dow, with 1,749 stocks gaining.

In the end, the stock market and financial system didn't collapse on Tuesday. Although trading losses—mainly in takeover-related stocks —ran into hundreds of millions of dollars, no major securities firm defaulted on its obligations to customers or was rendered insolvent. A few specialist firms merged or were forced to find new infusions of capital; most survived. But privately, key participants say they were deeply shaken by how close to catastrophe the system came.

And the crisis in the financial system revealed glaring weaknesses that are being closely examined in Congress. The New York Stock Exchange specialist system—despite some heroic efforts—proved inadequate to meet the demands of huge international flows of capital, nearly triggering a shutdown of the exchange and a public crisis of confidence. Though there is little to suggest that program trading or portfolio insurance caused the crisis, both contributed to a degree of volatility that the system couldn't handle.

"The markets will be nothing but an open casino if you let this continue," Mr. Phelan says.

More worrisome, many officials note, is that the crisis occurred in the absence of any true calamity. What might happen to the markets in a major political or economic crisis? Could a real meltdown happen?

"I won't even get into that," the Merc's Mr. Melamed says.

GLOSSARY OF TERMS

Index Arbitrage: *The simultaneous trading in stock-index markets and the underlying groups of stocks to take advantage of temporary discrepancies in prices.*

Margin Call: *A demand upon an investor to put up more collateral for securities bought on credit. The lender, usually a bank or brokerage firm, makes the call when the equity in the investor's account falls below a standard set by a stock exchange or firm.*

Options: *A "put" option permits a holder to sell a stock at a specified price within a limited period. A "call" option permits an investor to buy stock at a specified price within a limited period. An index option lets the investor buy or sell the "basket" of stocks represented by a stock-market index.*

Portfolio Insurance: *A method of hedging a stock portfolio, usually by selling futures contracts on stock indexes when the market falls.*

Stock-Index Futures: *Contracts for future delivery of an amount of cash based on an index of stock prices, such as the Standard & Poor's 500 index or the Major Market Index. A trader buying a December S&P 500 stock-index futures contract at a price of $200 today, for instance, would be agreeing to take delivery next month of 500 times that amount in cash, or $100,000. Traders would almost always close out that position by selling an offsetting futures contract.*

If the stock market—and corrrespondingly the stock index—rose before the trader closed out his position, he would make a profit because he could sell an offsetting contract at a higher price, taking in more money than he had to spend. If the market fell, the trader would lose money because he would have to sell an offsetting contract at a lower price. Futures are used to hedge against fluctuations in stock prices or to speculate on market moves.

(The Major Market Index encompasses 20 blue-chip stocks, including 17 that are also in the Dow Jones Industrial Average. Futures on the MMI are traded on the Chicago Board of Trade. Options on the index are traded on the American Stock Exchange.)

THE WALL STREET CAREER OF MARTIN SIEGEL WAS A DREAM GONE WRONG

DISGRACE OF ARBITRAGER WAS SELF-FULFILLING PROPHECY; IT ALL BEGAN WITH BENDIX

DINNER AT THE BOESKY ESTATE

TUESDAY, FEBRUARY 17, 1987

BY JAMES B. STEWART AND DANIEL HERTZBERG

NEW YORK—Last Nov. 14, 38-year-old Martin A. Siegel, one of Wall Street's leading investment bankers, was spending the afternoon in the Park Avenue offices of Martin Lipton, an eminent takeover lawyer and a man Mr. Siegel had come to regard almost as a father.

Suddenly a federal marshal burst in upon the two men, thrusting a subpoena into Mr. Siegel's hand. When Mr. Siegel read the subject matter of the investigation—Ivan F. Boesky—and the accompanying list of his own takeover deals at Kidder, Peabody & Co. in the 1980s, he knew his career was over. He began sobbing, as a horrified Mr. Lipton rushed to comfort him.

The public end to Mr. Siegel's career, once one of the most spectacular success stories on Wall Street, came last Friday. He resigned his year-old position as co-head of mergers and acquisitions at Drexel Burnham Lambert Inc. and pleaded guilty in federal court to two felony counts for his role in the Boesky scandal. Coming just a day after the stunning arrests of three top Wall Street professionals, Mr. Siegel's pleas still managed to shock Wall Street. More than anyone else so far implicated in the scandal, Mr. Siegel personified the American dream.

He also embodied the new breed of investment banker who has ridden the take-over boom of the '80s to the top. Inside information was inextricably linked to his own rise, and he is cooperating fully in the government's continuing investigation. His testimony has already implicated the three men arrested last week, and he has described the pressure for profits from high-level Kidder Peabody officials that allegedly led to the misuse of inside information by the firm's arbitrage department.

In sum, Mr. Siegel's testimony is a vivid chronicle of how systemic the abuse of inside information has become on Wall Street.

This is the story of Mr. Siegel's rise and abrupt fall. It has been pieced together from scores of interviews with people who know Mr. Siegel and with people who are familiar with at least portions of Mr. Siegel's recent statements to the government as well as those of others who have testified in the government's continuing investigation.

(Mr. Siegel couldn't be reached to comment on this account. The government wouldn't identify his whereabouts, citing his continuing cooperation and importance as a potential witness. His lawyer, Jed S. Rakoff, declined comment.)

In the eyes of many Wall Street observers, the takeover boom came of age on Aug. 26, 1982, when Bendix Corp. launched a $1.5 billion hostile bid for Martin Marietta Corp., the opening salvo in what became the now-legendary four-way battle involving Bendix, Martin Marietta, United Technologies Corp. and Allied Corp. And thrust into the center of the action, in his role as Martin Marietta's chief strategist, was a young, hitherto little-known merger specialist at Kidder Peabody named Martin Siegel.

By the time of the Bendix bid, Mr. Siegel had known Ivan F. Boesky for years. Kidder Peabody, where Mr. Siegel was the key mergers and acquisitions strategist, didn't have an arbitrage department so Mr. Siegel couldn't use his own firm for the information about stock positions and company valuations that is crucial to take-over strategy and is the arbitragers' stock-in-trade. He had come to rely on Mr. Boesky, whose persistent phone calls had led to a close relationship. Indeed, they spoke on the phone for five years before they met in person in 1980.

Mr. Siegel had become awed by the vast wealth he saw Mr. Boesky amassing. Two years before the Bendix bid, Mr. Siegel had been invited to dinner at Mr. Boesky's sprawling estate in suburban West-chester County; the Boesky house dwarfed the house that Mr. Siegel was planning to build on Long Island Sound. On two other occasions, Mr. Boesky had come out to the Siegel home to play tennis, a game Mr. Siegel loved and played well. Mr. Boesky arrived in his pink Rolls-Royce.

Mr. Siegel's awe at Mr. Boesky's possessions was all the more pro-nounced because he came from a modest family background that had been marked by financial struggle. When he was 20 years old, his father, then in his 40s, had filed for bankruptcy, an event that left an indelible impression on the son. Indeed, friends say that Mr. Siegel was haunted by the fear that someday, like his father, he would fail just as he reached the prime of life.

For the same reason, he saved money compulsively. For years, he had lived as a bachelor on his relatively modest $50,000 annual salary at Kidde·Peabody, saving all of his much larger bonuses. But in 1981 he married his second wife, another investment banker at Kidder Peabody, and they had their first child the next year. They built a large home in Greens Farms, one of the most exclusive enclaves on the Connecticut coast. They had a New York apartment as well and hired a nurse for the child. Mr. Siegel's salary wasn't enough to cover these burgeoning expenses; he was depleting his carefully saved capital.

Several days before the Bendix bid, Mr. Siegel, then 33, trim, dark-haired and strikingly handsome, pushed through the double doors of the grill room at New York's Harvard Club. Mr. Siegel spotted Mr. Boesky and the two settled down for what would become a fateful conversation.

Mr. Siegel aired some of his personal financial concerns to Mr. Boesky. He must have known that to do so in front of an arbitrager was like placing red meat before a lion. "I'll make some investments for you," Mr. Boesky volunteered, and one thing led to another. By the end of that conversation, the two had forged an agreement: In return for information furnished by Mr. Siegel, Mr. Boesky would pay him an unspecified percentage of Mr. Boesky's own profits from trading on the information.

THE 'PACMAN' DEFENSE

At the beginning, Mr. Siegel didn't expect to be leaking inside information; he thought he would simply be using his expertise as an investment banker to identify companies he deemed likely takeover targets. Indeed, Mr. Boesky had agreed that to trade on inside information just before a deal was publicly announced, or during the course of a deal, was too risky. The goal was to get Mr. Boesky into a takeover stock so early that the purchases couldn't possibly attract the interest of the Securities and Exchange Commission or other market watchers.

Bendix/Martin Marietta, however, provided an opportunity too good to resist. Martin Marietta, Mr. Siegel's client, had responded to the Bendix bid with the most audacious of tactics: the "PacMan" defense, named after the video game, in which the target tries to devour its suitor with a counterbid. Martin Marietta offered to pay $1.5 billion for Bendix.

In some ways, the tactic showed Mr. Siegel at his best. Although it wasn't the first time it had been employed, "it was wildly creative to do it on this scale," recalls one participant. Says another colleague, "You see the creative impulse in the literary and artistic worlds, only rarely in law or business. Marty had it."

But the PacMan defense, to be effective, needed some market momentum to get Bendix into play, pushing up its stock price so it would realize the market was taking the Martin Marietta attack seriously. So just before Martin Marietta's bid was unveiled, Mr. Siegel called Mr. Boesky and leaked the top secret plan, fully aware that he had just crossed the line of illegality. It was the last time he ever used the telephone to convey inside information to Mr. Boesky; shortly after, his feelings of guilt manifested themselves in a paranoid belief that his phone was tapped.

Using Mr. Siegel's information, Mr. Boesky bought Bendix stock, eventually realizing a profit of about $120,000. The PacMan defense succeeded. Bendix lost its independence and was acquired by Allied, and Martin Marietta survived, though at a cost so high that the PacMan defense has never again been attempted on such a scale. The battle was a coup for Mr. Siegel, thrusting him into the limelight just as the nation's takeover boom erupted. And it put Kidder Peabody, considered an established but sleepy firm in decline, at the forefront of merger-defense work.

THRIVING PRACTICE

Mr. Siegel parlayed that fame into a thriving defense-oriented merger practice, modeled in part on the successful takeover law firms. Mr. Siegel tirelessly traveled around the country, persuading chief executives of major corporations to pay Kidder Peabody a retainer to defend them should they become the target of a hostile corporate raid. Over time, he succeeded in scores of instances. "Marty was the most persuasive, most charming investment banker I'd ever met," recalls one chief executive who joined the Kidder Peabody fold. "He had a terrific bedside manner with [chief executive officers] and boards."

But his success wasn't immediately reflected in a significantly higher salary. Over the years he complained about Kidder Peabody's stinginess, its refusal to recognize his contributions to the firm and its penchant for doling out money to unproductive senior partners. In December 1982, a few months after the Bendix/Martin Marietta battle began, he turned to Mr. Boesky and asked the arbitrager for a cash payment of $125,000.

Mr. Boesky readily agreed even though the sum exceeded his profits from Mr. Siegel's information about Bendix. To avoid detection, Mr. Boesky placed the cash in a suitcase and gave it to a courier who met Mr. Siegel in a public place. Mr. Siegel gave the courier an agreed-upon password, and he handed over the suitcase. Mr. Siegel kept the cash hoard, dipping into it throughout the year to pay employees, such as his child's nurse, and for spending money. He thought of the money as a "consulting fee."

'LET'S HAVE COFFEE'

With the exchange of money, Mr. Siegel's relationship with Mr. Boesky settled into a pattern. When Mr. Boesky wanted information, or when Mr. Siegel had information he wanted to leak, the two got in touch by telephone. The signal was "Let's have coffee," and they then met in person to exchange the information, first in an alley behind 55 Water St., the financial-district building where Mr. Boesky worked, and later, after Mr. Boesky moved into the former Fifth Avenue offices of fugitive commodities trader Marc Rich, at a nearby midtown coffee shop.

In early 1983, Mr. Siegel leaked inside information about a bid by Diamond Shamrock Corp. for Natomas Inc. and a bid for Pargas Inc., later acquired by Freeport-McMoRan Inc. In September he told Mr. Boesky that Gordon Getty, one of Mr. Siegel's clients, was dissatisfied with the management of Getty Oil Co. and that a sale of the company was likely; it was eventually acquired by Texaco Inc. In 1984, he told Mr. Boesky about a bid for Midlands Energy Co. and used inside information about Carnation Co. to predict it would be sold. Nestle S.A. eventually acquired Carnation, and Mr. Boesky earned a profit of more than $28.3 million on that deal alone.

The insider trading in these instances was extremely clever. In at least three cases, Natomas, Getty and Carnation, Mr. Siegel used inside information to make an educated prediction that a major corporate transaction would ensue. Mr. Boesky was thus able to take enormous stock positions ahead of any final decision to make a bid. Even if detected by the authorities, such trading didn't look like it could possibly be insider trading. And in every instance, it could be argued that Mr. Siegel's leaks actually worked to his clients' benefit by driving up the stock price at which they were eventually acquired, and to Kidder Peabody's benefit by boosting its fees that were based on the sale price.

INCREASING ANXIETY

At the end of both 1983 and 1984, Mr. Boesky and Mr. Siegel met to tally up Mr. Siegel's fee. Mr. Boesky began by saying, "What did you do for me this year?" and Mr. Siegel responded with an analysis of his leaks. The two end-of-year cash payments totaled $575,000.

Mr. Siegel, however, was becoming increasingly anxious about the scheme; and during the summer of 1984, he received a tremendous jolt from an article in Fortune magazine. Buried in the text of an otherwise-flattering profile of Mr. Boesky was one sentence: "Boesky's competitors whisper darkly about his omniscient timing, and rumors abound that he looks for deals involving Kidder Peabody and First Boston."

Panicked, Mr. Siegel hastily sought a meeting with Mr. Boesky. But the arbitrager was unfazed, noting that the magazine had nothing specific and suggesting that he could set up a foreign bank account for Mr. Siegel if he was really worried. Mr. Siegel demurred, appalled by the image of himself as a fugitive. He vowed to stop passing inside information, even though he couldn't bring himself to tell Mr. Boesky, and he accepted the 1984 payment.

The Carnation deal, details of which Mr. Siegel leaked from April through June 1984, was the last about which Mr. Siegel passed information to Mr. Boesky. Indeed, the pattern of Mr. Siegel's leaks is almost as conspicuous for the deals in which he didn't leak inside information as for those in which he did. For example, one of Mr. Boesky's greatest windfalls came when he correctly anticipated that Lenox Inc. would give in to a hostile bid from Brown-Forman Distillers Corp. in 1983. Mr. Siegel represented Lenox, but he wasn't the source of any leak. Mr. Boesky apparently had inside information even before Mr. Siegel knew it.

VALUABLE INFORMATION

Similarly, Mr. Siegel defended Richardson-Vicks Inc. in a hostile bid by Unilever in 1985, but he didn't pass information to Mr. Boesky. Rather, Mr. Boesky passed valuable information about the transaction to Mr. Siegel indicating the presence of another source. The Richardson-Vicks transaction has been named in government subpoenas related to the Boesky investigation.

In these and other transactions, Mr. Siegel learned the value of inside information in the day-to-day workings of mergers and acquisitions. He continued to listen to Mr. Boesky, even after he stopped giving him inside information. At the end of 1985, when the two met for their annual session, Mr. Boesky told Mr. Siegel that he wanted a written list of the deals Mr. Siegel had helped him on, indicating that he was disappointed in the arrangement. "Don't you love me anymore?" Mr. Boesky asked.

By then, Mr. Siegel had allegedly forged a far more valuable relationship, one in which he was able to tap into one of Wall Street's greatest repositories of inside information: Goldman, Sachs & Co.

At Kidder Peabody, Mr. Siegel had developed into the model investment banker, idolized by many he worked with. The firm began having its annual summer party for interns at Mr. Siegel's home in Connecticut, the message being, as one participant recalls, "that if you come to Kidder and work hard, you're going to be like Marty—a beautiful home, beautiful wife, beautiful kids. It was like a stage set for 'The Great Gatsby.' "

Mr. Siegel commuted from the house to lower Manhattan by helicopter. At home, he pursued his two hobbies, tennis and sailing on adjacent Long Island Sound. Colleagues say Mr. Siegel was never swept up into the fast-paced whirl of Manhattan society. "He disdained the charity-ball set," says one friend. "He was not a social climber. He didn't globe-trot. His main interest was his children." (In addition to a daughter, the Siegels had twins, a boy and a girl, who were born in 1985.)

MOUNTING PRESSURE

Despite his growing success, Mr. Siegel was coming under mounting pressure from within Kidder Peabody. Many of its areas were not doing well, and many partners feared for the firm's future. In March 1984, Ralph DeNunzio, the firm's chief executive, told Mr. Siegel that in addition to his merger and acquisitions work, Mr. Siegel had to help create an arbitrage department. The firm allotted $30 million to that effort.

The directive seemed to undermine the "Chinese Wall" that is supposed to limit the exchange of information between arbitrage departments and mergers and acquisition departments at investment-banking firms. Evidently in recognition of the inherent conflicts in having the firm's top mergers and acquisitions specialist directly involved in trading on takeover rumors, Mr. DeNunzio also indicated that Mr. Siegel's involvement in arbitrage not be disclosed publicly; it never was. Indeed, when the government identified Mr. Siegel as the Kidder Peabody arbitrager it had previously identified only as "CS-1," it came as a shock even to some Kidder Peabody employees who had no idea that Mr. Siegel was involved in arbitrage.

Repeated efforts to reach Mr. DeNunzio, both at home and in the office, over the holiday weekend were unsuccessful. A Kidder Peabody spokesman denies the account of Mr. DeNunzio's involvement. The spokesman says Mr. DeNunzio's role in arbitrage at Kidder Peabody "is the same as any chief executive officer who supervises departments of a firm." Any inference that Mr. DeNunzio was aware of, or condoned, any misuse of inside information or other wrongdoing "is false and absurd," the spokesman adds.

Despite pressures from the firm's officials to generate large profits, Kidder Peabody didn't have the resources to succeed at arbitrage. Assigned to officially head the new unit was Richard Wigton, generally regarded as a loyal but plodding trader; assigned to work with him was Timothy L. Tabor, a young and headstrong former accountant. (Messrs. Wigton and Tabor were among the three arrested by the government last week.) Mr. Siegel despaired that the unit could generate legitimate profits and complained at the time that his own role in arbitrage was untenable.

EXTRAORDINARY PERFORMANCE

Apparently, the result was the alleged arrangement with Robert Freeman, the head of arbitrage at Goldman Sachs, who, when he was arrested by the government last week, was charged with entering into an agreement with Mr. Siegel to swap inside information. It was information that gave Mr. Siegel a tremendous edge in his own merger and acquisitions work. Mr. Freeman, too, became a highly valued strategist on Goldman Sachs merger deals.

The arrangement turned Kidder Peabody's arbitrage unit, virtually overnight, into one of the firm's principal profit centers. In an extraordinary first-year performance that aroused amazement within the firm, the arbitrage unit accounted for more than 25% of Kidder Peabody's pre-tax profits the first year it existed. Although that percentage declined slightly in subsequent years, the unit generated "millions of dollars in illegal profits to Kidder," the government charged last week. Confidential profit figures from Kidder Peabody obtained by this newspaper show that arbitrage profits in 1985 were $6.9 million out of total profits of $47 million, or 15%, the firm's third-highest profit center. In 1984, arbitrage profits were also about $6.9 million out of a total profit of $39 million.

The alleged arrangement with Mr. Freeman seemed foolproof. The idea was that Kidder Peabody would trade on information from Goldman deals and that Goldman Sachs would trade on information from Kidder deals, so there were no obvious leaks within the firms. (The government, however, hasn't said whether there was any trading by Goldman Sachs on information Mr. Freeman allegedly received from Mr. Siegel. It did allege that Mr. Freeman traded in his own account, which, if true, breached the alleged understanding with Mr. Siegel.)

NO MESSY EXCHANGES

Moreover, arbitrage departments took positions in so many stocks rumored to be takeover targets that a few striking successes wouldn't appear unusual. There were no messy exchanges of cash, no unsavory-looking couriers. Goldman Sachs said last week that its own internal investigation suggests no wrongdoing on the part of either Mr. Freeman or the firm.

During 1985, as the alleged Goldman Sachs/Kidder Peabody scheme flourished, Mr. Siegel's communications with Mr. Boesky diminished. They didn't meet until the end-of-year session, and it didn't result in any more money changing hands. Mr. Boesky kept pressing hard for more information from Mr. Siegel, but Mr. Siegel resisted.

Then, in January 1986, Mr. Siegel decided to move to Drexel as co-head of its merger and acquisitions department, in part because the pressures of sustaining the Kidder Peabody arbitrage operation while building the firm's mergers and acquisitions practice had become nearly unbearable. Mr. Siegel arranged to meet again with Mr. Boesky, fearful that Mr. Boesky would be furious that he had made the decision without consulting Mr. Boesky. Mr. Boesky *was* furious, though apparently for reasons unrelated to Mr. Siegel's concerns. Dennis B. Levine, then an investment banker at Drexel, was already leaking inside information to Mr. Boesky; Mr. Siegel was far more valuable to Mr. Boesky at Kidder Peabody. (Last year, Mr. Levine pleaded guilty to four felony counts and is scheduled to be sentenced tomorrow.)

Even at that meeting, Mr. Siegel couldn't bring himself to tell Mr. Boesky that the relationship was over. Mr. Siegel's paranoia about the scheme had continued unchecked, and he increasingly viewed Mr.

Boesky's swarthy, muscular couriers as potential hit men. Behind his usual cheerful, outgoing facade, Mr. Siegel lived in a state of fear.

SEVERED TIES

But at Drexel, Mr. Siegel put insider trading behind him. He severed his ties with Mr. Freeman. He had come to Drexel to wed his defense expertise to Drexel's legendary financing capabilities, and the result was hugely successful. Mr. Siegel represented blue-chip clients like Lear-Siegler Inc., Holiday Corp. and Goodyear Tire & Rubber Co.—the kind of client Drexel desperately wanted to attract. Ironically, Goldman Sachs was furious when Goodyear, a longstanding Goldman Sachs client, insisted that both Drexel and Goldman Sachs represent it in its defense against a hostile bid by Sir James Goldsmith.

Last summer, Mr. Boesky tried several times to get in touch with Mr. Siegel. In August, almost exactly four years after their fateful Harvard Club meeting, Mr. Boesky called to say, "I must meet with you" to discuss their "arrangement." Mr. Siegel resisted, then suggested a public place—the Harvard Club. Mr. Boesky said it had to be private; Mr. Siegel declined. Mr. Boesky was presumably wired at the time, but the government never obtained convincing recorded evidence of Mr. Siegel's guilt.

On Nov. 14, the question of the government's evidence became moot. After news of Mr. Boesky's settlement with the government and after he sobbed in Mr. Lipton's office, Mr. Siegel determined almost immediately to plead guilty. He returned to Drexel's offices that evening, where, without going into details, he offered to take a leave of absence. Frederick H. Joseph, Drexel's chief executive, wouldn't hear of it, saying the firm would back him.

But Mr. Siegel's career was effectively over. Though he kept coming into the office, he ceased active participation in pending transactions. The Connecticut home he loved was hastily sold. He moved his family away from New York. He quickly agreed to the government's offer of a guilty plea to two felony counts; negotiations with the SEC over the financial terms of his settlement took longer. Under his agreement, he is paying $9 million to settle the charges. When he resigned from Drexel, he also forfeited approximately $11 million—$7 million in compensation due him and about $4 million in Drexel stock.

CROWDED PRESS CONFERENCE

On Friday morning Mr. Siegel, flanked by his lawyers, Mr. Rakoff and Audrey Strauss, appeared in Manhattan federal court. He was dressed like an investment banker, in an expensive dark gray suit, blue shirt and red tie. Occasionally wiping tears from his eyes, Mr. Siegel pleaded guilty to a single count of conspiracy to violate securities laws, as well as to one count of tax evasion for failing to declare the Boesky payoffs on his tax return.

Later, U.S. Attorney Rudolph Giuliani and Gary Lynch, the SEC director of enforcement, held a crowded press conference to celebrate Mr. Siegel's guilty plea. Said Mr. Giuliani, "His cooperation is very valuable, and Mr. Boesky's cooperation is very valuable. The value of this will be apparent as time goes on."

Mr. Siegel's negotiations with the U.S. Attorney's office didn't include any explicit promises to name others in the scandal, but he is cooperating fully in the government's continuing investigation. He is familiar with the inner workings of Kidder Peabody and has implicated Messrs. Wigton and Tabor. He is expected to provide testimony about the involvement of other Kidder Peabody executives in the firm's arbitrage activities as the government considers possible criminal charges against the firm.

To a lesser extent, Mr. Siegel is knowledgeable about the inner workings of Drexel, a firm also under investigation for reasons unrelated to Mr. Siegel's activities. As for Goldman Sachs, it is known that Mr. Siegel is not the government's principal witness against Mr. Freeman, but his testimony could be valuable corroboration if the government's case against Mr. Freeman goes to trial.

In addition, Mr. Siegel is intimately familiar with many important takeover deals, including the role inside information may have played in them. For government investigators, Mr. Siegel's guilty plea is thus the biggest coup since the capture of Mr. Boesky.

For his part, Mr. Siegel faces a maximum of 10 years in jail and a $260,000 fine on the two charges. He also settled, without admitting or denying guilt, SEC charges that he tipped Mr. Boesky about six takeover stocks. Mr. Siegel was permanently barred from working in the securities industry. In a statement read afterwards by Mr. Rakoff, Mr. Siegel said, "I hope that, by accepting responsibility for my mistakes, I have begun to make up for the anguish I have caused my family, friends and colleagues."

In the end, it was Mr. Siegel, seemingly blessed with nearly every attribute for success, who was his own worst enemy. By embracing the use of inside information for personal gain, to advance his career, and to benefit his firm, Mr. Siegel sealed his fate. Mr. Siegel's fears that his career, like that of his father's, would end in financial ruin, proved self-fulfilling.

FOURTEEN

LAX LABORATORIES

1988 WINNER IN THE SPECIALIZED JOURNALISM CATEGORY

"For a distinguished example of reporting on such specialized subjects as sports, business, science, education, or religion . . ."

The Wall Street Journal
Walt Bogdanich

Walt Bogdanich of *The Wall Street Journal* didn't just interview experts. He sent samples of his own blood to be tested at medical laboratories, where he uncovered a chilling fact: Public and private labs frequently make gross errors that can endanger the lives of thousands of people.

My cholesterol test was reassuring. "Nothing to worry about," my doctor told me as he looked at a computer printout of a lab report. "Your count of 265 is well within the lab's normal range."

With a family history of heart disease, I thought that was great news. But six months later, the news wasn't so good. As part of a regular physical exam, another doctor using another lab told me, "Your count of 245 is much too high. The lab says you're in the high-risk group for heart disease."

I was confused. "How can 245 be too high and 265 be normal?" I asked. My doctor didn't know. "I guess every lab is a little different," he said.

So began what would ultimately blossom into a year-long investigation of lab test accuracy. By the end, I had interviewed more than 500 people, learned more about statistics than I ever did in school, and nearly fainted when I had a doctor draw what seemed like a gallon of my blood so I could have it tested simultaneously at five New York City labs. (Each lab reported a different result.)

In the beginning, I never envisioned such a long, involved project. In August 1986, I told my editor, Don Moffitt, that I simply wanted to do a narrowly focused story examining the reliability of cholesterol tests. With his blessing, I went forward, making my first reporting story at the Cleveland Clinic.

I found a researcher there with a good story to tell. "The lab industry doesn't want to confront its problems," he told me. "The physicians aren't demanding accuracy, and patients don't even know enough to question their test results."

He proceeded to tell me how manufacturers were turning out poorly calibrated blood test equipment and that lab workers often didn't know how to use it. Proving this, he cautioned, would be difficult.

At this point, I began wondering if the problem wasn't bigger than just cholesterol tests. Several years earlier, when I was a reporter in Cleveland, I knew a pharmacy board investigator who enjoyed telling stories about a lab owner who was a convicted felon and who continued to cheat the government. Couldn't be much government regulation, I thought at the time.

If I could find some state or federal regulation, I might find the documentation I needed to prove there was a problem. All too often, however, my conversations were like the one I had with an Ohio health department official:

Q: Who inspects your labs?

A: All our work is subcontracted out to Ph.D. laboratories.

Q: I'd like their names.

A: We don't give that out.

Q: You have to. The law requires it.

A: So sue me.

Ohio, like most states, had no meaningful lab regulation. Fortunately for me, one state—New York—did. Not only did its lab division have extensive documentation on laboratory errors, but New York officials also were eager to help.

I quickly learned that bad cholesterol testing was only a tiny piece of a national laboratory system that was out of control. New York State records showed some of the best known hospitals and laboratory chains had been barred from conducting particular tests in New York State because they failed proficiency exams.

"What's really frightening," said one New York official, "is that these same labs continue to test specimens from other states where there are no regulations."

Only a few states even bothered with proficiency requirements. And those that did viewed such requirements as an educational tool for labs, not a means to stop a lab from testing. California collected proficiency test results, but didn't bother to look at them. "We aren't advertising that," a California official told me.

Pennsylvania, on the other hand, did examine proficiency scores, and found that half its physician-owned labs had erred in analyzing a test for bacteria. Looking through state lab records, I found one doctor who had failed 24 of 40 individual proficiency tests, including six in a row for blood glucose, yet the state didn't restrict his testing. In fact, the state had never issued a single stop-test order against a physician's-office lab.

The best, however, was yet to come.

Mary Anne Gardineer, a New York State lab official, said somewhat cryptically: "If I were you, I'd look at the Pap smear. Its error rate is higher than you'd ever believe." A few phone calls later, I was on the line to the president of a pathologists' group. When he mentioned the word "sweatshop," I thought I had misunderstood.

"You mean there are laboratory sweatshops analyzing slides for cancer?" I asked. He assured me it was true.

By now, I had spent three months investigating lab procedures, and my editors were expecting some stories. I decided to write what I had, and get back to the Pap smear story later.

It was a good strategy, because breaking open the story on Pap smears took another three months of interviewing and record searching. It was worth the time. Not only did I locate studies showing the Pap smear to be notoriously inaccurate, but I had the good fortune of finding an extraordinarily dedicated group of professionals who helped guide me through the hidden world of Pap smear screening.

While the medical profession largely kept silent about bad labs, it was this low-paid group of cytotechnologists who courageously spoke out. Reaching them wasn't easy. Many were paid so little that they had to work at two or three labs. Consequently, many of my telephone interviews were done around midnight, the only time they were available.

In the end, my gratification in seeing the main story on Pap tests published was secondary only to another event that same day, November 2. It was the day I became a father, to Nicholas, 8 pounds, 10 ounces.

—Walt Bogdanich
The Wall Street Journal

FALSE NEGATIVE

MEDICAL LABS, TRUSTED AS LARGELY ERROR-FREE, ARE FAR FROM INFALLIBLE

HASTE, MISUSE OF EQUIPMENT, SPECIMEN MIX-UPS AFFLICT EVEN BEST LABS AT TIMES

REGULATION: WEAK AND SPOTTY

MONDAY, FEBRUARY 2, 1987

BY WALT BOGDANICH

It was 4:30 a.m. when cancer finally choked the last breath of life from Janice Johnson. She was 34 and a mother of two, and she died never knowing why her disease had been so unforgiving. An autopsy report called her abrupt decline "quite unusual."

Later, an important clue would be discovered: A hospital laboratory in Arlington, Va., had erroneously reported two successive Pap tests as noncancerous. Undetected, the cancer spread rapidly through Mrs. Johnson's body.

"The lab was never shut down or criticized," fumes Daniel Schultz, a Johnson-family lawyer who in 1984 settled a wrongful-death claim against the hospital and several doctors for $600,000. He asks: "How many other Janice Johnsons are there?"

No one knows. For in many states, including Virginia, the clinical laboratories that test body fluids and tissues aren't licensed—and thus enjoy a freedom from regulatory scrutiny not accorded even to hairdressers. Some 20 years after Congress declared war on incompetent clinical labs, many researchers say that inaccurate and unreliable testing remains a serious health hazard, as well as a waste of millions of dollars.

HARD DATA

In recent years, dazzling advances in computerized diagnostic testing have lent a comforting air of precision to the healing arts. Whether concerned about blood cholesterol, cancer, genetic flaws or diabetes, Americans spend an estimated $20 billion a year on clinical laboratory tests, often receiving impressively detailed printouts on the state of their health.

For the most part, such testing is a great boon to diagnosis and treatment. But along the way, patients have come to regard lab work as infallible—a dangerous assumption, critics say. "Every lab is producing some errors," warns Paul Fischer, an Augusta, Ga., physician and authority in the field. "Human error is inherent in this process. . . . I don't think the public realizes that."

The problem affects not only fringe laboratories in inner cities but also prestigious hospitals, publicly traded laboratory companies and labs in doctors' offices, according to an analysis of thousands of pages of government reports, court records and previously unreleased test data. The recent surge of testing in doctors' offices is particularly troubling, critics say, because these small facilities are often entirely free of regulatory oversight.

FALSE STARTS

While sloppy lab work isn't as obviously dangerous as incompetent surgery—errors are often caught by a patient's physician—it can do great harm. An Ohio baby developed mental retardation after a lab failed to detect a genetic condition that required a special diet. An Arizona man died after a biopsy slide of his malignant thyroid tumor was misread by two different labs. A California couple's marriage broke up after one spouse was mistakenly diagnosed as having syphilis.

Nor is health the only issue: A urinalysis that falsely tags someone as a drug abuser can sabotage the person's career.

Studies repeatedly have turned up substantial rates of laboratory error, as well as overworked or ill-trained technicians. But abuses are hard to prove, and accountability is scant. By the time an illness has progressed far enough to suggest earlier test error, the slide or specimen often has been discarded.

LITTLE REGULATION

Government hasn't come to grips with the problem. Regulation is so weak and uneven that labs barred from one state can simply do business in another. In some cases, a federal agency has no choice but to reimburse certain labs for tests that it has found them incompetent to perform.

Concern over such problems prompted Congress to pass the Clinical Laboratories Improvement Act in 1967. Although the law covers only a fraction of the nation's labs—those conducting interstate business—legislators hoped it would be a model for state regulation.

However, only about half of the states have enacted laboratory regulation, and most of it is feeble. In 1979 the Senate Labor and Human Resources Committee concluded that the public "cannot have confidence in clinical laboratory testing, despite its critical relationship to good health."

Faulty tests can occur for many reasons: A machine loses its calibration; testing chemicals lose potency or get used improperly; human specimens are inadvertently switched. Even if a test is performed properly, it may be misinterpreted.

Over the years, the medical profession has developed standards to minimize such mishaps. Conscientious laboratories test chemicals and machine calibrations daily. They frequently test "master" specimens of known value to detect any glitches in equipment or procedures. But without oversight, adherence to these standards is left to the whim of the individual lab.

THE JOHNSON CASE

If, for example, Mrs. Johnson's Pap smears had been analyzed at a hospital in New York, where government standards are among the toughest, they would have been screened by workers who had faced proficiency tests and had to have 10% of their work checked by supervisors.

Such safeguards didn't exist at Northern Virginia Doctors Hospital, whose lab supervisor conceded, in a deposition filed in Virginia state court, that Mrs. Johnson's two Pap tests were reported incorrectly one year apart by the same lab worker. The supervisor also said quality-control reviews weren't routine. The hospital declines to comment on Mrs. Johnson's death or her family's suit.

Some researchers worry that Pap-test "sweat shops" impair accuracy by overworking technicians. "I can't deny they are out there," says Thomas Bonfiglio, the president of the American Society of Cytology. "I think you'd have to be crazy not to be concerned."

The society recommends that, in the case of Pap tests, a full-time screener review no more than 10,000 to 12,000 slides a year. But about one-third of labs responding to a survey some years ago exceeded that workload, and records show that screeners at a lab just outside New York City currently have workloads three times greater. The Johnson family lawyer asserted that the worker who called Mrs. Johnson's Pap tests benign had an excessive workload.

Technicians must scan dozens of cells on each slide for abnormalities. "It's a very meticulous job," Dr. Bonfiglio says. "The error rate goes up as people get fatigued."

'SINK TESTING'

Boston researchers studied 10 women with cervical cancer who had had negative Pap tests in the preceding two years. A re-examination of their slides found that five had been misinterpreted and two slides were too poorly done to read; only three were clearly negative. Researchers at Harvard Medical School and the Boston Hospital for Women did the study.

An even worse situation occurred in the late 1970s at a lab that had won a contract to screen Pap smears for the Air Force. An Air Force pathologist charged that screeners at the lab, Automated Medical Services of Ohio Inc., were overworked. When government doctors reexamined slides it had processed, they found 5,949 "discrepancies" or "mistakes," says Patti Turner, a spokeswoman for the Air Force surgeon general. A search for women who had gotten false reports found most of them, though not all. The lab has closed, and its former officials couldn't be reached for comment.

Now and then labs have even reported on specimens without checking them at all—"sink testing," it is called. A Hempstead, N.Y., lab is alleged to have reported phony results for more than a year on blood tests for rheumatism, tuberculosis and various chronic infections. In September a state grand jury indicted the company, Reiss Health Laboratories Inc., on fraud-related charges. The lab, which has pleaded innocent, declines to comment.

Fraud, however, is much less pervasive than error. Nearly one in six labs tested recently by the Centers for Disease Control didn't properly identify several common strains of bacteria. One in seven failed to identify various fungal growths properly. "So many things can go wrong, even in the best labs," says Josephine Bartola, the director of Pennsylvania's laboratory improvement division.

DOCTOR'S-OFFICE LABS

Nearly half of outpatient lab tests now are done in physicians' offices, because of cheaper test equipment and changes in hospital economics. There are estimated to be between 40,000 and 100,000 such small labs, compared with 13,000 hospital and independent labs. The trend alarms many experts, because only 13 states even attempt to regulate labs in doctors' offices.

As a result, in all but a handful of states, their personnel needn't meet any training standards. Dr. Fischer, the authority on office laboratories, says that in as many as two-thirds of small doctor's-office labs, work is done by employees lacking formal lab training, including medical secretaries and receptionists.

When Idaho officials tested unregulated doctor's-office labs in the 1970s, fully half of them submitted erroneous or unacceptable results on a simple pregnancy test. "You'd get the same results throwing a coin in the air," Dr. Fischer remarks. (Their performances improved after they were instructed in the need for quality control and proficiency testing.)

Physicians with labs in their offices generally contend the new equipment is accurate and makes for faster diagnosis and better treatment. But David Yates, a pathologist in the Nashville, Tenn., area, says that "doctors don't realize how difficult it is to consistently generate accurate test data. People think it's a computerized situation where you always get a 100% accurate result; that's simply not true."

TWO STUDIES

Michael Kenney, a health-policy analyst, studied California clinical labs for the CDC in 1985 and found "a systematic pattern" of poorer accuracy by unregulated labs than by government-regulated ones. Another study, by Robert Grayson in 1984, reached a similar conclusion.

Even where office labs are regulated, the monitoring is usually superficial. California requires doctor's-office labs to submit proficiency-test scores—but doesn't review them. "We aren't advertising that," confides Ronald Harkey, of the state lab division. He says his office lacks the computers needed for the task.

Pennsylvania, which does review proficiency tests, recently found that nearly half of the doctors sampled had erred in analyzing a test for bacteria. The state has some of the nation's toughest rules for doctor's-office labs, but its officials say they have never disciplined a doctor for faulty testing.

Ms. Bartola, the director of the state's laboratory improvement division, says her office will order a lab to stop offering a procedure if it fails four consecutive proficiency tests. She says this has never occurred, so no stop orders have ever been issued. However, state records show multiple instances of doctor's-office labs failing four or more straight tests. For example, the lab of a doctor in Johnstown, Pa., Dinesh Mathur, failed 24 of 40 individual proficiency tests in 1984–85, including six in a row for blood glucose, yet the state didn't restrict his testing.

Asked about these records, Ms. Bartola says some failures may have escaped her attention because of a staff shortage. Besides, she adds, "We don't police them; we work with them until they come up to snuff." Ms. Bartola also says that many doctor's-office labs aren't licensed, as required by state law, and that she hasn't the staff to do much about it.

Dr. Mathur, who recently did pass a glucose proficiency test, says that his is a small lab doing few tests and that the state has never told him to stop. He also says he uses the best available equipment.

NEW YORK'S PROGRAM

The federal government is even more lenient. To get Medicare reimbursements, commercial or hospital labs must submit to proficiency testing and inspections. Not so doctors, if they confine their testing to their own patients.

New York state, employing about 170 medical doctors and Ph.D.s, runs probably the nation's most stringent program of laboratory proficiency testing. Yet it doesn't oversee those in doctors' offices.

As for the labs New York does oversee—independent ones and those in hospitals—when the state last February tested their ability to measure 18 parts of a standard blood-chemistry analysis, 11% of the results were either unacceptable or only marginally acceptable.

New York has issued more than 150 orders since July 1984 barring labs from testing in areas where they have failed to show proficiency. Many prominent labs, some with international reputations, have felt its regulatory sting, including the cytogenetics laboratory at Thomas Jefferson University Hospital in Philadelphia. That major referral center twice failed to pass New York's cytogenetics proficiency test in 1985, committing "major errors," according to Ann Willey, a scientist who heads New York's Laboratory of Human Genetics. Although barred from testing New York residents, it can continue to process specimens from other states.

Laird Jackson, the director of Thomas Jefferson's lab, says New York's proficiency tests were flawed. Besides, he adds, cytogenetics testing is subjective, akin to "judging ice skaters." Dr. Jackson says his lab has passed a proficiency test conducted by a major testing service outside New York.

A COMMERCIAL LAB

Another lab that has sometimes failed New York tests is the nation's largest publicly traded company exclusively engaged in testing human specimens, International Clinical Laboratories Inc. The Nashville-based company's clients include 40 hospitals with 8,700 beds. In a recent two-year period, ICL's major referral lab failed New York state's proficiency tests for toxicology, which detects drugs subject to abuse, and mycology, which identifies molds sometimes associated with severe infections. Paul Ottaviano, an executive of ICL, says it passed proficiency tests administered by others, as well as government inspections, and has since passed New York's tests.

What are the consequences of laboratory error for patients? A cytogenetics test (for genetic abnormalities) may lead a woman to terminate a pregnancy. "If that diagnosis was wrong, it's a wrongful death," Ms. Willey asserts.

Laboratory mistakes needn't be unusual to be devastating. Caroline Keklak, of Columbus, Ohio, says she suffered through two unnecessary operations because she was erroneously reported to be pregnant. According to a suit she filed in Ohio state court, the following occurred: Ohio State University Hospitals in Columbus admitted Mrs. Keklak with abdominal pain in January 1985 and a blood test determined that she was pregnant. When an ultrasound exam detected a pelvic mass, doctors, thinking she had a tubal pregnancy, performed emergency abdominal surgery. But instead of an embryo surgeons found a cyst, and they removed her right ovary.

Mrs. Keklak's suit says that as a result of the surgery, she later developed an abscess on a Fallopian tube and required a second operation to remove it. Except for the erroneous pregnancy test, the suit asserts, the cyst would have been treated with medicine and "no surgery would ever have been performed."

The suit attributes the faulty pregnancy test to a mix-up of specimens. A spokesman for the hospital declines to comment.

MEDICARE LOOPHOLE

The federal government tries to reduce errors by inspecting labs. But it is hampered by a surreal tangle of contradictory regulations.

Sharon Harris, of the federal Health Care Financing Administration (HCFA), says that if "people's lives are in danger," her agency can revoke a lab's Medicare certification. But the effect is merely to halt reimbursements for tests on Medicare patients; the lab can continue testing other patients.

St. Clair Medical Laboratory in Belleville, Ill., for instance, remains open seven months after federal regulators called it a health hazard and revoked its Medicare certification. (An attorney for the lab says it has never been a health hazard and notes that it has remained licensed by the state.)

Another inconsistency: In 1985, after St. Ansgar Hospital Laboratory in Moorhead, Minn., failed proficiency tests, the HCFA barred it from doing a kidney-function test on specimens sent across state lines.

Ms. Harris says such a stop-test order indicates patient safety is at stake. But because failing to demonstrate competence on a single procedure isn't deemed serious enough under Medicare rules to warrant regulatory action, the HCFA can't stop St. Ansgar from performing that test on Medicare patients, nor can it stop reimbursing for the test.

St. Ansgar says the lab has passed Minnesota proficiency tests. It won't comment specifically on the federal agency's action.

Since January 1985, the HCFA has issued more than 90 orders prohibiting labs from doing certain tests on interstate specimens, according to records obtained under the federal Freedom of Information Act. Most of these labs participate in the Medicare programs, so many of them continue to get federal reimbursement for the prohibited tests.

"It does seem very inconsistent," says the federal agency's Ms. Harris. "I'll admit it's a problem."

TRADE GROUPS

The government has also drawn fire for ceding regulatory oversight to private medical groups that, critics say, are lax in policing laboratories. For example, it essentially exempts from Medicare regulation labs in more than 5,000 hospitals accredited by the Joint Commission on Accreditation of Hospitals, a trade group. California's chief of laboratory field services, Roderick Hamblin, says the commission "doesn't always adequately identify deficiencies in performance or . . . get them corrected." A Joint Commission official calls that notion "ridiculous."

Many states accept Joint Commission inspections in lieu of their own, but not New York. When a commission team inspected the Moses Ludington Hospital in Ticonderoga, N.Y., on Aug. 30, 1985, it reported nine laboratory deficiencies; New York state inspectors who checked the lab a few months later found 38. The Joint Commission won't comment on the case but says different inspections may emphasize different aspects of labs. Margaret Warden, the hospital's administrator, says hers is a small rural facility that is "doing the very best we can."

Under current rules, if the Joint Commission wants to decertify a lab, it must revoke the accreditation of the entire hospital. The commission hasn't revoked any accreditation solely because of lab performance in recent years. "We . . . don't see ourselves at all in a policeman's role," says Jack Coale, a Joint Commission spokesman.

This view is shared by the College of American Pathologists, which runs its own accreditation and proficiency-test program for labs. It has revoked the accreditation of just one of 3,800 labs since January 1985. "The whole basis of our program is education and laboratory improvement," says John Duckworth, a doctor who heads its accreditation commission. "Ours is not a regulatory program."

Since Congress passed its laboratory legislation 20 years ago, it has tried five times to strengthen the law. Each effort, opposed by organized medicine, failed. The HCFA would like to see states take a bigger role, but organized medicine makes its presence felt in state capitols, too. Its influence, along with the issue of costs (New York spends $2.2 million a year to oversee labs) has helped keep state laws limp.

OFFICE MACHINES

Many doctors argue that technological advances make regulation less important. They note, for example, that new glucose-monitoring machines are so simple to operate that diabetics use them at home.

But the machines don't inspire universal confidence. In the past two years, the Food and Drug Administration has received about 1,200 reports of problems associated with glucose monitors. In one such report, a hospital complained that its machine wasn't working right; when the manufacturer checked, it found employees had apparently been using the device even though it was broken, dirty and held together with a rubber band. In dozens of other cases, technicians were found to be using the machines improperly. An FDA task force is investigating.

Growing evidence of testing abuses, along with fear of malpractice litigation, has begun to stir concern in some quarters of the medical establishment. Since late 1985, the Journal of the American Medical Association has been running a series of articles on office testing. Physicians, the authors have written, "are unfamiliar with . . . the subtleties of testing, the idiosyncratic personalities of 'foolproof' electronic equipment, or even the basic concepts of quality control."

Observes Walter Johnson, the director of the cytogenetics lab at Case Western Reserve University in Cleveland: "Most of us would prefer that regulation be on a voluntary basis. But frankly, voluntary systems don't work worth a damn in the long run."

INACCURACY IN TESTING CHOLESTEROL HAMPERS WAR ON HEART DISEASE

SOME DIAGNOSES ARE SKEWED BY GLITCHES SUCH AS USE OF ILL-CALIBRATED LAB GEAR

MISSING THE MARK BY 100%

TUESDAY, FEBRUARY 3, 1987

BY WALT BOGDANICH

In September 1985, a research group called the American Health Foundation hit upon a way to publicize the link between high blood cholesterol and America's No. 1 killer, heart disease. It co-sponsored a five-day "health fair" in New York offering free cholesterol checks.

Organizers, who expected maybe 2,000 or 3,000 visitors, were stunned by what happened. Nearly 30,000 people showed up, some waiting in line for three hours. The sponsors hired a plane to rush in extra lab equipment, but still had to turn away half the crowd.

Americans in large numbers are finally beginning to comprehend what heart researchers have been telling them for years: High blood cholesterol can kill. But while heart researchers publicly urge cholesterol tests, they privately worry that their battle against heart disease is being undermined by inaccurate or misleading laboratory tests.

WAY OFF

When a physicians' group in 1985 asked 5,000 of the nation's top laboratories to run cholesterol tests on identical samples, nearly half produced results that a leading expert calls "unacceptable." Some labs weren't even close.

In the test, the College of American Pathologists sent each lab a sample with a known cholesterol value of 262.6 milligrams per deciliter. The laboratories came back with reports ranging from 101 to 524.

Cholesterol, a substance needed for such functions as making cell walls, is produced in adequate quantities by the liver. But many people have an excess of it circulating in their bloodstream, usually traceable in part to a diet high in animal fats. It now is clear that too much cholesterol increases arterial deposits that can restrict blood flow to the heart. Each year 550,000 Americans die from coronary heart disease, more than from all forms of cancer combined.

High cholesterol is of course only one heart-disease risk factor, along with such things as smoking, high blood pressure and family history. Until a few years ago, there was much controversy over what danger a patient faced if cholesterol was high. But the National Institutes of Health has reached a consensus that 50% of adult Americans have levels high enough to worsen their risk of heart disease, and many leading cholesterol researchers believe the figure is even higher. For those with elevated levels, the NIH calculates, each 1% reduction in cholesterol lowers heart-disease risk 2%.

A COMMON TEST

About 100 million blood-cholesterol tests were performed in the U.S. last year, at a cost to patients and insurers of between $1 billion and $1.5 billion. In the future, the test is expected to be done even more frequently. Already it is among the most common clinical laboratory procedures.

Without accuracy in these tests, however, treatment is problematic. "We will never have good cholesterol therapy unless the doctors know that they can depend on the laboratories," says Gerald Cooper, a physician at the U.S. Centers for Disease Control.

Patients who falsely test low may forgo diet or drug regimens that their doctors otherwise would prescribe. Patients who falsely test high may face the unpleasant side effects of cholesterol-lowering drugs, to say nothing of an unnecessary cost of up to $125 a month. "That's a car payment for many people," notes one researcher.

WHAT CAN HAPPEN

Why do some tests mislead? Laboratory experts say some companies scrambling for a share of the growing market for cholesterol-measuring devices are selling machines they haven't taken the time to calibrate precisely. In addition, the people doing the tests may use equipment incorrectly, or they may buy chemical supplies not meant for their model of analyzer. And physicians may not properly interpret test results, in part because some lab reports include outdated information on what is "normal."

This reporter sent samples of his blood, all drawn at once, to five randomly selected New York City laboratories. Each reported a different cholesterol level. One gave a reading of 220, which, by NIH guidelines for his age group, falls on the borderline between average and moderate risk. Another lab reported 245, putting the reporter in a high-risk category. The variation could mean the difference between modest dietary changes and expensive drug treatment.

This informal experiment involved just a few laboratories, but the one done by the College of American Pathologists tested 5,000, many of them hospital labs. The egregious misses—50% too low or 100% too high—weren't common, but almost half of the labs did miss the result by more than 5%, says Herbert Naito, a clinical biochemist at the Cleveland Clinic and a leading authority on cholesterol testing. He says such a deviation is unacceptable.

Mr. Naito, who heads an NIH panel investigating testing procedures, adds that "many commercial and private labs—even medical centers—have as much as a 20% margin of error."

The pathologists' group won't release names of labs participating in its test, but records of a regular New York state test of laboratory proficiency illustrate Mr. Naito's point. One lab owned by Roche Biomedical Laboratories Inc. was 24% too low on a 1985 test sample. But another lab owned by the same company was 42% too high, state records show. A spokesman for Roche, a unit of Swiss-based Hoffmann-La Roche Inc., says the two labs have performed very well in subsequent proficiency tests and have never run afoul of government regulators.

In assessing a patient's risk, many doctors want to know what portion of the cholesterol is packaged as LDL (low-density lipoprotein) and what portion as HDL (high-density lipoprotein). LDL is the dangerous type that can clog arteries. HDL is essentially used cholesterol on its way out of the body, and a higher level of it is thought to be a good sign. But measuring these fractions requires an extra laboratory procedure, and researchers say such testing is even more subject to error.

CHEMICAL CHANGE

In tests for overall cholesterol level, some of the skewed reports are believed to result when a lab uses inappropriate chemical "reagents." During testing, reagents are added to the specimen and produce a byproduct, the color of which is measured by the analyzing machine. In their marketing, manufacturers occasionally discount the machines themselves, intending to make up the lower price through sales of reagents. But Robert Rej, a biochemist who heads New York state's clinical chemistry laboratory, says labs sometimes cut costs by buying less-expensive reagents not designed for their model of machine.

Labs often confuse doctors by noting in their test reports whether the cholesterol level is "normal," or within an acceptable reference range. These "normal" ranges differ widely and can run as high as 330 —far above what cholesterol experts agree is safe. "No wonder the physician does not get excited and intervene" in many cases, Mr. Naito says.

Labs commonly use the reference range supplied by the maker of their testing equipment. However, many manufacturers don't base the range on established links between cholesterol levels and coronary-artery disease. Instead, they may simply set up a statistical curve after testing new equipment on employees or others who appear healthy.

Robert Galen, chairman of the Cleveland Clinic's biochemistry department, believes "normal" ranges for cholesterol shouldn't be used at all. With total blood cholesterol, in most cases more is worse, he says, "so the notion of normal is not operative."

Some testing problems may result when equipment performs well in factory tests but poorly in the field, researchers say. "The laboratories are very dependent on what comes out of the factory and whether it will maintain its performance later," says Basil Rifkind, a physician at the National Heart, Lung and Blood Institute.

OFFICE TESTING

Of particular concern are the newer, cheaper models, called "black boxes" by some in the laboratory business. Aimed at physicians' offices, these analyzers can cost as little as $5,000. (More sophisticated machines cost well over $100,000.) "You are going to see these little black boxes coming out of the woodwork from all over because they [makers] see a market," says one researcher.

Many in the medical field welcome the low-priced devices. They say the analyzers are accurate and are so quick that patients can receive test results in minutes instead of days. They can also be used at health fairs, like the one in New York, for large-scale screening. A physician who has his own cholesterol analyzer can bill for the test instead of passing the work on to a laboratory.

But quality varies widely among these analyzers as well as others, test data show. "The problem here has to do with the science of laboratory medicine and pathology. There is more than one way to measure cholesterol," says the Cleveland Clinic's Dr. Galen. More than 30 different machines are currently sold, using somewhat different chemical processes.

After the College of American Pathologists proficiency test, researchers studied the performance of different machines used in the test. Some scored well, but others did not.

The Beckman Astra 8 analyzer, for example, had an average margin of error of 27%. A spokesman for the machine's manufacturer, Philadelphia-based SmithKline Beckman Corp., says that the test sample was flawed, and that if any problem existed, it has since been corrected.

SETTING THE DIAL

A major cause of inaccuracy, scientists say, is the sale of poorly calibrated instruments. George Bowers, a member of the NIH panel investigating cholesterol testing, notes that making properly calibrated equipment is time-consuming, and he says it is possible some manufacturers truncate the process for fear of losing market share. "If physicians don't demand accuracy—and by and large they don't—then manufacturers lack the incentive," Dr. Bowers says.

Manufacturers needing help with calibration can get it from the CDC and the National Bureau of Standards. Says the CDC's Dr. Cooper: "We offer industry a standardization program. We have invited them and done everything in our power. But, to put it bluntly, we have had a limited response."

Nathan Gochman, a manager of clinical instruments for a unit of SmithKline, replies that manufacturers can't count on this assistance because it isn't always available. He concedes, however, a need for manufacturers to agree on a "standardized protocol" to ensure that different machines produce the same results.

Richard Flaherty, vice president of the Health Industry Manufacturers Association, says he knows nothing about manufacturers refusing calibration assistance. He says his membership recognizes the need to standardize test results and is working with the scientific community to do so.

The NIH panel investigating cholesterol testing says its goal is to help manufacturers and labs get to the point where the margin of error is no more than 5%. It hopes ultimately to reduce the rate to 3% or less.

Not that such accuracy would be the end of the cholesterol battle. About two years ago, the American Health Foundation, through cholesterol screening, identified individuals at high risk of heart disease. Six months later, those who had subsequently seen a physician were asked what happened. In most cases, a foundation spokeswoman says, "their doctor told them not to worry about it."

FEDERAL LAB STUDYING TRAIN, AIRLINE CRASHES FABRICATED ITS FINDINGS

HIGHER-UPS WERE WARNED, BUT FAA UNIT CONTINUED TO PROVIDE PHONY RESULTS

SQUANDERING A BLOOD SAMPLE

FRIDAY, JULY 31, 1987

BY WALT BOGDANICH

Last January, at a Federal Aviation Administration laboratory in Oklahoma City, two men worked long into the night, finishing just before dawn. Their job was important: to tell the nation whether drug use was a factor in the worst railroad accident in Amtrak's history.

Along with an assistant, the lab's supervisor, 52-year-old biochemist Delbert Lacefield, was trying to test the blood of a railroad engineer involved in the Jan. 4 train crash just outside Baltimore that left 16 people dead and about 170 injured.

Their work hadn't gone well. For months, unbeknown to his superiors, Mr. Lacefield had been fabricating test data in other train-crash investigations, reporting results of blood tests that had never been performed. Now, with top government officials swarming over the Amtrak case, the lab supervisor knew that he had to produce.

FUZZY REPORT

But there was a problem: Neither Mr. Lacefield nor anyone else in the lab knew how to use the sophisticated equipment needed to perform such a test. The assistant would later say that he felt like someone "who had to learn to fly an aircraft already in operation."

Mr. Lacefield went ahead, but his fuzzy test report led the Federal Railroad Administration to investigate his operation, the Civil Aeromedical Institute, or CAMI, the premier drug-testing lab of the U.S. Transportation Department. (Both the FAA and the railroad administration are Transportation Department units.)

Investigators found that CAMI's forensic toxicology department had fabricated the results of 17 train-wreck blood tests during a nine-month period last year. Transportation officials stress that in the case of the fatal Amtrak crash in Chase, Md., the results weren't phony, just sloppy. In fact, Federal Railroad Administrator John H. Riley, whose agency began using CAMI for post-accident testing in February 1986, boasts that his internal-control system, although flawed, worked because it turned up the lab's shortcomings.

But according to internal government investigative files and interviews with lab experts, problems at the lab were far worse than transportation officials have publicly admitted. Moreover, though some government supervisory personnel were informed of the deficiencies nearly a year ago, corrective action wasn't taken until the Amtrak disaster focused attention on the problems.

MANY QUESTIONS

CAMI's work was so shoddy that accident investigators say they will never be sure whether drug use by the engineer played a role in the Amtrak tragedy. Moreover, investigators now wonder about the accuracy of hundreds of post-accident lab tests that CAMI performed on airplane crews over 20 years.

The case raises a number of other questions as well: Why did federal transportation officials give such an important task to an unqualified laboratory? How could widespread evidence of the lab's dishonesty and incompetence go undetected month after month? And what does the episode suggest about the U.S. government's ability to run a large-scale drug-testing program? Later this year the Transportation Department is scheduled to begin random testing of up to 30,000 of its employees.

In retrospect, there is little doubt that fraud and incompetence at CAMI could have been detected well before the Amtrak accident. The situation was so bad that lab technologist Mary Miller would later tell investigators that during her pre-employment job interviews last year at CAMI she "was twice approached by employees concerning questionable practices," including the reporting of phony test results.

NUMEROUS COMPLAINTS

In fact, three of the lab's four laboratory technologists say that they complained—without result—to Mr. Lacefield's supervisor about such problems as failed testing methodologies, outdated procedures and a lack of quality control.

At hearings held by a House subcommittee on transportation, the chairman, Rep. Thomas A. Luken of Ohio, called the government's casual supervision of CAMI "shocking," particularly in light of the Reagan administration's plans to embark "willy-nilly" on the testing of Transportation Department employees. Mr. Riley, the railroad administrator, cautioned against overreacting. He argued that calling off "the alcohol and drug program because of Del Lacefield is the rough equivalent of using Jim Bakker as a reason not to pray." But Mr. Riley and Rep. Luken did agree on the need for national certification of laboratories to weed out the good from the bad. Currently, only a few states regulate drug-testing labs—a process that laboratory experts say would have uncovered CAMI's problems much sooner.

In the case of the Amtrak crash test, CAMI's workers reached different conclusions using improperly calibrated equipment, then promptly lost the computer data backing their findings. Worse yet, they squandered the entire blood sample taken soon after the accident from train engineer Ricky Gates. With no blood left, retesting by a competent lab couldn't be done.

Mr. Gate's urine tested positive for marijuana, but lab experts say that without the more precise blood test, there is no way of knowing whether Mr. Gates was drug impaired at the time he pulled his Conrail engine in front of an Amtrak train carrying about 600 people at 105 miles an hour.

The botched analysis also means that the government can't use blood-test results in its prosecution of Mr. Gates, who faces 16 counts of manslaughter as a result of the crash.

CAMI's big lie began to unravel within days of the Amtrak crash, according to railroad administration records. Recognizing the unusually high level of public interest in the accident, railroad administrators made a point of reviewing test procedures with Mr. Lacefield before lab analysis began. Even so, transportation officials in Washington found Mr. Lacefield's eventual report imprecise, and the lab later admitted that documentation for its findings was gone. ("I have a confession to make . . .," Mr. Lacefield said in broaching the subject to investigators.)

But a major break in the case came on Feb. 6. Two railroad administration officials called Oklahoma City to ask Mr. Lacefield about terminology he had used to report blood-test results in the Amtrak case and in other cases. Because Mr. Lacefield wasn't available, the officials talked instead to laboratory chemist Ron W. Beckel. They then heard what they call the "startling" news that Mr. Beckel, whom they thought had been preparing blood for the tests, had not done so. Recounting this conversation in a memo, one of the officials said that from "the tenor of the conversation and Mr. Beckel's careful choice of words" he inferred that Mr. Beckel had no knowledge of Mr. Lacefield's having done blood work either.

WORKER INTERVIEWS

The next Monday, railroad officials flew to Oklahoma, where they reviewed CAMI's files and interviewed lab workers. Soon after, the Transportation Department's inspector general was called in to investigate and his findings were turned over to the U.S. attorney's office.

As part of a plea bargain, Mr. Lacefield, who no longer works for the government, pleaded guilty to three felony counts of providing false information to a federal agency. He was sentenced July 23 in federal court in Oklahoma City to two years' probation and was ordered to perform eight hours of community-service work a week for one year. FAA spokesman John Leyden, who says he knows nothing about higher-ups ignoring warnings of the lab's deficiencies, says that none of Mr. Lacefield's supervisors has been disciplined.

After the fraud was exposed, the railroad administration received what one of its officials calls "a considerable amount of credit" inside government for breaking the case. But some laboratory experts say that the episode never would have occurred if the railroad administration had used better judgment in selecting a lab and the FAA had more closely monitored its lab's performance.

Railroad administration officials say that they chose CAMI because it was part of the Department of Transportation and therefore a known quantity. Its forensic toxicology lab had conducted tests on cockpit crews involved in most serious U.S. plane crashes, and the National Transportation Safety Board had often considered its results in attempting to determine the cause of crashes. (CAMI also does general aviation research unconnected with its forensic toxicology lab.)

MAKING CHOICES

In the absence of a national certification program for drug-testing laboratories, a Transportation Department facility was preferable to selecting "an unknown—probably a low-bid outside contractor," Mr. Riley, the railroad administrator, says.

Although transportation officials say that CAMI was selected because of its top reputation, government accident investigators told The Wall Street Journal that CAMI's airplane work sometimes contradicted the findings of other labs. "That should have triggered the attention of management," says an accident investigator. "It was an island unto itself."

Richard Prouty, the chief forensic toxicologist with the medical examiner's office in Oklahoma City, recalls an incident several years ago when his lab results differed from CAMI's. "We got one set of values on subject A and B, and CAMI got a set of values on A and B that were essentially reversed," Mr. Prouty says. After retesting, he adds, CAMI's error was "demonstrated conclusively."

An FAA official says that specimens from the same subject may differ because of contamination or deterioration, so it isn't unusual for two labs to report different test results on the same individual. But a laboratory expert who has seen CAMI's work says that discrepancies were so "substantial that they raise the issue of who was right and who was wrong." This expert cites the case of a 1984 airplane crash near

Laredo, Texas. CAMI reported that the pilot had a blood alcohol level of .406, while a nearby hospital found only about a quarter of that amount. It would be "virtually impossible," the expert says, to fly a plane with the alcohol level reported by CAMI.

EQUIPMENT GAP

The railroad administration picked CAMI to run its post-accident program knowing that the facility lacked a device called a gas chromatograph/mass spectrometer that is needed for sophisticated blood testing. CAMI promised that it would subcontract blood tests out to a nearby nongovernment laboratory, but it never made good on that promise. None of its employees knew how to extract a test sample from blood plasma, a necessary first step before an outside lab can analyze the fluid.

Under pressure to produce results, Mr. Lacefield decided on his own to fabricate data. Investigators, still puzzled by his motives, speculate that the biochemist was eager to demonstrate competence in a sophisticated technology, got in over his head and falsified data to cover up. Mr. Lacefield, whom acquaintances describe as short, chubby and affable, had worked at CAMI for 21 years. Financial gain didn't figure in his actions; the railroad contract was simply another assignment handed to his lab. Mr. Lacefield declined to comment.

The situation didn't improve when CAMI finally obtained a gas chromatograph/mass spectrometer in late 1986. CAMI began using the device immediately—even though according to John W. Melchner, the Transportation Department's inspector general, "it can take as long as two years to develop a good feel for how to use the instrument."

Patricia A. Roberts, a CAMI technologist, told investigators that the new instrument "had some design and engineering problems" and that therefore its findings weren't "consistent enough for us to have confidence in our results." It was apparently while trying to use the instrument that Mr. Lacefield and his assistant squandered the Conrail engineer's blood sample.

FAA'S JOB

Mr. Riley, the railroad administrator, defends his agency's selection of CAMI, saying that much research went into the decision. "Assuring program integrity was a key issue for us from day one," he says. He also notes that the FAA was hired "lock, stock and barrel" to run the technical side of the program and was supposed to oversee the lab's activities.

But quality control was practically nonexistent at the laboratory, government records show. In June 1986, the Armed Forces Institute of Pathology reported to FAA officials that CAMI's forensic toxicology laboratory lacked certain safeguards, and it urged that the lab undergo proficiency testing by an outside group. These suggestions were ignored, and the railroad administration says that the FAA never informed it of the findings.

CAMI's own employees tried to alert authorities to the lab's incompetence. Medical technologist Claudia Ryan said in a sworn statement that she mentioned the "lack of quality control and outdated procedures" to one of Mr. Lacefield's supervisors but "was rebuffed. Therefore," she added, "I did not approach [him] with information concerning the falsification of reports."

A SLOPPY SHOP

Meanwhile, CAMI continued to run a sloppy shop. Following a Long Island Rail Road crash in New York City last December, CAMI incorrectly reported that a railroad worker's blood had tested positive for alcohol. The report was withdrawn before any action was taken because investigators concluded that the employee hadn't been drinking, government investigative files show. The laboratory attributed the mistake to a testing error. In an unrelated admission, Mr. Lacefield told the inspector general that CAMI workers had at times improperly cleansed test vials.

The railroad administration says that it doesn't know of a single railroad worker who was actually accused of using drugs or alcohol because of a false-positive test. Transportation officials say that in each case where leftover blood permitted retesting of CAMI's work, the error proved to be a false negative—that is, CAMI hadn't detected drug use when it was present. To critics, though, this is hardly reassuring. "Do we want junkies driving our trains?" asks a laboratory investigator. "What's the point of the program?"

After the fraud was exposed, transportation officials temporarily reassigned Robert Dille, CAMI's overall manager. The forensic lab has been shut down, and all post-accident rail and airline testing has been transferred to a nongovernment laboratory in Utah. The department's future random drug testing will be done by laboratories approved by the Department of Defense, which government officials believe has more expertise than the FAA.

Nevertheless, as more people call for drug and even AIDS testing, Rep. Lukens says that CAMI should serve as a sobering example. "We have to worry about having some way of assuring the public that these [labs] are following standards," he says. "No one wants to see careers shattered and innocent lives ruined" by shoddy lab work.

LAX LABORATORIES
THE PAP TEST MISSES MUCH CERVICAL CANCER THROUGH LABS' ERRORS

CUT-RATE "PAP MILLS" PROCESS SLIDES USING SCREENERS WITH INCENTIVES TO RUSH

MISPLACED SENSE OF SECURITY?

MONDAY, NOVEMBER 2, 1987

BY WALT BOGDANICH

The Pap smear. Over the past three decades, it has sharply reduced deaths from cervical cancer. Women and physicians trust it, so much so that the Pap smear has become one of the most common laboratory tests in America.

It is also one of the most inaccurate. No one knows how many women die because a lab botches the analysis or a doctor takes an inadequate specimen. The test, as it is being done today, fails to detect roughly one in every four cases of cancer or precursor cell abnormalities.

Linda MacNeil was one victim. A Florida store manager, Mrs. MacNeil suspected cervical cancer after experiencing bleeding, but a Pap-test report reassured her. Four months later, another test found cancer. Mrs. MacNeil died at age 36.

Cindy Gray's Pap smear wasn't analyzed in a laboratory at all but in the home of a lab employee, in violation of a federal regulation. There was no supervision and no pathologist to consult. Although the test reported no malignancy, the North Carolina mother of three was found soon after to have cervical cancer. She died at 34.

Barbara Arbuckle, of Seattle, was luckier: She is still alive. The 25-year-old woman received negative Pap-test reports, from two different labs, in the months before finding out she had invasive cervical cancer.

INCENTIVES TO HURRY

To find out why the Pap test falls so short of its promise, this newspaper visited labs, inspected records and interviewed doctors, lab workers and government officials. What emerges is a picture of a Pap-screening industry kept afloat by overworked, undersupervised, poorly paid technicians. It is an industry that often ignores what few laws exist to protect women from slipshod testing.

Across the nation, high-volume, cut-rate laboratories, sometimes called Pap factories or Pap mills, allow technicians to analyze up to four times as many specimens per year as medical experts recommend for accuracy. Many of them pay screeners on a piecework basis that encourages them to rush the analysis.

Some technicians work two or more jobs, earning as little as 45 cents to do the key analysis on a test that may cost the patient $35. In some cases, they say they are penalized if they resist the pressure to screen more slides in a day.

WORK AT HOME

"I think women would be horrified to learn what's happening out there," says Dwight Golann, former chief of consumer protection for the Massachusetts attorney general's office.

Women and their doctors might be surprised to learn that labs often let employees take slides home to screen. "That borders on fraud," says Myron R. Melamed, a physician at Memorial Sloan-Kettering Cancer Center in New York.

Pap mills prosper by underbidding competing labs, charging as little as $1.50 per test. They are sought out by some gynecologists, who profit by marking up lab fees on patient bills.

COST PRESSURE

But their bargain rates also appeal to budget-conscious administrators of group health plans and government-funded clinics. Thus, at a time when pressures are great to restrain medical expenses, problems with Pap-testing accuracy exemplify the possible trade-off in quality of care.

The consequences of faulty testing pose disturbing questions for the medical establishment. An estimated 60,000 women this year are expected to develop cancer of the cervix. If caught early, the disease is nearly always curable. Yet it kills about 7,000 American women a year.

"It is time for the medical community to acknowledge the failures of cervical cancer screening in the U.S.," says Robert Hasselbrack, a pathologist who runs a clinical laboratory in Seattle. Another physician, San Francisco pathologist Eileen King, complains: "Women have been told for many years that a Pap smear will tell them when they have cancer and when they don't. That is a big falsity."

Heightening the urgency is the fact that some doctors now believe cervical cancer develops faster than previously believed. Also, they see it turning up in more young women.

Citing an "alarming number" of cervical-cancer cases in women with recent negative Pap smears, the American College of Obstetricians and Gynecologists has criticized the American Cancer Society for advising women that they need a Pap test only every three years after two consecutive negative annual tests.

"Nothing merits total faith, but nobody can doubt its [the Pap test's] value," says Robert Hutter, a physician who is a past president of the society. Still, the society is considering recommending that women take the test more frequently.

Leading cancer specialists say about half the Pap-test failures result because physicians take inadequate cell samples. But efforts to better educate doctors in taking specimens have been "spectacularly unsuccessful," says the obstetrician and gynecologist association.

Labs could help by rejecting inadequate slides sent to them. But "even good labs" are reluctant to do so, for fear of losing business, says Dr. S. B. Gusberg, another past president of the American Cancer Society.

WALLPAPER CHALLENGE

The Pap test is named for George Papanicolaou, who developed it in the 1920s. To prepare a specimen for the test, a doctor smears cells from the female genital tract onto a glass slide, in some cases two slides. Most aren't analyzed by a doctor but by a cytotechnologist, who ordinarily is a college graduate with a year of special training. Unlike some kinds of medical tests, Pap smears aren't checked by chemical or mechanical means but depend on human visual examination of the specimen.

A slide may contain hundreds of individual cells, each of which should be studied under a microscope. It is tedious work and, if done properly, time-consuming. Louise Newton, an Albany, N.Y., "cytotech," likens the job to examining wall after wall of flowered wallpaper.

"Imagine trying to look at every flower and see how buggy you get," she says. "Tired eyes make mistakes."

Accordingly, the American Society of Cytology recommends that no full-time cytotech examine slides from more than 12,000 patients a year. A 1980 conference of cancer specialists convened by the National Cancer Institute also supported this limit. But it is flagrantly ignored.

WORKLOAD CONTROVERSY

An analysis by this newspaper of government data found that more than half of the Pap smears sent to New York state-regulated labs are screened in places where technicians exceed the recommended workload. Kyto Diagnostics Inc. of New City, N.Y., a large private lab run by a prominent cytopathologist, Ralph Richart, reported average workloads of 35,000 cases per screener last year—nearly three times what the cytology society thinks is safe. Most of his screeners aren't even full-timers.

Dr. Richart and other critics of workload limits say some cytotechs can accurately screen more than others. They argue that those who make excessive errors will be caught if a lab randomly rescreens at least 10% of negative slides.

Other medical experts disagree. Because only a small percentage of slides are likely to be positive, they say, and because everyone makes some errors, finding a problem employee might take years using a random 10% rescreen. "It's a seriously flawed quality-control technique," concludes Robert R. Rickert, vice chairman of lab accreditation for the College of American Pathologists.

Even as Pap-smear volume is rising, the number of qualified screeners is shrinking. Fewer people are choosing the field, and many are leaving it for better pay. Nearly half the schools that train cytotechs have closed in recent years; hospitals no longer find them economical to run.

"It is approaching a crisis," says San Francisco's Dr. King, who is studying the problem on behalf of California pathologists. Nearly 50% of advertised positions for cytotechs in California remain unfilled, she has found. Paul Krieger, director of anatomic pathology for MetPath Inc., a laboratory unit of Corning Glass Works, says that if the American Cancer Society decides to recommend more frequent Pap testing, "I don't know how we or anyone else is going to handle it."

To cope with the labor squeeze and to lower their costs, labs are turning increasingly to piecework, promising cytotechs that the more slides they screen, the more they will earn. Nowhere else in laboratory medicine is this method of payment so prevalent. "It's very bad practice. It makes quality control difficult," says Dr. Melamed of Sloan-Kettering.

Some big commercial labs pay almost exclusively by piecework, avoiding many employee costs. Even labs with salaried cytotechs, such as MetPath, usually let them do extras on a piecework basis.

Karen Sanford, a cytotech in Stockton, Calif., left a high-pressure piecework lab in the Los Angeles area after learning from a patient's doctor that she had failed to catch some abnormalities. "It really freaks you out," she says. "What do you say? It happened to me twice. That's when I decided to get out of there."

Not everyone is so conscientious. A particularly dangerous, yet very common, practice among cytotechs is to piggyback Pap-smear screening jobs, doing the maximum allowed at one lab, then meeting another lab's quota later in the day.

MIDNIGHT OIL

"Over 50% of the people I know have two jobs. Some have three or four," says Jason Betterton, a cytotech in Sylmar, Calif. Ms. Sanford tells of a technician who screens at three labs, working from 1 a.m. until late the next afternoon.

Labs frequently let workers leave for the day as soon as they reach their quotas—another incentive to screen slides as rapidly as possible.

Lon Barr, a cytotech in Poway, Calif., says that when he joined a San Diego Pap lab he was "astonished" to see workers screen 100 slides in 3½ hours, then leave. "It was inconceivable that someone could screen that fast," he says.

Dr. Hasselbrack, the Seattle lab owner, says that in Pap mills, screeners lose sight of the fact that "you are looking at somebody's life, and if you make a mistake, it may be all over."

Piecework pay scales also encourage overwork. At 50 cents a slide, one who stuck to the cytology society's workload limit would earn only $6,000 a year.

LITTLE REGULATION

Only one state, California, even attempts to prevent workload abuses. Its law states that "no cytotechnologist shall be required to examine more than 75 one-slide gynecologic cases, or 50 two-slide gynecologic cases per day."

But labs often violate or skirt this law. Start with the biggest Pap lab in the country, Cancer Screening Services, of North Hollywood. Almost a million Pap cases were processed last year by this unit of American Cytogenetics Inc. (which a West Coast business magazine in 1985 dubbed California's hottest stock).

Cancer Screening's full-time employees are required to do 100 slides a day, says Shahla B. Sadeghi, medical director. It has mostly one-slide cases. Reminded of the state's legal limit, Dr. Sadeghi says: "It's not really a law—they just suggest it. . . . They know it's not possible." She adds, "Every year we have passed the [state] inspection."

At Central Diagnostic Laboratory in Tarzana, Calif., says former employee Betty Jo Thompson, "there was no such thing as you couldn't do your 100 cases." Moreover, screeners were expected to do extras at $1 a slide, she says. California law lets workers analyze an unlimited number of Pap smears a day if they "volunteer," but Mrs. Thompson says that when she resisted doing extras, the lab cut her salary.

Cyrus Milani, a Central Diagnostic medical director, says workers are sometimes required to do 100 cases daily. He declines to be interviewed further, except to state that the lab does quality work. Another company official denies that the lab violates any laws.

At Yosemite Pathology in Modesto, "100 slides is what we consider the minimum," says spokesman Robert Colletti. He doesn't feel he is violating the law because "everybody interprets it differently."

FEW PROFICIENCY TESTS

Stephanie Harner, past president of the California Association of Cytotechnologists, says she has complained repeatedly to state health officials about pressures on cytotechs to exceed quotas, but "got mostly a non-response." Kenneth Kizer, director of California's health department, denies that his office has received complaints from cytotechs. He promises to investigate.

The federal government doesn't care about workload or piecework issues. It does prohibit labs under its jurisdiction from letting "kitchen cytologists" analyze Pap tests at home, but many do so anyhow. At the home, pathologists aren't available for consultation, and no one checks how carefully slides are examined. "Cytology is done in so many nooks and crannies—places we don't even know of," says Susan Yokota, a cytotech.

Cancer Screening Service, for example, is federally certified as an interstate lab, yet it concedes that workers in the past took slides home. The company says that happened only a few times and is no longer permitted. A Tulsa, Okla., laboratory permitted home screening of smears from government-financed clinics until a Journal reporter began inquiring about the practice.

The only equipment needed for Pap screening is a microscope. But as one lab worker points out, "It's not something to do after a day's work in between washing dishes, with kids screaming for attention."

Patients believe the government is watching over Pap testing, says Lawrence Bergner, a physician at the National Cancer Institute, "but it ain't so." The government sets some standards for interstate and Medicare-certified labs, but the Pap test is the only common lab procedure for which federally licensed labs needn't undergo periodic proficiency tests.

As for the states, only one, New York, requires screeners to pass such tests.

Doctors seeking quality work often turn to professional groups that evaluate and accredit labs. However, the largest group overseeing commercial labs, the College of American Pathologists, doesn't set any overall workload limit. The American Society of Cytology, which does, has certified only about 40 of the more than 1,000 labs analyzing Pap smears nationwide. Many of the largest labs have never sought accreditation.

With weak laws and scant professional oversight, there is little to protect women from the kinds of misfortunes suffered by Mrs. MacNeil, Mrs. Gray and Ms. Arbuckle. In all three instances, their Pap slides were misread, according to testimony in lawsuits filed in their state courts. Ms. Arbuckle's suit is pending; survivors of the other two women received large monetary settlements.

ELUSIVE SLIDES

It often is impossible, however, to determine what went wrong— whether the specimen was misread by the lab or whether, perhaps, it was poorly taken by the doctor. Pap slides are often kept only as long as the law requires. In states without laboratory laws—which is nearly half of them—a lab needn't keep slides at all unless it operates in interstate commerce or is Medicare-certified. In that case, it must keep them two years.

Patricia Ashton, a cytotech and consultant to a major national laboratory, says that her lab's lawyers instruct workers to "get rid of slides as soon as possible" to limit liability. "I don't think it's medically ethical," she says.

Even if a suspect slide exists, retrieving it can be a problem. A now-defunct Boston laboratory called Elm Medical Lab, after having failed to detect a woman's cervical cancer, covered up the error by substituting a negative Pap slide for a positive one in her file, according to evidence presented by the Massachusetts attorney general in a state court. A jury last year found the lab had violated state consumer-protection laws; the case is on appeal.

Mr. Golann, who handled the state's case, also presented evidence that slides were improperly prepared at the lab; that one screener spent just seconds on each specimen; that slides were examined at home; and that the lab had failed to find the abnormal cells on 10 of the first 12 positive slides checked by investigators in a rescreening.

The dimensions of some abuses have been stunning. A Mansfield, Ohio, lab in the late 1970s was discovered to have sent out nearly

6,000 erroneous Pap-test reports. A world-wide alert located many, but not all, of the women affected. And this past September, health authorities in Britain issued an international alert for 911 women who had Pap smears misdiagnosed by a leading pathologist there.

PLANNED PARENTHOOD

Bad lab work is currently a paramount concern for Planned Parenthood Federation of America, which last year took 1.4 million Pap smears through affiliated offices and clinics. Early this year, Planned Parenthood warned affiliates of "a rapid rise in the number and cost of claims" due to laboratory errors, specifically Pap smears.

A few years ago, it tried to catch a lab it suspected of misreading Pap slides. Twice it sent the lab, which it won't name, slides from women known to have cervical cancer or its precursors, and twice the lab failed to report abnormalities. When Planned Parenthood tried to retrieve the specimens, one set was said to be lost and the other came back smashed. It was as if "they beat them up with a hammer," recalls Louise Tyrer, a physician who is vice president for medical affairs.

With complaints about lab work pouring in, Planned Parenthood has begun trying to identify problem Pap labs. One lab that has come to its attention is International Cancer Screening Laboratories in San Antonio, Texas. Among the largest in the nation, ICSL processes about a half-million slides annually from 49 states. In 1985, it was banned from operating in New York after failing the state's proficiency test in cancer screening.

ICSL, operating out of a modern building on the outskirts of San Antonio, employs 42 screeners full or part time. It pays the part-timers 50 cents a slide and gives salaried employees 45 cents for each slide they screen after meeting the daily quota.

BIG PRODUCER

One screener is recorded as having analyzed 4,710 slides in June. That is a rate more than four times what the American Society of Cytology considers the maximum safe workload. Even if he worked all 30 days in June, the screener would have to have done 157 slides a day.

At such rates, "I wouldn't expect a cytotech to screen effectively or reliably," says George H. Anderson, a physician at the Cancer Control Agency of Vancouver, British Columbia, which has a highly regarded Pap screening program. Says Dr. Hutter of the American Cancer Society: "If such things are happening, then I would say that's terrible."

ICSL's president, Robert Boughton Jr., says that his lab's work "is the best humanly possible," and that he spends more money than other labs do on quality control. He also says the especially prolific screener's error rate is well within acceptable ranges.

But in a business where one mistake can have tragic consequences, the technician, who declined to be interviewed, last year made at least 93 errors—41 of them "major," lab records show. And those are just the ones uncovered in a routine rescreening of 18% to 20% of his negative slides. No one knows his actual error total.

Mr. Boughton attacks workload limits as the creation of physicians who "sit up in their ivory tower with a bottle of wine" and issue pronouncements. Lending authority to his attacks on workload limits is a Ph.D. degree he says he earned in biology from the University of Mexico in Monterrey "in 1981 or 1982." He is identified in state and federal regulatory records as having a doctorate.

The University of Mexico, however, doesn't have a branch in Monterrey. And no record of Mr. Boughton's Ph.D. could be found at two other universities in that city. Mr. Boughton declines to provide a copy of the diploma, saying, "I am telling you that I have it, and that is all I have to say."

Present and past screeners, who ask not to be identified, say that despite ICSL's huge volume, its medical director works only part time. They also say that 10% or more of the slides sent to the lab are broken in transit. "You could easily miss an abnormality on the broken spot," says one ICSL cytotechnician.

Mr. Boughton says the breakage rate is "5% to 7% at the most." He says that while his medical director holds another job with a state mental hospital, she puts in nearly full-time hours at ICSL. He also makes no secret of the fact that he continues to operate in New York state, even though it banned his lab in 1985 after it failed the cancer-screening proficiency test. "Who's going to stop me?" he asks.

A spokesman for the state, Mary Anne Gardineer, says, "If we can verify that [ICSL] is accepting samples from New York state, we will stop them."

Amid growing criticism of laboratory work, the American Society for Cytotechnologists is pressing for tough government workload limits—even though they would reduce many screeners' pay. "Just as the public needs protection from fatigued truck drivers," the society says, "it needs protection against life-threatening mistakes in the laboratory by overburdened personnel."

Meanwhile, the society has begun a campaign to urge women to ask their doctors where their Pap smears are analyzed. At the very least, women should be told that their Pap test may fail to detect abnormalities, many health experts say. This way, women may be less likely to skip their next gynecologic exam.

FAILURE RATE

The American College of Obstetricians and Gynecologists, citing studies of hundreds of women, puts the Pap test's "false-negative" rate —the failure to reveal or report abnormalities—at 20% to 40%.

The Pap test's reliability compares unfavorably with that of other lab tests. Drug tests, for example, have been criticized as being inaccurate. But labs measured in a nationwide proficiency test last year had a much lower false-negative rate of about 5%. Even under the best of circumstances, says Dr. Anderson of Vancouver, a Pap test will have a false-negative rate of at least 10%.

To help bring error rates down, San Francisco's Dr. King argues for better pay and working conditions for cytotechs. "The field has become unattractive to intelligent, dedicated people of the kind we have always had," she says.

Above all, people in the field don't want Pap testing to remain laboratory medicine's errant stepchild. They prefer to think of it as a test so important that a commemorative stamp was issued in its name in 1978. At the White House ceremony marking the event, Postmaster General William Bolger said of Dr. Papanicolaou: "He wanted to eradicate those awful words so many doctors have quietly voiced: 'If only we had known sooner.' "

Mrs. Gray, the North Carolina woman who got a negative Pap-test report before finding she had cervical cancer, felt the tragic sting of that lament. After the cancer had spread through her body, she underwent several operations, chemotherapy and radiation. As part of a lawsuit, Mrs. Gray gave a videotaped deposition from her sickbed, describing in detail the agony of her struggle for life. The deposition ended with her vow: "I made some plans to beat this thing."

Two months later, Cindy Gray died.

PHYSICIANS' CARELESSNESS WITH PAP TESTS IS CITED IN PROCEDURE'S HIGH FAILURE RATE

TUESDAY, DECEMBER 29, 1987

BY WALT BOGDANICH

The case involved a 34-year-old North Carolina woman who had died of advanced cervical cancer. The woman had conscientiously visited her doctor for regular Pap tests that should have—but didn't—reveal her disease while it was still curable.

Last year, William W. Johnston, professor of pathology at Duke University Medical Center, was called as an expert witness in a wrongful-death lawsuit filed by the deceased woman's family. His opinion: A critical Pap test had been improperly prepared by the woman's doctor. "If the smear is not satisfactory, you have no assurance of anything," Dr. Johnston testified in the case, which was later settled.

Studies show that the Pap test fails 20% to 40% of the time to detect cervical cancer or precursor cell abnormalities, making it one of the most inaccurate of all clinical laboratory procedures. Each year an estimated 60,000 women develop the disease, and about 7,000 die from it. Much of the blame for the high failure rate rests with labs that fail to detect abnormal cell growth in screening the tests, as reported in a recent Wall Street Journal article on problems in the Pap test industry.

DOCTORS' ROLE

But physicians' carelessness—and in some cases, physicians' ignorance—has compounded those problems, many medical experts say. Nearly half the lab errors apparently result from inadequate cell specimens obtained by physicians or other health-care professionals, according to the American College of Obstetricians and Gynecologists, or ACOG.

"The laboratory can only read what is submitted to them," says S. B. Gusberg, a doctor and past president of the American Cancer Society. (In very rare cases, even a properly taken Pap smear will fail to show cell abnormalities.)

The Pap test involves smearing cells from the female genital tract on a glass slide, which is then sent to a laboratory for microscopic analysis. Despite the test's high error rate, it has sharply reduced deaths from cervical cancer and has become an indispensable part of women's health care.

The failure of some physicians to master such a common procedure confounds many in the medical field. The use of refined sampling techniques can sharply improve the accuracy of the test, but "after more than 30 years of physician education, this effort has been spectacularly unsuccessful," says the ACOG.

Some suspect the problem lies in the nature of the Pap test, which is a screening, rather than a diagnostic, procedure. "Physicians are so busy taking care of sick people they are not perfectly geared to preventive medicine," says Dr. Gusberg. "When it comes to screening [patients who are healthy], they do it in a hurry, so the smear may not be taken adequately."

Moreover, because the Pap test is so common, there "may be some assumption that everyone knows how to do it," says physician John Graham, director of program services of ACOG. "It's possible that some people who take Pap smears get a little casual about it as the years go by."

An accurate Pap test depends on a physician's knowing which areas in the female genital tract are most likely to yield cells that will show the presence of disease. The physician must also quickly place the cell sample in a fixing solution and avoid mixing in excess blood or infected material. Failure to do this can obscure the cells, making subsequent analysis problematic.

DETECTING CANCER

"When a woman goes for her Pap smear, it should detect everything that a Pap smear properly taken is able to detect," says John Frost, of Johns Hopkins Hospital in Baltimore. That includes, he says, different types of cancers and certain other ailments.

While the Pap test is most effective in detecting cervical cancer, Dr. Frost says skillful sampling and analysis can triple the chances of its finding signs of endometrial cancer, an abnormal cell growth in the lining of the uterine cavity. Endometrial cancer, which typically affects older women, kills about 3,000 annually.

Not everyone agrees that physicians take lousy Pap smears. "I don't know that there is any objective evidence that people who obtain the Pap smears are obtaining them in a way that is inappropriate or unskilled," says Ross Berkowitz, associate professor of obstetrics and gynecology at Harvard Medical School.

However, when Alan Ng, a leading pathologist, surveyed the quality of Pap testing in this country in the late 1970s he reported finding a "serious defect" in physician techniques—specifically, failure to sample enough parts of the genital tract. Pathologists say such a comprehensive survey of the field hasn't been done since.

Whether medical schools properly prepare students for taking Pap smears is a matter of dispute. Malcolm L. Margolin, a West Coast official with ACOG, says he believes many physicians aren't adequately trained in the latest Pap test procedures. The doctor says he was taught techniques in the 1960s "which we now know" are insufficient.

Myron R. Melamed of Memorial Sloan-Kettering Cancer Center in New York says he believes students and physicians were better trained in Pap testing in the 1950s and 1960s when the procedure was just beginning to gain wide acceptance. He speculates that the test now receives less attention, and that students "really aren't taught how to do it as they once were."

Other doctors say the teaching is sufficient. Dr. Berkowitz says he doesn't know of any problems in training, and adds, "It should be part of basic medical school curriculum." Harry L. Metcalf, president of the American Academy of Family Physicians, a professional group that includes medical-school faculty, says his organization's 59,000 members are required to have specific training in Pap tests. But he acknowledges that many general practitioners may not have such training.

FEAR OF LOSING BUSINESS

In many cases, Pap test errors made by physicians should be caught by laboratory workers and the pathologists who supervise them.

"The laboratory pathologist has to have the guts to send specimens back, to say this is unsatisfactory," says Dr. Melamed. Many labs are reluctant to do this, however, out of fear of losing a physician's business.

The physician who gets a sample back can either ignore it or admit an error and call the patient back for another visit. "That is no fun for anybody, so there is a natural reluctance to return the test to the doctor," Dr. Melamed says.

Adding to the problem, communication between the doctor and the laboratory may be impaired when physicians, seeking bargain prices, send specimens hundreds of miles away for analysis, according to a 1980 report issued by a National Cancer Institute panel of experts. The use of such labs by physicians has increased in recent years.

Robert Hasselbrack has seen both sides of the issue, first as a family physician and now as a pathologist running a commercial lab in Seattle. His lab tries to help doctors by giving them monthly grades on their Pap specimens. "We give them a lot of feedback. The good ones want to know how they are performing."

"Surprisingly," Dr. Hasselbrack adds, "some of the best Pap smears come from non-physician health-care professionals, like nurse practitioners. They simply take the time and want to do a good job."

THE PTL SCANDAL

THE CHARLOTTE OBSERVER

Charles E. Shepard, 33, was hired by *The Charlotte Observer* as a reporter in December 1977. He was made an investigative reporter in 1984 and has been covering the PTL organization and its finances since July 1984.

A DEATH IN THE FAMILY

THE ALABAMA JOURNAL

Jim Tharpe, 34, has been managing editor of *The Alabama Journal* since December 1985. Before coming to *The Journal*, he worked as a reporter for two years in the state capital bureau for *The Greenville* (S.C.) *News*. He has also worked for several newspapers in Florida.

Ann Green, 34, has been city editor of *The Journal* since February 1987. Prior to that, she worked at the *Raleigh* (N.C.) *News & Observer* and other newspapers in South Carolina.

Frank Bass, 24, covers health, state government, the environment and national politics for *The Journal*. He worked at *The Lubbock* (Tex.) *Avalanche-Journal* and the *Columbus* (Miss.) *Commercial Dispatch* before joining *The Journal* in October 1986.

Emily Bentley, 23, covers the state Legislature and state politics for *The Journal*. She joined the paper part-time in 1985 after working as the Auburn correspondent while attending Auburn University.

Susan Eggering, 26, has covered the education beat for *The Journal* since June 1987. She previously worked at *The Anniston* (Ala.) *Star* and *The Washington Missourian*.

Peggy Roberts, 29, joined *The Journal* as a business reporter in 1986. Previously, she worked for several publications, including the *Houston Business Journal* and *The Norwich* (Conn.) *Bulletin*.

WHEN FURLOUGHED MURDERERS STRIKE AGAIN

THE LAWRENCE EAGLE-TRIBUNE

Susan Forrest, 28, has been a general assignment reporter for the *Lawrence Eagle-Tribune* since October 1983. She also worked as a reporter for the *Los Angeles Daily News* from September to December of 1987. Previously, she was assistant editor of the *Concord* (Mass.) *Journal*.

Barbara Walsh, 29, joined the *Tribune* in 1984, working first as a town news reporter and later as a general assignment reporter. She previously edited a weekly newspaper in New Hampshire.

Daniel J. Warner Sr., 51, has been editor of the *Tribune* since 1980. He joined the paper as managing editor in 1973. Before that, he worked for four years as night managing editor of *The Philadelphia Inquirer*.

THE SPOILS OF POWER
C H I C A G O   T R I B U N E

Dean Baquet, 31, joined the *Chicago Tribune*'s metropolitan staff in 1984 as an investigative reporter. In 1987, he was promoted to associate metro editor/chief investigative reporter. Previously, he worked as a reporter in New Orleans for *The Times-Picayune/The States-Item*.

Ann Marie Lipinski, 32, joined the *Tribune* staff as a summer intern in 1978. Following her internship, she was made a full-time reporter in the features department at the *Tribune*.

William C. Gaines, 54, has worked for the *Tribune* since 1963. He was among a team of *Tribune* reporters who won the Pulitzer Prize for investigative reporting in 1976 for their exposé of conditions at two Chicago hospitals. From 1960 to 1963, he worked for the *Chicago Daily News* as a correspondent in northern Indiana.

REBELLIOUS GENES
THE ATLANTA CONSTITUTION and
THE CHARLOTTE OBSERVER

Doug Marlette, 37, spent 15 years as editorial cartoonist at *The Charlotte Observer* before joining *The Atlanta Constitution* in March 1987. In addition to his cartoons, Marlette draws a comic strip called "Kudzu." He has been drawing newspaper cartoons since he was 16.

THE PENTAGON'S SECRET CACHE
THE PHILADELPHIA INQUIRER

Tim Weiner, 31, was among the staff reporters at the *Kansas City Times* whose reporting on the collapse of the Hyatt Hotel's skywalks earned the paper a Pulitzer Prize in 1982. Later that year, he joined *The Philadelphia Inquirer* where he has covered local, national and international new stories.

BITTER POLITICS IN THE MIDDLE EAST
THE NEW YORK TIMES

Thomas L. Friedman, 34, won his first Pulitzer Prize in 1983 for coverage of the Israeli invasion of Lebanon the previous year. He joined *The New York Times* in 1981 as a reporter in the business section. He was named bureau chief in Beirut in early 1982. Two years later, he was appointed bureau chief in Jerusalem.

THE RESCUE OF BABY JESSICA
THE ODESSA AMERICAN

Scott Shaw, 24, joined the photo staff at *The Odessa American* in November 1986. A journalism graduate of Southern Illinois University in Carbondale, Illinois, Shaw previously worked at the *Paragould* (Ark.) *Daily Press.*

THE GRAVEYARD
THE MIAMI HERALD

Michel duCille, 32, joined *The Miami Herald* photography staff in September 1981. Five years later, he shared the Pulitzer Prize for spot news photography for coverage from Colombia showing the devastation caused by a volcano eruption.

FLORIDA'S SHAME
THE ORLANDO SENTINEL

Jane Healy, 38, joined *The Orlando Sentinel* in 1973 as a reporter. She held a number of jobs, including regional coordinator, editorial writer and chief editorial writer, before being named associate editor in 1985. She was a Pulitzer Prize–nominated finalist in 1985 for editorial writing.

CHILD OF THE TELEVISION AGE

THE WASHINGTON POST

Tom Shales, 39, joined *The Washington Post* in 1972 as a writer for the Style section. He was named chief television critic in July 1977 and appointed TV editor in June 1979. Before joining *The Post,* Shales was entertainment editor for the (Washington) *D.C. Examiner.*

DAVE BARRY'S QUIRKY 'YUK SYSTEM'

THE MIAMI HERALD

Dave Barry, 40, began writing a syndicated humor column in 1980. He was hired in 1983 by *The Miami Herald,* which distributes his column to more than 100 newspapers. He previously worked briefly as a reporter for The Associated Press and as a teacher of business writing at Berger Associates, a consulting firm.

AIDS IN THE HEARTLAND

ST. PAUL PIONEER PRESS DISPATCH

Jacqui Banaszynski, 35, joined the *St. Paul Pioneer Press Dispatch* as a labor reporter in January 1984. A year later, she was named special projects reporter and feature writer. She was a 1986 Pulitzer Prize—nominated finalist in the international reporting category for her personalized account of famine in Africa.

SCANDALS AND SCARES ON WALL STREET

THE WALL STREET JOURNAL

Daniel Hertzberg, 42, joined *The Wall Street Journal* in 1977 as a reporter in the New York bureau covering the New York City fiscal crisis. In January 1978, he was named deputy news editor. He previously worked for *Newsday* and the *Buffalo Evening News*.

James B. Stewart, 36, joined *The Journal* as a reporter in 1983. A graduate of Harvard Law School, he previously worked at the law firm of Cravath, Swaine & Moore in New York. In 1979, he became executive editor of *American Lawyer* magazine.

LAX LABORATORIES

THE WALL STREET JOURNAL

Walt Bogdanich, 37, was hired as an investigative reporter by *The Wall Street Journal* in June 1984. He previously worked for the *Dayton (Ohio) Daily News,* the *Cleveland Press* and *The Plain Dealer,* in Cleveland, Ohio.

ABOUT THE EDITOR

Kendall J. Wills is a Gannett Foundation fellow at the University of Hawaii, where he is studying Asian Affairs. Previously, he was assistant editor of the Op-Ed page at *The New York Times*. Mr. Wills earned a bachelor's degree at Columbia College and a master's degree from the School of International and Public Affairs at Columbia University.

"Committees Work a Little and Spend a Lot" by Ann Marie Lipinski and Dean Baquet, October 5, 1987. Reprinted with permission of *Chicago Tribune*.
"Public Office a Boon to Private Interests" by Dean Baquet and William Gaines, October 8, 1987. Reprinted with permission of *Chicago Tribune*.
"Zoning Makes the Alderman a King" by Dean Baquet and William Gaines, October 1, 1987. Reprinted with permission of *Chicago Tribune*.
"Ready for Reform?" by Dean Baquet and Ann Marie Lipinski, October 18, 1987. Reprinted with permission of *Chicago Tribune*.

Introductory essay on editorial cartooning by Doug Marlette. Reprinted with permission of Doug Marlette. Adapted from an essay in *Shred This Book! The Scandalous Cartoons of Doug Marlette,* Peachtree Publishers, Ltd., 1988.
12 Editorial Cartoons by Doug Marlette published in *Atlanta Constitution*. Reprinted with permission of *Atlanta Constitution*.
4 Editorial Cartoons by Doug Marlette published in *The Charlotte Observer*. Reprinted with permission of *The Charlotte Observer*.

Pulitzer Prize nominating letter by Tim Weiner. Used by permission of *The Philadelphia Inquirer*.
"A Growing 'Black Budget' Pays for Secret Weapons, Covert Wars" by Tim Weiner, February 8, 1987. Reprinted with permission of *The Philadelphia Inquirer*.
"Planning for World War IV" by Tim Weiner, February 9, 1987. Reprinted with permission of *The Philadelphia Inquirer*.
"Covert Forces Multiply, and Some Run Amok" by Tim Weiner, February 10, 1987. Reprinted with permission of *The Philadelphia Inquirer*.

Pulitzer Prize nominating letter by the editors of *The New York Times*. Used by permission of *The New York Times*.
"Palestinians Under Israel: Bitter Politics" by Thomas L. Friedman, January 12, 1987. Reprinted with permission of *The New York Times*.
"An Islamic Revival Is Quickly Gaining Ground in an Unlikely Place: Israel" by Thomas L. Friedman, April 30, 1987. Reprinted with permission of *The New York Times*.
"Ariel Journal, One West Bank Plan: Mix Concrete and Yuppies" by Thomas L. Friedman, June 2, 1987. Reprinted with permission of *The New York Times*.
"Fight Builds Over the Shape of Religious Future in Israel" by Thomas L. Friedman, June 29, 1987. Reprinted with permission of *The New York Times*.
"A Forecast for Israel: More Arabs than Jews" by Thomas L. Friedman, October 19, 1987. Reprinted with permission of *The New York Times*.
"Israel's Arab Army of Migrant Workers" by Thomas L. Friedman, December 6, 1987. Reprinted with permission of *The New York Times*.
"Palestinian Cause Turns to Fury As it Passes from Fathers to Sons" by Thomas L. Friedman, December 28, 1987. Reprinted with permission of *The New York Times*.

Introductory essay on spot news photography by Scott Shaw. Reprinted with permission of Scott Shaw.
Photo of Baby Jessica by Scott Shaw published in *The Odessa American*. Reprinted with permission of *The Odessa American*.

Pulitzer Prize nominating letter by Pete Weitzel. Used by permission of *The Miami Herald*.
12 photos by Michel duCille. Reprinted with permission of *The Miami Herald*.